PENGUIN BOOKS
THE RIBBON AND THE RAGGED

Linda Christmas was born in Middlesex in 1943. After a brief
spell working for M I 5, she spent twenty years in newspapers,
eleven of them as a feature writer on the *Guardian*. During this
period she travelled widely, making frequent visits to the United
States of America and to Europe, and less frequent visits to
Albania, Cuba, the USSR, South America and the Far East. *The
Ribbon and the Ragged Square* is her first book.

THE RIBBON AND THE RAGGED SQUARE

An Australian Journey

Linda Christmas

PENGUIN BOOKS

Penguin Books Ltd, Harmondsworth, Middlesex, England
Viking Penguin Inc., 40 West 23rd Street, New York, New York 10010, U.S.A.
Penguin Books Australia Ltd, Ringwood, Victoria, Australia
Penguin Books Canada Ltd, 2801 John Street, Markham, Ontario, Canada L3R 1B4
Penguin Books (N.Z.) Ltd, 182–190 Wairau Road, Auckland 10, New Zealand

First published by Viking 1986
Published in Penguin Books 1987

Made and printed in Great Britain by
Richard Clay Ltd, Bungay, Suffolk

To
Australia and the Australians

Here perhaps, more than anywhere, humanity had a chance to make a fresh start.

Alan Moorehead, *Cooper's Creek*

In shape, Australia resembles a ragged square, but the real Australia where people live and work is a ribbon.

Professor Geoffrey Blainey,
Daedalus, The Journal of the
American Academy of Arts and Sciences
(Vol. 114, No. 1, Winter 1985)

Contents

Acknowledgements

I wish to thank warmly the hundreds of Australians I met in my travels; many gave me hours of their time and some generously allowed me to become part of their lives for several weeks.

I'd also like to thank:

Qantas for flying me to Australia in November 1982 and for flying me and a weighty sack of books back to London in August 1983.

The Australian High Commission which, when processing my visa application, became interested in my plans and offered the help of the Australian Information Service. This meant that in every major city I received a warm welcome and help in making appointments.

Professor Geoffrey Bolton, former head of the Australian Studies Centre at the University of London, and now Professor of History at Murdoch University, Perth, for reading the manuscript and offering advice.

And John Higgins who fed the terrapins while the words tripped all too slowly from the typewriter.

DARWIN
Rum
Inr
Bradshaw
Kununurra
Broome Derby
NO
TE
Port
Hedland
Monte Bello Islands
Marble Bar
Dampier
Nullagine
Tom Price
Docker
River
Ayer
Roc
Giles
Carnarvon
WESTERN
Wingelina
AUSTRALIA
Blackstone
Warburton
Mt Will
SO
Geraldton
Kalgoorlie
Ma
PERTH
Bunbury
(Margaret River)
Albany

Jungle
Jabiru
Katherine
nesvale

NORTHERN
TERRITORY

Mount Isa

Alice Springs
Curtin
Springs
Marla Bore
Oodnadatta
oughby
Coober Pedy

SOUTH AUSTRALIA
aralinga
Woomera
Port Augusta
Orroroo
Port Pirie
Clare
ADELAIDE
Nhill

Broken Hill

VICTORIA
Ballarat
MELBOURNE

QUEENSLAND

Lizard Island
Cooktown
Cairns
Green Island
Karumba
Townsville
Charters
Towers
Hayman Island
Hughenden
Mackay

Rockhampton
Gladstone
Morven
BRISBANE
Byron
Bay
Coff's Harbour

NEW SOUTH WALES
Newcastle
SYDNEY
CANBERRA
Wollongong

TASMANIA
Strahan
Queenstown
HOBART

CHAPTER I

The Poor Who Got Away

Priscilla was recovering from what she described as the worst 'flu of her life. She hadn't bothered to enlist the help of a doctor; instead, she had shed the virus her way, with fresh air, Aspro and chocolate. I was on the point of asking her to reveal the secret healing power of chocolate when she started to cough again. 'I'd love some coffee,' she whispered between attempts to evict the irritation from her troubled lungs. 'Whiteandtwosugars,' the words tumbled out on the shortest possible breath.

It wasn't late, a shade after ten p.m., and as the ferries were still running a stall was still serving coffee. The terminus of Circular Quay was dusty, scruffy with the debris of the day's crowds and somewhat desolate, as is the way of places denied the bustle and movement for which they are designed. For all that, it was less forlorn than any night-time airport, or many an early morning railway station. Or so it seemed to me. Perhaps that was fanciful thinking, aided by my knowing that outside, beyond the arms of the jetties, was one of the loveliest of sites. A harbour like no other harbour. A harbour not shrouded in smoke, nor scarred with cranes; not unduly bothered by the business of freight, nor bunged up with the uglier sort of boat. Out there, most days, yachts with coloured spinnakers catch and hold the eye as they skirt the ferries and drift across an oak-leaf-shaped sheet of blue.

Priscilla needed the coffee. 'I'll drink half of it now and keep the rest warm in a plastic bag for later. I don't find it easy to sleep these days. I worry. There are so many pickpockets about. Look over there. See those two? The one on the left is the best pickpocket in Sydney.'

For the moment, at any rate, the two were asleep, huddled within the paraphernalia of the vagrant, umpteen layers of clothes, rugs, newspaper. Priscilla seemed an apt name (meaning as it does 'ancient') for an elderly lady whose head was wrapped in a plastic hood and whose figure was padded into the shape of a rotund toy, the sort with perfect equilibrium which budgerigars are given for company and which they smack around, amused to watch them rock from side to side but never keel over.

Manny appeared. 'Touch you for a coffee, did she? Hello Priscilla. Have you seen a youngster around here, a woman in a white jumper? They say she is off the planet.'

'Seen no one.' Satisfied, Manny, who had already carried out his own inspection, hopped back into the van he'd parked on the concourse and together we sped across town to Ansett, the airline, where trays of buns and biscuits, sandwiches and fruit awaited our collection. The well-fed businessman might have waved them away during the day but they'd make a fine breakfast tomorrow for the folk at Sydney City Mission. Manny and I had spent the evening combing the streets for drunks and drug-addicts and those in need of a bed.

We found only one in the gutter and he had a home; but drinking on top of new pills – so he said – had made him incapable of reaching there without our help. He thanked us warmly as we taxied him home and waited while he fumbled with his keys to a neat front door in the poorer part of the inner city. And we left only one in the gutter. His name was Dawson and, as we were ferrying him to a hostel, he changed his mind and made a fuss in the back of the van, yelling to be let out. So we let him out and watched him stagger towards a brick wall. 'We can't take that right away from him. If he wants to stay out he can. Maybe I'll drive back and look for him later.'

The public ring the Mission's headquarters if they see someone in difficulty in the streets, and that is how we came to comb Circular Quay seeking the girl in the white jumper; but many find their own way to the Mission's Hunt Street headquarters. They begin arriving at five-thirty; some merely need a cheap meal or somewhere to chat, others need a bed; and if the Mission is full, it acts as a clearing house to other hostels, detoxification units or drug-rehabilitation programmes. That evening, mostly men hung around the entrance, docile, funny and affectionate, happy to tell me of their gambling prowess, and constantly apologizing for swearing. Howard, clutching a paper bag containing Mars bars, was full of the day's triumphs. He'd won enough at cards that morning, he said, to have had a big feed at Woolies' cafeteria at lunchtime.

It could have been a depressing evening, but it was not; humour helped as always, but so did Manny. He never for a moment allowed sentiment to swamp our discussions. He knew the score. Born in Malta, he had been a truck-driver before he got into heroin. 'Damn the stuff, it's so easily available in Sydney, and for a long time the police seemed more concerned busting the guy who grew a little dope, rather than busting the big peddlers.' It had taken him fifteen months to break the habit with the help of a Mission Programme, and now he was more than happy to repay that help. Many other hostel workers had arrived by the same route. He was just right for the job. He knows it is all too easy to take the wrong path: he does not pass judgement, does not moralize and, above all, doesn't despair. He knows it is possible to turn back. A sign on the wall of the Hunt Street headquarters says: 'God give me the serenity to accept things I cannot change; and the courage to change the things I can.'

Every city has its Priscillas and Dawsons and Howards. Every city where there is freedom has winners and losers. Few cities are kinder to losers. I don't mean that Sydney teems with Mannys and with money for reform programmes, but it is easier to be down on your luck in a city where the climate and the surroundings and the prevailing mood raise the spirits and defy the soul to hug its sorrows. Sydney does not worship work, nor debase leisure. People relish their free time and drive around in cars with stickers announcing 'I'd rather be sailing'; and the central business district is numb from four p.m. on Friday – indeed, it is quite often numb from noon. The city's mood is casual and carefree and it has always been so. Australia was the first country to adopt the eight-hour day, as long ago as the 1850s, and has jealously guarded a balance between work and play, a balance which some other countries admire and suggest could provide a model for many other societies, now that unemployment has become a permanent feature. That mood is promoted by the weather, which is perfect for leisure. Other parts of the country may suffer from unpredictable extremes, but on the whole Sydney veers between pleasantly cool and comfortably hot. On my second day it chose, however, to be uncomfortably hot, the temperature playing tag with the mercury and not stopping until it reached 108°F (42°C). People *phewed* and puffed and complained to strangers, and a stillness came over the city as people hid inside their homes or clung to air-conditioned offices. But even then, at around four p.m. came relief with the southerly buster, bringing with it a *wosh* of cold air which lowered the temperature by twenty Fahrenheit degrees, and it came so quickly, and the drop was so sudden, that one shivered.

If the climate is responsible for the city's relaxed attitude, so are the surroundings. Sydney has a remarkable natural beauty which it entices its citizens to share. It starts with the harbour, a stretch of water, of sea, which, as it skips in and out of bays and inlets, scallops the land into an edge of flamboyant prettiness. It is not easy to paint a landscape in words; to paint loveliness is impossible. Others have tried and given up in exasperation, including, most notably, Anthony Trollope. 'I despair', he wrote in *Australia and New Zealand* (1873), 'of being able to convey to any reader my own idea of the beauty of Sydney harbour. It is so inexpressibly lovely that it makes a man ask himself whether it would not be worth his while to move his household gods to the eastern coast of Australia in order that he might look at it as long as he can look at anything.'

The harbour and its beaches which are numerous act as a magnet. Sydneysiders gravitate to the water, not to sit in cars and stare blankly through half-open windows, but to embrace what they see. They may want to jog, or picnic, or sail, or surf. They may choose a quiet cove or a deserted headland or the bustle of Bondi. Because Bondi is internationally famous, one expects it to disappoint – but it does not. There are no stones, no rocks, no piers, no jetties, no oil-slicks, only a massive curve of white sand and magnificent surf. Occasionally – if the sewage workers are on strike – there may be signs warning the swimmers to beware, but rare is the summer's day when Bondi is bereft of bodies, both young and old, from dawn to dusk. The beaches are used more than ever. They are free and fitness is back in fashion.

The sea has never been out of fashion; it is after all the symbol of life to Australians. There are few rivers, and the rainfall is low and the centre remains a desert. Australians may talk about the Outback, the much-romanticized, challenging, unconquerable and, to me, utterly lovable Outback, but they don't want to live there. The population of 15 million has chosen suburban living and settled the edge of this vast island, some eighty per cent living within fifty miles of the sea; a ribbon within an island shaped like a ragged square. I too wanted to live by the sea, in a room with a view, as I planned my journey. I settled all too quickly for a room without a view, but only a two-minute walk from a bay where I could go and sit from time to time and try to imagine how it must have seemed to the first Europeans.

That great sailor, Captain James Cook, surprisingly did not find the harbour when he sailed the east coast in April 1770. He found Botany Bay, which pleased him enough. Back in London there was no scramble to stake a claim to his discovery until the American War of Independence in 1776 deprived Britain of a place to send its convicts. Then Botany Bay came into focus as a dumping ground.

Australian historians now argue about this. In the mid-1950s when they first began in any number to delight in their own history, some found it hard to accept that a convict settlement was the British government's sole aim. Surely back in London in the eighteenth century they were perceptive enough to see that New South Wales would be a good base for trade with China and with Japan and with the Spice Islands? Surely they could see that it would make an excellent naval station in the Pacific and that neighbouring Norfolk Island was awash with flax and pine, both of great value to a seafaring nation? Other dons disagree. Canada could supply all the timber necessary, so why worry about tiny Norfolk Island, except to backload ships already in the area off-loading convicts. And the British had no need for a naval base to service ships as Bombay already provided such facilities. Many a Ph.D. later, the only fact upon which all agreed was that, no matter what subsidiary interests there might have been, New South Wales was colonized to provide a home for the riff-raff.

And so, on 13 May 1787, the First Fleet sailed from Portsmouth, consisting of eleven vessels and 1,000 people, three-quarters of whom were convicts. Captain Arthur Phillip, at the head of the fleet, arrived in Botany Bay on 20 January 1788 and grumbled at what he saw. The land seemed barren, swampy and uninviting. He sought something better and discovered Sydney Harbour, 'one of the finest harbours in the world, in which a thousand ships on line might ride in perfect security'. It made him optimistic as it does us all, and so he moved the fleet to Sydney Cove, now Circular Quay, Priscilla's home. He raised the flag on 26 January and then set to – to trample European boots over what is geographically the oldest continent in the world, peopled at that time by some 300,000 Aborigines who had inhabited the land for at least 30,000 years.

The first settlers had no easy task; for many years Sydney was a camp rather than a town. The first architect did not arrive until 1814: he was an Irish convict, Francis Greenway, transported for forgery. Within five years his work had earned him a complete pardon. Now Greater Sydney boasts a population of more than 3 million, spreading across some 1,500 square miles (4,000 square kilometres). Sydneysiders are proud of their city. The harbour, they say, would be beautiful without Sydney, but not half as beautiful as it is now, with Sydney added. They would not want the world to think they are incapable of embellishing nature's best work. Far from it: to the harbour they added a bridge, a latticed curve of steel, and then they flanked one side with an opera house of such glorious design that it has earned its place among the great buildings of the world. The two provide the best-known images of Australia and a focal point for Sydney, behind which lies a city centre with large open spaces and skyscrapers and smart hotels and paved plazas, and beyond that an inner city of hills, of steep hills where streets swoop and dive and round corners to leafy roads and plain terraces, to pockets of perfectly restored Victorian architecture with double-storey houses fronted by lacy cast-iron balconies provoking thoughts of New Orleans.

I stayed for my first few days in a hotel in King's Cross, the 'red light' district where soliciting even in daylight is open and obvious and where by shamelessly eavesdropping I could catch some moments of intricate bargaining.

'How much?'

'What do you want?' Silence. 'What you you *want*? Then I'll tell you how much.'

Then I moved to a room in an apartment in Double Bay, one underground stop further from the city, where the prices in a score of boutiques and restaurants have earned the area the nickname Double Pay. This section has been cornered by the Jewish community, and any morning at a popular coffee shop named the Cosmopolitan, I could watch bejewelled fingers cuddle cups on the covered forecourt, or inside become aware of regular huddles of expensively dressed older men gossiping over the morning papers. Compared to parts of Europe and North America, Australia did not attract a large number of Jewish refugees. Maybe a couple of thousand before the war, and then in 1940 a very special shipload, a present from the British government in one of the more unnecessary, shabbier scandals of the war. Presumably in a moment of panic, in mid-1940 the British rounded up so-called enemy aliens and shipped many of them to Canada and Australia. Some 2,000 were herded into the *Dunera* and wound up in Australia, to be shunted into internment camps; most of them were anti-fascist, most of them were refugees from Hitler. Once again, it seems, MI5 had made a hash of things and many had been wrongly classified. By and by the mistakes were unravelled, some were repatriated and others were freed from their camps to join the Australian army. At the end of the war, around 1,000 chose to stay and, so it is argued, began to teach the Australians the benefits of non-British immigration.

Double Bay is but one small part of the inner city, a mere speck on the map of Greater Sydney which stretches for miles to the west and for miles to the north. Indeed, Sydney could well be described as three cities. The first comprises an inner ring, the fortunate 700,000 or so who live within four miles (six kilometres) of Sydney Cove and have all the advantages of an environment which is visually stimulating, cultured and convenient. Such people are favoured; they live within a stone's throw of the Opera House, the University, the theatres, the major shops and offices, the beaches and the restaurants.

Beyond this and over the harbour bridge is the outer ring, the north shore providing comfortable leafy living in single-storey houses with car-ports fringed with palm trees. The wise on the north shore work on the north shore; the unwise trundle each day across the bridge and sit, bad-tempered, in traffic jams while planners pursue thoughts of a second bridge and residents, whenever the shadow threatens, rise up and fight as though they were being asked to accept a mental home or a monumental airport.

And then there is the third city of Sydney, the Western Suburbs. You do not need a bridge to go west – and in any event the colony's first railway line struck out in that direction over a century ago in search of soil suitable for market gardens. The flat and windy plain was once famed for its oranges. It is now famed – at least according to the inhabitants of the inner ring – for being a wasteland of cheap, ugly housing; a dull place for dull people, and a problem for the State since it has the lowest level of educational attainment, the highest unemployment, the greatest number of single mothers and of deserted wives. Sydney has been moving west since the war, with migrants and lower-income families seeking a block of land, but neither services nor jobs have in any way matched the march of people.

It takes about an hour by rail from central Sydney to Blacktown, now recognized as the demographic centre of the city. At the end of the day the trains are crowded, and I stood for much of the journey. Above my head a message from the State Rail Authority asked surfers to keep their boards clear of other passengers and off the seats, and another message suggested that 650,000 passengers a day travelled the suburban networks and had nothing better to do than study the advertisements. But they had. The girls beside me gossiped about five-day wonder diets, or crocheted and ate nuts, or did the crossword and ate crisps. A handful of men read newspapers with over-large, quarrelling headlines: 'This dingo took Azaria', and 'My Dingo didn't do it', both references to a bizarre murder case a few years before when a mother claimed she had not killed her baby, but that the dingoes were responsible. For some reason this story caught people's imaginations and although the mother, Lindy Chamberlain, was found guilty, there is an ongoing campaign to free her and any fresh thread is worth reporting.

By journey's end the crowds had thinned; those left neither sighed nor yawned, they accepted the tiresome travel with good grace. The residents of Blacktown were warm in their greeting and glad to have the chance to put their own case; they hate the image they have acquired from the condescending concern of inner-city dwellers and are ready to go for the throats of those who rubbish their community. They may have problems – but they also have a fierce community pride and a commitment to a way of life which is acceptable to them. All they need is a fairer allocation of resources. They do not wish to be told what is good for the Western Suburbs by people whose own quality of life is, to them, questionable, and this shows most clearly in cultural development.

Blacktown prefers to concentrate on local history (it was once a place to which the aborigines were herded, hence its name), local theatre and local crafts, rather than worry about whether Joan Sutherland is coming to sing in the park. And the place is not ugly, just flat and all too new with neat fibro houses amid well-kept gardens. No one in Blacktown is bothered by the flatness or the newness. They are more concerned with the lack of jobs and hospitals, bus routes and child care facilities. And now that the Western Suburbs as a whole house 1.3 million people, with further expansion expected, much has been promised including a recreational park, an amusement park which claims to be Australia's answer to Disneyland, and maybe even a cultural centre. There's talk too that sand and gravel pits near Penrith are to be made into huge lakes. It may not be Sydney harbour – but beaches and big city trimmings are no attraction. Some people admitted that they had not been to Sydney in ten years. If they yearn for sight of the sea, they prefer to go south to Wollongong; but on the whole they prefer to visit the Blue

The Ribbon and the Ragged Square

Mountains, half an hour's drive further to the west. And what they like best about Blacktown and the rest of the Western Suburbs is the people. 'We're friendly, honest and fair dinkum,' they said; and friendly, honest and fair dinkum is how I found them. There wasn't a trace of suspicion, and yet they could have been forgiven for fearing that yet another writer might produce yet another tale of 'poor Westies'.

I'd met greater suspicion in Sydney. The forthright question, 'What exactly are you doing here?', accompanied many an introduction. I'd explain that my aim was to write a portrait of contemporary Australia by travelling for some eight months in a clockwise direction around the country from Sydney to Sydney. No one responded to the concept of the journey itself which was an integral part of my plan (and had been since I'd spent a weekend reading Jonathan Raban's *Old Glory* and Gavin Young's *Slow Boats to China*, whose adventures by Monday morning had left me envious and longing to be rid, at least for a while, of the constraints of a daily newspaper routine). Instead, my questioners shot back: 'Why Australia? Are you an Australian or do you have links with Australia?' Their supposition seemed to be that only Australians were interested in Australia. I assured them that I was a complete stranger, but none the less fascinated by a country about which the world seemed to know so little.

For many years people in the United Kingdom, if they thought about Australia at all, were content to assume that it was more or less Greater Britain on the other side of the world, not different enough nor exotic enough to command attention and interest. Indeed, even those who chose to emigrate skimped their homework, assuming that they would automatically feel at home and, as a result, often experienced an unnecessarily difficult period of adjustment. But all that is changing; people, not just in the United Kingdom, are becoming curious: they admire Australian films; they have seen the odd television programme, and they are keen to know what lies behind these images and beyond the mocking, deprecating humour of Barry Humphries and Paul Hogan. With the approach of 1988, the bicentennial year, this curiosity will grow and many people will consider visiting the land. Most of my questioners were content with an explanation of this sort, but a small number would mow me down with razor-sharp retorts: 'We don't want the Poms here'; 'We don't want the Poms to know about us'; 'We don't care what the Poms think of us, in fact we are sick of their views'.

Such remarks were upsetting, but not without foundation. The Poms have a reputation in Australia for complaining, for making unfavourable comparisons and for generally behaving in a supercilious manner; while not condoning the sensitivity that this has caused, I must admit that in part the reputation has been well deserved. Over the years Australia has suffered from a hefty dose of Old World superiority.

From the first, many visitors flinched at what they saw; they moaned that the gum trees looked melancholy because their leaves hung down and offered little shade; they said that the birds had no song and the flowers no scent and that the scenery was monotonous. As time passed, there were other things to bewail. Beatrice Webb savaged the illiterate speech, the ugly manners and the women: 'The women of Australia are not her finest product'; Sir Thomas Beecham was brief: 'A nation of oafs'; even D. H. Lawrence, who showed a rare empathy towards Australia, said of Sydney: 'I don't like it, it is so raw and crude. The people are so crude in their feelings – and they only want to be up to date in the conveniences – electric light and tramways. The aristocracy are people who own big shops and there is no respect for anything else.' Indeed, time and again it is Sydney that has suffered most from the pen of foreigners. Jan Morris had kindly thoughts of several cities but with Sydney she let rip: 'The origins of Sydney are unsavoury, her history is disagreeable to read, her suburbs are hideous and her politics often crooked, her buildings are mostly plain, her voices rasp on the ear ...' and this is just part of the opening paragraph! Jan Morris claims to have received hate mail for five years after her views were published in the 1960s.

And yet the Australians claim they don't care. They do, of course; they are as quick to take offence as they are to give it. Rudyard Kipling, after one visit to Australia in the 1920s, included in one of his stories an apt exchange between a group of First World War ex-servicemen. An Englishman asks an Australian: 'Have you started that republic of yours down under yet?' The Australian replies : 'No. But we're going to. *Then* you'll see.' However, on being told, 'Carry on. No one's hindering you,' he scowls and says: 'No. We know they ain't. And that's what makes us all so crazy angry with you. What *can* you do with an Empire that – that don't care what you do?'

This legacy of neglect, indifference and slights in the end drove Donald Horne, one of Australia's best-known social critics, to England to redress the balance. In 1970 under the (ironic) title *God is an Englishman*, Horne savaged Britain's self-importance and her capacity for self-delusion; he suggested that no war, no catastrophe, seemed capable of knocking the arrogance out of the British whom he portrayed as folk full of pride, bellowing 'Land of Hope and Glory' from great black lumps of cities, and who were content to be governed by a series of advertising copywriters who dashed off slogans for products that did not exist. Welfare State? Bah! Swinging Britain? Bah! *Touché*, but no truce. Some fifteen years later, another Australian journalist, Margaret Jones, who had been based for some time in London wrote a book in which she admitted that she felt disadvantaged to be an Australian; indeed, she often felt as persecuted as the Irish and included in *Thatcher's Kingdom* five pages of patronizing and snide references to Australia that had appeared in the British press over three years in the early 1980s. She suggested that the origin of all this nonsense would make an excellent Ph.D. thesis. It would indeed; and yet both sides prefer to make light of their attitudes and often prefer to deny that any antagonism exists, rather than face exposing the odd mixture of affection and exasperation that binds the two nations. Les Murray, a leading contemporary poet, has tried. He suggested that 'much of the hostility to Australia shown by the English above a certain class can be traced to the fact that we are, to a large extent, the poor who got away'.

And the poor who got away had no intention of imitating those whom they had left behind; they were glad to be rid of the old world and its restrictions and refinements. They wanted Australia to be the land of the common man with a new life-style and new attitudes. Before long, the effete Englishman had come to represent all that was irritating about the old world, and when that Englishman came to Australian shores he was in turn irritated, and thus a stereotype was born and a battle begun which it is easy enough to trace in the pages of Australian literature. It was a battle between the genteel and the robust, the refined and the crude, the men of paste and the men of steel, the old world and the new.

This battle lost much of its heat years ago, but the remnants remain just below the surface, ready to erupt whenever the Australian feels that the English are about to lord it over him. My English accent made some people fear that I was yet another Pom who had come to sneer; having been made aware of this in some very uncomfortable moments, I could see more than mere humour in car stickers which said: 'Grow your own Dope: Plant a Pom' ... 'Keep Australia Beautiful: Shoot a Pom'. A prescient Australian writer, A. G. Stephens, said in the 1890s that imported antagonisms would last longer than men thought. 'Our children bow instinctively to the fetishes of their fathers, for the heredity of centuries is not eliminated in a generation or in half a dozen generations.' He was right.

And these fetishes, which primarily reveal an unpleasant class-consciousness, are further complicated by political undertones. Many of the first poor to get away were Irish. The Irish have a good many reasons for disliking the English – together, the two have a history of mixing about as successfully as red wine and chocolate – and in those early years when anti-Pommery was more overt, it was the Irish who led the chorus. The Irish have been a great influence on Australia. They know this and they are proud of it; they do not take it for granted since it is only in the last few decades that Australian historians have analysed their contribution and made them aware of it. Before, the early settlers were merely classified as 'British' and the strands were not separated. But during the first 100 years, Irish convicts and free settlers comprised one in four of the population and, where the small minority of Irish Protestants were quickly assimilated, the Irish Catholics were not. They were different; they had a different religion and they now wanted the power and influence that had in the past been denied them. The Irish Catholics produced four Prime Ministers and one man who was to have as much influence

as the four put together. His name was Daniel Mannix and he was
Archbishop of Melbourne. He came to Australia in 1913 and within
a few years had made his name as a rebel leader by whipping up a
storm over conscription for the 1914–18 war. He advised the Irish –
and anyone else who would listen – to have nothing to do with
Britain's problems in Europe. Twice a referendum on conscription
was lost; those who fought in the First World War did so voluntarily.
After this early success, Archbishop Mannix settled down to pursue
his passion: emancipation through education was his slogan and he
fought doggedly for State aid for Catholic schools. It sounds a laudable
and harmless aim, but it caused gigantic waves through Australian
politics.

Mannix's first strategy was to battle through the Labor Party,
whose supporters were largely but not solely Irish Catholics. But this
did not work; State aid was not given to Catholic schools even when
Irish Catholic Prime Ministers were in office. Disappointed, Mannix
and his followers then decided to try and purge the Labor Party of
its leftish and communist leanings by founding a Catholic social
movement which infiltrated the unions in an attempt to take control.
For his pains, Mannix and his supporters were expelled from the
Labor Party; but they survived to form the Democratic Labor Party,
a split which kept the Labor Party out of office from 1955 until 1972.
It is not surprising that Robert Gordon Menzies, the Liberal leader,
with victory in the balance in 1964, granted State aid to Catholic
schools, indeed to all private schools. But by 1964 something else
had happened: post-war migration had brought in many European
Catholics, and Irish influence was no longer dominant. It was thus
that much easier for Menzies and the rest of Anglo-Australia to
support a move which no longer benefited solely the Irish.

So much for the stuff of politics. The Irish have made other marks,
too. They provided one of the few enduring heroes, Ned Kelly; they
were the ring-leaders of the only rebellion to take place on Australian
soil (of which more later), and they have contributed a considerable
number of strands to the Australian character. I felt this to be so, but
it was only on returning to London and opening Donald Connery's
book *The Irish* that I became certain. Connery was, of course,

discussing the Irish in Ireland, but he could well have been describing the Australian. He suggests that the Irish are fatalistic and never surprised when things go wrong, being convinced that all will work out in the end; that they are given to improvisation and are able to cope and thrive in adversity; that they see life as a dance rather than a race and look with suspicion upon excessive expenditure of energy or too obvious a display of ambition; that they are not a demonstrative race and are embarrassed by displays of feeling – emotions are for the sporting field, and on the sporting field they show a self-confidence that is missing elsewhere.

The Irishman is elusive, evasive, eager to please; in an oriental way he will not disagree with you directly nor reveal his full feelings. You will learn about them later from a third person. An Irishman will never say anything about you to your face that he would rather say behind your back. We shy away from speaking the truth. And we are a great people for disliking; we never speak well of each other and we have developed the habit of belittling and back-biting and we like to drag down what is most lofty.

This habit of belittling is most disconcerting for a newcomer. People would ask me whom I was meeting and interviewing; when I offered a name or two, the response would be: 'Oh, not that dill' or 'he's a dickhead'. The Australians have a colourful way with colloquialisms; these two were the first of many to be collected. But in the end it was not disconcerting back-biting that moved me from Sydney; it was physical discomfort.

I found, towards Christmas and a month after I arrived, that I had difficulty breathing – that I wheezed through the day and gasped for breath during the night. It was most embarrassing. Many explanations were offered: that my difficulties were psychosomatic; that they were caused by the histamines in wine; that they were provoked by cats or house mites. No one mentioned that Australians (second only to New Zealanders) suffer more than any other nation from hay fever and asthma and that the culprit is pollen. I discovered this by visting a doctor who said that I was probably allergic to any number of pollens; ryegrass was high on a list that was so long that I didn't try to memorize it. He gave me a prescription for an inhalant and some pellets to be fired down the back of my throat. I took them home, read somewhere that Australians spend $A7 million a year on such things, and decided that, rather than alleviate the symptoms, I'd prefer to tackle the cause. I'd go to Tasmania.

The timing was right. I'd become interested in the Sydney-to-Hobart yacht race and had made friends with Neville and Valerie Chidgey, who referred to themselves as a geriatric sailing couple and who were taking part in the race in their boat *Mystic Seven* with the help of four much younger crew members. Their enthusiasm was infectious; the race dominated their calendar. The event had first taken place in 1945 when a group of friends, wondering how to spend that dreary week between Christmas and the New Year, decided to cruise to Hobart and then, to heighten interest, decided to make it a race. From a nine-yacht 'friendly', over the years it has become an ocean-racing classic across 630 nautical miles of the wildest and most unpredictable waters. The start of the race is one of the great spectacles of Australian sport, a Boxing Day tradition for thousands who take to the harbour in ferries, yachts and canoes to escort the fleet to sea. If the sun is shining and the winds demand a spinnaker, then the sight of well over a hundred boats weaving their way down the harbour, through the Heads for the turn southwards to Hobart, is said to be stunning.

That Boxing Day morning was hot, cloudy and dull. There were no spinnakers and the sea was grey and the sky was grey, even the sails seemed grey. None the less there was a carnival atmosphere. The press boat, to which I had attached myself, was for the first time allowed to sail in front of the fleet, dead centre of the course – in previous years it had had to keep alongside. We left an hour before the starting gun and sailed down the harbour, filming the fun all round. There were parties on every spectator boat, much music, much noise, much drinking – and the inevitable naked lady attempting to catch the attention of television cameras.

For the start, the fleet was spread right across the harbour; for a while the spectator boats were well behaved and kept their distance, to allow the competitors a clear run but, as we approached the Heads, restraint broke down. It became difficult to distinguish between competitors and onlookers; the tempers of crews were tested to the limit as they screamed and waved in an effort to get a clear passage. Choppy seas added to the confusion, at least one spectator craft capsized, and several competitors were forced to tack. The muddle made an amazing picture: there were boats as far as the eye could see and all much too close together. Could the Armada have seemed more menacing?

And then they were gone. The excitement was over for Sydney; the action had moved to Hobart, and I was glad to be able to follow the fleet.

CHAPTER 2

The Wilderness and the Dam

There has always been a gulf between Tasmania and the rest of Australia. It is called the Bass Strait and it produces differences and difficulties out of all proportion to its width of a mere 100 miles (160 kilometres). Tasmania has mountains; they may not be high, peaking at 5,000 feet (1,525 metres), but they are numerous; it has rivers and grand forests and lakes, and there is plentiful rain and a gentle climate with temperatures which rarely drop below freezing or climb above 75°F (24°C). Earlier this century, the residents of Sydney and Melbourne flocked there to avoid the summer heat, but since the advent of air-conditioning and cheap flights to Bali, the numbers have decreased. Now when they cast a thought southwards, it is usually to moan that the island hanging off the edge there is a drain on the family purse.

Over the years the Federal Government has given Tasmania more money per capita than any other State, because it is the smallest (about the size of Sri Lanka), because its population is tiny (less than half a million) and because that strip of water causes economic difficulties which at times seem insuperable. One Prime Minister became so exasperated that he said he wished he could get a piece of rope and haul Tassie to the mainland or else cut her loose and hope she would float away. But Tassie is unmoved and refuses to allow dollars from Canberra to bribe her into subservience. She is fiercely proud and independent of thought. Sometimes her origins cause her to wince: she was founded in 1803 as a penal colony for the worst of convicts; but on the whole she manages to turn this to her advantage by proclaiming a pronounced sense of history. Most of the

State's early development work was done by convicts: they built roads, bridges, churches and many public buildings, and these have lasted. The guidebooks to Hobart are cluttered with references to the work of convicts and, 100 miles south at Port Arthur, the original penal settlement has been restored for all to admire.

There is only one way to get to Hobart from Sydney and that is by air – unless of course you sail with the fleet or persuade the Australian National Line to shove you in with the freight. I sought both alternatives and ended up flying. The bus from Hobart to the centre of town skirts Constitution Dock, and there, through the window, I saw them. *Mystic Seven* had arrived a day earlier than expected, and the crew were celebrating their success munching lunch on deck. They had not been first over the line; that honour is always reserved for the maxi-yachts, but they'd done well enough within their class. The atmosphere on the dock was so heightened you'd have thought every boat had won. The great boat race was about to become the great booze-up.

Hobart loves the race. Its citizens turn out at all hours to line the dock and cheer the arriving boats: the event keeps Tassie on the map and brings around $A1 million into the town. Not everyone, however, is well pleased. The local newspaper columns were full for days with letters signed 'Lemon Squash' and 'Sad Crewman', and arguing that there is a fine line between high-spirited celebration and behaviour that is offensive even to tolerant locals. And that behaviour includes obscene language, urinating in public, vomiting over boats and drunkenness to the point of incapability. 'Lemon Squash' knows where it will end: 'One day Australia will finish just as other countries have finished – destroyed by their own greed and drunken behaviour.'

He (or she) has a point. Paul Hogan has never dared show it like this. That New Year's Eve the whole place buzzed, the pubs were full, the restaurants happy to squeeze another chair into the space between the tables and the noise from Constitution Dock surely was acceptable only to those busy making a buck selling fast food and trashy fluorescent headbands from stalls encircling the wharf. The filth floating between the yachts was distressing, and while some of it may have been tossed there by passers-by eager to shed a beer can, most of it had to have come from the yachts themselves.

That night there was to be no sleep: bands were playing on the wharf and each boat had its own party; the general rule seemed to be, the smaller the boat the bigger the party, and the success of that party was determined by decibels and by the number of drunks who ended up in the dock. Space being limited on yachts, those who wanted to dance (or who wanted to pretend to dance in order to kiss and cuddle), and those who wanted to kick beer cans around, moved to the wharf. A real rage. On *Mystic Seven* we had our share of fun and champagne, and at three a.m. I made a final circuit of the dock which was by then midcalf deep in rubbish, and then attempted to sleep on board the boat. By eight a.m., those without hangovers were eating breakfast, delighted to see that the Hobart authorities had already cleaned up the mess. No doubt they feared the wrath of 'Lemon Squash', out for an early morning stroll.

The party was not over, however. We were to start again at ten a.m. New Year's Day would not be the same without the Quiet Little Drink. I'd been hearing about this event for weeks. Not to be missed, they all said, referring to the fact that one lucky pub would be able to rid itself of 14,000 beers in one session. The early birds, arriving at ten a.m., also got a cabaret – the yachties each doing their party piece to entertain the others. By the time I arrived – it cost $A3 to cross the threshold, some of which goes to charity, and for that you get a Fosters sticker plonked on your bosom – the floor was already awash and men were elbow to elbow and God knows who could hear anything. Did someone say that the minimum shout (round) was $A100! Outside, there was a beer garden where enterprising sailors were selling hamburgers and steak sandwiches – that's a hunk of steak slapped between two pieces of sliced white bread. It seemed to go well with beer and high spirits.

After an hour it was time for me to leave the yachties and join the Greenies (Conservationists). The boat race was not the only event keeping Tassie firmly in focus on the mainland. But no one at the pub was much interested; Greenies, to them, were dole bludgers, and their cause the butt of jokes. There was even a mickey-taking T-shirt on sale. It showed Tasmania looking huge and Australia looking tiny, and imposed on the map were the words 'Save the Tasmanian Kevlah'. The Kevlah looked like a beaver. Kevlah is the cloth from which sails are made.

The Greenies' cause was a dam, a dam which the Tasmanian Government thought it would like to build across the Franklin River in a pretty part of south-west Tasmania, home of one of the world's last temperate rain forests and one of the world's last wild rivers. They call this area Wilderness, and it is magnificent. It is an area of grand river valleys as unspoilt as the first Eden and still remote enough to evoke a sense of awe. There are no detergents to be found in these waters, no heavy metals or sewage, no beer cans or broken bottles. And this rare river is hedged by magical banks of trees: of myrtle, of sassafras, of dogwood, of leatherwood, of native laurel. And, of course, of Huon Pine, a tree which matures at 500 years and lasts for thousands. It is the colour of pale honey; it is close-grained, strong, silky and aromatic. It has been under threat since the first settlers arrived and felled the pine for boats. Now, if the Franklin were to be dammed, it would destroy thirty-five per cent of the known habitat of the Huon Pine.

All this rare and natural beauty few have seen, for it is accessible only to outdoor types given to rafting down wild rivers. Many fear such places. Tasmanians, like mainland Australians, live in towns and cities. The Wilderness frightens and provokes ridicule. The Premier of the State called the Franklin a 'brown ditch, leech-ridden, unattractive'. But that's because he wanted to make it his, destroy it and create electricity and jobs to ease the highest unemployment rate in Australia – a full two per cent above the national average of nine-and-a-half per cent. The Greenies argued that the dam was not needed; that the energy forecasts were based on questionable statistics; that there were many other ways of solving unemployment, and that the wishes of the Tasmanian people had never been properly sought. The Government at one time offered the public a referendum which permitted a choice between two dams, at different points on the same river – but there was no 'no dam' option. The result was a remarkable forty-four per cent informal vote – spoiled ballot papers, many with 'No Dam' written in.

This may sound like a parochial squabble, but it was not. The dam issue became the most important clash between conservation and development that Australia had ever seen. The mountain rivers are among the gems of the landscape, while cheap hydro-electricity is sacred to Tasmania's economic policy. The row had smouldered for years, each side growing more entrenched until, finally, the fight erupted into the kind of drama reserved for episodes of *Dallas*. Self-interest, intrigue, greed, lies and misrepresentation all flourished. Families were wrenched apart as members took opposite sides; towns turned against one another; politicians threatened resignation and one swore that he had never before experienced an issue where the parties were so unwilling to listen to each other. Such was the distortion and animosity, I felt I was certainly in need of what Hemingway had once recommended, a built-in shock-proof shit detector, before clambering aboard the bus for the six-hour journey to Strahan.

The 'bus' was an eight-seater van loaned by a travel agency to the Tasmanian Wilderness Society (TWS), an organization founded in the mid-1970s to save the Franklin from the hands of the Hydro Electric Commission (HEC). Its growth was slow in the early years, but during 1982 it doubled its membership to 6,000, increased its volunteer permanent staff to around forty and acquired a handsome house as its headquarters. The society bought the house by appealing to members to make a $A1,000 investment. A hundred did, providing enough to buy the $A70,000 property and leaving the rest for renovation. The scheme was masterminded by a local business-woman who makes furniture and who is dedicated to the Franklin. Tears came to Judy Richter's eyes as she talked of old ladies sending $A5 bills with notes of regret that they had never seen the Wilderness. And now never would. 'Gee, I'm proud to be an Australian at moments like that.'

The society's income, she explained, came from three sources: donations, membership and profits from the sale of T-shirts and postcards and so forth. She claimed a million-dollar turnover and denied, as they all do, that the TWS gets funds from East Germany or from oil companies who would prefer Tasmania to get its energy from their sources. The organization's aim was to get the Federal Government to intervene and stop the Tasmanian Government building the dam; this the TWS hotly argued the Federal Government had the right to do, since the region is listed as a World Heritage Area; and not merely the right, maybe even a legal obligation as a signatory to the World Heritage Convention. Such an obligation would take precedence over a State's right to do much as it pleases.

To publicize its point, the society began organizing demonstrations which, it turned out, drew crowds as big as the anti-Vietnam rallies. Its efforts then moved on to organizing an impressive blockade of two sites, one where the HEC had begun building a landing stage on the river, and another on an access road where the workers' village was to be constructed. The blockade became a well-orchestrated media event, grabbing headlines in newspapers and on television screens. And as publicity grew, so too did the number of blockaders, mostly young folk from all over Australia, aided from time to time by a celebrity, including the British naturalist David Bellamy, a Cockney botanist who talked of Tasmania as though it were his own backyard.

They assembled in their hundreds at a camp site in the tiny west-coast town of Strahan and, after several days' training in the skills of non-violent action, went upriver by boat. As soon as they set foot on land owned by the Hydro Electric Commission, they were arrested for trespass or obstruction. (Increased police powers, and also increased penalties for trespass, had been introduced specifically to deal with the protesters.) Once arrested, they were taken to court and asked to accept bail conditions not to appear in the area again. Many signed; others did not do so and went to jail, and there they stayed until they signed or until their case came for trial, which was often several months after the arrest.

Such people left Tasmania politicized. They had arrived somewhat bewildered, uncertain what to expect, and armed only with suitable gear plus commitment and passion and aching to do something that proved that, as individuals, they were not impotent, that with effort they could exercise a degree of control over their own lives, or at least their environment – and, yes, they ached to give the wielders of power a punch on the nose. They looked alike, young, shabby and longish-haired; few appeared to be committed politically; some had established careers and were using their annual leave; some were students eating into their long vacation; some were new graduates beginning the dispiriting search for jobs.

The forty or so working for the TWS also seemed of a kind: a trifle lost, stumbling a little, not having found careers that caught their imagination; or having found careers which disappointed. These people were seeking to save a river, and they were also seeking to find themselves. Rob, for example, was a zoology graduate from the Australian National University in Canberra. More than two years earlier he had decided to take a break from job-seeking and to have a walking holiday in Tasmania. A chance encounter led him to the TWS, and there he stayed. He worked part-time for the Conservation Foundation, preparing fact-sheets on rain forests, and lived well enough on the $A80 it paid him, sharing a house with other society members. The joy of being involved kept him there, and he intended staying now to the end, telling me proudly that both his parents were on their way to Hobart to blockade and be arrested. His father is a retired, high-ranking public servant from the Department of Defence, and his mother an academic.

Felicity went to university and ended up teaching in primary school; she hated it, and taught meditation instead. She now has a child and lives off her weekly $A100 single-parent allowance. Her mother paid the deposit and organized the mortgage on the house, and she is repaying the loan from the rent provided by fellow Greenies. This house welcomed me warmly and gave me a bed while I was in Hobart.

Chris had been a trainee reporter on the local newspaper but deserted after two months, having found that he didn't fit in and that he disliked parochialism. He had turned himself into one of the society's spokesmen. Vince, too, had come to dislike his job as a wages clerk and again, while on a walking holiday, looked in to say 'Hello' and stayed, living off his savings and odd jobs. 'The dam is an issue which shows what is wrong with the world – economic mismanagement – and it's not enough to sit around and talk about it. We are all disillusioned with party politics; we all feel powerless. This is an issue where we can exert influence and we can win.' When it is won, he will study law.

A wild river brought these people together. What *kept* them together was to become apparent during the next few days.

We didn't talk much on the bus to Strahan. Instead we sat back and admired the undulating green hills peppered with farms, which led gradually to the Central Highlands. Just before darkness fell and just before we became sated with scenery, we came upon a shocking sight: miles of wreckage, of battle-scarred ground where trees had been flattened and lay in lifeless piles. For some the amputation had not been neat and stumps jutted accusingly into the air. Others, unwanted, diseased perhaps, dying, had been left, looking as though napalmed.

The sight caused Bob Burton, secretary of the TWS, to turn in his seat and explain: 'Admire the work – the forests being chopped down for pulp, for newsprint and writing-paper. Tasmania is like a Third-World country in decline, her forests are being given away as woodchip to the Japanese. They say the Tasmanians were born with a match in one hand and an axe in the other.' The worst sight of all, he added, we'd been spared that night because of the darkness. I was, however, to see it another day.

It was midnight by the time I arrived at Hamers Hotel, the cheapest in town (and indeed the cheapest in the whole of my eight-month stay): $A16 a night for a single room and a huge breakfast. The bar was still open and outside it hung a sign: 'All rooms are noisy because they are over the bar and drinkers like to sing.' They didn't bother me; I was just thankful that the bed had an electric blanket as it was much cooler in Tasmania.

Next morning I was woken to take a phone call in the bar. It was from London, and a cross voice reported that whoever had answered the phone had said: 'Can't you call back later – I'm cooking breakfast.'

Mr Ryan and I were not to become friends. This was a pro-dam hotel and the Ryans of this world have no time for journalists whipping up a storm. His wife served breakfast without a smile.

I asked her about the dam. 'Well, people want their power, you know. We must have it. We have enough power cuts as it is. One Christmas we were without electricity for the entire holiday.' On the tables there were plastic mats with views of Lake Pedder. Lake Pedder was created from the last dam scandal. 'No one had heard of this place,' said Mrs Ryan, pointing to a mat, 'until the lake was created, and now they come in their hundreds. A Greenie the other day said to my husband that he hoped the Hydro didn't get their hands on Pedder. He thought it was a natural lake. Most of them don't know what they are talking about.'

Her husband went on television to complain about the Greenies. He said they sat in his pub and hugged a soda water all night, keeping good drinkers out. It was not true. For the next week I was to join the Greenies drinking his beer and cider and wine, and eating his counter meals when they got bored with lentils at the camp. The counter meal is ubiquitous; it is a meal ordered at the counter and collected by the customer when his number is called. Cuts down on service. In Hamers there was one bar where the Greenies gathered and another for the pro-dammers. They didn't mix. I was the only person who moved between the two.

The Warden of Strahan got up from his chair and turned away. Hugh McDermott's life in recent weeks had been fraught. He was tired and turned away to avoid revealing the tears in his eyes. 'Who cares if they want to oust me. What have I to lose? Face, that's all.'

Face *is* all. Tasmanians are proud and they go to great lengths to keep their pride intact. They are a stubborn and fiercely independent people, and none more so than those on the west coast. If the rest of Tassie is busy holding its own against the mainland, Strahan is busy holding its own against the rest of Tassie. The State was first settled in 1803, but there wasn't a road linking the west coast to Hobart until 1932. That cuts you off and makes you independent and prideful.

Hugh McDermott has been Warden of Strahan for twenty years,

re-elected each year by his fellow councillors, of whom there are eight. He's been a councillor for twenty-seven years. Strahan itself is only just 100 years old, and this means that McDermott has been concerned with running the place for more than a quarter of its existence. To be thrown out now would be a blow.

'I've been anti the dam for ten years, long before the environmentalists were around, and I've been anti because of the effect it will have on tourist traffic. It's all we have now. This tiny town of five hundred people swells to fifteen hundred during the season – and that's only a couple of months a year. Way back, Strahan was a thriving port handling all the minerals mined on the west coast: copper, silver, lead and zinc. Gradually trade frittered away because of competition with the deep-water port of Burnie in the north. The final blow came in 1970. Consolidated Goldfields had taken over the copper mine up the road in Queenstown, and in 1970 decided to close the smelter and the refinery and ship concentrates to Japan. Burnie won again.'

Hugh McDermott was Wharf Superintendent until 1970, and then with sixty-five others he was made redundant. That may not sound many, but it was half the town's working population. Some moved to Burnie. McDermott, with his brother, built flatlets to rent to holidaymakers. 'It's a great credit to the people that this town didn't die. We got to a low ebb and then dug our heels in. People are like that.

'There used to be fishing here too; but each year the copper mine disgorges two million tonnes of solid waste into the rivers, and that finally ends up in the harbour and has turned it into a marine desert. The only fishing now is deep sea, and that is in trouble. The Japanese started abalone fishing and we know what they are all about. They get the thing off the ground by offering big money, and then they gradually pull back on quotas and prices. And what can we do but accept the situation? No one else wants abalone.

'Tourism is all we have and that was started by a man with vision, Reg Morrison. He was a timber cutter and knew the beauties of the river, and he bought a boat so that others could see it, too. It is a slow journey from here because it takes more than an hour to get out of the harbour. The round trip takes six hours.'

It is a slow journey. I made it on the *Denison Star*, joining the Greenies on a day off, and tourists on a day out. You see the merest edge of the forest and a fraction of the river. It is better than not seeing it at all.

'We are aware that people find it a bit much; they all seem in so much of a hurry these days. So now another operator has bought a faster boat which cuts the trip to three hours. But that does harm, you know. The wash from a boat going at twenty-five knots damages the banks, little landslides are created and you can see trees tipping into the river. Going up the river on that fast boat is like going through the botanical gardens on a motorbike. And if the dam *is* built, it will provide access much more easily by road, cutting out the need for tourists to bother with the harbour or with Strahan. All this might sound mean and selfish, but people's jobs and the town's survival are at stake.'

It sounded neither mean nor selfish; Hugh McDermott was the only person to admit self-interest, and it was refreshing and helped me to sort out the confusing stands taken by others in the town. Two boat operators, for one thing, were on opposite sides of the dam fence. 'Ah yes, the fast boat operator is pro-dam and people do say that he has already been given the concession to operate a boat on the lake when flooding has taken place! It seems more likely that his interests are merely short term. By the time the dam is built he will have made his money and left Strahan.'

The Warden was upset that morning because, the night before, pro-dammers at a meeting in Queenstown had voted to get up a petition to have him removed. His main sin was allowing the Greenies to use the People's Park.

'I didn't hesitate. The TWS has been coming here for their Wilderness Festival for several years and there has never been any trouble. There is no trouble now, except that the numbers have grown. The park is really only suitable for sixty, and some nights there are a hundred and twenty people there. This bothers the permanent residents in caravans and at first caused problems with the toilets and showers and washing machines. But the Greenies saw that and have been using the facilities sparingly and have provided chemical toilets for their own use. The cry now is, where are they being emptied! The Health Inspector is happy, but to take the heat out of the situation we are finding them a larger space, a field on the outskirts of town.'

I had been at the previous night's meeting, and the heat would not be taken out of the opposition by such a move. The Greenies were simply unwelcome to the pro-dammers.

That morning another problem had arisen to blight the life of Hugh McDermott: a group of Aborigines had arrived in town and pitched their embassy on the beach and asked to have their flag flying from the council building. 'Well,' said Hugh McDermott, breaking into laughter, 'the council doesn't have a flag-pole, so that is one decision I won't have to make! The only pole is in Memorial Park and the Returned Servicemen's League will have to face up to that one!'

The Aborigines in Tasmania have a peculiar problem. The more blinkered persist in maintaining that they don't exist; that they are extinct, effectively wiped out by the white man; and they can even put a date on it: 1876. But with growing awareness during the early 1970s, an increasing number have been openly asserting their Aboriginal identity – although there are no fullbloods and some do look white. The Aboriginal Centre, with offices in Hobart and Launceston, claims 3,000 Aborigines in Tasmania. In 1971 there were 700. It was members of the Centre who were now camped on the beach. No one is supposed to camp on the beach. The police had been to look and had passed on by.

I invited myself to the embassy, and sat on the floor of the tent, to try to discover why the movement had attached itself to the Greenies so late in the day. The answer was that they had only recently realized the significance of the sites that would be flooded. 'Only a few of us have been up there to see the caves and now that we have we realized. In one cave there were beams of light coming in from two angles and we didn't need a torch to see and as soon as we got inside we felt at home, as though we had been there before. We kept silent, not knowing what the others were thinking, but we were all feeling the same. Now we must save the river because the land is ours and we don't want a fucking dam on it when it is eventually handed back to us.'

It is because the river is so inaccessible that the caves have taken so long to find. Once discovered, they appear to be a prehistorian's dream. They say the caves have been preserved like sealed laboratories; damp-sealed for 15,000 years, and that they will now provide the world with a glorious opportunity to study a unique Ice-Age community.

The Aboriginal camp was on the road that leads to the Greenies' new camp – soon to be christened Greenie Acres. It is nowhere as pretty as the People's Park which is deep and narrow, extending only a few yards on either side of a central gravel path. The cleared space then terminates among a canopy of tall eucalyptus and blackwoods and fern. There were many small tents and two large ones for food (vegetarian food at $A1 a meal) and a security tent where people tended to gather. The Greenies were happy there and slow to see the wisdom of a move. Slow, too, because every decision was made by consensus, a time-consuming and frustrating process, but one which at least gave each a chance to contribute and participate and which avoided backroom politics and encouraged openness. This did not mean that there were endless mass meetings. On arrival, newcomers were divided into Affinity Groups, and it was these groups which thrashed out decisions and then appointed a spokesperson to attend another meeting. And it was inside these Affinity Groups that the non-violent action training took place.

I asked to observe such a group and was readily accepted, provided I joined in rather than sat on the sidelines. Together then, we learned how to make decisions under pressure and by example. Here we were blockading the road, blocking the path of a bulldozer which suddenly started to move towards us. Should we remain still and sing? Should we link arms and stand silently? Should we link arms and walk slowly backwards – or would that signify retreat? As we ploughed through many such examples, so it became easier for each to offer a view and all to come to agreement. We also discussed how to talk to the HEC workers and the police, what tone of voice and attitude to adopt in order to convert rather than alienate. Then there was a significant amount of role-playing and scene-sketching; we became the press asking questions, an aggressive policeman, an angry pro-dammer – all of which enabled the blockader to anticipate problems and not be thrown by situations.

There were also games to change the pace and the mood, and a fascinating exercise in active listening: in how to observe tone, gestures, eyes and expression while a person is talking, how to concentrate on what was being said rather than evaluate and judge midway. For this we divided into pairs and for five minutes one of the pair talked about his or her reasons for joining the blockade; for a further two minutes the listener gave a précis of what she had heard and then, finally, the original speaker corrected the mistakes. An invaluable lesson in how much we fail to hear.

My Affinity Group had a special problem. It was university vacation, the camp was full and it was rumoured that not everyone would be able to take part in a blockade. And yet all were anxious to go up the river, to see it and to experience several days in a daunting base camp which, when I saw it in the rain, could not be described as enticing, especially when I learned that you were likely to be awakened by a kiss from a leech. In the event of a surplus of blockaders, who decided who should go? That was what my group wanted to know. The answer seemed to be that the non-violent action trainers made the choice. My group denounced that and said that, if weeding-out had to be done, the group itself would make the choice. That seemed fair.

I enjoyed my membership of this group; I enjoyed watching the dominant personalities surface and recede, and the quieter ones gradually allow themselves to be drawn out, and most of all enjoyed the difference it made to my stay in Strahan. We'd meet in the street and hug each other, share a drink and a chat. I was no longer an outsider.

That helped as I waited for Bob Brown to be released from jail, and I had no intention of leaving until I met the man who was behind this campaign and who had been nominated 'Australian of the Year', by one of the country's two national newspapers. The Greenies described him as the first among equals; but they wrapped the words up in the kind of awe the young and idealistic reserve for natural leaders. The Tasmanian Wilderness Society *is*, in most eyes, Dr Bob Brown. He was among the first to be arrested and, since he refused to accept bail conditions, he had spent several weeks in jail, to mounting pressure from his supporters. They felt he was of greater use to the cause outside jail and that he should sign the conditions. In the end he accepted their argument and drove straight to Strahan to rally his followers.

We met at one of the town's few meeting places, a shop which doubles as a fast food outlet. And there, clutching two hamburgers and a chocolate milk shake, he sat on a wooden bench and explained how he had discovered, by accident, the cause which was to take over his life.

Dr Brown is the son of a New South Wales policeman who grew up to love gum trees and the great outdoors while his father was posted from one country police station to another. He became a doctor because that is what his father wanted. 'There was no altruism in it. I did it because my family thought it was a good idea and I was much too shy and withdrawn to argue.' He hated university and medical school, but none the less completed his studies and began to practise. In 1970 he went to London as a locum. 'By the end of the trip I had overcome the urge to pursue a conventional career. A friend in Australia offered me his practice – which was worth fifty thousand dollars a year – and I said no.'

Instead, he took a leisurely passage back home on a cruise ship as its doctor, and then, one day while browsing through a newspaper, he saw an advertisement for a locum in Launceston, in northern Tasmania, and off he went. 'If you stay more than a few weeks in Tasmania, you're done for. Here, I'm right. I bought a house with a mountain at the back and a river at the front.' And he discovered the Dam. 'It was 1975 and a friend asked me to raft down the Franklin. What's that? I asked. I'd never heard of the river, few people had, and I'd never seen a rubber raft. When he'd answered my questions I still wasn't keen. I like to get to places under my own steam. In the end I agreed to go rafting with him if he came bush walking with me first. And those two weeks of rafting turned out to be the best in my life.

'We'd spent eleven days without seeing anyone and then suddenly we turned a bend in the river and there they were, men with chain-saws looking for a dam site.'

The movement to save the Franklin was born immediately with sixteen people in Dr Brown's house. In 1978 he gave up his medical practice, to live on his savings and concentrate on the river. 'I had many doubts. What was I doing giving up medicine to save a river, when all those bombs were being aimed at mankind? What finally convinced me was seeing it all as part of the same argument – man's inability to handle technology. If you can't save a river, then you haven't got much chance of saving mankind from nuclear weapons madness.'

Dr Brown is a modest and likeable man. He has pared his needs to a minimum, hardly ever sees his own home and travels with a sleeping-bag, willing to stay anywhere. Furthermore, he has the charisma to encourage others to do the same. For this reason, he reminded me of the early days of Ralph Nader's success in the United States. He liked the comparison. The big difference is that Nader would never have stood for parliament.

'I decided it was necessary but I hated doing it. I hated all the campaigning and the self-promotion.'

In any event, he lost to Norman Sanders, a flamboyant American who had settled in Tasmania and who was also a leading light in the fight to save the Franklin. However, Mr Sanders got tired of the job; got bored with giving 'geography lessons to drunken bums' and quit, and so Dr Brown became an MP. He thought the salary would be useful; it would enable him to hire several people to work out detailed options for employment, based on tourism and labour-intensive small industries.

The Organization for Tasmanian Development sneered at the thought: 'Those Greenies are trying to turn us all into tourist guides and rafting instructors.' Kelvin McCoy, who founded the OTD in order that 'the silent majority' should have a voice against the TWS, had no time at all for Greenies. He disliked their clothes, the food they ate and their middle-class attitudes. 'Who can afford to raft down the Franklin – very few people. When the dam is built and there is a lake and roads, many, many more people will be able to enjoy the scenery.'

But secretly he envied their middle-class ability to put their case across, to win the media over. 'We know they have the edge on us there, and the best we can do is organize demonstrations so that thousands of Tasmanians will take to the streets to show what they want for their State. The pro-dammers increase in numbers every time another Greenie arrives from the mainland. We don't care what they think – it's Tasmania for the Tasmanians.'

I suggested that the sight of so many people from all over Australia coming to fight for the Franklin showed a commendable unity in a country where national feeling was lacking; where each State was more concerned with itself than with the welfare of the country as a whole.

He paused for a long while and then conceded that I might just have a point.

Kelvin McCoy was just as passionate and committed as any conservationist, and in many ways more likeable. The Greenies were so *certain* that they were right; Kelvin McCoy had doubts and occasionally showed a glimpse of bewilderment. He couldn't understand how this river issue had grown to command mainland, let alone international, attention. I spent many enjoyable hours with him, listening to his side of the story, and one day hitched a ride with the mail van to visit him at his home in Tullah where he lives with his family in isolation; where there is nothing to do at the end of the day but watch television. And when the rain comes down on the tin roof, it's quite difficult to do even that. He was there building a dam. He works for the HEC.

There are thirty-nine dams and twenty-six hydro-electric stations in Tasmania. The HEC is a victim of its own success. Decade after decade for more than fifty years, it has provided its own consumption estimates, chosen its own projects, and received the support of an unbroken succession of Labor governments between 1934 and 1982. The Premier at the time was Liberal, and just as ardent a supporter.

Kelvin McCoy was also a victim of the HEC success. It was drilled into him at school that the HEC was responsible for converting

Tasmania from an agricultural economy to the most highly industrialized, power-consuming State. In the same classroom he was also
taught that Tasmania had attracted world-class industry through its
cheap power. And so it had. But one set of figures showed that the
seventeen largest users of electricity take their profits out of the State,
and that while they may use sixty-seven per cent of the electricity,
they provide only six per cent of jobs. Other reports show that in the
last twenty years few new industries had been tempted and that this
indicated that hydro-industrialization had run its course.

The HEC, of course, cannot agree. They are convinced that by
1991, when the Franklin dam would be completed, the power would
be needed otherwise there would be rationing. Said Bill Gaskell, the
second-in-command: 'No one would destroy the countryside without
good reason. We are not unappreciative of what is there, nor of what
will be in its place. What this comes down to is that we need power,
and hydro-electricity is cheaper – once built, it goes on creating
electricity for hundreds of years – *and* it causes less pollution.'

The State is proud of its environmental record. The tourist brochures boast that fifteen per cent of the area is given over to national
parks, nature reserves, wildlife sanctuaries and so on. It's a pity about
Queenstown. It's the ugliest place on earth, a monument to ignorance
and to greed and growth. It's the sight I missed on the journey to
Strahan because darkness had fallen. Queenstown is dominated by
a copper mine; and uncontrolled pollution during the early days of
copper smelting, plus the demand for wood to feed the furnaces, has
left the town with a lunar landscape. The hills have no grass, no
greenery, no trees; the slopes eroded long ago. The residents love it.
They say that when the sun shines, the denuded hills change colour –
just like Ayers Rock. It is rumoured that they have refused grants to
replant because what they have instead is a tourist attraction.

I hitched another ride to see for myself. The car's driver was a
proud Queenstowner, driven to Western Australia by lack of work,
but back on a visit, and still proud. He kept stopping the car and
suggesting I take photographs, and then as we arrived he said, 'I
must just show you something before you go ...' We stopped by a

football pitch. 'Have you ever seen one like that – made of gravel? The grass won't grow. I had many a sore knee as a kid, playing on that.'

It began to rain again. Fortunately the pavements in the main streets are covered by wooden awnings and give partial protection. I found a café called The Miners' Crib Room and sat drinking coffee, watching the rain come down; watching it swirl through the gutters carting with it cigarette ends, straws, anything light. A squashed beer can remained nailed to the spot where a heel had ground out the last breath. The wooden awnings were linked by drenched triangles of bunting in orange and green and purple and pink. There were fairy lights too and a sign saying 'Welcome to Queenstown'. And lots of postcards of denuded hills. Forlorn ... the place is forlorn. A victory for violation.

In early 1983, Malcolm Fraser was Liberal Prime Minister of Australia. He refused to ban the dam, but he did try and persuade the Liberal Premier of Tasmania, Robin Gray, to find an alternative. Mr Gray refused. In March of that year an election was held and Bob Hawke led the Labor Party to victory. The Labor Party was opposed to the dam and took the matter to the High Court, where it was decided by four to three that the dam should not be built. The Court ruled that the Federal Government had the power to overturn a State's decision because it had ratified the World Heritage Convention and thus had authority to make decisions relevant to the protection of the environment. No one denies that the Federal Government has power over external affairs, but some were displeased to see that the signing of foreign treaties could mean that Canberra had found a back door through which to advance its power over the States.

The States loathe Federal intervention; each of them, not just Tasmania; and this battle over the Franklin River has reopened the rivalry between the States and the Commonwealth Parliament which had existed since the colonies came together to form a Federation in 1901. They had done so reluctantly; only sixty per cent of Australians bothered to vote – which meant in effect that only forty-three per cent of electors said 'Yes' to federation. And they did so because at the time Australia was feeling vulnerable and insecure. For twenty years before the turn of the century, the colonies had debated coming together, but the movement only gathered momentum when the country was experiencing a hideous depression, with banks crashing and high unemployment. Businessmen then put their weight behind the idea of federation, for they could see it as a way of getting rid of customs ports at State borders and guaranteeing free trade between the States. At the same time as being stunned by the depression, Australia was also realizing for the first time its proximity to Asia. There was much talk, most of it hysterical, about the yellow hordes which surrounded this western nation. Federation seemed the best step, the midway path between those who were agitating for closer ties with Britain (the Imperial Federation League, set up in 1885, was urging some sort of political unity between the two countries) and those who were agitating for Australia to become a republic. Australia whole-heartedly rejected both such suggestions and half-heartedly accepted a weak central government and strong independent States. It was a strictly limited bargain with specified powers given to a Federal Government and the residue, unspecified, remaining with the States. Since 1901, however, central government has encroached slowly and steadily upon the States. The Franklin dam decision was yet another example.

The Federal Government paid $A277 million in compensation to Tasmania for the loss of the dam and agreed to subsidize another power development, should it be necessary, later this century. The Greenies, heartened by their new-found power, turned their attention to wood-chipping and uranium mining. And Tasmanians made ready to welcome the thousands of extra tourists from the mainland and abroad who would, they hoped, come to the west coast to see what all the fuss had been about. The dam controversy had been worth its weight in State advertising.

CHAPTER 3

Bush Capital

Canberra has never been much loved. Her early years teemed with troubles, leaving her wounded by bickering and scarred by uncertainty. It was ages before she felt the warmth of even a half-hearted embrace and it is only in recent years that people have been prepared to admit that they positively enjoy living there, rather than curse because their career demanded a short stay. Even so, the effects of that early lack of commitment, both to the place and in turn to the notion of federalism, are obvious and perhaps will never be erased. For Canberra was created by the Constitution which created the Federation: a neutral capital like Washington, Ottawa and Brasilia. It's common enough in federal countries for the seat of government to create its own territory, detached from the local interests of individual States.

The senior State, New South Wales, won the battle to house the capital so long as it was not within 100 miles (160 kilometres) of Sydney. There was much competition for the spot outside the forbidden circle and much gossip about the group of Parliamentarians who were responsible for choosing the site: they appear to have had a merry time at the tax-payers' expense. Finally they chose Canberra – the name is said to derive from an Aboriginal word for 'meeting place' – a pretty limestone plain 600 feet (180 metres) above sea level, occupied then by a few sheep and surrounded on three sides by an amphitheatre of hills and mountains known as the Australian Alps which, at 5,900 feet (1,800 metres), rise high enough to be snow-capped and to provide a winter playground for skiers.

The planning of this purpose-built political centre was decided by international competition in 1911, a competition boycotted by the British because it was not limited to qualified architects and the assessors were not named in advance. First prize went to an American, Walter Burley Griffin, a pupil of Frank Lloyd Wright. His plan was grand, but it was not thrust upon the landscape. His admirers said that he had a magical sympathy for the nature of materials and the possibilities of the site. But magic is not enough. Just because he had won the competition did not mean he was going to be invited to build the city. For reasons discernible only to bureaucratic minds, a government board produced a modified plan with features from several designs; and this hotch-potch was not abandoned until a 'Save Canberra' campaign fought to have Griffin brought from America. Once there, the thwarted board clipped his wings and constantly quarrelled – quarrelled about everything from the sewerage system to the form the lakes should take. The conflict was, in part and with hindsight, the usual struggle between tiny minds that wanted to start small and a man with a vision who had no time for village planning. But there was also some genuine concern that Griffin was planning only for political effect and had no interest in mundane day-to-day living. Before he quit, starved of money and of support, he was clever enough to achieve one thing: he built the main roads to ensure development on the basic principles of his triangular design.

From these inharmonious beginnings, a disrupted future sprang. People did not have their hearts in this bush capital, and any excuse and any event, including war and the Depression, held back progress. In the end, only 6,000 people bothered to turn up to the opening of the provisional Parliament House in 1927, causing a massive catering surplus; some 20,000 meat pies had to be buried in a mass grave, and the incident has been the butt of jokes ever since. The provisional Parliament House will finally be replaced in 1988, the year of the Bicentennial celebrations, a fact which clearly underlines that early lack of commitment. It shows, this sporadic attention, this hiccuping history. Uncertainty adds lines to a face and wrinkles to a plan. The result is a planned city totally lacking in architectural cohesion.

At first I thought Canberra's past was the sole reason for this, but then I realized that deeper forces were at work. Featurism, Robin Boyd called it. Throughout history, he says, there have been two basic schools of architecture: one school designs buildings which gently lie down with nature; the other designs buildings which proudly stand up in contrast. Featurism is a third kind: it is neither sympathetic to its surroundings nor challenging. It is evasive, a nervous chattering as opposed to a statement that is bold, straight-forward and honest. And it is not lack of imagination or sensitivity or originality which causes this, but an over-abundance of these qualities without the discipline of a common artistic aim. Freedom and unruliness are essential to its flowering.

Within this definition, Canberra is a featurist city. It has little consistency of atmospheric quality – and yet there are plenty of numbers on the tourist map guiding visitors to places of interest; all self-consciously different; all determined to be arresting; all showing off their isolated moments of conception. And this isn't merely to be found in public buildings. If anything, domestic architecture has caught the disease with even greater determination. I found a booklet on Canberra which boasts that in housing no pattern is repeated, that each has its own character: 'No nightmare here of the kind familiar to London's Bloomsbury in which part of the surrealist horror is the problem of trying to recognize your own home in an endless vista of identical buildings.'

Robin Boyd wrote a book about all this and called it *The Australian Ugliness* – for featurism is not confined to Canberra – and when it was first published in 1960 it caused a stir. Australians were not used to criticism, least of all by fellow Australians, and they didn't like it much; thought it was unpatriotic. Boyd did his best to soften the blow by writing with wit and by pointing out that other countries suffered from featurism too – although, in the end, he had to admit that Australia suffered more than most. Why? Why not? This is what Australia is about – a self-centred, careless freedom. An easy, unrestricted freedom. Why bother with restrictions and confining control, or common aims, artistic or otherwise? Let each follow his own star. And then there's the landscape. Whenever one is lost for a convincing explanation for the way things are, one looks at the landscape. Perhaps this nation confuses symmetry and unity with sameness and monotony, and fights the latter with all its being. There is enough of *that* in the landscape.

In the end of course, architectural approval is a matter of personal preference and open to endless argument. Well, others can take delight in the buildings: I will remember them. I will remember gazing up at the High Court Building and the National Gallery, sited a mere 300 feet (ninety metres) apart, completed in the same year in the early 1980s and designed by the same firm of architects, and wondering if they had wilfully decided to ignore Boyd, or had simply never heard of him. The huge, intimidating High Court, dwarfing people and aptly symbolizing most people's view of 'The Law', offers competition rather than kinship with the National Gallery, which in itself is full of broken planes and interrupted lines: a building which will not let the eye rest and which has been described, by those who are supposed to know about these things, as a high-speed version of the idiom known as New Brutalism – aggressive concrete planes and deep slots of shadow – to which has been added some invocation of palace and fortress architecture.

In other words, it's ugly. Inside is different; the space has been well divided into manageable segments and the main floor offers an arresting juxtaposition of paintings. But what startles most is the crowds and the atmosphere. In London, unless there is a special exhibition, crowds are rare and the mood of a gallery resembles a church in which a voice raised above a whisper is frowned upon. Here, on a Sunday, the place brimmed with families, including small children, wandering, chatting, glancing, stopping. At first I cynically thought that the air-conditioning was the chief attraction, such was the heat of the afternoon, but it was not so. Every survey analysing the arts scene in Australia shows the wide appeal of the visual arts, and in particular Australian painting. Australians may be ignorant of their novelists or their playwrights, but they know their painters. A man who hardly ever reads a book, who has never been to the opera or ballet, will suddenly reveal that he has tried his hand at painting. There is even a Flying Arts School where teachers from the cities settle in tiny Outback towns for a week or a weekend and offer courses to bush dwellers. Reflecting this interest, newspapers devote much space to exhibitions, interviews, and criticism at an accessible level addressed to a wide audience; and each year around Christmas there is much razzmatazz surrounding the announcement of the Archibald prize for portrait pointing and the Wynne prize for landscape painting, together known as 'The Archibald'; it makes television news and front-page headlines.

The history of painting in Australia is just the reverse of other art forms: Australian painters were not swamped by an intimidating mass of imported Anglo-Saxon achievement. Distance protected them; Grand Masters stayed in their European galleries, far too precious and far too costly to transport by sea to such a hot country with no air-conditioning. Australians had to create their own works – and this they did from the early days of settlement, free from belittling comparisons. And the people, with few counter-attractions, supported local and popular artists and accepted them as part of the community. They did not – and they do not – see painting as esoteric, needing knowledge and analysis. By 1860, most States had their own galleries. They were not filled with hallowed names; they were filled with unintimidating attempts to commit Australia to canvas.

In those early years there was so much to capture; the displacement of Aborigines was a favourite topic, and so was the landscape. It was so different; the trees were different, the flora was different, the fauna was different and all of it was just that much easier to capture with a paintbrush than to re-create in words. The first painters did not capture too successfully the colours, the hinted hues, the faded greys, olives and ochres; they tended to plump for the more vibrant tints, particularly the greens, of Europe. It is argued that this revealed their entrenched thinking, their backward glances to the homes they had left, although a few art historians suggest that this colour-blindness had as much to do with fashion. Until the late nineteenth century, until the Impressionists, no painter was particularly aware of, or interested in, the effect of light upon colour. Whatever the reason, it is fascinating to wander through a gallery and notice the transition from an overcoloured Australia to an Australia of more delicate, subtle shades.

Unfortunately very little early Australian painting has been shown in Europe. China has fared better. She received an exhibition in the early 1980s called 'A Century of Australian Landscape, 1830–1939'. It included some particularly lovely late-nineteenth-century works in the Impressionist style by such painters as Charles Conder, Tom Roberts, Frederick McCubbin and Arthur Streeton. They tended to paint around Heidelberg outside Melbourne; it was not until the 1930s and 1940s that Russell Drysdale, Albert Tucker, Lloyd Rees and Sidney Nolan took up the challenge of the Outback. And in the 1950s, just as other art forms were crawling out from under foreign domination, painting in Australia fell prey to the influence of American abstract expressionism. It's hardly surprising; most of Europe was also conned by New York's fanatical promotion of modernism. The Australian Government went so far as to buy Jackson Pollock's *Blue Poles*, a controversial move, involving a controversial sum of money, $A1 million. It is in the Canberra Gallery looking large, a mere glance away from Monet's *Water Lilies* and Sidney Nolan's series of paintings on Ned Kelly.

During this flirtation with the avant-garde, portrait and landscape painting were never totally abandoned. Over the years, Fred Williams, Arthur Boyd, Clifton Pugh, and more recently Colin Lanceley, John Olsen and Salvatore Zofrea, have been fighting it out for the $A10,000 prize which Archibald, the founder of the magazine the *Bulletin*, initiated in 1919. And the public remained constant to Australian painters and the first art form to flower without an unholy struggle against a flood of imports.

The War Memorial was not crowded with track-suited families in search of their past. I didn't want to go inside either. Such monuments – even though they set out to commemorate the dead – always seem to end up glorifying war. But then one afternoon I met Professor Manning Clark, a historian I much admire, and he asked me if I had visited the Memorial. I told him that I had not and I told him why. He smiled in what I took to be an approving way, but suggested that I spend just five minutes glancing around the Hall of Memory, looking at the stained-glass windows and noting that the fifteen figures portrayed there each typified what were judged to be admirable Australian qualities. And then he wanted me to go and stand for another five minutes in front of William Dobell's painting, *Billy Boy*. I took his advice. The fifteen qualities are resource, candour, devotion, curiosity, independence, comradeship, ancestry, patriotism, chivalry, loyalty, coolness, control, audacity, endurance and decision. Only one quality is portrayed as a woman: devotion. The fourteen male figures are all slim, young and certainly handsome, some almost patrician.

Billy Boy is ugly, overweight and grinning, his tattooed arms folded across his singlet. *Billy Boy* is a portrait of an ocker. It is wise, I think, to let the *Macquarie Dictionary* define an 'ocker': 'the archetypal uncultivated Australian working man; a boorish, uncouth, chauvinistic Australian; an Australian male displaying qualities considered to be typically Australian, good humour, helpfulness and resourcefulness'. Dobell's brush is full of compassionate realism. The stained-glass windows are full of imaginary, somewhat pious perfection; out-dated and decidedly Anglo-Saxon.

I walked outside to admire the trees – to praise them, in fact. Canberra is the only city I know to have a tree index: look up a street and it will tell you what trees are growing there. In Franklin Street, Forrest, where I lived for several weeks, there were sweet gum, pin oak and plum. Parks and gardens and trees were very much a part of the original plan, and so were the experiments carried out to determine which trees and shrubs best suited local conditions. There are English oaks and elms, North American firs and birches, cypresses from the Mediterranean, and of course eucalyptus and wattles. The variety, and particularly the inclusion of foreign deciduous trees, help mark the seasons. Winter in Sydney is leafy; winter in Canberra can be leafless. Spring is a mass of yellow, white and pink; autumn is the time of reddish tints, of gold and purple. Canberra folk advise you to visit in the spring and autumn.

Canberra folk are unusual. There are 250,000 of them now, forming the largest inland city. There are so many Ph.D.s in the place, and so many of them like to use the prefix 'Dr', that it is something of a distinction to be just plain 'Mr'. Canberra is unbalanced in that way. The tenacious National Capital Development

Commission is constantly trying to persuade private industry to come to town to provide jobs for the less well-educated as well as a balance for the public sector. A technology park is their dream. And the Commission's propaganda suggests that the city could be a perfect base: it has clean air, good water, is research orientated (the Commonwealth Scientific and Industrial Research Organization has its headquarters there) and academically minded; the Australian National University can attract the best. Success, however, is elusive; growth is more likely to be achieved by offering convention facilities and by tapping tourism.

Meanwhile there are plumbers and clerks and shop-assistants and hairdressers, but they live in their own suburbs and seem swamped. Canberra belongs to the machinery of government, to politicians and public servants. The academics and the scientists all add their share of 'Drs' to the electoral roll, but they appear to form an outer circle. The inner circle is clearly labelled – and I doubt if I would wish to live in Canberra unless I were a part of it. *Then* the place is fun. Public servants are accessible and interested in talking about their tasks; politicians, at least those in office, are somewhat less accessible, but those I managed to meet talked with relish and without undue recourse to platitudes and press aides. Then there are the lobbyists, a surprisingly high-profile group who act at best as intermediaries and interpreters and at worst as messenger boys between government and governed; between government and government; between government and billion-dollar Japanese businesses. And it's easy enough to be drawn into this political web, and this I loved.

Another country's politics, like other people's families, always seem more interesting. The background is different; faces are fresh and the problems, for there are always problems, may be inherently similar but, for a while at least, they seem sparklingly novel. So while in Canberra I indulged, knowing that enthusiasm for political chat begins to evaporate at the city boundary and, by the time you get to Sydney, interest has thinned dramatically. It's back to gossip and topics of the day, and if politics is mentioned at all it is restricted to state affairs, local and immediate interests.

Political scientists are for ever saying that Australians express little interest in politics. They add, by way of emphasis, that two per cent are members of parties, half the electorate have never attended a political meeting, and one-third pay no attention to political news even during an election campaign. They offer any number of explanations. These include: that Australia is a fundamentally united and conservative country where there is little difference between the two main parties, the Coalition of the Liberal and National Parties (Conservative) and the Labor Party; they suggest that compulsory voting, backed by the threat of fines, ensures a high turn-out and reduces the need for party membership whose main function, after fund-raising, is building a body of workers willing to spend hours on doorsteps identifying voters and dragging them to the polls; they say that the electoral process is too complicated: it involves a system of preferential voting for the House of Representatives and a system of proportional representation plus preferential voting for the Senate. Finally, they admit that there are far too many elections.

This is more to the point. The States and Territories hold them every three years but not at the same time, and this gives the impression that there is always an election going on somewhere. It may be thousands of miles away, but it hogs media attention. The House of Representatives is re-elected every three years and so is half the Senate, but not necessarily at the same time. Voters can go to the polls once a year – and that does not include local elections or referenda. The electorate is sated rather than excited.

There is a move to synchronize the Senate and House of Representatives elections and to lengthen the life of Parliament to four years; but both changes require a referendum, which more often than not results in a resounding 'No'. This could have something to do with compulsory voting, which encourages the Don't Knows and Don't Cares – a large number when it comes to such 'technical' matters – to vote for the status quo.

Fewer elections and longer Parliaments could help to promote greater interest. It would also help if political scientists stopped labelling the electorate as apathetic. This has a poor effect on politicians; it makes them believe that the only way to succeed is to appeal to self-interest, to feed dollars into wallets with tax concessions and to offer a railway here and a tourist development there for those who look beyond their personal pockets. This attitude encourages the voter to even greater self-interest, and so the downward spiral continues: apathy breeding cynicism breeding cynicism breeding apathy – a vicious circle in which the politicians appear to treat the electorate as simpletons and the electorate hold politicians in low esteem.

I witnessed one election, a particularly interesting election in which the Liberals lost office after eight years, and was disappointed to find little discussion in the newspapers and on television on policy issues, on what changes a Labor victory might bring. Instead the campaign concentrated on the assessment of two personalities, that of the incumbent, Malcolm Fraser (respected but not liked) and that of Bob Hawke (popular but temperamentally unpredictable), and of course on money, with Fraser telling the electorate that if Labor won, their money would be best kept under the bed, it would not be safe in the banks. When I queried the low level of debate I was told that Australians did not relish discussion nor like 'ideas' and were certainly not interested in ideals and grand visions. This is a community of casual existentialists, concerned with the present. Life is to be lived and not thought about, not prodded and poked and made better. They can be critical – indeed they can – but also incredulous, incapable of believing that anything else is much better; incapable of believing that idealistic passion can be translated into social progress. Australians have a deep-rooted sceptical streak. How this got into the bloodstream we will explore in the next chapter. Meanwhile suffice it to say that such scepticism prevents them from investing anyone with magic powers. Indeed, they have invented a phrase for those who are outstanding in any way – 'tall poppies' – and the national pastime is to cut them down. At this they are skilled. When Dame Nellie Melba returned to Australia at the height of her operatic career, she was quickly labelled a drunk. For a while, such is the power and popularity of films, Breaker Morant looked in danger of gaining special status for being the Boer War soldier executed by the British for killing prisoners of war. Before you could say 'hero', the knives were out, showing that he was an amoral drunkard, a liar, a coward and a bully, a champion pugilist, a vicious racist and yes, even a murderer who shot the Boer prisoners as retribution because they had killed and mutilated his best friend. The only praise that might be acceptable was that he died gloriously with 'Shoot straight, you bastards!' echoing in the ears of the firing squad. Of course this could be seen as fashionable debunking, but it is more than that: Australians have no use for heroes or exemplary figures.

Sportsmen are different. Their success is physical and it is beyond question, beyond scepticism and therefore understood. You can *see* one man run faster than another; you can see a swimmer beating another swimmer; a tennis-player flooring his opponent; a cricketer knocking everything for six; a yachtsman winning a race. This is acceptable; other sorts of achievement are not.

There did appear to be one exception to this rule and it bothered me for a while: Ned Kelly. If you ask a schoolchild to name a national hero he might just come up with Kelly, about whom he would know very little. But Kelly has been painted by Sir Sidney Nolan, turned into a film with the help of no less a figure than Mick Jagger, and indeed recently he has been deemed worthy of operatic treatment. Who then is Ned Kelly? They said he was a kind of Robin Hood. But Kelly was no swashbuckler; Kelly was no politically motivated visionary, disregarding personal safety and devoting his life to his own brand of wealth distribution. Ned Kelly was a victim: what he achieved he achieved by default, not by design. He came from a huge family of petty troublemakers and drunks; his father, transported for stealing pigs, was one of seven, his mother one of ten, and he was one of twelve. All caught in a hopeless web, scratching a living from the land while others got rich in the Gold Rush. Ned Kelly did not start trouble, but he was always there on the fringe, easily fingered by the police, eventually rebelling into crime and finally forced to become an outlaw from which he knew there was no return. And so he talked – about himself and how he had been persecuted. He railed against the corrupt police whom he saw as agents of the Crown. He hated the Crown: he was Irish. And English domination dogged the Irish across 12,000 miles. The promised land was full of pitfalls.

He was caught after two years and much Keystone Coppery. He'd robbed one bank – or was it two? – and spread the money among his numerous Irish dependants, his mother's family, and the families of his brothers and sisters. He died well, with the words 'Such is life' upon his lips.

Ned Kelly is not so much a hero, more a symbol to remind people of their own history of oppression and poverty and disappointment. He changed nothing. No one has magic powers. And to get back to politics, least of all politicians. All that the electorate ask of them is that they should offer stability, moderation and not become too self-important. And since the electorate is not expecting too much, they do not become indignant about injustice or inefficiency, and they have surprising tolerance for political malpractice. Scandals seemed startlingly frequent during my stay. No one else seemed startled. Perhaps that is fair enough if it is the sorry saga of the chairman of a Peanut Board accused of taking some Sheila on an overseas 'selling' trip at the taxpayers' expense; or a junior minister accused of trying to avoid paying duty on a colour television set he was bringing into the country. But I didn't hear much of a gasp of injured innocence when the Premier of one State was accused of making phone calls to court officials in an attempt to get a friend off a fraud charge. A Royal Commission resulted, which acquitted the Premier – and the most commonly heard snipe was that the Commission was a waste of money, taxpayers' money. If stability and moderation are what is demanded, then it is not surprising that anyone who starts an unsettling, radical, high-minded pursuit of the Holy Grail will suffer. He will be cut down. And he *was* cut down, as the mesmerizing events that closed 1975 showed.

There is a four-letter word in the Australian language which does strange things to men and to women; it is even known to turn the dullest, most taciturn, non-communicative person into a sparkling orator. And it breaks all the rules; it is the one occasion in living memory when politics became the stuff of life – for a few weeks.

The word is 'Kerr'. On 11 November 1975, Sir John Kerr, the Governor-General, the Queen's representative in Australia, sacked the Prime Minister, Gough Whitlam. He called him into his office and gave him his cards. This moment is to Australians what the assassination of J. F. Kennedy is to Americans. They will tell you exactly what they were doing when they heard the news, exactly how they felt and what they thought. A decade later, it takes little to revive that memory, and academics are still arguing and publishing their opinions as to What Happened. Relations between Britain and Australia will never be the same again.

When Gough Whitlam came to power in 1972, the Labor Party, through quarrelling, dividing, splitting, had been out of office for twenty-three years. The long reign of the Liberal Party was due almost entirely to the mighty figure of Robert Menzies, who gave the country what it loved most: stability and moderation, a touch of paternalism, no cause to worry and no reason to think. A couple of pale shadows followed him and gradually it became obvious, as is the way of these things, that the tired old Liberals needed a rest and that the time was right to give the Labor Party a whirl. Not surprisingly, the Labor Party was hungry and ready for power. Whitlam had had years to refine his policies and indeed had put them before the electorate once before, in 1969, and thus, when he secured office in 1972, he had every right to hope that the voters were giving him a mandate for his policies.

Off he went. Ideas, absent for so long, were best weighed by the ton. And they were dumped on people like a dust storm or a tropical downpour. Not just any old ideas, but radical ideas reforming society, away from its acquisitive, competitive, capitalistic character, into a humane, cooperative society which was socialist. Whitlam wanted Australia to sever legal and constitutional ties with Britain and become a republic; he wanted a one-storey central government, which meant the abolition of the Senate of the Commonwealth Parliament; and he wanted to do away with the Parliaments of the six States and replace them with seventy-six regional councils. And the electorate voted for this. Either they were so comatose they did not read the not-so-small print, or else they believed that he could do none of these things without a referendum or two, and that would give them ample opportunity to say 'No, thanks'. What they may not have foreseen was that there are many ways of engineering a centralist government before reaching the point at which constitutional change is needed.

By the time the end came, they were punch-drunk. The arm of the Federal Government was everywhere: there was even a commission looking into Human Relationships and someone fussing over Consumer Spending. 'The Australian Government is finding it hard to stop people consuming goods which do not make them happy and which they do not need.' If they weren't too busy at the beach, that sentence must have sent shivers down the spines of this materialistic society.

But this is to make light of many, many impressive achievements: the introduction of Medibank, a health-care system, reforms to benefit women, migrants and Aborigines, the setting up of the Schools Commission, the Film and Television School, the Australia Council. Let Whitlam speak for himself:

But for my Government's initiatives would we have had FM and colour TV? Would there yet be equal pay and maternity leave for women, assistance for single parent families, indexation of pensions? Would there be a Heritage Commission or a Barrier Reef National Park? Would we have a floor price for wool? Would there be grants for local governments or for national highways? Would there be a regular redistribution of electorates? Would we yet have the High Court and National Gallery in Canberra, a new railway to Alice Springs?

All this – and more – had been achieved, and yet there were still twenty-one bills before the Senate, awaiting approval, in November 1975. The twenty-one bills were designed to give more power to central government. And they came before a Senate where the opposition had the edge. This is not unusual in Australian politics; indeed most of the time the Senate is in the hands of the Opposition, a fact which Prime Ministers have learned to put up with. In this instance, however, Opposition control had been achieved by provocative action from New South Wales which had flouted a convention which says that if a senator dies in office he must be replaced by someone from the same party. In this instance an Independent was appointed. And in Queensland another death saw the appointment of an old Trade Unionist opposed to Whitlam's trendy Socialism. The Liberal leader, Malcolm Fraser, swung into action, determined to force an election.

The Opposition did not like the look of the twenty-one bills, nor did they like the scandals that were bugging the Labor Party: a minor one involving the Deputy Prime Minister's relations with a member of his female staff; a major one involving Whitlam's attempts to borrow $A4,000 million from non-traditional sources to fund his spending. The money was to come from the Arabs, and in order to get it an unknown Pakistani financier was sent globe-trotting with his hand held out. Unorthodox money ... unorthodox methods. All secret, of course, and when the details began to leak out through the press, a slight smell turned quickly into a mighty pong.

Malcolm Fraser's method of forcing an election was to block Supply – neither to pass nor to reject, but to defer the most important bills of all, the bills which grant funds for the day-to-day running of government and therefore of the country. There is provision for this extreme action in the Constitution; however, in seventy-five years no one had exercised the right. Gough Whitlam thought that the Opposition were bluffing and that his best course was to tough it out. He would not agree to an election and he set about borrowing dollars from the banks to pay the bills after the money ran out on 30 November.

Days of high political drama followed: neither side would budge. On 11 November 1975, Sir John Kerr sacked Whitlam and an election was called for 13 December.

Kerr's timing was curious. The country was not going to run out of money until 30 November, and he could have waited to see if Whitlam was right in his view that the Opposition's nerve would break. Now we'll never know. Kerr argued that leaving the decision any longer would have meant interfering with the nation's Christmas and with the long summer vacation which follows and which is sacrosanct. One view is that Kerr acted on 11 November out of the fear of being sacked himself, believing that if Whitlam realized that his position was in any danger, he would make a pre-emptive strike and fire Kerr.

No Greek tragedy offers a better story. Two powerful and talented men, the victims of hubris, losing to a ruthless political schemer. For the election on 13 December gave Malcolm Fraser a resounding victory, and he soon replaced Kerr. The election seemed puzzling at first. Surely the people of Australia would have been so annoyed at the Queen's *unelected* representative sacking their *elected* Prime Minister that they would have voted him back? Australian anger is like a bush fire: soon over. And besides, Gough Whitlam had not offered them stability – he had brought about a political and constitutional crisis; he had not offered moderation – he had charged ahead with reform after reform; and he had become so self-important that he didn't even see that he was heading for the sack. His political nous got clogged up. The nation lost a man of talent and vision and an innovative thinker. Not that they cared: they told themselves that they had been right all along. They'd had their fling with men of intellect, men of ideas, men who dreamed of a better society, and look what happened. They were happy once more to acknowledge that they preferred the prosaic and the pragmatic and to get on with painting the bathroom and planning the weekend barbie.

Not all of them, of course. The events of November 1975 radicalized a small minority and gave a boost to the Republican movement, and started many arguing for at least some constitutional reform that would ensure that November 1975 would never happen again. They managed only one immediate reform: it is now no longer possible to stack the Senate; if a senator dies he must be replaced by someone from the same party. The bush fire was firmly put out, but it left a legacy. The next Labor Government, however strong its desire for change, would have to act with extreme caution.

Bob Hawke was elected in March 1983. He became leader of the Labor Party after the election had been called. It was Malcolm Fraser's turn to lose his political head. His timing was wrong and he felt that his Liberals could win against Labor's Bill Hayden. He didn't realize that, such was Labor's desire to win, they would dump their leader at the eleventh hour and install a man with a mere two years' parliamentary experience. A rare man. A man known to everyone in Australia for his leadership of the Australian Council of Trade

Unions. A man not only widely admired but widely liked. A man who made no secret of his past weakness for beer and for women; a man so emotional that he cries in public and loses his temper on television. A real larrikin: a mischievous bloke who, in spite of his background (his father was a Congregational minister) and his education (he was a Rhodes Scholar at Oxford), has a loutish accent and a hair-style more suited to a second-hand-car salesman. A man so steeped in the ways of back-room bargaining and in the ways of men that he was not going to bungle himself out of office.

In case anyone had forgotten the errors of the Whitlam years, Malcolm Fraser saw to it that they were reminded during the election campaign. Remember what happened last time, he kept saying. And he deployed basic scare tactics: he branded Hawke a Commie-lover who would turn Australia into a republic and spend, spend, spend. All the leading newspapers with the exception of the *Age* of Melbourne told their readers to vote for Fraser. Bob Hawke romped home. Fraser wept on election night. And resigned.

Political scientists had better stop telling the electorate that they are apathetic. They may not relish debate but they know what they want; and in his first term in office, Bob Hawke studiously gave it to them. At every turn he risked the wrath of his left wing and showed himself to be steadfastly moderate, cautious and pragmatic. He rid himself of the legacy of spend-and-change and offered instead government by consensus and consultation. This allowed him to introduce a new health scheme, give Ayers Rock back to the Aborigines, permit a limited amount of uranium mining, float the dollar, deregulate the financial system. He had watched Menzies pinch Labor policies when it suited him; now it was his turn to pinch Liberal policies and prove that he too could be a man of the centre. That his style of government and its content met with approval was reflected in the opinion polls, which gave him a consistently high personal rating and kept that of his party at the level which won the election. Within eighteen months, Hawke had established the credibility of Labor, particularly in economic management, and had killed the Liberal coalition's image as the party born to rule. This was no mean achievement, even if Labor's detractors put much of it down to luck:

luck that the drought broke, luck in having a weak Liberal leader, Andrew Peacock, and a good run with the economy which could not be expected to last. Riding high on this success, Bob Hawke called an early election in 1984 and got a surprise. While the opinion polls predicted that Labor would be returned with an increased majority, they were in fact returned to office with a reduced majority. This was in part caused by an unusually high number of spoiled ballot papers. The electorate got in a muddle; changes had been made to the Senate voting system, and all too many people thought they applied to the House of Representatives as well. A black mark for those responsible for publicizing the change. But the reduced majority could also have something to do with Tall Poppies. Hawke had become too confident and the electorate did not like being dragged into yet another election: an opportunist and unnecessary election. It was meant as a warning.

The warning may hamper Hawke. If he had intended using his second term to re-establish Labor as the party of reform, he may now be less inclined to pursue such a course. Instead he will coax much-needed taxation changes through detailed and prolonged consultation, he will chivvy a restructuring of Australian industry, and he will slowly seek a more just and equitable society. And Labor will lose its tag as the reformist party.

It is the oldest party in Australia and, when it was founded in 1890 from the Trade Union movement, it was decidedly radical. It wanted '... nationalism of all sources of wealth and all avenues of productivity and exchanging wealth'. Since then it has gradually watered down its policies, partly because any form of nationalization is against the Constitution, which guarantees the freedom of inter-State trade, and partly because successive waves of self-interested migrants have made the country more conservative. Unless policies were changed, the party would have little chance of power. Indeed, since 1901 the Labor Party has been in office at federal level for only a couple of decades, but it has been much more successful at State level. This can only be because at State level the party is limited in the amount of change it can pursue while its willingness to fund many unprofitable enterprises that the private sector will not contemplate is welcome.

Ever pragmatic, the electorate can understand that 'state socialism' works to its benefit. At federal level it threatens.

It threatens because of Labor's underlying desire for Australia to become a republic; it threatens because of Labor's woolly views on defence; the party dislikes kow-towing to America and yet has not come up with an alternative defence strategy to make this white Western nation feel secure in Asia; and it threatens because it keeps a watchful eye on foreign investment to which Australia has become addicted, believing it is the only way to the good life, to the maintenance of its all-important standard of living. Bob Hawke has calmed fears on the last two points; he has made it clear that he has no intention of upsetting America or foreign investors, and whenever he is asked about Australia's future as a republic he shrugs and says that he is occupied with more immediate concerns.

In 1979, however, when he was President of the Australian Council of Trade Unions, Bob Hawke gave a series of radio lectures in which he advocated radical constitutional changes similar to those advanced by Gough Whitlam. He said he felt that for reasons of national identity it would be better for Australia to break her links with Britain and have her own president as head of state. He said he wanted the constitution altered to give central government much wider powers, to abolish State governments and to strengthen third-tier local government which is more responsive to the needs of citizens. He said he wanted to improve the body politic by offering one-quarter of cabinet positions – seven out of twenty-eight – to people outside Parliament.

It is a powerful list; just the kind of thing the electorate is said not to like. No wonder Hawke shrugs and says that perhaps the year 2001, the centenary of federation, would be the time to consider such changes. The Australians are ignorant of their Constitution: they adopted it half-heartedly and then forgot it. It isn't a lovable pet like the American equivalent which is always being stroked, patted and quoted, especially all that lovely stuff about the people having the right to life, liberty and the pursuit of happiness. Most Australians haven't read their Constitution which is short and readable, even though hardly full of quotable sentences. Ignorance is causing the fear of change and it will take a massive educational campaign to make the electorate realize that a constitution is nothing more than a set of rules which needs dusting down and changing occasionally to suit the times. In the past, since 1901 thirty-eight referendum questions seeking change have been put to the people and only eight passed, a pretty poor record which either means that the electorate is so conservative that nothing will ever change or that politicians have not been perceptive enough to realize that ignorance is the problem and education the answer. I'd prefer the latter explanation because it is more hopeful. Politicians ought to abandon the received wisdom that the electorate can take only the most perfunctory political debate and slowly, patiently and persuasively mount a campaign of explanation and advice. It won't enable Hawke to put the clock back to the days when the Labor Party was formed amid radical zeal, but it might leaven the conservative lump; it might even counteract the cycle of cynicism and apathy.

CHAPTER 4

Wanted: Men with Muscles

It was the last day of January and hot, uncommonly hot, for Melbourne. Most of the month had shown a seemly maximum of 80°F (26.5°C), on the low side. That day the temperature was to abandon decorum and rush above 100°F (38°C) – and it would get worse. We were warned. That night was to be the hottest on record, the daily maximum becoming the nightly minimum; and the next day, 1 February, was to be a sweltering 105°F (40.5°C). That sort of heat brings problems; people arrange their day, if they can, to enable them to stay within air-conditioned buildings – that in turn causes overloading and power cuts, but it's better than being outside. Not even the trams were running. Some 150 conductors and drivers walked off the job.

I took refuge in a newspaper library, determined to ignore the heat and the heat-talk. And it was possible until mid afternoon. Then Melbourne came to a halt. Those in the streets stopped walking and shielded their eyes and, if they couldn't get inside, squashed their bodies against the sides of buildings. Those inside looked out and watched the clear blue sky turn an eerie red; watched a bright summer's day turn to night. Lights came on.

It was a sudden dust storm.

Strong northerly winds had whipped up the dust from drought-stricken areas of northern and north-western Victoria and with great theatrical force dumped a load on Melbourne. Australia's climate is not benign and not always beautiful. It can be violent and wilful and, above all, unpredictable. And this dust storm seemed a fierce gesture of exasperation: a wile to remind city-dwellers that, even though their gardens were scorched, their parks scarred and their water restricted, all this was nothing compared to the plight of farms and bushland, parched by the longest drought for many a year.

High up I watched this vicious little scene; watched the huge dark cloud roll towards the city. 'A bush fire?' queried someone, knowing that it was not. It looked more like the aftermath of an exploded bomb. There was a second's fear and then, this being a newspaper office, out came the flip remarks about The End of the World – an allusion to Ava Gardner's comment, when filming *On The Beach*, that Melbourne was indeed a suitable place for a story about the end of the world. You could hear tomorrow's headlines being written.

It was over in half an hour. The wind gradually changed to south-west and the temperature dropped ten degrees Fahrenheit, and we cooled a little and rearranged our minds from thoughts about the unfathomable ways of nature to more prosaic concerns: windows left open at home, and dust dancing on the washing left on the line.

But on the last day of January, dust storms were tomorrow's excitement. For the moment there was heat. And a day off, a long weekend. Australians have more public holidays than most nations and they are all arranged for Mondays, earning the country another euphonious title, The Land of the Long Weekend. This was the closest Monday to 26 January, the day Captain Phillip hoisted his flag on Sydney Cove; they call it Australia Day. Professor Manning Clark was on the radio explaining what it all meant, while everywhere women struggled into as little as possible and men poured them-selves into shorts, T-shirts and thongs, standard Aussie heat-wear, not at all attractive – and not that cool either. And off they all went to the beach. (I wonder if Australians know why Arabs wear long flow-ing robes which look so elegant and which would certainly grace even an award-winning beer-gut in a way no T-shirt ever can?)

I set off for Ferntree Gully Community Centre, in the city of Knox, a distant suburb of Melbourne. There, they were holding a citizenship ceremony turning immigrants into New Australians.

Once Ferntree Gully in the Dandenong Ranges was far enough from Melbourne to be considered 'bush', and it was beautiful. So beautiful that it caught the imagination of Eugene von Guerard and

73

he, in 1857, painted the Gully in oil on canvas. I saw it in the Australian National Gallery in Canberra. Today the green growth has been tamed for suburban living, but still the Dandenong Ranges frill the edges of the settlement. Outside the Community Centre, chairs had been arranged to catch the shade around the edges of a slab of concrete. There was music and dancing, and at regular intervals men wandered to their cars to catch the score in a one-day cricket match.

Then the Mayor arrived with local politicians and the Town Clerk and an official from the Immigration Department, and they lined up on one side of a long table and called the New Australians to come forward in groups of six. He, the Mayor, asked each candidate to hold the Bible in his or her right hand and to repeat the oath of allegiance: 'I ... renouncing all other allegiance swear by Almighty God that I will be faithful and bear true allegiance to Her Majesty Elizabeth the Second, Queen of Australia, her heirs and successors according to the law and I will faithfully observe the laws of Australia and fulfil my duties as an Australian Citizen.' The candidates retain the Bible as a gift from the council, along with a flag and a native tree to plant in their garden to mark the occasion. Bottle brush is the most popular. Those wishing to make an affirmation rather than an oath waited until the end and, of course, did not get a Bible as a present. It was an odd experience for me to hear the term 'Queen of Australia' used for the first time, and even more odd to see the Mayor dressed in a long, velvet, fur-trimmed robe and lacy jabot. In that heat! Why cling to such ritual?

A lady in a red hat walked forward. She had a Union Jack pinned to her dress. The Mayor said, 'I think you can trade that in now,' and leaned across the table and unpinned it. I followed her. Her name was Jean and she had been in Australia since 1955 and had five children. She had heard a rumour that the Government might make citizenship compulsory or else send immigrants back to where they had come from, and she didn't want that. Did she like it in Knox then? 'God put me here,' she said. God had loomed large in her life, and we chatted about that while a hundred people 'renounced all other', and waited for the speeches.

74

A graceless and inappropriate speech from an inappropriately dressed Mayor: 'We used to be known as the Lucky Country, but the dream has become a nightmare. There is drought, unemployment, inflation; but citizenship means accepting the hard times as well as the good times. We used to be a trading nation, now we have lost the desire to compete: our pride is restricted to the sporting field. We seem to have gone overboard in seeking a fair day's pay for a fair day's work ... there is more to Australia than meat pies and tomato sauce and Holden cars. People must re-think their goals, must regain the work ethic. You are one of us now; let's all get down to it; let's get this country going again.'

The proceedings ended with 'God Save the Queen' played on an electric fiddle by a young man with long hair and his shirt hanging outside his trousers. The fiddle made a melancholy sound.

There are more than one million people in Australia who have the right to citizenship which they can claim after two years, provided they have a clean criminal record and a basic knowledge of English. They have not bothered. It is argued that the one million resist swearing allegiance to a figure whom they identify as Queen of the United Kingdom. There have been several attempts to change the wording – which is clearly a good idea in a post-imperial age and in a country where twenty-five per cent of the population are of non-British origin. The last attempt in 1984 tried to make it possible to swear allegiance to the Commonwealth of Australia, but the proposal failed in the Senate. However, 'God Save the Queen' is no longer the National Anthem; 'Advance Australia Fair' with newly penned words, less sycophantically pro-British, has taken its place. It is but a small change; the flag remains unaltered and those who wish to see the Union Jack banished from its corner will have to fight on; for the moment, sixty-eight per cent want the flag left intact. Change in this conservative country has to be piecemeal and painfully slow. The clingers, those who need symbols to remind them that they are still part of one of the 'great races in human history' (and that is one Australian's view of the British), must be left with something to which to cling.

What causes such conservatism? It must be in the very nature of the people who settled the country. Were they noble pioneers, their luggage crammed with ideals, their hearts and minds seeking religious, political and social freedom? On the whole, not. The first wave were criminals, the second opportunists in search of gold, and a good many of those were so helpless and destitute they had to be encouraged by assisted passages; and the third wave, the post-war migrants, were being booted out – or tempted away – from an overcrowded, ravaged Europe. Australia was not necessarily their first choice, and again they were attracted by the lure of free or cheap passage. Australia had a hard time, until comparatively recently, finding anyone willing and eager to pay their way to the new land. And the majority of those who finally ended up there went desiring only to put their heads down and work and then return to their native lands with their economic position enhanced. Even political refugees hoped that the circumstances that had caused them to flee might change and permit them to return. They didn't go, all these people, to get involved in a new community. They went, their horizons limited, their aspirations humdrum, their goal personal gain.

The first wave were obviously the most unwilling. They were sent as an alternative to reform or hanging. The British Government, unable to come to terms with the need to reform its overflowing prisons, side-stepped the issue and sent the overflow to Botany Bay. From this it could be argued that Australia inherited a reactionary disposition. For those convicts wanted only one thing – their free-dom – and to them freedom meant a plot of land. Personal acquisitive-ness was their motivation. Community spirit was not their concern. What did they know of that? Some thirty per cent of them were under nineteen years of age, uneducated errand-boys from the slums of London. And the rest were hardly the heroic martyrs to English injustice so often described by romantic Australian nationalists. Whatever may have been the case of the relatively small numbers transported before 1815, after that date, as both criminal law and administration were steadily reformed in Great Britain, most of those sent out were aptly described as 'the dregs of society'. Political offenders were few: they included the Tolpuddle Martyrs and some Chartists.

Australians do not like too much being made of their convict origins, nor should too much be made of them. Nor, however, should their influence be ignored. For the first fifty years their numbers outweighed those of free settlers; they intermarried and became interwoven into society; they set the tone. And the last convicts did not die until the 1920s. Their influence is profound, and indeed their very arrival was vital to Australia. If, from the beginning, the country had had to rely on free migration, it would have attracted but few. Those thinking of quitting Britain and other parts of Europe clearly preferred America – it was a much shorter and much cheaper sea journey, and it was free from British rule. The fact that Britain paid the passages of selected convicts at least started something, and when this stopped there were problems.

By 1840, the 400,000 inhabitants of Australia were eager to give away the land in order that others should join them. But newcomers still hesitated. What was the point of owning land when there was a shortage of labour to work it? The answer, according to Geoffrey Blainey who wrote a most influential work called *The Tyranny of Distance*, came from the pen of Edward Gibbon Wakefield, as he languished in Newgate Prison charged with abducting a schoolgirl heiress. Instead of giving the land away, he suggested that a relatively high price be charged for it and that the money raised be used to pay the passages of a work-force. In 1842, Crown land was sold at twenty shillings an acre, and in that year the British Parliament passed a law which apportioned half that land revenue for encouraging immigration.

They came but slowly. Wakefield's idea was botched: the price of land was pitched too high. An acre in America cost only five shillings, so Australia still remained second choice. The discovery of gold in the 1850s helped. As Blainey says, 'Gold built an escalator across the ocean, but thousands would not have stepped on it unless they had been given a free ticket or a bargain fare.'

But as the escalator got busy, other changes occurred. The colonies became self-governing and the new parliaments took control of the money raised by selling land. And these men, all immigrants, and the men they represented, all immigrants, resented the arrival of further immigrants to compete for jobs and depress wages. They did not want to dilute what they had; they knew their bargaining power was strengthened by the scarcity of labour. Wakefield's policy crumbled; first one colony opted out of the scheme, and then another. The seeds of self-interest, sown so early, began to shoot. Blinkered men thought only of protecting themselves and there was no need. The discovery of gold had made Australia wealthy, confident and optimistic, and the country could easily have supported a larger population without anyone suffering. But gold made men blind and greedy. Land prices rocketed and there was much speculation and heavy borrowing by colonial governments from banks in London to fund every kind of development, some worthwhile and some worthless. It was a giddy time and visitors like Trollope were much impressed by what they saw – the emergence of a paradise for the working man.

Inevitably the bubble burst. Drought affected the primary sector; there were serious strikes; London became cautious about lending money. Between 1891 and 1893, forty-one land companies went bankrupt; there were runs on the bank and many suspended payment. There was much misery; the country received a knock from which it never completely recovered. It was the end of an era; the dazzle departed and with it any thoughts of radicalism, and Australia was moulded into a middle-of-the-road mentality. Social commentators suggest that it was the Great Depression of the 1930s that made Australians cautious and conservative, but I believe that the depression of the 1890s was the more significant. The appalling suffering of the 1930s, with thirty per cent of the work-force out of work, was psychologically hampering for those who lived through it, but it merely compounded a loss of confidence that had occurred in the early 1890s: the turning-point years.

The massive post-Second World War migration was not born of renewed confidence or a flash of insight or a desire to prove Wakefield right – it was born of fear. The Japanese bombed Darwin in 1942 and made Australia once again aware of her position in the world – at the tail-end of Asia; the cry went up 'Populate or Perish', and the country appointed its first Minister of Immigration. Opening the

doors to the dispossessed and destitute of Europe was only in part a
defence policy – the United States became Australia's real protector –
it was just as much an economic policy, a mechanism for growth.
Australia needed men with muscles to build up the nation and to
stock factories. It seemed a perfect marriage: people with no homes
and no jobs came to a country where the Commonwealth Employment Service listed 100,000 positions vacant each day. Unending
jobs for the work-starved. Work was once again the word – not
involvement; not politics – work.

In 1947 Australia was still ninety per cent British and wanted to
keep it that way, and such a massive immigration policy could only
be sold to the people by stating clearly that, for every foreign
immigrant, there would be ten from the United Kingdom. It didn't
work out that way; eagerness for numbers broke the barrier and the
ratio became four to one. South and East Europeans triumphed and
the composition of the population changed significantly. Some 3.5
million immigrants have arrived since the war.

TABLE I: *Origin of the Population of Australia*

	in 1947 (%)	in early 1980s (%)
British	90	75
South European	1.5	8
North European	6	7
East European	0.9	4
Asian	0.5	2
American	0.2	0.2
Aboriginal	0.8	1

Melbourne is a good place to glean an understanding of the
immigrant situation. It has nineteen per cent of its population born
overseas (not counting Anglo-Saxon immigrants); this is a higher
percentage than any other city. As a manufacturing location, it offers
jobs: four of Australia's car makers have plants in the city. At first
glance Melbourne may seem more British than any other city, but
that is because the British are more British; underneath, however, it
is truly cosmopolitan, with Greeks and Italians forming the largest
communities. Everyone knows that Melbourne has the largest

The Ribbon and the Ragged Square

gathering of Greeks outside Athens and New York. The Italians, however, form the largest non-British ethnic group in Australia. They were not welcomed with open arms. The first British settlers had pretty thin smiles of welcome for the later British immigrants, so it is scarcely surprising that they had severely limited appetites for the differences and diversity offered by true foreigners. The new arrivals were supposed to become ockers overnight. If they spoke anything but English on the Melbourne trams in the 1950s they were inviting a spit in the face.

Giovanni Sgro, the first Italian-born immigrant to enter state politics, recalls it vividly:

I didn't want to come here in the first place. I was working in an olive factory in Calabria and one day I came home and found that my father had put my name to a piece of paper. He wanted his sons to have a better life and so four of us came here in 1952, and just like ninety-nine per cent of the Italian people we came here with one objective: to work seven days a week and then go back home and buy land. We were peasants and that is all we knew about – land. I intended to stay for four years and work, work . . . no movies, no girls, just work.

For the first three months we were all in a camp 400 kilometres [250 miles] from Melbourne. There were 10,000 of us and as the weeks went by we became desperate. Where were the jobs? We used to lie on the railway line to block trains because we wanted to get to Melbourne and complain. And twelve of us formed ourselves into a committee to say, 'Give us jobs or send us back.' During this time six young men hanged themselves, such was their desperation, and we were told that their deaths were from natural causes. Bullshit. So we set fire to a couple of barracks and organized a demonstration. We were confronted by 200 soldiers and four tanks. It was the first time since Eureka that they had used the army against civilians. No, you won't find anything about the incident in books and newspapers. I think maybe the local newspaper might have mentioned it.

The day after the demo, I was found a job as a painter in Cobra and all twelve of the committee were split up and sent to different areas. That's how I got involved in politics and it was twenty years before they allowed me to take citizenship. That's one of the reasons I stayed, to get back at the Establishment that had given me such a hard time. They didn't destroy me and since then I have worked to persuade a lot of South European immigrants to become involved in politics and the trade unions. At first, most couldn't speak the language and didn't have the right to vote, so they were no threat. But as time went on it became more and more important to see that people became involved; they should participate fully and fight for equal jobs and opportunities.

If I had to start all over again, I wouldn't come here. I don't think people should leave their own country for purely economic reasons. Italy wasn't poor, but the wealth was not distributed. We should have stayed and fought for change there. What is the sense of coming here and having to fight the same battles? And many of my generation of immigrants feel the same.

Was the battle easier here, you ask. Isn't the society more equal to start with? Bullshit. It isn't even equal among politicians. As a Parliamentarian I am entitled to a gold pass to attend sporting events and travel on trams and so on and when a white Australian pulls out the card everything is OK. But for me the questioning begins – what's this Wop doing with such a pass? I won't take any nonsense from the bastards. I battle. I'm equal in law all right, but that doesn't cover people's attitudes and suspicions. I call myself Giovanni, not John, and I can tell you it cost me a lot of bloody votes from Australians to start with.

Sgro may sound aggressive; he didn't seem aggressive, merely passionate and committed, as is the way of some politicians. And anyway, what he said somewhat stridently, many others told me softly. They arrived in a hostile environment and they had to battle against many a prejudice, and improvements took time, took years. For all that, Australia's immigration policy has been successful; tensions there have been – and still are – but they rarely erupt and, for a country which has absorbed settlers from a hundred different nations, this is no mean achievement.

The policy of assimilation was of course offensive and doomed to failure, but who was to be that wise in 1947? Who anywhere knew any better? Who could have realized that it is impossible to expect people to shed their skins like snakes? They didn't and they huddled together in pockets for support, until one fine day people realized that such a policy posed a real threat of alienation and division. At which point a new word crept into the language: multi-culturalism. Instead of a melting pot to produce a bland and homogeneous stew, Australia would try a new recipe: it would try and produce a salad, a good salad in which every ingredient keeps its own flavour.

Multi-culturalism is more than a toleration of diversity. It sees diversity as a quality to be actively embraced, a source of social wealth and dynamism. It means you not only stop sneering at spaghetti, but you learn to eat it with as much relish as a meat pie covered in tomato sauce. And of course, it is supposed to be about equality of opportunity and everything else. Such a policy is derived from hard-nosed realism: if particular groups feel they are condemned to occupy the worst jobs and houses and suffer the poorest health and education, then the society in which they live is bent on a course which will cost them dearly.

Where did it come from, this change of heart? It came with the Whitlam era, the early 1970s. It took all that time for the immigrants to look up from their machines and become politically aware; it came with the emergence of the second generation from schools and universities. It took all that time for political parties to see that there were more than one million non-British votes to be sought. And what Whitlam started, the Fraser government embraced whole-heartedly, and proceeded to make the immigrants' lot into a growth industry. Much money was spent on setting up institutes, publishing reports and starting an ethnic television channel which showed foreign films, concentrated on overseas news and made document-aries in which second-generation immigrants were taken back to the land of their ancestors. All good stuff and much applauded.

The timing was right. They say the technological age is somewhat responsible. Technology has given us mass-produced cars, clothes, cinema, magazines, music, lotions and creams; and, in the end, such homogeneity becomes unattractive. People come to dread being melted down and pressed tight into a common alloy – and that applies just as much to the Anglo-Celtic community as it does to immigrants. Differences, once feared, could now be embraced – a little.

There is no doubt that the immigrant communities have benefited much, particularly the second generation who (though born in Australia) were still not entirely accepted and who, in order to make themselves acceptable, deliberately scorned their ethnic roots and found themselves in no man's land, adrift from their families and from society. An Italian Australian now in his late twenties would have spent his school years not speaking a word of Italian, denying his love for pasta, embarrassed by the salami sandwiches his mother packed for his lunch; reluctant to invite non-Italians into his home where his mother expected to be greeted with a kiss. On the whole, he would have felt more comfortable in the company of other migrants, Greeks and Yugoslavs, whose family life was similar. Today, such a schoolboy could well be learning Italian alongside an Australian of Anglo-Celtic origin; he might be sharing the salami sandwiches and occasionally inviting his schoolmates home – but only occasionally: there is still a tendency for the immigrant communities to remain together.

The steps seem small. To some, they are *too* small; they argue that encouraging cultural differences is deluding people: it is a ploy designed to keep people busy with festivals and folk-days and, along with token gestures of ethnic representation on committees, its aim is to keep immigrants from true involvement and the pursuit of social change. There is some truth in this. Promoting ethnic identity sounds good and it means you won't get spat at for speaking Italian on the trams, but it does not necessarily lead to improved opportunity and real equality.

Multi-culturalists are now questioning what has been achieved in the last decade, in order to decide directions for the future. And they find themselves facing a wall. It is called backlash and it does not come just from those who still support assimilation and who find multi-culturalism a nasty North American word. It is wider than that and embraces those who have watched the multi-cultural growth industry eating vast sums of public revenue. They argue that there may well be low-income families among immigrants, but that there are also low-income and no-income families among the rest of the community. There's not much sympathy around.

There is not much sympathy around because there is high unemployment – which at one stage reached ten per cent; and there's not much sympathy around because of the changing nationality of the latest wave of immigrants. There has been a decline in European immigration and an increase in Asian immigrants. Between 1961 and 1970, eighty-three per cent of immigrants came from Europe, compared with seven per cent from Asia. In contrast, between 1971 and 1980, the proportion of immigrants from Europe dropped to forty-eight per cent and those from Asia increased to twenty-five per cent. There are now some 250,000 Asians in Australia, more than half having arrived since 1976, and the greatest number have come from Vietnam.

Shung, a young doctor from South Vietnam, saved for six years to bring out his wife and two younger brothers: 'We can't live under communism. Australia looked peaceful and the country looks a little like my country, people live in houses with a garden.' He intends to work in factories for as long as it takes to educate his younger brothers and sisters and then he intends to re-qualify as a doctor. 'I am happy to work hard in this country, free and kind.'

He smiled when I asked how he felt about working in factories when he was used to something intellectually more satisfying. He wouldn't admit that it was a problem. No Vietnamese is inclined even to hint at problems, let alone criticize. I talked to a number of them at Springvale Migrant Centre, near Melbourne, one of twelve such Centres where new arrivals go to learn English and to live until they find jobs and homes. The centre holds 1,000 people; it is basic and pleasant enough for temporary accommodation. The Centre's organizers were unstinting in their praise for Asian attitudes. It was the Polish immigrants who were causing problems, they said. Once they had been anti-communist, but now they are intellectuals, Socialists, and demanding. They were arguing for separate English lessons because of their ability to learn faster and because, unlike the Asians, they do not need to concentrate on pronunciation.

'Asian determination is amazing. It is little short of a miracle how they find houses and jobs and start to rebuild their lives. They are eager to learn and never skip classes. And they are something of a challenge to the welfare agencies since they do not like hand-outs and believe in self-help and family support. And of them all, it is the Chinese Vietnamese who shine. They are so industrious and ambitious. They are going to be of great value to Australia.' Not everyone agrees with that, least of all the Vietnamese Vietnamese. They sneer; they call them the Jews of Asia; they say that the Chinese would be happy anywhere, so long as they can make money.

The Quach family are Chinese Vietnamese. They by-passed the arrival centre and went straight to a neat estate, aided by a church organization which works alongside government services. They were happy to talk to me, so long as I was careful with questions about Vietnam. There had been suggestions in the press that many immigrants were sending back money, hoping that the present regime would be overthrown. A romantic notion, I was assured. A few might feel that – the fiercely nationalistic Vietnamese – but not the Chinese Vietnamese. Their interests were concerned solely with a home and a job and education for their children.

The Quaches served me with Coca-Cola from a cup, and the wife did all the talking. She had learned English at school; her husband was still struggling with the language after two years in the country. Their son already had an Australian accent. The family had owned a shop in Saigon selling building materials. They lived over the shop and were wealthy enough to employ a girl to look after their child while both of them looked after the business. They first tried to escape in 1976 in a boat of their own, but they were caught and thrown into jail. There they stayed for six months, until they had handed over all their possessions, including their gold and jewellery, and then they were freed to start again. It took three years to save the money to buy places on a boat laden with thirty others. It took forty-eight days to get to Hong Kong, and there they stayed in a refugee camp for two years. On arrival in Melbourne, the husband got a job in a carpet factory, but that lasted only a year and unemployment followed. He now stays at home and his wife works in a factory.

'Australia first choice. Australia good country, no war, no trouble. We read some books in Vietnam. Here weather is cold and job is hard for me. I work all day for food for us. We both need to work. Lady work, man stay at home, not good. In future, I like to work in Post Office or in shop. Maybe we have another business one day.'

They have no Australian friends outside the church they attend, and their Vietnamese friends are of Chinese origin. 'I was born in Saigon, but my parents were Chinese, and so my blood is Chinese. We were in Vietnam for business and one day we intended to go home to China. But now we are in Australia to stay. My son loves school. He has an Australian accent. You hear it?'

They smile all the time. Unemployment is just one more hurdle in their long struggle. Gratitude dominates their thinking.

The Chinese came to Australia during the Gold Rush because greedy merchants did not like their ships to sail empty. The ships came into Melbourne full of British immigrants, and there were not enough exports to fill the ships for the return journey, so they headed for Hong Kong and other Chinese ports to collect tea for Europe and tea for Australia – Australia with her tiny population was the fourth-largest tea importer in the world in 1850. But before long, too many ships were calling at Chinese ports in search of cargo; rather than sail away empty, they began accepting human freight: poor Chinese in search of gold.

By 1880, the Chinese formed four per cent of the population, and it would be difficult to overestimate the extent to which they were loathed, feared and persecuted. They were seen as an inferior race with vile habits: opium smoking, prostitution and sodomy. And of course they were willing to work long hours for small wages. They were prepared to comb the soil discarded by white gold-miners and they often prospered on such pickings; they were prepared to work in the tropical north where the climate proved difficult for Europeans. But once the Depression came, competition from the Chinese could not be tolerated. Their drive set them apart and so did their skin.

Australians, feeling vulnerable and lacking in confidence as their dazzling progress was halted in the 1890s, became paranoiac about the yellow races surrounding them. Dr Charles Pearson, an English don who for some time was Director of Education for Victoria, finally struck the match which lit the fire. In 1893 he published a book entitled *National Life and Character* – a dull title to an unreadable and arrogant volume – in which he divided the world into inferior and superior races and said that it was inevitable that the inferior races – both black and yellow – would one day swamp the superior races.

He therefore urged that the workings of a few mines and sugar plantations be sacrificed, rather than endanger the British way of life in Australia. 'We are guarding the last part of the world in which the higher races can live and increase freely for the higher civilization.' The White Australia Policy came into being in 1901 and remained until 1973. Australia, instead of acknowledging her place in the East and befriending her neighbours, slammed the door on them.

The fears which brought in and sustained such a policy have not disappeared. The interdenominational church group responsible for bringing in the Quach family freely admitted that they had had to curb their own racist fears before they could agree to act. Their first thought had been to let the refugees stay where they were. They had had to be cajoled into helping the first family and slowly, through contact, they have overcome their fears. For some it isn't so easy. One woman told me that she couldn't bring herself to tell her in-laws about the work she was doing; they wouldn't understand. Others said that, when they went to rent houses on behalf of refugees, they were told: 'We won't let this house to a dog, let alone an Asian.' Yet another told of firms that stipulate 'European labour only'.

For a long time, newspapers kept alive compassion for the plight of the refugees with regular reports of their appalling struggles; but there was no discussion in a general way about the increase in Asian immigration. Not even when population projections showed that by the year 2008 the Asian community will have grown from two per cent to eight per cent.

TABLE 2: *Projected Origin of the Population of Australia*

	in early 1980s (%)	in 2008 (%)
British	75	70.6
South European	8	7.6
North European	7	7
East European	4	4.1
Asian	2	8
American	0.2	1.2
Aboriginal	1	1.5

In other words, all communities will have shrunk in size except the Asians and the Aborigines. Such a realization sends a (not surprising) shiver of apprehension through those who have bothered to absorb the figures. Just as Australia was coming to terms with 'foreign' Europeans, the game changes. It changes not just for the Anglo-Celtic majority, but also for the ethnic groups. They are aware that their power base is eroding as numbers dwindle. The Italian community emphasized that it was becoming increasingly difficult for Italians to get entry visas, and the statistics bear this out. The Greeks, Yugoslavs and Italians add 1,000 new immigrants a year to their communities, but this does not balance the death rate among the early post-war immigrants.

The more I discussed these matters, the more surprised I became that it was not and never had been a matter of public debate. Then, one day, Professor Geoffrey Blainey, the most widely read historian and a much admired academic, made a speech in which he questioned Asian immigration policy and suggested that the numbers coming into the country were running ahead of public opinion, and that at a time of high unemployment there might be difficulties. All hell broke loose: Blainey was branded a racist; his academic colleagues dissociated themselves from his views; students picketed his lectures; and politicians shouted at one another, even though there is no basic difference in their immigration policies. The Liberal governments had started and encouraged the increase and the Labor Government was following through under the umbrella of family reunion. The media went to town, too. They fuelled the debate by playing with the figures – the recent figures which showed large annual increases rather than the overall figures which, when all is said and done, show that the Asians are a mere two per cent of the population. But most of the time they castigated, crucified even, Blainey for daring to mention the unmentionable. They said it was wrong of him to have raised the subject. When I dared to suggest that Blainey as a historian (rather than a scaremongering politician) had been right to air a subject that was simmering below the surface, I was told in no uncertain terms and with the help of four-letter words to go home. 'Look where "Debate" over immigration has got Britain,' I was told by any number of well-informed opinion-makers.

A taxi-driver provided comfort. When I got into the cab, he was listening to an immigration debate in Parliament on the radio.

'What to you think of all this?' I asked.

'Well now, I've given this a lot of thought. Look at my arm. Those marks are cancers just from sitting with my arm on the open window. Our skins are not suited to this climate. And I've looked around me – and I get plenty of opportunity in this job – and I've decided that Australians are ... um ... ugly. Then I've looked at those Asians – and you've seen the Singapore Girl Ad, haven't you? – and I've decided that many more of them should come here and marry Australians and that way we'll have more suitable skins and we'll end up a better-looking lot.'

Pearson might have thought of that.

CHAPTER 5

Made of Gold

Melbourne is a stolid city sagacious rather than sparkling. It radiates a certain tweedy confidence, a kind of horn-rimmed cleverness; all the world knows that its brilliant doctors do remarkable things for infertile women, producing babies from test-tubes and deep freezes and goodness knows where else. And all Australia knows it prides itself on playing St Petersburg to Sydney's Tinsel Town. Clinging to its 'wowser' (killjoy) image, it sanctioned nude bathing only recently, likes its pubs to shut early and steadfastly refuses to welcome casinos or permit poker machines. It prefers its citizens to go home at night, leaving the city centre deserted. For twenty-seven years, until the early 1980s, it clung to a Liberal (Conservative) Premier.

It wasn't always so – the very opposite in fact. There was a time when Melbourne men lit their cigars with a £5 note, played skittles with bottles of French wine and shod their horses with golden horseshoes. Melbourne was made out of gold. For the first twenty years – until gold was discovered in 1851 just sixty miles north – settlement was slow, having started with a handful of pastoralists who hopped across from Tasmania and discovered that the soil was suitable for sheep. Sylvan solitude gently gave way to primitive village, to tiny port, to modest town. And then came gold, driving the place at a dizzy pace to premier position. By 1880 Melbourne reigned supreme, having outstripped Sydney, fifty years her senior, in every way. It became the country's focus; the country's financial capital; the tap through which a torrent of British capital watered a whole chunk of South-East Asia. It wasn't long, however, before Sydney recovered her breath and raced up behind, determined to

regain supremacy to match her seniority. The Depression of the
1890s helped Sydney to a neck-and-neck position.

The Depression hit Melbourne hard, harder than other States;
speculation ensured that she had much to lose. The buoyant optimism
of her boom years had land-prices, both within the city and without,
shooting to outrageous heights; thousands borrowed money and
bought acres of far-flung land which, when the crunch came, they
found unsaleable. The rapid transition from boom to bust had a
profound effect on the personality of the place. Melbourne was once
seen as an American-style city, aggressive and self-assertive, and
Sydney was portrayed as quieter and more civilized, a respectable,
sleepy hollow. A century ago, a traveller wrote, 'There is a bustle and
life about Melbourne which you altogether miss about Sydney. The
Melbourne man is always on the look out for business, and the
Sydney man waits for business to come to him.'

The reverse is true today. The pendulum began to swing firmly in
Sydney's favour when America discovered Australia's investment
potential and chose to make Sydney its headquarters. The Japanese
followed suit. Melbourne watched resentfully as Sydney bustled and
brimmed with new money. Then came the Sydney Opera House.
Poor Melbourne, she'd regarded herself as the cultural capital, and
it now appeared she had lost that title, too. But she did not give up
the fight; rivalry remained, surfacing whenever possible and often in
the most puerile way. At one stage when no real issues could be
found, Melbourne was reduced to boasting that she had a winter,
while Sydney had only a pale imitation of the season. And a Sydney
newscaster, relaying the saga of a windsurfer who had struggled
from Melbourne to Sydney, added his own footnote: 'I knew people
were desperate to leave Melbourne, but not *that* desperate.' With that
sort of silliness, it was something of a relief when the two centres had
some tangible reasons for reviving their rivalry. It came with the
decision to allow foreign banks to operate in Australia. Here was
Melbourne's chance to re-establish herself as the financial capital;
and here was Sydney's opportunity to deliver the final blow and
assert that she was the hub of that arcane and, to the layman, eye-
glazing world of hedge rates, spot rates and forward rates. Both the

Victoria and New South Wales governments set up large committees in attempts to ensure that their respective capitals became the base for the new banks. In the end, the first sixteen newcomers decided to spread their largesse between four cities: Adelaide and Perth, as well as Sydney and Melbourne. Stalemate. But not to worry; something bigger was emerging along St Kilda Road.

As soon as Sydney's Opera House became an international talking point, Melbourne took to the drawing board and began to scheme her $A225 million reply, all the while mocking Sydney's building for being twenty-five times over budget, for having a stage too small for opera and for omitting a car park. In 1982, the concert hall opened – a concrete bunker of a place on the outside, but opulent inside. It was, they said, a reflection of the city and of its citizens: solid and discreetly hiding their wealth, in contrast to Sydney, showy on the outside and nothing much within. Two years later came the second building, housing three theatres of varying sizes, a huge underground park for 1,500 cars, and – yes, of course – in the largest of the theatres, a stage so vast it could accommodate eight suburban houses. The inside is once again lavish, dripping with art works and demanding to be admired, and the outside remains something of a puzzle. The architect, the late Sir Roy Grounds, who also designed the concert hall, was said to be anxious not to detract from his location in tree-lined St Kilda Road, and thus put most of the building below ground, causing umpteen problems for engineers as steel piles disappeared into unfriendly silt. But if this was his thinking, why the 375-foot (115-metre) spire with its anodized aluminium base, described by Grounds either as a ballerina with her skirts swirling or as a see-through negligée? It dominates the skyline for miles and there are those who would like to embellish the spire further by adding lasers projecting beams into the sky to form a giant firework which would be activated one hour before a performance and for half an hour afterwards. Such a tower, Eiffel or eyeful according to taste, would give those soaring sails in Sydney some competition.

Both cities have now spent decades and millions of dollars exorcizing their edifice complex and convincing themselves that beautiful buildings stimulate artistic excellence. And it is upon this that they will finally be judged. Sydney claims that its building has rejuvenated the arts scene. It has certainly made it livelier – but what with? The lyric theatre, from musicals through to opera, is still heavily dependent on imported material. It is no coincidence that Melbourne's vast computerized stage was first trampled by *Fiddler on the Roof*. It's all the fault of J. C. Williamson, an American actor-manager who arrived in Australia as early as 1874 with his actress-wife, Maggie Moore. They brought with them something called *Struck Oil*, and in their first season made £22,000 before heading to London with the same product and making a further £30,000 and returning to Australia with a mint of money and the rights to the Savoy Operas of Gilbert and Sullivan. They promptly bought four theatres, two in Melbourne and one each in Sydney and Adelaide, and set about shaping public taste with a steady diet of imported work. Indigenous musical works did not get a chance. The legacy of Williamson and 'the firm', as it was called, is still discussed today. As a theatrical manager, he did much to help establish local artists, but their dependence on English theatre was a high price to pay. The lyric theatre has not recovered to this day; imports of the previous year's successes from Broadway and London's West End dominate. There is no such thing as an Australian musical; there are a handful of musical plays, but they are slight stuff indeed.

Williamson had much the same effect on opera. By 1900 'the firm' prospered by not only importing foreign works, but also importing foreign companies to perform those works, a policy which no doubt played its part in encouraging audiences to believe that 'foreign is best', which in turn caused singers from Nellie Melba to Joan Sutherland to find their voices and fly away. The first Australian opera company was not formed until 1956. Today, the opera is still dependent on the European nineteenth-century repertoire – but then that is the case with most opera houses around the world. Composers are rare creatures and operatic composers are rarest of all. Australia's two leading names, Peter Sculthorpe and Richard Meale, are more inclined to orchestral works. None the less, there are two operas in the pipeline, one by Richard Meale based on Patrick White's *Voss*, and the other by Edward Cowie with the legend of Ned Kelly as its subject. What is less understandable is Australia's dependence on imported directors and designers, although I did see one splendid all-Australian production of Verdi's *Il Trovatore*, produced by Elijah Moshinsky, designed by Sir Sidney Nolan and conducted by Richard Bonynge with Dame Joan Sutherland leading a home-grown cast with only one exception (Manrico was the British tenor, Kenneth Collins). It was a memorable occasion, made more so in Sydney by a delightfully unstuffy, largely female audience who, if young, came in jeans and, if elderly, showed their relaxed view of the whole occasion by knitting as they waited for the curtain to rise.

I hope they take such an attitude in Melbourne, for the building is inviting, not intimidating like so many European opera houses. It doesn't have Sydney's site advantage; the neighbouring landscape does not etch itself upon the eye; but for all that it has elegance. Melbourne as a whole is elegant; it is a Victorian city still, in spite of redevelopment. At its height, of course, it was exclusively and enthusiastically Victorian; indeed, its rise and fall coincided exactly with the reign of the queen who gave the state its name. Now it sprawls, as every city sprawls, but it has retained a real centre, a heart. Here, every street is straight, all the main streets run parallel to each other and all the secondary streets run at right angles to the main streets. They are proud streets, wide enough for trams to trundle down the middle. And everywhere there are large open spaces and public gardens. Each morning and each evening, I would walk to and from East Melbourne through Fitzroy Gardens, a pleasure I did not have in Sydney.

Robert Louis Stevenson felt sickened by all this neatness: 'When I think of Melbourne, I vomit. Its flatness; its streets laid out with a square rule are doomed to have a detrimental effect on those who are condemned to dwell by the yellow waters of the Yarra.' He might have been right about the Yarra. For years it was a dump for factory effluent and sewage, and derided by all. The upside-down river, they called it, because all the mud and muck was on the surface. But since the early 1970s a massive clean-up has been in operation. The Yarra is now a pleasant river with lawns planted to the water's edge, with trees along the footpath to provide shade for picnic tables and with strategically placed electric barbecues which, activated by a coin, allow steaks and sausages to sizzle. And grand plans are afoot to transform the South side with waterfront houses, hotels, shops and restaurants.

Stevenson would no longer be sickened by the yellow waters, but then he should never have been sickened by the square-ruled streets. The magic of Collins Street clearly eluded him. Collins Street is the heart of the heart. It is a great street, with a grandeur and presence that enable it to hold its own with many a grand street anywhere. Jan Morris said that a morning walk down Collins Street is like a conversation with a continent. I felt I could have that conversation from one spot; standing outside Number 360. Every company of any stature seemed to have offices in that building, and by turning my head I could also embrace the Stock Exchange opposite, at 367. The country hums the tunes played inside these two buildings. The tunes are often orchestrated further down the street, at the Melbourne Club.

This was founded early in the city's life to provide for the needs of the landed gentry when they came to town, many of them Scots. The Scots chose Melbourne as their city and became merchants and landowners. Today, the club is still to some extent dominated by graziers, as a glance at the list of vice-presidents and presidents reveals, although judges, doctors, professors, bankers and a few leading merchants are allowed through the portals. Some people argue that Catholics and Jews are not all that welcome, but the club denies this. It does not deny, however, that membership is universally acknowledged as the social apex. Its equivalent in Sydney, founded in the same year, does not have the same aura; it is not to the same extent an anachronistic bastion of wealth and privilege. The very existence of the Melbourne Club gives the lie to the much-publicized view that Australia is an egalitarian society, for no amount of money or distinction will automatically earn the right to membership.

The myth of egalitarianism is so well entrenched in Australia, and so well exported and so much believed in other lands, that it needs the mightiest of hammers to knock it down. Australia is neither socially egalitarian nor materially egalitarian. There are class distinctions and there are wide variations in income and wealth. These distinctions might be less obvious and the variations smaller than in many other Western industrialized societies, but they are there. Jack may like to believe that he is as good as his master; and Jack may also like to believe that birth and family do not entitle anyone to a leading role in society; but Jack deludes himself. There is a self-perpetuating ruling elite, and this is abundantly apparent in Melbourne. It is also readily acknowledged and freely talked about. Those at the top of industry and commerce all come from a handful of schools, they have cemented themselves into an establishment, and they do not welcome outsiders. And this is one very good reason why newcomers head for Sydney.

I met this problem myself. I wished to meet a few members of the financial community, and to this end I wrote letters which were not answered. I followed the letters with phone calls and these were met with evasive messages from secretaries. In the end I asked friends for help. They telephoned an 'insider', someone who was not in fact on my original list, and he agreed to see me. He also, at the end of our discussion, phoned the others. Of course he knew them: he'd known them since schooldays. I got my meetings and the point was finally driven home when I walked into the office of the Chairman of Charlton and United Breweries. (They make Fosters.) Sir Edward Cohen said to me: 'You wouldn't be in here if we hadn't checked you out and found you to be OK.' Some Tall Poppies remain untouched. They are too tall – out of Jack's reach. So he pretends they are not there.

There is much less pretence surrounding material equality. Australians have never really cared about or yearned for material equality. They accept that people are born with unequal abilities and they believe that everyone should have the right to develop those abilities fully; and if some get rich in the process, well, so be it. Few appear to believe that taxing the wealthy is a way of making life better for the less fortunate. Indeed, the tax system favours those with higher incomes; a capital gains tax has only recently been introduced and, in most states, there is neither gift tax nor estate duty.

But if there is less pretence about material equality, there is much ignorance; few Australians have any idea of the disparity of incomes and wealth within their own country. One set of figures published in 1985 claim that 1.4 per cent of the population own some twenty-nine per cent of the nation's net wealth. The nearest equivalent set of figures for the United Kingdom claims that the richest one per cent own eleven per cent of the wealth.

Maybe this head-in-the-sand attitude was acceptable during the good years when the general standard of living was high and unemployment non-existent. In the 1950s, Australia ranked fifth in the world after the USA, Canada, New Zealand and Switzerland. Her current position is fifteenth, and falling. The differences matter now, as the gap between rich and poor is getting wider and the Hawke Government seems determined to revise the tax system and use it to redistribute wealth. The widening gap has much to do with what is clumsily described as the feminization of the work-force – highly educated, high-earning men with secure jobs tend to marry women in a similar position, while the poor do the best they can on one income or, at worst – and all too often – on the dole.

It is easier to define poverty in Australia than in most countries because a Commission of Inquiry into the subject in the mid-1970s established a poverty line. This line is in fact a sum of money on which families are supposed to be able to exist; and the formula on which it is devised takes into account weekly earnings, size of family, housing costs and so on. In 1985, the poverty line for a family of four was $A252 while average male weekly earnings for the same period were $A397 and average weekly earnings for females stood at $A325. The poverty line was set low, to avoid contention, so that no one would dare argue; it is austere enough to be unchallengeable. Those below the poverty line are classed as 'very poor' and those twenty per cent above are described as 'poor'. At the time, the Commission found that ten per cent of the population were very poor and another eight per cent were poor. By 1985, the Government's own statistics revealed that one Australian in five lives below the poverty line; that is, 2.8 million people. They cover all categories, the elderly, single-parent families, recent immigrants, the disabled, large families and the unemployed. At worst, their plight is absolute, they are homeless and have nothing; at best, it means a home with a television and a fridge, but inadequate meals, second-hand clothes, no car and certainly no money for even an occasional glimpse of the good life.

No wonder they stormed the Melbourne Club – twice, in fact, during my stay in Australia. The first time was a non-violent affair. Seventeen unemployed people distributed leaflets outside which said: 'The Melbourne Club is the best-known and most obnoxious retreat of the spoiled rich. While Victorian Liberal party leaders and press barons can gorge themselves on two-hour business lunches served on expensive silver, many unemployed and pensioners are worrying where their next meal is coming from.' Finally they walked through the door chanting, 'Jobs for all, not just the rich,' and then sat on the floor and presented a petition containing six demands: that members should make a donation to a rally against poverty and unemployment; that the club should be opened to women, the unemployed and pensioners at no cost and that free meals, child care and accommodation be provided; that the club management instruct its members to create jobs by approving a thirty-five-hour week; that the club management instruct members not to lay off workers and not to cheat the public through tax-avoidance schemes; and that members who did not comply should be expelled. The seventeen were evicted and eventually charged with trespassing on private property.

The second occasion, one month later, was violent. Some 2,000 members of the Coalition against Poverty and Unemployment marched down Collins Street to the Stock Exchange building and then to the Melbourne Club.'Work or Riot' was their slogan and a handful of the demonstrators forced their way through the door, smashing windows and overturning bookshelves and furniture. 'We want them to know we are very angry. That is the ruling class in there, that's the tax evaders.' Guests at the club were moved to the rear garden and served drinks and canapés while the police restored order. Some time later, four men were charged with riot, criminal damage and unlawful entry. The Golden Mile, as Collins Street is called, winced at such flamboyant gestures. Some spluttered, 'It's bloody silly. If they walked into your home you'd object, wouldn't you? This is our home.' But some took the point: the ruled were telling the rulers that they hated being have-nots. And they were doing so in the time-honoured way. Indeed, the first class clash in Australian history took place not a hundred miles away.

When gold was discovered at Ballarat, it acted like a magnet. Men who toiled all day in shops and on farms and down mines saw their chance and rushed lemming-like in search of the lump that would change their lives. At the height of the Gold Rush, 500 men a day were arriving on the gold fields. The government was beside itself: to whom did the gold belong? Who should be allowed to dig? Who should administer the fields, and how could order be maintained? They decreed that money should be raised for administration by making the miners, the diggers, take out a licence. At first this was £1 a month and then it was raised to £3 a month in an attempt to stop men abandoning other occupations. The diggers refused to pay and had to be hunted down by police, and when caught they were treated none too kindly. As gold became more difficult to find, the surface exhausted, the diggers grouped together in a reform league under Irishman Peter Lalor, pressing for a lot more than the abolition of the licence fee. The government's response was to step up the police hunt. Then one day corrupt magistrates acquitted an ex-convict publican of the murder of a miner. The miners rioted: some were arrested and convicted; others, their tempers high, built themselves a crude stockade at a place called Eureka. One morning, at dawn, the police attacked, killing more than a score of men. The Eureka Stockade is often painted as a great fight for the rights of the working man – a fight which they won, for several reforms followed. The storming of the Melbourne Club, 130 years later, by a Coalition against Poverty and Unemployment, was not without historical echoes.

Inside that walled garden that night, standing beside the huge oriental plane tree (said to be the most splendid specimen of its kind), I wonder what was being discussed: the need for reform? The on-going struggle with Sydney for financial leadership? The unemployment figures; or the latest monthly statistics showing how much foreign capital had flowed into the wide brown land. Australians are addicted to foreign capital. They firmly believe that development, and in turn the maintenance of high living standards, cannot be achieved without massive injections of foreign capital.

Australia now has the highest level of foreign ownership and control of all the advanced countries except Canada. Figures on this are most unreliable, not least because the section of the Australian Bureau of Statistics that measures foreign ownership was closed down for four years between 1978 and 1982, but also because the situation is remarkably easy to fudge with the help of nominee companies and all the other loopholes available to the world of high finance. Some argue that three-fifths of the mineral industry is under foreign control; one-third of the manufacturing, general insurance and non-bank finance; for motor cars it is one hundred per cent; for oil ninety per cent; basic chemicals seventy-eight per cent; black coal fifty-nine per cent; brown coal eighty-four per cent; iron ore forty-seven per cent.

The process of selling off Australia has been going on apace for forty years, having started with a Labor Government decision in 1945 to accept General Motors Holden's proposal to build an automobile plant financed by an overdraft from the Commonwealth Bank. Menzies opened the floodgates during the boom years when money was much needed to service the needs of millions of immigrants as well as the opening up of the country's resources. It is easy enough to argue that the money was indeed needed, but the point is that it went unchecked ... it was assumed to be a good thing and so went unchecked. Until it began to create bogey men. GMH was the first; that company became – to some at least – the symbol of multinational exploitation of Australia; and every time enormous profits were declared and large sums of money left for the United States, squeals of protest were heard. In the end, GMH is said to have taken refuge under a law which did not require it to publish profits if there were no local shareholders, and so the few remaining were bought out.

While there might have been some squeals, nothing was done to temper the open-door policy until Gough Whitlam came to power with the laudable nationalistic objective of 'buying back the farm'.

A Foreign Investment Advisory Committee was formed and rules began to emerge. The aim is fifty per cent Australian equity, but this is subject to waiver if the money is not available. And there's the rub. The Committee, now a fully fledged Foreign Investment Review Board, reviews all investment proposals worth more than $A5 million and all real-estate proposals worth more than $A350,000. It claims to assess each application on its merits and there isn't, for example, a ceiling for each sector. The Board is referred to as the Foreign Investment Attraction Board since it turns down so few. In one recent year there were 1,256 applications: 847 were unconditionally approved; 362 were approved, subject to conditions, and a mere 47 were rejected.

There is no real will to curb the flood. The Hawke Government has adopted a soft line, ignoring official Labor Party stipulation that Australian participation in key areas such as gas, oil, minerals and farming should be extended to a controlling fifty-one per cent. He does not wish to frighten off foreign money and argues, once again, that Australia will continue to need overseas capital if the rate of growth of the economy is to be maximized. Those who think this is wrong, those who supported Whitlam's Government in its attempt to 'buy back the farm', continue to argue for a more balanced approach; and this includes some important leaders of the financial community who feel that more ought to be done to encourage Australians to invest, to own shares in Australian companies. It is·a slow process, changing the attitudes of people who have become used to seeing others make the effort and take the risks – first the British, then the Americans and now the Asians – while they concentrate on buying a home or two and then sit back and enjoy life in a modest way. Again, caution and conservatism result in a lack of enterprise and adventurous spirit.

Men as dynamic as Rupert Murdoch in creating wealth and in redressing the balance of ownership by acquiring newspapers in Britain and America have been rare. I asked Rupert Murdoch if I was right in thinking the Australians lacked enterprise.

'Well, you have to understand we got the worst in this country. We got the criminals and we had a pretty slow start. Until gold was found there was little more than a few farms, and that wasn't much more than a hundred years ago. We are still a desperately young country. None the less, attitudes are changing. The 1980s have seen Australian companies moving out into the world. And if you look at the survey carried out by the *Business Review Weekly* and listing the two hundred richest people in Australia, you will find very little old money there. If you leave aside the three media families, you will find that most of the money has been made since the war and much of it has been made by migrants.'

To examine the list is indeed interesting. Of the twelve who have been classified as having wealth in excess of $A100 million, a list headed by Rupert Murdoch with $A300 million, six names belong to newcomers to the country: two from Poland, and one each from Russia, Italy and Germany, and Mr Robert Holmes a Court from South Africa. In the list of those with wealth in excess of $A50 million there are three from Poland, three from Hungary, one Romanian and one German. Below $A50 million and in excess of $A10 million, the Hungarians and the Poles still head the list, although there are six from Britain, most of them Jewish.

The immigrants, then, with their different attitudes to work and to the sacrifices necessary for long-term gain, have had a major influence on the country. They set an example, showing that risk can equal profit and advancement, for a further glance at the survey of the richest 200 shows that while the immigrants were busy creating wealth, so too were a large number of Australians. The survey is dotted with references to 'the former telegram delivery boy from Brisbane', 'the butcher's son from New South Wales', and 'the grocer from Melbourne'. The climate of the three decades, the 1950s, the 1960s and at least part of the 1970s was conducive to money-making, the opportunities were there. For the press barons it was the coming of television, but for a large number of those listed it was property development. The list of the wealthy mirrors the development that has taken place in Australia since the Second World War, particularly in Sydney and in Perth. New South Wales has the highest number of multi-millionaires in the list, a total of seventy-four, while Melbourne has fifty-seven and Western Australia, with less than a third of the population of the other two States, has twenty-nine.

The coming together of opportunity and the emergence of men willing to grasp it has started something. Rupert Murdoch believes it will continue. 'There is something happening that Australians don't want to talk about, something that is good even though they think it is bad, and that is oriental immigration. These people are terrific: energetic, intelligent and entrepreneurial. They will pick up any opportunity.'

And with these changes perhaps, in time, there will come a lessening dependence on foreign money. There was jubilation, at least in the media, when Australia's largest company, Broken Hill Proprietary (BHP), nibbled at another American giant, Utah Development. BHP raised $A2 billion to buy out General Electric's interest in Utah, and this meant that five of the world's most lucrative coal mines were passing from American to Australian control and largely into Australian ownership. There was no jubilation – indeed there was shock – when some time later it was discovered that an American company held the North American performing rights on the words and music of 'Waltzing Matilda'. The sale took place in the 1930s. There's much buying back left to do.

If Melbourne has lost the title of financial capital and if she is struggling to regain cultural supremacy, there is still one crown that is indisputably hers. Melbourne started, and continues to host, more significant sporting occasions than any other State. She has a famous cricket ground; she is the home of Australian Rules Football, and on one day of the year she has the distinction of uniting the interest of the whole of Australia. That occasion falls on the first Tuesday in November and is called the Melbourne Cup.

Mark Twain described the Melbourne Cup as the Australasian Day. 'It would be difficult to overstate its importance. It overshadows all other holidays. I might say it blots them out. Each of them gets attention, but not everybody's; each of them evokes interest, but not everybody's; each of them rouses enthusiasm, but not everybody's. Cup Day and Cup Day only, commands an attention, an interest, and an enthusiasm which are universal. Cup Day is supreme – it has no rivals.'

Today it has rivals, but the two-mile handicap which was established in 1861, as Melbourne was beginning to glow with gold, has retained its special place. Maybe it is no longer the flashy affair which Twain chronicled, with women decked out in finery ordered months before, champagne flowing free and crowds piling in from the countryside ready to dance all night in the week leading to the Cup and then returning to the bush whacked and lamenting that they would have to wait a whole year before they could have such fun again. Maybe it is no longer quite so exhausting, but it is still the one day of the year when the eyes of Australia are trained on Melbourne. The track at Flemington, all emerald turf and rosebeds, does its best to repay the nation's interest and by 1988 it will have, at the top level of the grandstand, a 130-foot- (40-metre-) long mural of gigantic proportions depicting the development of horse-racing from the early passion of the Romans and Greeks through to the present, via the day in January 1788 when the First Fleet arrived with seven horses on board, and men eager to transplant the British love of horses and of racing. It didn't take long. The first recorded horse race dates from 1810, and now it is big business.

I wonder how much money has changed hands over the years on Cup Day? Even during the Depression of the 1930s, men were not deterred from their annual desire to change their fortunes on the back of a horse. In fact, during the Depression interest was heightened by a horse called Phar Lap; a phenomenal horse that stood seventeen hands, weighed half a ton and possessed a heart twice the size of any hefty army horse. This heart, weighing fourteen pounds, is preserved behind glass in Canberra and the hide is mounted in a Melbourne museum. Phar Lap gave hope to a nation during those appalling years; 'Big Red' they called him, although his name in fact means 'Wink of the Sky' or lightning. As befits Australia, his early days were unpromising. When he was bought for 160 guineas (£168), he resembled a scrawny mongrel dog with boils round his mouth and bruises on his chestnut hide; his first nine races brought only one win and he lost his first Melbourne Cup. But then as a four-year-old he found his form and won fourteen races in a row, including the Cup. By then he wasn't racing other horses, he was racing the clock and would sometimes win by thirty lengths. Frightened men who could not cope with the competition tugged at the winsome creature and placed impossible weights upon him. And still he won. In the end his greedy owners, needing new challenges, took him to America. He won his first race, the Agua Caliente Stakes, held over the Mexican border from California. He died before his next race. His death is a mystery. To a nation that mourned him behind newspaper headlines which simply read 'He's dead', he was poisoned, but the evidence is inconclusive; he may merely have eaten a quantity of grass dampened by fog which caused large amounts of gas to fill his intestines.

The truth will never be known, and the Australians will never forget. They were rapidly forming the opinion that Americans would do anything to ensure victory. A prize Australian boxer, Les Darcy, had died in 1917 in America, and the memory of the two, Darcy and Phar Lap, is coupled in Australian minds and resurrected whenever the country finds itself in sporting combat with the United States. They were recalled in 1970 when a boat called *Gretel* made a valiant attempt to win the America's Cup; the yacht won the second (of seven) races and the victory was greeted with howls of protest from New York Yacht Club. They were recalled in 1983 when many unsporting accusations and much silly nonsense from the same club were in danger of marring Australia's successful attempt to prise this glorious trophy away from New York where it had rested for too long. It was a magnificent victory.

All nations take pride in their sporting prowess, and small nations take great pride in achieving victory over superpowers with populations twenty-five times their own. On the playing fields they can achieve influence that is denied them in other spheres; and with victory they can shine for a while in a world which is otherwise content to ignore their presence. When Australia won the America's Cup the whole nation cheered, delighted to have up-staged a world power upon which it is dependent. And a whole nation cheered, delighted that it had not lost its reputation for sporting achievement.

Australia had gained a love of sport early, mainly because the work-force had more leisure than other countries, the eight-hour day being introduced for some skilled workers as early as 1856, and this work-force, disinclined to follow intellectual pursuits in its spare time, found sport the perfect antidote to labour. By 1875 it had nurtured its first world champion. His name was Edward Trickett and on the River Thames, on Tuesday, 27 June 1876, he became the world sculling champion; and for the first time since the commencement of international rowing contests in 1863, England had to reconcile herself to defeat in home waters. *The Times* next morning was rather churlish in suggesting that Trickett could not have beaten the English champion, James Sadler, at his best, but that the poor man on that memorable Tuesday was suffering from a cold and feeling his age which was thirty-seven. Trickett, six foot four inches, fit and healthy and only twenty-seven, owed his success, so the newspaper claimed, to the two months of training he had received since his arrival in London! Trickett returned to Sydney to a hero's welcome. It was the first taste of victory over the mother country and it was sweet.

The second followed swiftly; less than a year after the sculling victory, in March 1877 at Melbourne, Australia won the first Test Match to be played between the two countries and not surprisingly writers began dreaming of producing a race of super sportsmen in a land full of leisure, sunshine and fresh meat.

The cricketing contest, as all the world knows, continues at regular intervals and at times England's desire to defeat her former colony has resulted in behaviour no more gentlemanly than the displays put on by the New York Yacht Club. The word 'bodyline' needs no explanation to an Australian, whether a cricket devotee or not. The events of the 1932–3 Test series caused serious talk of severing Imperial ties. In 1984, Australian television broadcast a ten-hour reconstruction of the matches in which Douglas Jardine, the England captain, was portrayed as 'aristocratic, cold and disdainful, the cosseted child of the Raj', while the local Sir Galahad, Don Bradman, was drawn as the poor carpenter's son who taught himself to play cricket with a golf-ball in a dusty backyard. Harold Larwood, who pitched a good many of those balls at bodies rather than the wickets, now lives in Sydney; after the screening he received threatening and obscene phone calls and was said to be amazed that people should feel so strongly after fifty years. But then Don Bradman and Phar Lap, during the same period in the 1930s, were gods. That one should die in mysterious circumstances in a foreign country, and the other be pelted in the chest by supercilious Englishmen claiming they were playing cricket, was more than the nation could bear.

Not all Australia's sporting joys are silhouetted against a background of unpleasant international petulance. Indeed Melbourne's most regular sporting treat, occurring every Saturday through winter, involves no other country and, for a while, involved no other State. Australian Rules Football was invented to keep cricketers fit during the winter. Tom Willis devised the game. He'd been to Rugby in the 1850s and there he had played a rough sort of a game which he decided was not quite suitable for Melbourne: 'Boys have plenty of time to nurse their wounded shins, and now and then their broken limbs, but men, however their courage might prompt them, cannot afford to become victims in such a cause, especially as there is little skill required in a scrummage, but rather any amount of brute force.' Aussie Rules, then, is not a brutal game – indeed, it seemed to me after only one visit, to be preferable to other football and Rugby because, with no off-side rules, interruptions were less frequent, and at times the players made glorious leaps into the air to catch the ball. The higher the leaps, the more the crowd roared. Melbourne hopes that its invention will one day become the national game. Two States have yet to be convinced: Queensland and New South Wales have not succumbed with the same passion as the rest of Australia. Meanwhile, the Grand Final which takes place on the last Saturday in September has the same effect on Australia as the Melbourne Cup. It draws a raucous capacity crowd and glues the rest of the nation to the TV screen.

On such an occasion, television comes into its own, allowing millions to share the excitement. On other occasions, television has played havoc with sport, turning it into big business and one-time participants into stodgy watchers. In 1956 when the Olympic Games were held in Melbourne, Australia performed well, but by 1976 their performance was so pathetic that the government announced an inquiry. The Duke of Edinburgh was displeased: 'The idea of Australia holding an official inquiry into the country's performance at the Munich Olympics is deplorable; it is not for a government to worry about how many medals are won – this is taking sport far too seriously.' But it is not: all countries worry about their medals, and Australia had not been worrying enough. She needed to sort out why her sportsmen had dominated after the war and then, inside twenty years, had slipped so badly. She had been dozing, basking in her easy success and taking things for granted, and had not realized that the rest of the world had been pouring money into improved facilities and improved opportunities for talented sportsmen and women. The pursuit of medals had become a serious study; sunshine and fresh meat were no longer enough. The inquiry resulted in the setting up, in 1981, of the Australian Institute of Sport, in Canberra, with world-class facilities and coaching aimed at helping young people to study and train without strain, and not be tempted to America with offers of scholarships. The eight-hour day and Edward Trickett started something which any nation would strive to keep alive.

CHAPTER 6

The Whore Strikes Back

That dust storm was more than a wile; it was a warning – a neat fifteen-day notice that the force of nature was once again about to overwhelm man, dwarf and humble him, and prove that Australia can be a harsh and sometimes savagely hostile land. That force was about to produce the biggest disaster since cyclone Tracy destroyed Darwin on Christmas Day, 1974.

South-east Australia is one of the most fire-prone areas in the world; the heat, the dryness and the wind make it so. A greedy threesome who when they decide to dine together find no shortage of food; indeed, all too often they find a feast of highly combustible fuel awaiting them. Bush fires are as much a part of Australia as the kangaroo. A land is not tamed, the elements are not intimidated, by millions of bungalows and miles of bitumen road. While the sun glares and the winds blow and the eucalyptus thrives, fires remain a threat. And they are frequent during the summer months; so much so that the sight of another blaze on the nightly television news-bulletins comes to have little more significance than another road accident. Most are snuffed out quickly; trained fire-fighters and experienced volunteers know their stuff; occasionally property might be destroyed, but rarely are lives lost. Until the day when man is put firmly in his place and fiercely reminded that this is a land of extremes: of drought, of fire, of cyclone and of flood. Until the day he finds the words 'Nature Rules OK' chalked in black across the landscape. And she has a sense of irony. This time, the day she chose for her display was Ash Wednesday.

South Australia was struck first. It was, of course, hot with temperatures reaching 110°F (43°C); the land was drought-crazed, some areas having not seen rain for five years. And then came the wind, a searing thirty-knot wind which sent shivers of apprehension through those with long memories. (Three years before, on the very same day, Ash Wednesday, fires had burned across the hills surrounding Adelaide, the dress-circle suburbs where those who like to combine city life with a touch of grass and green build their houses. That time no lives were lost, but seventy homes were destroyed.) The first fire was reported just before noon, and within two hours a corner of South Australia was in chaos. Fire is capricious; its course is difficult to plot. Some peope had little warning. First they heard a roar and then towards them rushed a fire wave, sometimes sixty feet (twenty metres) high and sometimes – such was the speed of the wind – the flames seemed horizontal, like a blowtorch.

Murray Nicholl, a journalist and volunteer fireman, rushed to the hills to help fight the fire and to report on it. His emotion-laden and smoke-choked words were relayed across Australia and out to the rest of the world:

I'm sitting out on the road in front of my own house where I've lived for thirteen or fourteen years . . . it's going down in front of me. The roof's falling in. It is in flames and there's nothing I can do about it. The flames are in the roof . . . goddam it. It's just beyond belief, my own house. Everything around is black. There are fires burning all around me, all around me.

The front section of my house is blazing; the roof has fallen in. My water tanks are useless. There's absolutely nothing I can do about it. My house is gone. It's exploding still and I just can't bear to look at it.

The last I saw of my wife, she was at the fire station, manning the radio. The man across the road from me thinks his wife is trapped in the house – and his house is burnt to the ground. He hasn't seen his wife since they left and she didn't come out of the house at all. He believes, and nobody can tell him to the contrary, that she may still be in there. Well, if she is in there, she's gone.

As Murray Nicholl told his story, Victoria's turn had come. It was three p.m. when the first fires broke out. By evening, they were out of control, areas were evacuated and firemen began praying for the 'cool change'. The wind did indeed change around eight-thirty p.m.

It whipped around from north to south-east at appalling speed; and it did not bring relief, it merely compounded the disaster. By then, standing in the garden of my temporary home in the centre of Melbourne, there was no mistaking the smell: the acrid, pungent smell of smoke, carried on the wind. The sky was a ghastly, gloating red. It was the evening of the next day before the fires were under control. Seventy-five people lost their lives in the two States, and the damage ran into hundreds of millions of dollars in lost homes, in lost stock, in damaged forest, roads, bridges and power lines.

Within thirty-six hours I was in Adelaide. With some trepidation I phoned the police and asked where I might go to witness the mopping-up operation. The television cameras had now gone and I expected short shrift, believing that the police would want to protect the area from prying eyes and be left alone to get on with the job. Instead, an officer, when he realized that I was new to the area, offered to pick me up from my hotel and personally show me the magnitude of the task they faced. The South Australian force pride themselves on their close ties with the public.

We went by police car to the hills. In places the land was grimly silent; it looked war-torn, bomb-blackened: trees napalmed, leafless; cars incinerated by the side of the road; signs buckled and unreadable. And people, dazed, crept back to the place they had once called home and sieved through the rubble for anything that might have escaped the flames.

Lyn Lamshed's legs were bruised and scratched and her husband Barry's face and clothes were covered with soot. They reckoned it would be more than a year before their home was rebuilt and a lot longer than that before Barry could rid himself of the image of Ash Wednesday when a ball of fire raced towards his home. 'I was on the roof filling the gutters with water, hoping that this would help the fire go over the house, when I realized that I had to get out.' He leapt into his car and fled to the nearby town of Gumeracha to find his wife and tell her that their home was gone.

Lyn felt empty. 'I have cried and I do feel anger, but most of the time I just feel empty.' For the next year they would be living in a caravan in the garden. It had been lent to them by the local postmaster and it had been stocked by the local doctor. 'And it wasn't just ordinary tucker either. There was the best breakfast tea, nice biscuits and veggies from his garden.' And as she spoke, neighbours and friends were working in the backgound rigging up an outside lavatory. An architect, sent by the insurance company to assess the damage, walked out from the ruins and announced that the remaining walls were still sound. All around, three acres of fruit trees – plums, apples, pears – sagged, seemingly lifeless. 'Maybe with a good prune, we'll be able to save some. We are lucky, really, that this is only a hobby farm. My husband still has his job.' Barry Lamshed works for the Department of Aboriginal Affairs in Adelaide. They had given him a week's leave and he had taken a further month. He needed all of that to sort out the mess.

Elsewhere in the hills, people busied themselves. Telephones were being reconnected; the highway department was taking down dangerous-looking trees. And behind a sign saying 'Indoor and Outdoor Plants', the police had set up a temporary headquarters. They had finished looking for bodies, but now they were flat out assessing damage, policing the area to deter looters and trying to determine the cause of the fires.

Detective Chief-Inspector Bob Potts, field commander, is also a volunteer fireman; for one day and night he fought the fire. 'We are all full of stories, but what I will remember is the sense of inadequacy. It was man versus nature and, although it may sound dramatic, no amount of resources or bravery would have helped. Nature overwhelmed us.' A blackboard behind him logged the damage: 1,000 sheep, 44 goats, 119 cattle, 160 fowl, 3 dogs, 1 pig, 60 beehives, 30,000 goldfish and 1 cat. 'Yes, the goldfish do look odd, but there was a goldfish farm. The fish were in open tanks and a branch from a tree fell on them.'

Bob Potts was not sure what caused the fire in this particular area. In others, it had been caused by electricity wires flung together in high winds; and in one a swimming pool pump had overheated. Here, he couldn't be sure. They had been having trouble with arsonists, people who find it amusing to leave a match by the roadside. He preferred not to speculate and to remain detached.

The Chairman of the Country Fire Brigade was anything but detached and readily admitted to being under considerable emotional pressure. His 105-year-old house was wrecked; only the thick stone walls remained. It was one of eight old houses in the area. 'South Australia's history gurgled down the ash pipe,' he said with ill-disguised bitterness. 'Our gardens used to be show-places. We won't bother to plant azaleas again. Asbestos trees would be better.'

During the previous year his organization of 38 full-timers and 1,200 volunteers had been under investigation for inefficiency and spiralling costs, and he had spent considerable time defending his organizations to auditors and committees.

Although we came out pure as the driven snow, our morale was low. We could have spent all that time educating people about fire. We spend enough telling them not to drink and drive, but we ought to be putting the fear of hell into those who are careless. And to arsonists. There is an unstable element in our community, and those people are getting their own back on society because they are unemployed or because they have been smacked by their headmaster. The fines don't even cover the cost of apprehending them. They are murderers. That's what they are. Would you prefer to be stabbed in the back or boiled alive in a vat of eucalyptus oil? ... because that is what happened here. I don't want them locked up with a colour television set. I want them put to work planting trees for every one that has been burned and I want them building houses for every one that has been destroyed.

His anger was healthy enough. It is the next phase after the numbness and shock and before the release of determination to rebuild lives and homes. His anger was healthy and it was real. It was also being experienced in Victoria, where the problems were identical. They too had been having trouble with arsonists. The police estimate that six per cent of fires are started deliberately, but this is most difficult to prove – unless, of course, they catch someone red-handed. Even then there are problems. The force was still smarting from the penalty served on someone they had not only caught in the act but who had also pleaded guilty. He was fined $A500 and given a good behaviour bond. The offender sold fire extinguishers and was a volunteer fireman. A sick man. But even allowing for sympathy, there was considerable outrage at the sentence.

And Victoria's fire-fighters had also been under a microscope. A new Labor Government, anxious to promote efficiency and cut costs – after all, they fund the brigades, together with the insurance industry – were determined to bring about closer links between the volunteer fire-fighters in the country areas and the professional fire-fighters in the metropolitan area. The relationship between the two had always been edgy, with little formal exchange of information, and, at the time of the fires, had been made worse by the threat of a merger. Accountants can always see the advantages of shared administration and so forth and can't always see problems of compatibility and pride. Such items do not figure on balance-sheets. And it would be hard for me to overestimate the pride of this band of men who had no intention of getting too close to the heavily unionized professionals.

And the effect of all this showed clearly through one newspaper paragraph.

The United Firefighters' Union of Victoria said that about 1,000 professional firemen in Melbourne were not called to help fight the bush fires.

Our members are irate that they didn't have the opportunity to help. The only Metropolitan fire brigade firemen who were fighting the bush fires were a small number who were with the Country Fire Authority units because they lived in the affected areas.

The union, needless to say, used this as an opportunity to renew its long-standng demand that the State's fire-fighting services be integrated. They will never be totally integrated. The volunteers would disband if a merger were ordered. But Ash Wednesday led to closer ties. It had to happen, with eight authorities in the State, each with some fire-fighting responsibilities, and no single body to oversee and co-ordinate the activities. Disasters usually bring about analysis and evaluation. And compromise.

The pride of the volunteer lies in his sense of uniqueness – nowhere else in the world are they unpaid – and of tradition. The volunteer dates back to the early days of settlement when men had nothing more than branches with which to fight – branches and the desire each to help the other. Even today, with a military-style operation and paid employees to worry about organization, training and the provision of equipment, there is no shortage of volunteers. Out there in the bush, you have to join; self-interest dictates that if you don't go to the aid of your neighbour down the track, he is not going to turn out for you. But that self-interest is also coated with community spirit which is strong. The brigades are often the social centre of a small rural community and the men like to feel that they are the fourth arm of defence. What they may lack in professionalism, they make up by an intimate knowledge of their area. They know all the fire-trails, where the hydrants are, whom to ring if they want a bit more pressure in one of them, and everything else a man should know. They resent, now, being told they must take a training course and pass examinations. Country people are always a bit touchy when they feel they are being pushed around by city-dwellers. They do not want their easy-going self-reliance further eroded. At other times I encountered a Boy-Scoutish boastfulness as men recalled past experiences – the roar of the fire through the timber, or the smell of eucalyptus – but perhaps this is understandable. Fire-fighting is not a hobby, it is a question of the survival of life and of livelihood. The dread of it encourages a veneer of casualness and the inevitability of it brings acceptance.

Fire has been a fact from the beginning. Certainly Captain Cook and his crew record having seen fires burning as they sailed up the Pacific coast in 1770. They describe witnessing Aborigines lighting fires almost daily; it was the core of their technology. They used it to roast meat, keep mosquitoes at bay, send messages, lighten their darkness, warm their nights *and* act as a land management tool. Fire acted as a cultivator – in the same way as the plough – and after the fire and the next rain, lush new green grass provided pasture for the kangaroo and other animals. The Aborigine depended for his survival on a ready supply of harvestable game.

Cook and his team claim that they never saw an Aborigine put out a fire, They appeared, it is recorded, merely to walk away and leave the fire to burn out. They had no possessions to worry about,

10 sheep, no permanent houses, no fences. Other early explorers, however, noted that this was not always so. They witnessed section burning, and marvelled at the dexterity with which the Aborigines managed fire; how, armed with green boughs, they beat it out if it moved in the wrong direction. Such was their ability, they appeared to be able to make docile this disruptive element. Men try it today: they call it prescribed burning, and it is much used by those who work the land and by the Forest Commission to clear the undergrowth so that, should a fire start, it is soon starved of fuel. Lose a little to save a lot, is their slogan. The results of this strategy are mixed; bush fires all too often start by prescribed burnings getting out of hand.

In the aftermath of Ash Wednesday, people were heard to suggest, once again, that European man is made to feel almost unwelcome in Australia. Of course this was a singularly bad time. Australia was not the only country to have it so hard; everywhere except Antarctica and Europe suffered from an aberration in the weather system. They called it *el niño* ('the Child'). The Child was a maverick, it broke all the rules; the trade winds faltered and the equatorial current reversed direction across the entire Pacific Sea; surface temperatures rose as much as eight degrees Fahrenheit until a great tongue of warm water stretched 7,950 miles (12,800 kilometres) along the Equator. It will be years before scientists fully understand what happened.

However, even without the excesses brought by the Child, Australians have had reason to be daunted by their environment. The response has been a few good jokes, a band of devoted scientists determined to understand it, and a larger band of hostility and indifference. The best joke indicates that Australia has to be the oldest land-mass since the Creator, if he'd had more experience, would surely have made a better job of it. He would then have plonked it at least ten degrees further south to take better advantage of the rain-bearing westerlies; or he could have supplied at least one decent mountain range whose snow-capped peaks might sustain rivers to water the arid land.

The first arrivals were truly baffled; their settlements floundered; the first explorers met with death and disaster. The land, to them, seemed defiant. And so they countered this with more defiance and some disrespect. D. H. Lawrence claimed that 'Australia is like a poor prostitute and the Australian just bullies her to get what he can out of her and then treats her like dirt.' A harsh judgement, but in part true. The first settlers certainly couldn't have cared less about the land. They came from the cities and had no real empathy with land. They saw trees; they cut them down to clear the way for farming or to use the wood for building. Small farmers lacked money and education to adopt good farming practices, and repeated cropping soon reduced the productive capacity of the soil. And the large landowner, with his merino sheep and cattle, was not intent on staying, but merely making his money – and such an attitude does not encourage conservation. Over-grazing continued and soil erosion is now a major problem. But this wilful disregard was mingled with some genuine bad luck. In 1838, an innocuous-looking cactus called prickly pear was introduced as a pot plant; and, before long, vast areas of eastern Australia were totally infested, which started a long struggle to find its natural enemy – a moth.

And what of the rabbit? Thomas Austin of Geelong earned himself an unenviable niche in history in 1859 by bringing in wild grey rabbits because he fancied a spot of hunting, thus starting the greatest animal invasion of any continent in history. Within twenty years, Victoria knew the extent of the menace; but by then poor people had come to value the creature for both its meat and its fur, and politics interfered with any serious attempt at eradication. At one point, Louis Pasteur suggested that chicken cholera would do the job, but nervous men worried about the effect of such a drastic step on other edible animals, and it was decided to stick with time-honoured trapping. This was such a lucrative business that the trappers made sure enough does were left to keep themselves in business. By and by, in 1919, a solution was offered by a Brazilian scientist – myxomatosis – but once more the carcass and fur lobby won the day. They did not want their rabbits totally destroyed. It was not until after the Second World War that the situation became desperate enough for men to put aside self-interest. By then, with so many away at war and unable to carry out trapping and shooting and poisoning, no one could argue against drastic measures. They just had to look: where there were rabbit fences, there was lush green grass on one side and, on the other, naked earth. The myxomatosis theory was revived. In 1952–3, Australia's wool and meat production jumped by $A68 million as pastures recovered from the ravages of rabbits.

Science is as often at odds with the greeds of men as it is in tandem with them. And Australia has never been short of scientific talent. In the early years, men relished the challenge of a new land; in later years, they relished the opportunity to be released from the limitations of their own countries. By 1850, each State had its own Meteorological Office, and, by 1900, each had its own agricultural department which included among its functions the spread of information about sound farming practices. And then in 1926, from a few small rented rooms in the suburbs of Melbourne, a major scientific research organization came into being: the Commonwealth Scientific and Industrial Research Organization (CSIRO). In the beginning there were forty-one scientists; there are now several thousands with a hundred laboratories and field stations dotted around the country; it is one of the most comprehensive research organizations in the world. It is a statutory body, government-funded, and its aim has always been to offer the resources of science to both the primary and the secondary sector; its battle has always been to balance pure against applied research in order to be seen to be worthy of its huge budget. It has had both impressive successes and noble failures and many a controversial problem in between. Probably its best-known success today is the Interscan aircraft landing system, which is gradually being introduced into airports around the world. Australia won international acceptance for this system against competition from both the UK and the USA, and proudly and justifiably boasts that it is a fine example of pure science (in this case astronomy) being applied for the practical good of modern man in a modern world.

Undoubtedly the CSIRO's most controversial project involves the humble dung-beetle. When the first English settlers landed five cows and two bulls, they clearly gave little thought to the effect that cow-pats would have on the land. Without the benefit of nature's refined waste-disposal system operated by a wide variety of dung-burying beetles, farmers eventually discovered that the pats dried on the ground and remained there for months, even years, until they disintegrated. Since the cow drops a dozen dung-pats a day and there are now millions of cows, it was argued that many hectares of grazing land were being spoiled. Furthermore, the unburied dung was a breeding ground for flies – and bush fly is more than just a corked-hat joke; it is a damn nuisance, giving rise to the Australian salute: that reflex flick of the hand which is needed all summer. What to do? Bring in the foreign dung-beetle, and it was not until 1967 that they were released on any scale. And now after millions of dollars' research, it is being hotly contested that the money is well spent. For one thing, some say, only about one per cent of pasture is spoilt by lingering pats; others add that the foreign beetle is no better at the job than the native kind. And what of the flies? They have far from disappeared.

The noble failure brings us back to the weather. After years of trying to establish drought patterns – every seven years is the most reliable of unreliable guides – man decided to play with rain. One of humanity's pet dreams has been to control the weather. The rain-makers had their first success on 5 February 1947; it was a day when deep cumulus cloud covered the country inland from Sydney. A plane dumped dry ice into one cloud, and within minutes rain started to fall while the cloud top-mushroomed explosively. The rain lasted several hours; surrounding clouds gave no rain. This is believed to be the first documented case anywhere in the world of an appreciable man-made rainfall reaching the ground and the first time that dynamic cloud growth had followed cloud-seeding. Thirty-five years later, seeding experiments were discontinued with a sad little note in the CSIRO's annual report:

Research has shown that meteorological conditions in many areas of Australia are either not conducive to the succcess of present cloud-seeding techniques, or are so variable that results are inconclusive. Also it is noted that since aircraft costs are rising well above the general inflation rate, it has become increasingly difficult to justify the program in terms of economic benefit to agriculture.

Only in science fiction can the sun and the rain be drummed up to order. Science will never control the elements.

The bush fires prove that. All the hi-tech surveillance apparatus, the automatic weather stations, the data banks stuffed with statistics came to little when faced with the flames. Such supremacy must tempt man to be fatalistic, to centre himself in the present and not fret too much about the future. It ought not to make him careless, but it does. Some of the devastation caused by the bush fires was not necessary. People had become careless, lulled into thoughtlessness; they were not obeying the rules of clearing land around their houses; they wanted ferns lapping their doorsteps and eucalyptus trees shading their lawns. And they tried to fight fires with water pumps dependent on electricity – and yet the supply is always the first to be affected. How many had an independent power source – a petrol-driven water pump costing a few hundred dollars? What a hero they made of the man who had invented a water-sprinkling device for his roof. The fire went over his house. Those who prefer the morning sounds of magpies instead of motor horns, even in the outer suburbs of the cities, should not take the bush for granted. The whore is likely to strike back.

Up to this point in my journey, my travelling between cities had been uneventful, unadventurous even. That was about to change. But through Canberra and Melbourne to Adelaide I had discovered and stayed with the bus. It was an obvious choice. I had no intention of flying; too expensive, and too dull, hermetically sealed above the clouds, deprived of any sense of distance, of space and of emptiness. Deprived indeed of the very essence of Australia. Staying on the ground enables one to savour all this and to sate oneself with scenery.

A car is not the answer. It is isolating, and anyway the strain of long-distance driving drowns the freedom to stop and start at will. The railway would always be my first choice. The train offers a certain freedom of movement and of choice: you can be solitary behind a book one minute, and sociable in the bar car the next. But trains do not stretch to every limb of Australia; and even when they are plentiful (as in the south-eastern corner) they are often on strike or they choose to take on the characteristics of the koala and come out only at night, to hug the tracks during the hours of darkness, again depriving the traveller of contact with the passing world.

The motor coach is a cheap and comfortable form of transport – but somehow too utilitarian, too severely practical to offer even a hint of glamour. Whoever heard of a heart-tugging romance, or a half-decent piece of literature germinating in a coach station or blooming on a bus? The train has *Brief Encounter*; the ship has *An Affair To Remember*; even the remorselessly disappointing aeroplane, with departure points like transit camps, now has *Emmanuelle*. The coach has nothing more than a gum-chewing *Midnight Cowboy* trundling to New York. Poor coach, too commonplace to excite the imagination. And too avowedly anti-social.

I arrived early to ensure a window-seat for my longish, ten-hour run from Melbourne to Adelaide. I needn't have bothered. I had already been allocated Seat 3B, and it was not a window-seat. 'We put men with men; women with women; and families at the back. You are 3B and there's no chance of changing.' The coach had started in Sydney and was going through to Perth, so I ought not to have been disappointed with the computer's choice of seat. I was, however, surprised by the segregation, and wandered outside to glance at my fellow travellers and see if I could spot the occupant of 3A. No trouble; my eye went straight to her. She wore a cardigan and stockings and had a mouth that had clearly never smiled; never been used for anything that would deflect its downward cast. A study in misery – and the computer had made us companions for the next ten hours. She took her seat, arranged herself neatly and didn't even look in my direction as I placed my typewriter on the rack above.

I rebelled by remaining standing until all the passengers were seated, well placed to spot a pair of empty seats that the computer had overlooked. And sure enough there were two. 'Sure – you can sit there,' said Alan, the driver, 'we've a number of pick-ups, but use it while you can.'

I used it all the way. Coaches have 'no-shows', too. Around me there was little chatter, little sign that on this Saturday morning anyone intended to do anything but sink into his or her own thoughts with the help of those tape-recorders with ear-muffs, a danger to hearing and a blow to conversation and communication.

Alan took us in hand, and in a Rolf Harris voice went through a list of dos and don'ts. The lecture started with the dunny. The dunny is a euphemism for lavatory. It is in fact an outside lavatory, in an unsewered area, usually some distance from the house and consisting of a small shed furnished with a lavatory seat placed over a can. The word comes shortened from 'dunnakin' or 'dunnaken', meaning 'dung place'. This dunny was at the back of the bus and Alan hoped we would use it sparingly. There would be road stops; the dunny was for emergencies and, if we found ourselves using it, would we please remember to lock the door. Last week, crossing the Nullarbor desert, he'd swerved to avoid a camel and the door had come open, plonking a woman into the aisle in considerable disarray, or, as Alan put it, 'with her knickers around her knees'. Parents were requested not to let their children play with the drinking water – otherwise we'd all be dying of thirst by mid-afternoon. On the other hand, we were all invited to play with our seats (which reclined like those in an aeroplane) and with the overhead lights (inadequately powered and designed to give eye-strain), and to beware of the ashtrays which had been sited too close to the curtains; a careless flick could cause a fire. The last two don'ts were important: no sleeping in the aisles – sounds odd, but it is astonishing how one longs to be horizontal after hours in an upright seat – and no alcohol. 'I don't make the rules; it is the law of the land: no alcohol in express vehicles. If I catch you drinking I'll put you off.' After the reading of the rules, Alan became friendly and insisted we pass by for a chat, enjoy the music and even submit our own tapes for playing. He also offered to point out the sites on the way, even though this was not a tourist bus. By the time Alan fell silent, the houses were thinning and the land was becoming flat and parched and dotted only by cable lines and a tree or three. The sleek silver bus sped on and we, each in our separate world, daydreamed to Ballarat.

Ballarat is one of the largest inland cities. It was created by a great gold find but, unlike many others, it did not die when the gold was exhausted. It became a service centre for many an industry: wool, cereals, fruit and vegetables, as well as factories producing bricks, tiles, furniture, industrial chemicals, paper, paint.

Alan wasn't much interested in all this but he was concerned that we should look out for McDonalds. 'You'll never see another one like it. It's new, but it has been built to look a hundred years old.' And so it had.

Ballarat is keen to preserve its glory from the gold days, and careful to preserve its 1860s atmosphere. The suburbs are dully uniform, but the town centre has style, the buildings accentuated by many tree-planted streets and avenues, often wide enough for flower-beds to parade down the centre.

We lingered not, sweeping through the town and out through a cream-coloured victory arch which led to an avenue of trees. Alan said that each tree had a name-tag and each was dedicated to a soldier who had died in a war far away. Actually there were 391 trees, one for each man and woman who enlisted during the First World War.

And on to Stawell. Doesn't look much, our driver confessed, but it is supposed to be a top tourist stop. A tiny tourist spot, perhaps, again created by the discovery of gold, named after a Victorian chief justice and now offering a few Aboriginal cave paintings and a rare example of a mid-nineteenth-century wool-shed.

We were now firmly in the 'mallee' district, in the north-western corner of Victoria, an area of flat, semi-arid sand plains which were originally covered by eucalyptus scrub called mallee. This scrub has been cleared to make way for wheat, leaving light, fertile soil, lush indeed after rain. But not just now. It was topsoil from this area that had blown into Melbourne during the dust storm. We stopped at Nhill, a tiny, neat wheat town, exactly halfway between Melbourne and Adelaide and boasting the world's largest single-bin wheat silo and the fact that it was the first country town in Victoria to install electric light. Our port of call was a service station where the sandwiches were said to be fresh. Most people preferred their own picnic and sat outside under cover, gazing at two azaleas in two pots and a host of blue-and-white triangles, standard service station decor the world over. There was nothing else to see. Flies, two boys riding the same bicycle; trees that were ever grey; miles of dusty road and few dusty sheep which blended beautifully with the dusty mallee.

I tried to talk to a couple of girls as we washed our hands in a soapless basin, but petered out pathetically. Perhaps we all needed a day of silence. I'd play a game, the first of many: if anyone spoke to me I would respond with enthusiasm, and if they did not I'd remain silent. I remained silent. I can't explain the anti-social behaviour of bus travellers; after all they covered all ages from tiny infant to OAP and there were as many lone travellers as there were couples and families. Perhaps it was the absence of alcohol to loosen timid tongues. Certainly Australians can be as reserved as any Englishman. More so: at times they are totally taciturn and incurious. Perhaps it was a low-tension day.

I'd read somewhere that the typical south-east Australian has a high-tension brain which alternates between energy and utter sloth. An animal that moves in spasms. On a high-tension day he is a man in furious motion, and on low-tension days he sits brooding with downcast head. How sensible to have a low-tension day on a bus. I didn't mind. By the end of the journey I had discovered the perfect Saturday: while the bus moved me to wherever I wanted to be and while others stared blankly at the passing scene, or slept or Sony-Walkmanned the hours away, I indulged my life-long addiction to newsprint, mentally munching my way slowly through a pile of neatly folded newspapers and periodicals, to emerge bloated with information – which might well have become scrambled in my mind but for another lifelong habit of cutting out and preserving articles of particular interest.

Some Australians worry about their newspapers. That's mainly because the bulk of the capital city publications are owned by three groups who also own television and radio stations. The owners of the three groups tend to be conservative-minded and the fear is that this uniformity of opinion may be passed on to the population. There is, of course, some truth in this: conservative newspapers reinforcing the already conservative views of the population. But then newspapers do have a tendency to exaggerate their importance as opinion-formers; and there can be few better examples than the election in March 1983 which brought Bob Hawke to power: as I have already mentioned, all the major papers except the *Age* of Melbourne advised their readers to re-elect Malcolm Fraser, and the readers happily ignored the advice. The *Age* and the *Sydney Morning Herald* are two of the oldest and most respected quality newspapers, and each serves its own State well. There are two national newspapers, the *Australian Financial Review* and the *Australian*, the latter started by Rupert Murdoch in the 1960s. On weekdays the *Australian* can be a little dull, with rather too many articles reprinted from non-Australian publications like the *Economist*. However, I bought it daily and applaud its assumption that Australia is one nation, rather than a handful of States given to rivalry and showing little interest in one another. The paper may change its sports and arts reviews, but the main contents are not altered between States; items on Perth reach Queensland and articles on Tasmania reach Darwin – and this is a much-needed service. The *Weekend Australian*, published on Saturday, is the bumper edition and is anything but dull. It is a most enjoyable newspaper, giving much space to features on life in country towns and the Outback, thus enabling city dwellers to have some idea of the problems of the rest of the country.

Overall, Australian newspapers' coverage of Australian affairs is first class, wide in scope, detailed in background and well written; coverage of Asia tends to be in outline and lacking in analysis, and coverage of the rest of the world is idiosyncratic. This to some extent mirrors Australia's view of the world and its own position in the world; it offers a contrast with British newspapers, whose extensive foreign coverage is often at the expense of domestic insights. There is no doubt that, during my travels, buying the *Australian* and one State paper each day, I felt well informed about the country I was in, but somewhat cut adrift from happenings over the rest of the globe. And it didn't seem to matter: I was, after all, studying Australia. I also bought, whenever I could, the *National Times*, a weekly quality newspaper with an impressive team of investigative journalists, *Australian Society*, another weekly concentrating on social issues, and the *Bulletin*. The *Bulletin* is special. It was once a literary magazine, but now is more akin to *Time* or *Newsweek*; indeed, it incorporates *Newsweek*'s Pacific edition, and the combination is irresistible. It has not forgotten its literary origins and regularly publishes a literary supplement, offering book extracts, short stories and poetry. So too does the *Australian*, with money provided by Esso.

This weighty bundle caused me to arrive at journey's end with tired eyes, but it demanded no depth of concentration. After a stab at an article or two, I'd daydream through the coach window of coloured glass and relish the joy of being in transit with time to mull over what was being left behind and to anticipate what was to come.

In South Australia there were no disappointments; no unanswered letters; no phone calls unreturned; just the warmest of welcomes. Adelaide is small enough not to swamp and just that much slower in tempo for people to have time for one another; to want to help and to welcome. I met this first, of course, from the police. And then there was John Parnell.

CHAPTER 7

Mobs of Nothing

He is a stocky man of middle height and neat appearance. His trousers, cream-coloured and made of moleskin, are always topped with a light-coloured shirt, the sleeves rolled up, and toed with ankle-high elastic-sided boots. A bushman's gear, bought from R. M. Williams, the bushman's outfitter.

I first saw him on television during my early weeks in Sydney. Watching television is as good a way as any to begin to absorb a new country, or at least to become familar with a few names of people and of places. And there he was, evening after evening, with a Cessna at his elbow, the way other men might have a Scotch, and with the incomparable glow of a desert sunset in the background. While a voice chattered over this pretty scene, he handed a wedding-anniversary gift to a couple who live in Innamincka in central Australia. Just in view was a petrol pump.

John Parnell, known as Jack, sells and distributes petrol. He has his own trucking company and the petrol comes from Ampol, Australia's only oil company. It is small, having only ten per cent of the market, and is of course dwarfed by the multi-nationals. To them a pump is just another bowser, but to Jack Parnell every pump is a person, a couple, a family, with a story and a life-style and with singularly fascinating problems that come with isolated, Outback living. His clients are spread across thousands of miles of South Australia, touching on the Northern Territory and on Western Australia, and when he visits them in his light plane, it is an event. He may stay overnight, such are the distances and such is the nature of his relationship with the people in the bush. He listens to their tales, learns of their tribulations and does his best to help in whatever way he can: writing letters, taking up their problems with the authorities in Adelaide, loading the plane with a much-needed spare part or a wedding-anniversary gift. He does much more than keep the petrol flowing: he offers an old-fashioned thing called service, and for this he has been awarded an Advance Australia Medal. Each night on the television he is advertising Ampol as a company offering much more than oil.

One morning, on impulse, I rang Ampol and asked the Advertising Manager if there was any way, once I reached Adelaide, of meeting Jack Parnell and of travelling with him to witness the Australian way of giving service and to learn of Outback life. Yes, said Ampol. Yes, said Jack Parnell. And so, several months later, I made my way to Adelaide's Parafield Airport where Peter Cox, one of Jack's employees, was to fly me to Port Augusta. From there I was to travel by road train carrying Ampol oil straight up the centre to Marla Bore, south of Alice Springs, where Jack and I would meet.

As I stepped into Peter Cox's Piper Cherokee at eight a.m., on a glorious morning with the sky resembling silk shot through with wispy hints of white cloud, I felt lucky and mighty pleased with myself for making that impulsive phone call. This beats the bus. Below lay a choice of roads for it to take, one straight and the other curving to encompass small communities. Up here, at 2,000 feet (600 metres), I could admire the irrigated market gardens, bright, over-bright green and tinged with yellow; giving way to the neat brown squares of cereals; and they in turn giving way to even neater lines of vines in the wine-making area of Clare. Before long, however, this pretty patchwork dissolved into belching smoke as we flew over the huge lead-smelting works of Port Pirie and on to Port Augusta. As a port, it is no longer of great significance, but for ground traffic it is *the* crossroads; all vehicles heading north to Alice and Darwin, or west to Perth or east to Sydney must pass through Port Augusta.

Peter calls his plane a bushwhacker. He hops in and out of it, the way others hop in and out of bed. His job is to keep Parnell's trucks in good order, but if they do break down on one of their long, long journeys, he can diagnose the problem with the driver over the radio and then dash into his plane with spares.

I took a taxi from the Aero Club to meet my road train, which was being loaded in a coupling yard on the edge of town. At a hundred feet (thirty metres) in length and weighing eighty-five tons, it is not allowed to amble through city streets; it remains a creature of the Outback. It is not a bit like a train, and it does not need a track – but then nor is it a truck. It is a cab plus several trailers and is used to transport livestock, produce and oil throughout the land. Anthony Jansen (alias Ike, because of a childhood smile that resembled that of Eisenhower) seemed amused that I should wish to travel in such a vehicle. But it had been one of my early ambitions and none too easy to realize. My first round of phone calls to the major haulage companies had met with a rudeness which I much disliked but a directness which I much liked. 'Madam, you sound as mad as a banana; go see a movie,' said one. And another suggested that truckies were not ambassadors for Australia and would not wish to put up with my company. I turned to the truckies' union and found to my delight that it was headed by a woman, who thought I was neither mad nor untenable company and went to great lengths to find me a refrigerated road train on which to hitch a ride. But that was some months away; Ampol's road train was an unexpected bonus, and Ike was worried about 'mobs of nothing'. 'That's what you're going to get for the next two days, mobs of nothing, hours without seeing another vehicle, or even a sign of life, not even a bird. You might see a roo, but it will be an event to wobble over the grids that divide the paddocks!'

And he was right. The land is stony, colourless, treeless, and there is scarcely any ground cover except for a few saltbushes, stunted and twisted. They say it wasn't always like this. They say it was much better – but then never exactly lush – before the great drought of 1864, from which it never recovered; from which it was never allowed to recover as sheep and cattle and horses and camels and rabbits ate and trampled their way through a covering of mulga and myall and saltbush. Trollope saw it a few years after the drought and was not much impressed.

I cannot say that the country is attractive to the visitor. There is very little to gratify the eye. I saw no grass and very few sheep, but with one sheep to ten acres [four hectares] this is not surprising. An emu running wild I never did see. I hardly saw any living animal. Just saltbush ... an ugly grey shrub about two feet [sixty centimetres] high which seems to possess the power of bringing forth its foliage without moisture. This foliage is impregnated by salt and both sheep and cattle will feed upon it and thrive.

It is still sheep country, and I saw very few. But I did see two emus running wild. And I loved it, the mobs of nothing. I loved the sense of space and of emptiness and of age. The land looked old and exhausted and weary, dejected. Maybe one ought to have found it sad rather than awe-inspiring, but that is how it seemed to me. Particularly in the early morning, in that still, cool moment when the sun creeps above the horizon, as yet without the power to offend with its heat; and again in the evening when, white with exhaustion, it sinks, ringing the land with a band of brilliant red. Such beauty is gratifying.

During the day we had little to bother us inside our air-conditioned road train. Normally, Ike travels through the night. He prefers it that way, and sometimes the heat can melt the bitumen and the stuff gets stuck to the tyres. Sometimes the air-conditioning can provide too great a contrast with the temperature outside. 'It pays to turn it off half an hour before arriving to off-load to give your body time to adjust, and if you blow a tyre you'll find it harder to cope with if your body is struggling to adjust to the heat as well.' It is difficult to know when a tyre has blown; there are forty-two, so you hardly feel or hear it. For this reason Ike stopped every fifty miles [eighty kilometres] and toured the wheels. He hadn't had a bad breakdown in a long while, except the time when the water pump packed up and bad weather made it impossible for the plane to fly out a spare. 'All I could do was sit it out for thirty-six hours, but I made it easier by radio-ing to the nearest roadhouse and asking if the next truckie down the track could bring me something to chew and to read.' They sent Coke and cigarettes. And rum.

Blown tyres are a common occurrence and no problem. You just change them and leave the lifeless tube right there on the roadside.

Abandoned. There's a line of them right through the centre of Australia, scarring the landscape. They are as nothing compared to the cars, left and soon gutted. 'If you break down here, it just costs too much for a tow, so you leave it and the traffic using the road descend like vultures and soon strip the thing of anything worth having.'

In fact, few cars attempt the journey; the bitumen road runs less than half-way and the motor car is unhappy on rutted roads. And people are a little afraid. They just don't see a journey from the coast through the Outback to the centre as an adventure to be undertaken with care but also with relish. Their minds are conditioned from schooldays with tales of tragedy surrounding the early explorers who, while searching for an inland sea, a river system or a route from south to north, met with death from an Aborigine's spear, or scurvy, or lack of water, or who simply vanished. And if they did return, they brought with them blindness and blackened skins. Not the best of images to feed to impressionable minds, especially when accompanied by the thought that the desert and the Outback did not always bring out the best in men. Anyone hearing the story of William John Wills and Robert O'Hara Burke and their struggles to make the first south–north crossing, or reading Alan Moorehead's account of that journey in *Cooper's Creek*, will be struck not so much with visions of courage and nobility as by the competitive spirit which existed with other expeditions, and the rows and rivalry that prevailed within their own team. The Outback thus becomes a sinister place, a destructive place where even the fight for survival does not make men pull together. It isn't a sinister place, it is much too bright and open – at least by day – for that, and such harsh conditions hardly touch today's traveller; none the less men fear the vast mobs of nothing and the notion that they might break down and spend hour upon hour fearing that it might be days before another vehicle will come along.

One day, of course, they will run the bitumen to Alice, but Ike is not too keen for that to happen. It would be boring. He likes the rough conditions, as they demand greater skill; and he dreads the thought of cowboy truckies belting along the bitumen. There are enough already. They are the ones who have little regard for their expensive vehicles and who get a bonus for arriving early. Often two drivers do the run from Adelaide to Darwin in five days non-stop, one sleeping in the 'dog-box', a bed which runs horizontally behind the seats, while the other drives. He knows them all, the other companies, the other drivers and their ways. Each gets a wave, a big circular movement with the left hand. Even an unknown car gets some recognition, a flick with the fingers without moving the wrist from the steering wheel.

Our first stop was at Pimber, 100 miles (160 kilometres) from Port Augusta. In the Outback, man does not always bother to surround himself with prettiness or neatness. Even so, Spud Murphy's road-house suggests a bad case of torpor and invites comment. People are always complaining because he never finishes anything. There are ugly shacks, partially blown down, leaning in all directions; and the house itself is surrounded by empty petrol drums and, of course, the odd battered car. Tethered outside were a donkey, a goat and a camel. Inside showed the same indifference, the same lack of regard. I bought some cigarettes and the girl didn't even smile or say 'Thank you'. Ike doesn't usually stop there. It's BP.

In the eleven years since he began driving this route twice a week, he has established his own routine. He'd been a motor mechanic once but couldn't take the shit. 'You're always in it. People never say "thank you" for a good job; you only hear from them when something goes wrong. My brother used to drive for Parnell and that's what gave me the idea. He drove smaller trucks and one day he went to sleep at the wheel on a journey from Melbourne to Adelaide. He was carrying a load of wool. He died, yup, but it didn't put me off. I dunno why. It gets in your blood.' One day he might try flying; he already does some for Jack. But the future is not something to which he gives much thought. He is thirty-one – and looks older, through the deep lines on his face caused by the wind and the sun and the fact that Outback Australians don't bother with dark glasses; they prefer to screw up their faces like a Roman blind.

Ike refers to himself as 'the dummy' which he is not, but perhaps he feels so in relation to his father who was a doctor and his elder brother who was a scientist before he discovered pottery. In any event, he is happy alone on the road and comfortable enough with my questions so long as they were widely spaced and did not appear intrusive. In return he asked but one: 'Live in London, do you?'

'Yes'.

'Black as ever, is it?'

We stopped at Glendambo to eat. There was a choice between Chris Wood's store selling snacks and Ampol or Grant Fox's roadhouse selling food and Mobil. We voted, at three-thirty in the afternoon, for steak and eggs. Grant Fox is a tall man with long greasy hair and sloppy clothes. His shirt was open to the waist revealing a large white belly and his shoes were untied and skipped up and down on his sockless feet. He was very talkative. I tried asking a question or two; but he answered without looking at me, so I decided that a female stranger was expected to sit and listen. So I sat and listened to gossip about how much he longed to get away for a break but scarce indeed are those willing to step in and be on call from five a.m. to two p.m. His wife looked miserable and didn't join us. Perhaps she didn't want to hear about shock absorbers and road conditions and her husband's deal with Mobil. 'I cross-examined them on this. I know I'm only a dickhead from the Outback but I cross-examined them until I got it all clear. Lately they've been buggering me around on credit, so if someone comes along and offers petrol at a cheaper rate, I'm taking it.' They drifted from the nature of Grant's relationship with Mobil to the nature of his relationship with Chris. I missed the nuances but caught the punch line: 'Arrh, he's all right in his place, but they haven't dug it yet.'

Back on the road, Ike explained: 'Chris and Grant both carry on like a pair of pork chops, but they'd be the first to help each other out. Mateship, y'know.'

It sounded more like self-interest: with only a handful of people around and no one else for hundreds of miles, men must help one another. Mateship implies friendship, however superficial, and the concept of this fine-sounding word and its origins have been much discussed by academics trying to weld together a set of characteristics into a national identity. Without doubt the word has its roots in the time when Australia was a man's country – which was indeed a lengthy period, the sexes not finally balancing until around 1900 and the imbalance in the far-flung areas lasting even longer. Some argue that the spirit of mateship was born among the convicts, largely working-class, largely Irish, when the outcast sought allies from among other outcasts in his war against his warders; that circumstances impelled the most individualistic of men towards collectivist behaviour; and that the symptoms became fully fledged once the convicts got their freedom and sought a life of true independence as far from the cities as possible. Mateship among bushmen or pastoral labourers – boundary riders, cattle drovers, sheep shearers – has been immortalized and romanticized in Australian literature. It existed too in the gold fields and between men who went to war together, indeed anywhere where men are forced to keep their own company. Whatever the bonds they shared, these differing groups, of work, of poverty, of war, of bondage itself, they surfaced and spilled over in drink. They were drinking mates. They shared the end of the day; the end of the week. Mateship exists today. From time to time I glimpsed it in the Outback, the remnants of a renowned myth, just enough to make me appreciate how the ideal once caught the imagination of writers. It exists today in the cities, but there it merely describes the relationship between men who meet in the pub each night after work and share little beyond the commonplaces of weather and sport. The word, of course, is constantly used, or misused, by those who like to think that it is still a national charac-teristic.

The bitumen road had ended now and there were some five hours to go before reaching Coober Pedy. Our speed was limited to nineteen mph (thirty kph), slow enough to ride the ruts – or corrugations as Ike called them – as smoothly as surfers and slowly enough to admire every detail of the scenery – mile upon mile of ankle-high scrub, cloaked in a fine film of white dust thrown up as our forty-two wheels pounded the road. Dust. Everywhere dust. When I looked into the side mirrors, all I could see was dust; fortunately nothing ever seemed to come up behind us, but on the rare occasion when a vehicle passed from the opposite direction visibility sank to zero as we ploughed through their dust path.

'Look, there's a horse,' said Ike, startling me out of a long silence. There was no horse. He was teasing me for having asked him earlier to identify a bird which flew in front of the truck: a pretty bird, grey with a pink breast and a pink head. 'That's a galah,' he said, astonished that I didn't know, 'silly birds, they swoop in front of the engine playing chicken. Y'know, last one to turn away is chicken.'

At seven p.m. the truck sprang a leak. Ike noticed it during a routine tyre check. A compartment in the second cylinder was leaking steadily, so he uncoupled the trailers, reversed alongside and pumped the remainder of the petrol from the leaking compartment into another which was not full. It wasn't meant to be full, as the weight would have been a touch heavy on the axle, but the alternative was to leave a trail of expensive petrol along the desert road. It took Ike half an hour to complete this operation while I watched a glorious sunset, a brief dusk and rapidly descending darkness.

We arrived at Coober Pedy at ten p.m., by which time Ike had discovered an air-leak which was upsetting the braking system; that had to be corrected and petrol had to be delivered, before he could shower in the nearby caravan park and relax for an hour or so, swopping gossip with another truckie carting horses from Alice to Adelaide, before sleeping in his dog box. I checked into the local motel chosen for me by Jack who was convinced that after hours in a shuddering truck I'd be glad of a proper bed, rather than a bedroll under the stars. The traveller, wishing to appreciate day after day of new places and new faces, needs sleep rather more than does the person facing a regular and familiar routine.

We met next morning at seven a.m., minutes before the sun rose. A light wind was blowing and dust, once more, was everywhere. Aborigines sat in groups on the pavement, dogs squabbled and chased each other and a tourist bus was about to leave. Not, however, before a group of Swedish tourists had taken pictures of Ike's truck and queried its load and declared that they had never seen anything so large, so long, so heavy.

Coober Pedy attracts tourists; every bus on its way to and from

Alice Springs stops there to look at opals or to look at men looking for them. They were discovered quite by accident in 1915 by a prospector named Hutchinson who was looking for gold, and it is still the world's largest opal-producing area. There is no other reason for being in Coober Pedy; the heat is notorious. It doesn't hold the record for the hottest place in Australia – but it runs pretty close, the temperature reaching 104°F (40°C) much of the time. A proportion of the population of around 1,500 lives underground in dug-outs, some spacious, with shafts to the surface to let in the air. The church is underground and so are several shops and a small hotel. Once, everyone lived underground and the place was the queerest-looking settlement in all Australia; and that is how it got its name, Coober meaning 'man' and Pedy meaning 'hole in the ground'. Newcomers are now building above ground – air-conditioning making that possible – detracting a little from the uniqueness of the place. But the miners continue to leave their special mark as in the white dazzle of the day they gouge through the white earth to the pink desert sandstone in search of their fortunes. From the air, Coober Pedy looks as if it is covered in large blobs of white bird-droppings and then, as you come in closer, the blobs seem to have bullet holes; closer still and you can see that the hole is where men have been gouging and the white is displaced earth. If they hit a good spot, then they continue to scoop and eventually move on. If they have not hit a good spot, they simply move on. No environmentalist talk of re-dressing the landscape; it is a costly enough business digging the holes without having to shovel the stuff back. Thus, as far as the eye can see, there are holes surrounded by mounds or mountains of earth. It is almost attractive; it adds something to a barren, featureless landscape.

The traveller can take out a Miner's Right and wander through the abandoned shafts in the hope of finding opal; for no charge at all he can 'noodle' on the dumps of operating mines, examining the heaps of crushed stone for an overlooked scrap. The town's Aborigines are said to live by noodling. The town itself is ramshackle, rough and raw, and full of characters as colourful as its product. In the early days it attracted a number of socialist miners, convinced that the newly triumphant Russian Bolsheviks had found the answer to the world's problems: the road valley that is a continuation of the main street is still known as Bolshevik Gully. Today, fewer than half the residents are Australian-born or English-speaking.

Kypros who runs the Ampol garage is a Greek Cypriot who, even after fourteen years, speaks in broken English and with a heavy accent. He also wears a large opal in a ring on his little finger to remind him of the days when he was a miner, a gambler and a big spender. It is still a gamblers' town. There are card games every night in which men can lose their money rather than let the tax man find it. They fight too, mainly over opal claims, and Kypros is full of tales of gun-battles and stabbings and dead men being shoved down mine shafts. They manage a murder trial once every couple of years, and indeed there was one taking place at the time. Exaggeration and boasting are of course part of the scene. They always have been. Trollope noticed it and called it 'blowing'. He met a man who was not in his company longer than an hour, and in that time had mentioned half a dozen times that he had shot a bushranger. The others who were listening to this 'blowing' thought no more of it than if he had confessed to biting his nails.

That morning we didn't linger. Ike got on with riding the ruts and I listened to stories of the hazards of long-distance driving. Bogging is the worst. When one of these huge road trains gets stuck in mud, axle deep, it isn't difficult to imagine the dilemma. Not all roads in the Outback are as firmly established as the Stuart Highway; often they are merely tracks.

Ike's worst experience had him stranded for five days, but fortunately he was travelling in convoy with two other trucks and together they displayed the resourcefulness for which bushmen are famed. First, they found a tree to cut down in an attempt to dam the water and help the road to dry. In the end, nothing worked, and one driver had to set off seventy miles (110 kilometres) in search of a bulldozer. It's just as well that the cabs have an icebox, between the two front seats, filled with necessities.

A major excitement for me that day was sighting the Dingo Fence, a six-foot- (two-metre-) high wall of wire netting and posts which runs 6,000 miles (9,650 kilometres) across Australia, rising northwards from the Great Australian Bight, across the Great Victoria Desert, bending southwards towards the border of Queensland and New South Wales, and then heading east to hit the coast south of Brisbane. It should be called the Great Dingo Fence. After all the Great Wall of China is only 1,500 miles (2,400 kilometres) long. It exists to separate the sheep from the dogs; it cordons off the south-eastern third of the continent for the sheep, and leaves the rest to the dingo. Dingoes savage sheep, going through thirty or forty at a time, just tearing them to pieces. Some say they do the same to babies, and scientists often wonder if they aren't partial to wombats and wallabies as well. The tawny-coloured creatures, with erect ears, bushy tails, a distinctive gait and a call resembling a howl or yelp rather than a bark, came to Australia thousands of years ago – probably with the Aborigine – from what is now Indonesia and New Guinea. They have few friends. Indeed, the word 'dingo' is used to describe a contemptible person, one who shirks responsibilities and evades difficult situations. They don't sound like dingo characteristics; none the less, people who have a failure of nerve are said to have 'dingoed out', and to 'dingo' on someone is to betray them.

The fence works well as long as there aren't any holes in it. And that's the problem: it is for ever under assault from the weather and from wild creatures like the kangaroo that wallops into it at great speed, punching big gaps. Men patrol the fence regularly, mending holes and shooting the odd dingo. Grant Fox's son, Murray, is one of them. He used to drive trucks, but he smashed three in one year.

Ike was, once again, slightly amused by my desire to dismount – that's what it felt like from such a high vehicle – and take photographs. To him the fence is nothing special; but he pulled up with a good-natured smile alongside the double grid upon which sheep fear to tread and across which dingoes cannot leap.

Midmorning, we stopped at Mount Willoughby where the sheep-station owner also had a roadhouse, a common practice giving the station an additional income and the traveller a source of petrol, water and snacks. Willoughby Roadhouse is run by a wild young man called Chris, who was anxious to show me the bullet holes in his ceiling and recall for me the night he drank rum and wine with a friend until he felt the urge to shoot down a plane which happened to be on a sticker on the ceiling. (It is a car sticker which says, 'I've survived the Stuart Highway', and for some reason there is a little plane in view.) Chris holed its wing that night on rum. Everywhere was dusty, untidy and seemingly uncared-for, but then repairs in distant places are expensive and often it is not worth while hauling the right materials from the cities. Men therefore make do with whatever is at hand, a practice which gives a temporary air to so many places, particularly those where the passer-by stops for only a few minutes and is not likely to be deterred by appearance.

Marla Bore does not look temporary, but then it is a smart new motel for overnight stops and it has long-term plans for itself. Jack and his colleagues saw the potential of the site a few years earlier when the new Ghan railway opened, following a different, somewhat shorter route from the old line. Oodnadatta, the town the track deserted, is in consequence dying, and Marla Bore hopes by the end of the decade to be a thriving township with a school and a hospital, a Department of Mines and a police station. For the moment it is a motel with a staff of between eighteen and thirty, depending on the season. Maybe a hundred people stop by in coaches and it's also the focal point for those within a hundred miles or so – the sheep stations, the opal mine at Mintible, the railway gangers and the Aborigines. Marla Bore is a tight community, generating a family atmosphere where it is impossible for anyone to get a letter or a phone call without everyone knowing. Anyone who doesn't fit in is not encouraged to stay, and that afternoon the staff dining room was relieved to have seen the back of one such misfit. When her character had been thoroughly dissected, the talk turned to tourists, an endless source of gossip, rivalled, as was soon to become apparent, by only one other topic.

The girls are full of smiles when the coaches have been through; they love the chat and the contact; and their smiles are even broader when the coaches stay overnight. 'Smoothing', the men call it.

'Your hair is looking a mess today, Pat, but then I'm not surprised after what I heard last night. Those demountables sure have thin walls.'

The Ribbon and the Ragged Square

Pat shot him down:'I have no intention of being discreet. I get it so rarely these days, I'm going to let go!' She'd passed by one day on the coach and liked it so much she wrote asking for a job as a general help. Divorced and approaching middle age, Pat is happy to wander from job to job, exploring her country.

So is Wendy, but she is much younger. 'It is a great way to save money. We are well paid and there is just no way to spend the money. One day off is enough a week because there is nowhere to go and $A30 to spend each week on drinks and cigs is quite enough. Anyone who spends more than that is a mug.' She will be off to Queensland at the end of the season, to play on the beach for a couple of months; meanwhile she is saving to go to Canada where she has heard the horses are good. Within a few days she is off to Alice to the races with a long shopping list from the others. She handed it to me while I stirred the gravy to go with the onions to go with the sausages for lunch. 'Black skirt, leg wax, Painting-by-Numbers, tapes, laundry basket, videos.' Videos are a huge success in the Outback, a must for station life where, until the satellite is well into orbit, many cannot receive even one television channel.

Wendy, with her bubbly personality and ready wit, is relied on to handle the tourists. 'They can be pigs. They come in here and order me around, demanding things and complaining all the while. One night after a difficult group had finished dinner I said goodnight and added, "Don't forget to strip your beds in the morning." And I went around ... and that was exactly what they had all done! It's the individual traveller who really gives us the bother. Some are real odd-balls. A man drove up in a wetsuit one day and said he'd been scuba diving up the road – I suppose he meant Darwin – and asked for an ice-cream for his dog. Horrible ugly thing. And then he got cross because I hadn't got an ordinary cone, only a choc-ice. When the dog wouldn't eat that, he asked me to take it back!'

The stories are legion and entertaining, and some of the problems are real. Station owners are fed up with city folk who wander the land, not knowing how to behave, and who are often caught washing their clothes with detergents in a precious bore. And filling stations like Marla have tales of similar ignorance. Graham, assistant manager and shareholder, showed me a drawer full of watches from people who needed petrol and had nothing else to offer. 'We've also been offered hi-fis and television sets. They may be stolen ... but it is more likely some guy shoves a few possessions in his car and heads north, either looking for work or running away from the wife. Darwin's full of those.'

Graham was soon to move on to *the* other topic of conversation: 'coons'. I was to get used to the term during my time in central Australia. City dwellers, who of course have little to do with Aborigines, would not dare to refer to them in such a way. Country folk whose contact is close and continual have no such qualms.

'They are a protected species, you know, like the kangaroo – only more so. We're not allowed to do anything to them. I can refuse to sell a white fella a drink if I think he's had too much, but if I do that to a coon they call it discrimination. And they can't hold their drink, two beers and they are pissed and ready to fight. And, boy, how they smell! We have to spray this place when they have been in here and we don't allow them in after five p.m. That's easy: we apply dress rules and that means a shirt, trousers, and shoes – which they don't have.'

Pat's view is a little less hard-edged. 'The moral standards of the elders ought to be copied by white society; the older guys are gentlemen. It's the half-educated young ones that cause all the problems. Two coons were fighting outside here one night, and a third goes prowling around the back of the motel to see if he can find a big stick or something to wield, either to separate the two others, or to join in. He sees this gun in Murray's car and takes it but he can't fire it because he can't get the safety-catch off. In the end Murray gets it off him and the guy keeps shouting, "Toy"; and it takes a while for Murray to convince him it isn't a toy. It's the first time I've seen a black man go white. His eyes bulged and the colour drained from his face and he runs, goes bush. But the elders find his tracks, they must have done because a few days later he's back in here with stab wounds in his hands and arms. We reckon that is his punishment from the elders. They won't touch a child under sixteen because they reckon he's too young to understand, but there is a strict moral code beyond that.'

Murray is an opal miner from Mintible. He used to mine in Coober Pedy, where he heard from a couple of Greeks about a new drill costing $A34,000 and off he goes to Adelaide to buy one, sharing the cost with his father and his father's brother. 'Within three months we got lucky and bought out my father's brother who had made enough to retire on. We went back, looking for more. When you find something that easy you think it will go on being easy, just like gambling. But it stops. Since then, we've hardly made enough to pay for the tools. I got fed up with Coober and came to Mintible. Sun's rough out there, so is the life. Men in shacks and no women.'

I had hoped to see the place. Although it is part of the land given by the South Australian government to the Aborigines in the early 1980s, the State retained this section for twenty-one years. Ike had petrol to deliver there but Bob, who had the bowser, was away and without his presence it was impossible to get to the tank. He ploughs up the nearby land to keep the fuel safe and bulldozes it back when access is needed. I don't suppose the miners are above helping themselves, but his measures are directed against the Aborigines. Petrol-sniffing has become a problem. It takes the edge off their hunger and relieves their boredom, according to Jenny who teaches at Mimili school.

Mimili in the late 1970s was a highly prized experiment. It used to be called Everard Park and was a cattle property which came into being in the 1940s. The white owners called upon the Aborigines in the area only for seasonal pastoral work and then left them free to follow their traditional ways, provided they refrained from drinking and camped away from the homestead. The Federal Government then bought the property and gave it to the Aboriginal community as part of a programme to return lands to their traditional owners. Somewhere between 100 and 150 people live on the station; but it is impossible to be specific, because people drift in and out to take part in ceremonies elsewhere and to hunt food – bush tucker, kangaroos, lizards, wild cats. The income of the families, derived largely from welfare benefits of one kind or another, is spent not on food, clothing and other goods, but on old cars bought on very bad terms from Alice Springs car dealers and used to ease hunting and to travel to and from ritual activities.

The cattle enterprise remains, but for this to work they need to hire a skilled white manager capable of operating an enterprise worth $A500,000. This is not meant to be patronizing, but merely acknowledges that the Aborigines have little concept of how to run such a place and the responsibilities that go with it. The idea is that they should learn. It was hoped that, although the enterprise looked the same as when it was owned and run by white pastoralists, it was now different: the manager worked for them, they were to hire him and fire him; the windmills and wells were theirs, and the cattle. It was designed as a clear invitation for the community to retain its traditions and take from white society only those things which served its purpose. At first they didn't want a school. They had seen enough of white teaching and how this alienated children from parents and created a rootless generation. However, in time, they realized that they needed some white-style knowledge.

Jenny's picture of the place is sad:

It's run down now; nothing seems to be working. The most recent white manager was caught ripping the place off and was fired, but no action was taken. The school has hardly any books, and those that are there are all wrong – they talk about city life and some are American! How do you relate that to life in a humpy? Yes, there are houses, but few people like to live in them, they prefer to be outside. And the kids are underfed because money is spent on soft drinks and junk food to which the Aborigines seem to have become addicted. I teach the girls and that means concentrating on reading and writing and speaking. And showing them how to use a shower and wash their hair! Some are quite bright but they don't concentrate. Maybe hunger has something to do with it. It is certainly why the boys sniff petrol.

Neville, who is also white and the station's book-keeper, said he was fed up with Aborigines breaking into his tank to steal petrol. He feels tempted to leave a canful by the side of the car. Petrol-sniffing is a relatively new nuisance. Jack Parnell, feeling that the petrol companies had some responsibility to help combat the misuse of their product, devised a solution which he told me about with great pride. He swears there is a substance which can be dropped into petrol to stop it being sniffable. 'I wrote to everyone about it, but people in cities do not understand. They wrote back and said that such a step would be attacking merely the symptoms and not the cause.' Nothing was done.

At least something has been done about drinking. Many Aborigines, well aware of the damage they are doing to themselves, have banned alcohol on stations and settlements, and the tribal leaders impose heavy fines on those found bringing it in. Of course it is easy enough to get into a car and drive to Marla Bore for a binge. The plight of 'pissed coons' – as Graham would have it – has been obvious since 1967 when a referendum gave Aborigines complete civil rights. Before that, through the mixed motives of racism and paternalism, they were banned from pubs and it was an offence to sell them liquor. Why alcohol affects Aborigines so easily and so badly is a matter for speculation. Some say it has to do with levels of zinc in the liver. The white man has had generations to lick his liver into shape and build up resistance; the Aborigine has not. In the past, their only narcotic was *pituri* made from a shrub which, after it had been dried and refined into a chewy black ball, became a mild drug.

To ask the question, why do they drink when it is not part of their culture, is to invite embarrassing replies: they drink to obliterate their being catapulted into the twentieth century in less than 200 years; they drink to forget the loss of their traditional ways and the irreparable damage done to their culture by the invasion of their country and the attempted imposition of an alien culture; they drink because they are a conquered people lacking direction; everything they cherish has been taken from them.

In *A White Man'll Never Do It*, Aboriginal writer Kevin Gilbert says: 'It is my thesis that the Aboriginal Australian underwent a rape of the soul so profound that the blight continues in the minds of most blacks today. It is this psychological blight, more than anything else, that causes the conditions we see on reserves.'

Few would argue against this. No one denies that uncalled-for atrocities took place. In the beginning the blacks were not hostile.

They thought, according to historians who have bothered to look at history through Aboriginal eyes (most notably, Henry Reynolds in *The Other Side of the Frontier*), that the white man wouldn't stay. Others had come and gone. Such was their early confidence, they felt that even if he did stay he might well adapt to their way of life, or at least be prepared to share the vast land. This passivity gave way to feuds and revenge only when they realized that the white man was out for total possession and that they were being totally dispossessed. And these feuds gave way to general conflict as the white settlers pushed further and further into Aboriginal land, moving them off into arid unwanted areas, depriving them of game, a main source of food, using their women and butchering any who resisted.

The Aborigines were not to know, in the beginning, that racism lay deep in white minds. How could they know that, to white Europeans, there never was a civilization of any other complexion than white. This view persisted for a shameful length of time, firmly lodged in some of the best brains. It is embarrassing now to read Trollope on what he describes as 'this disagreeable subject'. He tries to praise:

Their laws, especially with regard to marriage, are complex and wonderful; their corroborees, or festival dances, are very wonderful. Their sagacity, especially in the tracking of men or cattle, is very wonderful. The skill with which they use the small appliances of life which they possess is very wonderful.

For all this, his lack of sympathy is profound. He chides even their deportment:

That dignity of black deportment of which one hears not infrequently is simply the dignity of idleness.

They will not work for their bread, he exclaims. They will not learn white man's virtues.

Every effort has been made to teach them the lessons. But how can you teach any good lesson to a man who will only hold his head erect as he grins and asks you for sixpence, or a glass of grog, or a bit of tobacco, or a pair of old trousers?

He concludes:

Of the Australian blackman we may certainly say that he has to go. That he should perish without unnecessary suffering should be the aim of all who are concerned in the matter. But no good can be done by giving to the Aboriginal a character which he does not deserve, or by speaking of the treatment which he receives in language which the facts do not warrant.

It is hard to read these words, written in 1873, without wincing.

It is just as hard to read the opening paragraph of Alan Moorehead's *Cooper's Creek*, for it was written in 1963:

The land was absolutely untouched and unknown except for the blacks, the most retarded people on earth; there was no sign of any previous civilization whatever, not a scrap of pottery, not a Chinese coin, not even the vestige of a Portuguese fort.

If we do not know what to look for, and if what we find bears no relationship to anything we have known, we miss so much.

Ironically, 1963 was to be a turning point in the white man's attitude towards and understanding of the Aborigine and his culture. Until that date, he had either been killed speedily and directly by contact with the white population (a practice which persisted on and off through to the 1920s) or he was being killed slowly and indirectly by a policy of assimilation which destroyed his way of life and beliefs. Those who survived the early battles for supremacy were herded on to bits of land in the hope that they would die out or quietly disappear. Children of mixed blood, half-castes, had a different fate. They were taken from their families to the cities in the hope that dormitories and a dose of Christianity, education and eventual inter-marriage would breed out the remaining blackness. This 'civilizing process' caused a deep division within the Aboriginal community. The half-caste was taught that his tribal brother was inferior – a view which some accepted, thus casting themselves into no man's land, unwanted by either black or white. A few managed to overcome this huge personal loss of kinship and ties, and turn what was offered to their advantage: they form today's black bureaucracy. Charles Perkins, the first Aborigine to graduate and now head of the Department of Aboriginal Affairs, talks well and writes movingly about the personal scars he bears from that policy of the 1940s and 1950s, and of the need now to unite the tribal and non-tribal Aborigine as one people.

The first signs that the black minority would no longer accept the white whip came in the 1960s. In 1963 the discovery of bauxite in Queensland on two Aboriginal reserves resulted in the first petition to parliament. The mining leases had been granted without one word of consultation with the Aborigines. The petition achieved much public attention and led eventually to the first court case, which the Aborigines lost on the grounds that they were a conquered people and that the rights to the land belonged to the conqueror.

A short statement put out by the Aborigines said it all: 'The Australian law has said that the land is not ours. This is not so. It might be right legally, but morally it is wrong. The law must be changed.'

Meanwhile, in the same year of 1963, blacks working on white-owned stations went on strike for equal wages, and got them. And Charles Perkins, taking an idea from the American Black Power Movement, organized the first Freedom Ride through the country towns of New South Wales. All this generated enough public interest and concern for there to be overwhelming support for the 1967 referendum in which the Federal Government was given the power to legislate in Aboriginal affairs, a major step forward on the path to complete civil rights.

Since then, whether through guilt or good-will or self-interest or international pressure, much has been done. In 1967, the Federal budget for Aborigines was $A10 million; it is now around $A200 million for somewhere between 120,000 and 180,000 Aborigines (no one is certain of the number). In both urban and rural areas, standards of health, education and housing have improved and employment opportunities have increased. And, most important of all, most States have either given or are in the process of giving land rights to Aborigines, that is to say, freehold title to land which means something, land awash with sacred sites, rather than mere leasehold over land, which is meaningless. Each State has its own laws for establishing this and, as States' attitudes differ, some get better deals than others; Federal law is pending which will unify what is given and how it is given.

That much remains to be done is beyond doubt. Infant mortality, child and adult morbidity, life expectancy – indeed all measures of health – demonstrate that the position of Aborigines is inferior. Unemployment in some areas is still five times higher than among the white population. Although Aborigines form one per cent of the population, they form thirty per cent of the prison population. And the numbers in the higher levels of education, in the professions, in the bureaucracy and other positions of power and influence, are negligible.

None the less, Australians are given little credit for what has been achieved so far. Charles Perkins readily acknowledges that much has improved, but admitted that he could not afford to emphasize this in case people became complacent. Public spending on Aborigines is already inclined to encourage a white back-lash. And the media help in this respect. Anyone reading Australian papers would be forgiven for thinking that black/white relations were at an all-time low as reports of riots in the Redfern district of Sydney, murders in country towns, brawls in the Outback, squabbles over sacred sites and hostility between mining companies and Aborigines appear in the press.

After 180 years during which the conqueror hoped that one day the conquered would shape up, would agree to go to school, get a trade, live in a three-bedroomed house, marry and have kids, a mortgage and ulcers, and become a fully fledged member of a bourgeois society, it is not surprising that the policy-makers, however good their intentions, have had some difficulty finding and following an appropriate approach. The community's needs are so diverse that many policies have had to be tried and abandoned. The urban Aborigine has a different set of problems from the Aborigine living on the edge of a country town; he in turn has different needs from those of the tribal Aborigines in remote areas, some of whom wish to have nothing to do with Western ways while others are willing to embrace a limited amount of Western progress.

Some argue that the urban Aborigine has the worst deal: he has lost his roots and his kinship ties, even if he does have a better house and a few possessions. Others say that the poverty of those clinging to their ancient ways is as bad as anything to be found in the Third World; but then few have the chance to view this for themselves. For me to see Aborigines in settlements was no easy task. I could not just walk in; there are fines for whites who venture uninvited into Aboriginal areas. To be invited is not easy. Some of my letters went unanswered; others received a polite and evasive reply, saying neither yes nor no. I can understand. The Aborigine is sick of being prodded by anthropologists and welfare agencies and white do-gooders. Foreign journalists he can do without. But I was lucky; Jack Parnell's timetable for the next week included visits to five settlements where he supplied petrol, and I went along as Jack's friend. That was enough for them. And that was enough for me.

CHAPTER 8

Red Centre

We left Marla Bore for Alice Springs early one morning when the heat was such that everything shimmered, and I made the mistake of asking if anyone knew the temperature.

Jack stared at me blankly: 'What's it matter? We can't do anything about it,' he said as we clambered aboard his Cessna 182 and rose high into the sky.

He immediately rang home. It is easy that high, that early in the morning, easier than trying to make contact on the ground over a radio-telephone with a crackling line which requires two people to shout their greetings for all to hear. The air-to-ground equipment is expensive, costing $A4,000, but essential for Jack who spends so much time away from home, where he also has his office. Glenda, his secretary, answered his call and assured him that all was well and passed on greetings from June, his wife. He now has thirteen employees, eight trucks, fifteen trailers and three planes (two Cessnas and one Piper). A prosperous small businessman. It wasn't always so. Jack Parnell has known hard times.

His great-grandfather, Richard Thomas Parnell, first settled in Orroroo, several hundred miles north of Adelaide, in 1880. He came overland by bullock and opened a blacksmith's shop, eventually becoming a 'buggy' (coach) builder of high quality and known throughout South Australia. A Parnell 'buggy' is on display at the Alice Springs Telegraph Station which is now a museum. When the car came, the Parnells became agents for Ford and Dodge. Jack went straight into the business after leaving school and worked for his grandfather, Seth. Seth encouraged Jack's entrepreneurial aptitude and all was well; but when his father took over the firm, all was not well. They did not get on, and Jack came north to Alice to work on a cattle station as a stockman, returning when his father was ready to hand over. 'By then the business was in debt. They were worrying times and I would not wish to go through them again. June went through those rotten times with me. We don't talk about them now.'

The company had started carting cattle, but Jack considered this was not the way to make money, so he eased himself out of cattle and into freight and then into fuel. 'Those hard times developed in me the killer instinct. I wasn't naturally aggressive, but I forced myself to become like that. And way back in the piece when things were rough, we made a decision on standards – high standards; no shaky deals for us. Quality service is what we offer and genuine concern for our clients. If they give us business we offer them friendship.'

Jack Parnell is a religious man, a Mason and a staunch member of the Uniting Church which brought together the Methodist, Presbyterian and Congregational Churches. That week there had been an article in the *Bulletin* claiming that the Church hierarchy had been infiltrated by the Left. Jack was displeased. He phoned a friend and said, 'If this is untrue we should sue and if it is true we should fix it.'

Down below there was little to catch the eye; still the same stunted shrubby trees and still the gibber – iron-stained, wind-polished stones – strewn on the surface of the sand plains. The line of the road and the railway neatly scored the red-brown land and there were also a creek, a salt lake and a homestead. This might seem remote to some, but while there were such obvious features it was not remote to Jack. During the coming days we would be flying over desert where there was nothing, and special navigation equipment would be needed to guide us. Erldunda, the homestead and cattle station, belonged to Syd Stains, 'A good reliable customer. I deliver around half a million litres [110,000 gallons] of fuel to him each year. He used to be with Shell, but Ike would call on him from time to time, just to make sure he was satisfied. That way he got used to seeing us around and then, as soon as he became dissatisfied, we were ready to move. It's a good way of doing business – build up the contacts and then wait.'

Erldunda is two hours' drive from Alice – distances in the Outback are usually defined by travelling time – but flying at 150 mph (240 kph) reduced that to half an hour. And as we got closer I began to wonder why it is called the Dead Heart. It didn't look dead at all. In fact, *Dead Heart* was the title of a book published in 1906, and it stuck in the language. Maybe it did seem dead then, but not now. Red, but not dead. As we neared Alice, a range of hills came into view and trees appeared, looking like blobs of mould on a slice of brown bread. Stations became more numerous and turquoise swimming pools twinkled up at us.

Alice Springs is a surprise. Smack in the middle of Australia, 1,000 miles (1,600 kilometres) in any direction from a comparable settlement, I didn't expect to find her so big, so suburban, so prosperous and so green. The colour causes the first blink, although the surprise soon vanishes when one ponders the name. Alice is not a spring, but a deep, semi-permanent water-hole, so for most of the time it should be green.

The suburban feel takes a while longer to accept. The frontier-town myth is so entrenched that I expected to find a romantic outpost, roughish and a little haphazard and makeshift, like the settlements on the Stuart Highway. Alice is none of this; she is solid, brimful with brick veneer houses, each standing in its own small fenced garden, stretching to accommodate her 18,000 residents until stopped short by the Macdonnell Ranges. Some people find the place ugly, a discomforting contrast to the magnificence of the scenery which surrounds it. I do not, probably because I am too intrigued by a town that is not what it seems. The deception is not deliberate, there are obvious visual hints to the true character of Alice but, as with all hints, their significance takes a while to unravel.

On the surface Alice is a tourist town existing to service the needs of those who wish to visit the Centre, to experience the heat and the dust and the flies, and see and maybe climb the gigantic sandstone monolith called Ayers Rock which is not a short walk down the street as so many believe before they arrive, but a further 310 miles (500 kilometres) south-west – more than a day trip away unless you fly.

Alice then seems a good place for motel-keepers, tour-bus operators, opal merchants and those who can't resist selling boomerangs made in Taiwan and tea-towels sporting spear-carrying Aborigines. The main street, lined with two-storey buildings and coolabah trees (a species of eucalypt common inland), offers a little of everything: bookshops, camel rides, Cardin shirts, a cinema and a craft centre. Ice-cream is in short supply. Jean Paget searching for Joe Harman in *A Town Like Alice* was always slipping into milk bars for an ice-cream soda. Trying to follow her example was disappointing. Even Woolworths sold it only in large quantities, to be moved from one deep freeze to another. I walked the length of Todd Street before finding ice-cream *and* chocolate sauce in a service-station café.

But apart from ice-cream, Alice is short of nothing. Gone are the days when fresh fruit and vegetables were not to be found and all supplies had to be humped from Adelaide by camel. For the first fifty years, Alice Springs may have been a mere dot on the map, but the second fifty have shown constant growth. The dot on the map in the first place denoted a telegraph repeater station which was named after Alice, the wife of the Postmaster General of South Australia, Charles Todd, who supervised the building of the overland telegraph-line. He gave his name both to the river which runs through the town and to the main street. The line was designed to link not only Australia with itself but also to the rest of the world via submarine cable. For two years from 1870, 100 men toiled to set up 37,000 poles between Adelaide and Darwin at a cost of $A1 million. Between the poles repeater stations had to be placed, as morse signals could not be transmitted by wire for distances greater than 185 miles (300 kilometres). Thus Alice became a lonely outpost, and stayed that way until the railway line began to creep up the centre. It got as far as Oodnadatta by 1889, and then took another forty years to complete the 400-mile (650-kilometre) journey. Until 1929 the gap was filled by camel or on horseback; and that is how the railway got its name – the Ghan – for it served the same function as the camel trains led by their Afghan handlers. Even with the railway reaching

Alice it was no easy journey; the line ran on a cheaply engineered road-bed in country which was subject to serious flooding. The line would be washed out and the train flood-bound for several days at a time. The new line takes twenty-four hours in air-conditioned comfort.

What the railway started, the radio continued. It provided the Outback with a mantle of safety and so, by the time the Depression hit the south, Alice was beginning to look attractive to the settler who saw that the neighbouring land was suitable for cattle and horses. The Aborigines had to be displaced, of course, driven away from the major water sources, and before long roaming cattle had munched their way through much native flora, depriving the Aborigine of a significant part of his diet. To cope with this shortage of food, he was tempted to camp on the outskirts of the town and depend on hand-outs of a hopeless assortment of rations: flour, tea, sugar, jam and a little meat. The camps are still there, maybe as many as thirty, ragged settlements and clearly visible to those who arrive by train.

These camps are the first hint of the other Alice. The tourist industry is not the only significant feature of the town's wealth; she is also the urban focus for 13,000 central Australian Aborigines. Only 3,000 are listed as permanent, the rest drift in and out of Alice. There are no more food-parcels, but their place has been taken by numerous 'pensions', the Australian word for benefits, ranging from child endowments, single-parent and old-age allowance, to unemployment payments. Various government departments and statutory bodies dealing with Aboriginal welfare are to be found in Todd Street.

There is no other place in Australia where so much white business is dependent on black custom. One estimate reckons that thirty per cent of the work-force owes its jobs to the presence of the Aborigine – and not just the welfare bodies: the taxi-drivers do well ferrying Aborigines to their camps, and so do the second-hand car dealers and pub owners, particularly on pension day when the ragged come into town for their dole cheques. Liquor is a crucial issue. There was a time when it was common to see blacks sitting under the trees drinking all day; there was a time when the Todd River was described as a dangerous place. The river bed is dry most of the time, and the warm sand provided a home for black alcoholics and their families. Then came the day when it was deemed unseemly for such abject poverty to be so highly visible to affluent tourists and, as is the way of these things, a law came into being in the Northern Territory, where Alice is situated, which forbade drinking in public within a mile or so (two kilometres) of a liquor outlet. The law applies equally to black and white; the aim is to stop whites drinking in the streets, too – Top End dwellers are a notorious lot of drinkers – but the underlying aim of the law was to clean up Alice, to displace the problem from public areas to other sites where it could no longer be regarded as a public nuisance. Alice folk are pleased with this stroke of legal genius: the town and the Todd River look tidy.

The Todd River is in fact one of the town's major tourist attractions, for once a year it hosts the Henley-on-Todd regatta. This is a zany celebration, for there is no water – indeed, the organizers insure against unexpected rain. Instead, yachtsmen pick up their fabricated bottomless boats and run with them. For the rowers it is a little more complicated: they have to paddle through the sand. The whole town embraces this buffoonery – including the Space Base which enters a boat each year, and often the American Ambassador is present.

If you fly into the town, you get the second clue to the real nature of Alice. A nest of pure white spheres and oblong buildings is tucked conspicuously between two ridges in the Macdonnell Ranges, in a place called Pine Gap. The Gap, officially called the Joint Space Research Facility, is the target of gossip and guesswork. Prime Ministers may just know in detail what goes on there, but the population has to make do with scraps of information that do not endanger its Top Secret rating. Certainly it seems to be CIA-run and to form a crucial part of the American early-warning system. It receives, via space satellites, information about missile launchings. It can, they say, provide pictures of intercontinental ballistic missiles (ICBMs) in flight. It can also watch out for nuclear explosions, thereby monitoring the nuclear test ban treaty and offering support to non-proliferation measures. Other notions tossed around suggest that its listening facilities are not just restricted to the Russians and the Chinese but are turned upon other countries as well. The one fact upon which all unite is that the presence of Pine Gap, eighteen miles (thirty kilometres) from Alice, makes Australia a nuclear target. Prime Ministers no longer deny this, but add that the risk is an acceptable part of the alliance with the US, an alliance which provides Australia with nuclear protection. Furthermore – and politicians always like to add a touch of altruism – the base is supposed to make a contribution to world peace: the skills deployed at Pine Gap help to discourage nuclear war by making surprise attacks more difficult.

No one is much bothered in Alice. They are happy to accept all this, to accept that the operation is part of a genuine deterrent system, contributing to a stable nuclear balance and, if it makes Alice a target ... well ... if some clown pushes a button we're all dead anyway, so what's the difference? Who wants to make a fuss and ask awkward questions? The base is good for business – there are 250 people employed there: a handful of Australians in menial jobs like gardening, a handful of Australian technicians and, at the last count, eight scientists; the rest are highly paid Americans, who may wish to keep a low profile in Pine Gap, but who are happy to keep a high profile in Alice.

Alice likes Americans. And she is used to being used. She was garrisoned during the war and became a transit camp. It was a tedious business running the town on curfews, but there was money in it. And a road – the road linking Alice to Darwin, which had been planned for sixty-seven years, got sealed in ninety days, a black strip busting the bush wide open. All this was good for go-getting Alice; a bonza place, Joe Harman called it.

Baffling to me. The heat and the dust and the flies seem to generate energy, encourage initiative and bring forth inventions. The first road train came out of Alice in the 1940s. It was based on a surplus army personnel-carrier and the prime mover was a tank transporter. It could carry 100 head of cattle, but it didn't catch on too quickly; the men liked droving. The wine did, though. One family grow their own grapes and make their own wine and sell it in their own restaurant, improbably called Chateau Hornsby. And Bob Collins is busy creating a solar pond, which he hopes will one day generate electricity. Think of the saving in fuel. It won't threaten Jack for a while.

The Debutante Ball didn't cause him to raise an eyebrow either. I'd seen it advertised on my walk down Todd Street: a hand-printed bill in a shop window, above the notice of the next race-meeting which was bringing Wendy to Alice, announced a Debutante Ball at which the girls would be presented to the Northern Territory Commissioner – here in the land free of social snobbery; here in the suburb in the scrub! I scoffed silently. And by coincidence, Jack's sister was able to give me all the details. She and her husband, Grant, own Bond Springs, a cattle station fifteen miles (twenty-four kilometres) from Alice. Around the pool we ate barbecued steak and salad while two teenage daughters bubbled about the social scene. Tanya, a law student in Adelaide, thinks the social life in general – and the night life in particular – is vastly superior in Alice. There are at least two hotels, as well as the casino, where one can dance until the licence calls a halt and then move on to a Bojangles Disco until four-thirty in the morning.

Meliss came out at the previous year's ball, in a beautiful long white dress sent from Adelaide and long white gloves and a posy. Her brother, Brett, decked out in a white shirt, black trousers and bow tie, escorted her, which seems part of the tradition. Jan said that two girls in town had ordered dresses from Singapore, but they failed to arrive in time and a sympathetic shop in Adelaide sprang to the rescue. There was much preparation. There were lessons in how to bow and how to curtsy and how to waltz. As I listened, I pinched myself mentally, perhaps the heat was affecting me. But it wasn't – I can prove it. Later that night I found Brett in front of the video, showing a recording of the ball to two of his chums. I watched, too, as the girls each made their entrance in turn and, leaving their escorts standing with their hands behind their backs, walked the length of the floor alone to be presented. The ball began with the Waltz of the Debs, while adoring mothers, relatives and friends looked on. Brett was cross because the video showed only a minute of the waltz. 'All that practising and all those rehearsals and it was all over so quickly. It was a magic evening. The tops.'

The Deb Ball is quite a feature of life in country towns. It raises money for charity and gives young girls the opportunity to dress in white which may – or may not – prevent them from rushing towards that other white frock day. It is not intended to launch them on to or into the social scene, but it is intended to mark the transition from school to work; and no one had thought to make the link with the British equivalent.

Jack's business was soon completed. He needed to talk with the Ampol depot in Alice and to sort out a few cash-flow problems for Marla Bore, which was experiencing a slow start to the tourist season. With that settled, we flew to Curtin Springs, a cattle station an hour away, over a mountain called Conner and on the road to Ayers Rock.

The station has its own air-strip; the owners can both hear and see a plane circling overhead, which is the signal for Peter to drive to the strip and collect his visitors. Peter Savarin owns 16,000 square miles (41,500 square kilometres) and 4,000 head of cattle. He bought the place in 1957 and faced nine years of drought, which left him destitute. After that he decided to diversify, as a hedge against the threat of its happening again, with a roadhouse and a handful of demountable motel rooms. All the tourist buses stop for a beer; most cars stop for petrol, and some travellers opt for an overnight stay for $A12. The demountables are merely a wooden box with a wardrobe, a bed and an air-conditioning unit, and a short trip over wooden planks placed across the desert to the shower – a shower full of cobwebs and insects which fall upon you as you wash; a harmless but not a pleasant sensation. For another $A4, travellers can join the family around a large table in the kitchen for breakfast. For slightly more, they can share lunch, and for $A7.50 they can share dinner. The homestead itself is large and rambling, inelegant but most welcoming. It is difficult to get builders and carpenters in the Outback, much less architects, so stations like Curtin develop piecemeal and have to depend on itinerant bush workers who drop by unexpectedly looking for work and willing to make use of any available materials. Several men were working on new showers and lavatories. 'This lot had been on the grog for a week and had not eaten. All they asked for was food and a bed. We have to take these opportunities when they come up.'

The station has its own abattoir and cold store. Peter decided on this when he realized how much he was paying to send cattle to Adelaide; by doing his own killing and cutting, he could save the cost of transporting useless weight. 'It was all very easy until they started tightening up on TB and brucellosis. The Yanks were looking for an excuse not to buy our meat! Anyway, with that I had to put in a proper abattoir. None the less, it pays off.' He sells a fair amount to the neighbouring Aboriginal settlements and has his own plane to deliver the meat. 'I've cut everyone else out of the operation. Before, everyone was making a buck except me. No, not many people do it like this. They think a pastoralist is a pastoralist and not interested in all the rest. They think I'm strange.'

I could detect Jack's entrepreneurial influence at work, and indeed he had persuaded Peter to take the final step and buy his own plane, and he is now encouraging Peter to apply for a licence to carry passengers; there are many people who would like a ride in and out of Alice, and this would keep both the plane and the pilot busy.

The purpose of this visit was to take Peter to Warburton with us. Warburton, over the border in Western Australia at the point where the Gibson Desert meets the Great Victoria Desert, used to be a mission and is now a government reserve. All their supplies are trucked from Western Australia, but Peter would like to supply the meat and Jack would be happy to handle the fuel and other freight.

It is a three-hour flight from Curtin to Warburton. Jack and Peter sat in the front to plan their discussions and I sat in the back to enjoy, during the first hour of the flight, the splendid view of Ayers Rock and the Olgas. The Olgas, looking like slightly mis-shapen sand-castles, were named by the first explorer to set eyes on them. He was obviously something of an internationalist and chose to name them after the Grand Duchess of Russia. Ayers Rock, which resembles a vast upturned boomerang, was also named by the first explorer to view it, only he, being a State employee and of a rather more prosaic turn of mind, clearly thought it wise to name the monolith after the then premier of South Australia.

Ayers Rock also has an Aboriginal name, Uluru, and it is among the most sacred of sites. No white person knows the full significance of the rock. Few white men took any real interest in Aboriginal culture until the 1960s, but since then it has become a thriving industry with anthropologists and academics struggling to piece together the rich and complex beliefs of these ancient people. Their beliefs resemble, if they must resemble anything, those of Ancient Greece. In his writing, Hesiod describes how the visible order of nature arose, how the gods were born and how their spirits remain to guard their laws; and the followers of Hesiod's writing treated these legends as relics of a sacred history and believed in its doctrines and the practical duties it placed on men. The difference between the Ancient Greeks and the Aborigines is that whereas the former version is now merely literature to be studied by classical scholars, the Aboriginal version of the evolution of the universe, with its religious law and ethical precepts, continues today.

To the Aborigine, everything hinges on Dreamtime. Before Dreamtime there was nothing, merely a flat and uninhabited land. Then huge semi-human creatures arose out of the featureless plains and wandered the countryside creating plants and animals and humans. And as they passed on, or as Dreamtime came to an end, wherever these creatures had been active they turned into a mountain range, a hill, a valley, a watercourse. They left behind all the laws by which life should be lived and organized and also the supernatural penalties that would be suffered by those who disobeyed them. They also left behind their spirits to haunt the sacred places as invisible guardians of justice.

Since the creatures were both good and bad, the myths are sometimes poetic and sometimes grotesque, and at all times highly imaginative. They cover the origins of fire, the sun and the moon; and they include saucy tales of power struggles between the turkey and the emu which explain why the emu has no wings, and lustful tales of the pelican which explain why he is coloured black and white; and they offer reasons why Aborigines will not kill or harm a green frog for fear of flood and why they treat a dead koala with particular reverence for fear of drought. The koala myth is one of my favourite stories.

There was an orphan boy called Koobor who was badly treated by his relatives and given only the foliage of gum trees to eat and never enough water to drink. One day when the relatives went off to look for food, they forgot to hide their buckets full of water. Koobor took them and hung them in the branches of a tree, then climbed the tree and chanted a song to make it grow and grow. But not high enough. Angry relatives climbed the tree and threw the boy to the ground where they watched his shattered body turn into a koala and climb back into the tree. At that moment, koala-boy Koobor made the law that the koala can be killed for food but no bone in his body may be broken and he must not be skinned until he is cooked. If these rules were not observed, he would cause a severe drought in which everyone would die – except, of course, the koala. To this day the animal lives on gum leaves and does not need water to keep him alive.

The air-strip at Warburton was close to the main buildings – which was just as well since there was no one to greet us; no sign of life. The place was eerily quiet and abandoned. The community was either away attending to black fella business at another camp or sleeping off the heat of the day. We walked to the store and found it closed. It was noon. It was windy; the land was bare and the dust billowed. There was hardly a tree to be seen, presumably all knocked down for firewood. There were canvas lean-tos and shanty-style tin huts, and the ground was covered with ring-pulls from crumpled soft-drink cans. Robyn Davidson had passed through here with her camels as she journeyed from Alice westwards to the sea: she described the place as a hole – and it is. Numerous rusty old cars were abandoned in piles, and once again I had a vision of the desert disappearing, gobbled up by used cars. The Aborigines play cards as a way of distributing money: the winner gets enough to buy a car which is old anyway, and everyone then hammers it into the ground. They don't know how to maintain them and they don't try. When a car ceases to work they abandon it and play cards again. Jack said it wasn't worth anyone's while to cart the things back to the cities as scrap metal. He'd looked into it and he'd rather send his containers back empty.

We wandered across to see what they were charging for petrol: 60 cents a litre. That is about 18 cents a litre more than they had paid for it, but still not excessive, as the settlements use petrol as a revenue-earner.

The settlement's other revenue-earner, the store, is a large wooden warehouse, properly built. It also acts as a bank and is the only place where welfare cheques can be cashed. Joseph arrived and as he unlocked he explained that he had a degree in economics and had once worked for Coles, the big department store; while he hadn't asked to see Jack or Peter, he was always interested in cheaper prices and better service for the settlement. At the moment he received forty tonnes of goods every three weeks from Kalgoorlie and Perth. He'd love to have smaller deliveries once a week, but so far he hadn't found anyone interested because the place was so isolated and the cost prohibitive. Jack did some quick sums to see what it would cost to send twelve tonnes of goods a week on the train from Adelaide to Alice and then by road train from Alice to Warburton, a sixty-hour journey. The figure he arrived at was $A245 a tonne. Joseph smiled. He was paying $A160 a tonne now. Back to the calculator, and this time the figure emerged at $A178 a tonne, working on the premise that goods on the whole are cheaper in Adelaide than in Perth, that he would be able to undercut the price of petrol and that the meat would come from Peter. It began to look as though once a fortnight would be a better proposition, and Jack said he would do a detailed analysis of prices of everything from retread tyres and motor oil to food, and let Joseph have it within a fortnight. He invited Joseph to come to Adelaide at his expense to talk to the suppliers, but Joseph declined and said he'd be quite happy with a price-list.

The chat then dissolved into gossip. It seems the previous store-keeper had disappeared with $A30,000, leaving many unpaid bills, and nothing was done about it. Joseph argued that the settlement didn't want the public to know it had been ripped off, and the

Department of Aboriginal Affairs don't want it to be known that they do a bad policing job. I looked around the store at the tuna fish and Band Aid, the muesli, the tinned goods, soft drinks and frozen vegetables. Everything was priced in round figures: $A1 – $A1.50 – $A2. Joseph said that the Aborigines don't like dealing in small coins. They just throw them on the ground with the ring-pulls from the soft-drink cans.

The meeting was a little cool, but Jack and Peter seemed happy enough. Their job now was to supply figures that tempted Joseph to switch suppliers. Back on board, we nibbled the sandwiches we had bought for our lunch and arrived back at Curtin in time to shower before tea at six-thirty. Tea consisted of huge slices of beef with roast pumpkin and potatoes, followed by the most delicious apricot shortcake. A dozen of us sat at the long kitchen table, the men in sleeveless shirts showing unsightly tufts of hair, the women in cotton frocks. There were Peter and his wife, Dawn, and his son and daughter-in-law, and the governess who'd just left school and who looked after their young children. There were Syd and his wife who looked after the roadhouse, and Mary the cook, and other station hands. The chat concerned the high price of carting fresh milk from Alice – it was too much bother to have milk cows – and an item in the Adelaide *Advertiser* which was being passed from hand to hand: a judge had ordered a white man to pay $A75,000 in damages to an Aborigine, whom he had knocked down and, in doing so, had caused head injuries needing two operations. The accident was said to have affected the Aborigine's ability to receive and pass on accurately tribal secrets. The wording of the judgement, according to Jack and Peter, was in the language of the Freemasons. Peter is a Mason, too.

No one lingered over the meal. By eight p.m., Jack and I were by ourselves, Peter having been called outside to settle a dispute with an Aborigine who wanted to buy grog. He came back in a flurry. 'I get on well with those coons and they respect me. But I won't sell them grog when they are already full and likely to cause trouble. This lot weren't full, but they had children in the car and I told them that I was responsible for the safety of the children. One of those do-gooding type of women came here the other day and questioned me on why I refused to sell to coons, and I threw her out in the end. My solution to all these problems is simple: the blacks must kill the white do-gooders and we must kill the blacks.'

Peter enjoyed watching my reaction to such remarks; he enjoyed teasing a newcomer to the problems he has lived with all his life. There was no malevolence, as far as I could tell, in his words; he simply had little time for woolly liberal thinking that created as many problems as it solved. Jack's style was somewhat different: whatever he thought did not seep out in provocative sentences.

Peter also came back with the news that the Aborigine came from Jamieson settlement where, he claimed, the community adviser and his wife who ran the store had run off with $A9,000. This was the third time I had heard such a story in as many days, and I asked Peter for an explanation. The answer came quickly and took me by surprise. 'Those white fellas who hang around with the blacks are up to one of two things. Either they want to rip the blacks off financially, or they want to use them politically. Those blacks are being used by agitators who want to bring about a communist state. Haven't you read the book? We've all read it around here, passed from hand to hand.' And he introduced me to *Red over Black*, which I borrowed and read each night until the generator snapped off the lights at precisely eleven p.m.

The book is a slim volume with a clear message. It is written by Geoff McDonald who has spent a lifetime in the labour and trade union movement and who was once a prominent member of the Communist Party. He argues that although the Communist Party in Australia may look harmless, impotent even, crippled by splits into three camps (pro-Moscow, pro-China and pro-goodness knows what), nothing could be further from the truth. And the truth is that Marxist influence has never been stronger. Activists, mainly white but some part-Aborigine, have infiltrated Aboriginal organizations in both city and Outback and are now happily exploiting those whom Lenin described as 'useful idiots' in order, by and by, to bring about a communist state.

In the Outback, McDonald points his finger at the white advisers to the communities. Their strategy is simple, he says: they fight long and hard for land rights and, once the Aborigine has control over the land, he also has some say over the development of minerals and so forth. Only a say, because the Crown owns the minerals and, if the Aboriginal community were to give a firm 'No' to development, the Federal Government has the right of veto 'in the national interest'. None the less, public opinion sometimes makes it difficult for Federal action and, anyway, the Aboriginal community can do much to slow up the whole process in the hope that companies get so exasperated that they quit. The white adviser, according to McDonald, will do all he can to urge the Aborigine to oppose development of any kind. This is necessary not to protect them but to drag Australia down, since a prosperous land stands in the way of revolutionary objectives. Meanwhile, as Australia declines, the Aborigine, with possession of the land and some control over mineral and other wealth, can demand anything – say, an independent state which either Russia or China would be happy to aid. Pernicious rubbish to be swallowed only by those with a penchant for conspiracy theories? Or a grain of truth?

Peter and his friends see the grains. Here in the Northern Territory, Aborigines form twenty-six per cent of the population, and some thirty per cent of land has already been handed back to them, with more in the pipeline. Since 1976, when the first lands were returned, there is no doubt that the mining companies have been given a hard time. The processes of identifying traditional owners, seeking their permission to explore, identifying sacred sites and deciding which must not be touched, and agreeing compensation is hardly stream-lined. It is tedious and time-consuming and tempts some to walk away, and all to complain – even the most moderate of men with a genuine desire to balance the need for profit and economic growth with Aboriginal wishes. Guide-lines and some streamlining are obviously necessary, if only to stop the genuinely greedy and insensi-tive and unscrupulous from whipping up a backlash by arguing that, if exploration continues to be so restricted by land rights, then the resource-hungry countries of Asia may eventually decide to come and help themselves to Australian minerals – black bastards and yellow hordes neatly packaged in one threat!

It must be said that there is no conclusive evidence that the Aborigine is against mining. Provided the more sacred sites are not sacrificed and the compensation is suitably high, then many see it as a way of getting cash to improve their communities. Certainly they appear to approve of mining rather more than they do of tourist developments – which would be the only alternative money-raiser. From this it would be quite feasible to argue that white advisers are moulding the minds of rural Aborigines. Of course it is impossible to prove or disprove McDonald's theory. But then, as Peter says, 'You'd have to be blind not to see that some whites are making financial mileage out of the coons, so why is it so hard to believe that some are making political mileage?'

The next day, at six a.m., a smell of burnt toast greeted me as I entered the kitchen. Peter was in charge of breakfast (poached eggs, toast and honey) and then the men went off for a day in the slaughter-house, and we set out for Giles, a weather station in Western Australia, and the neighbouring settlement of Warakurna. Giles is a grand place with a swimming pool and a tennis court and five men and one woman who is the cook, and a baby kangaroo, a joey, who lives in a rucksack lined with sheepskin and is fed on Weetabix and baby food specially flown from Alice. Five men, it seems, need something to look after.

The function of this and other stations around Australia is to send up hydrogen-filled weather balloons and then track their course with radar to determine wind patterns and temperatures. The data is then transmitted to headquarters in Adelaide for analysis to aid predictions. It's an odd life, and most do it for six months at a time for the money and the tax advantages. Peter Dawson came for that reason and to see if he could survive the heat. He'd already done time in the Antarctic and loved it. He's happy in temperatures of 23°F to 41°F (− 5°C to + 5°C). Air-conditioning makes life that much easier in Giles, but even so he has to spend many hours outside, particularly as the radar had broken down. 'It's old and needs replacing, but Giles is not as important as it was when Woomera, the rocket range, was in full flight testing guided missiles. So right now I'm having to stand outside and watch the damn balloons and work out the calculations based on certain assumptions.' It sounded neither scientific nor particularly skilful.

All the food they need for themselves and for the joey is flown in every week from Alice, and so we sat down to a rare treat, newly made scones with jam and real cream for 'Smoko', as the Australians call the mid-morning break. The fuel is provided by BP and is negotiated by national contract, so there is nothing that Jack can do. Our call was purely social. Giles likes visitors – they don't get that many, and anyway Jack wanted to say 'thank you' to Peter and his team for hauling one of his trucks out of a creek. A hard one that; it took several days to dig him out.

Chris Clarke, the community adviser from Warakurna, drove over to pick us up. His first comment to Peter was that, after four months in the job, he intended to apply for an upgrade: the responsibility was greater than he had thought. He'd been a District Officer in Kenya at some stage in his life and had power to put people in jail. Here, he had much less authority, and that became obvious the moment we reached the settlement. We were inspecting a broken fuel storage tank when the commotion broke out. It was merely shouting at first, then men started going for one another and a woman charged another woman with a *nulla*. We stood on the side with the community's chairman and said nothing. Chris interferes only if guns are involved.

To avoid the petrol-sniffing problem, he has advised the community not to install a bowser. His fuel is diesel, which doesn't rate as sniffing stuff, and most of the vehicles belong not to individuals but to the community who share them. Housing or – perhaps a better word – shelter is formed by placing sheets of tin across a couple of empty barrels, or by tying canvas to a tree. There are also dog boxes. These tin boxes were once considered to be suitable housing in which the Aborigines could sleep at night to shelter from the cold. They prefer to use the huts for storage and sleep outside as they have done for thousands of years. If they don't have such huts for storage they hang meat in the trees, to keep it away from the dogs which are everywhere. To cook, they dig a hole in the ground and light a fire. There are no other facilities. There are many health problems:

bronchitis and other respiratory diseases are common; so is scabies, the outcome of insanitary conditions; and so are trachoma and other eye infections, caused by the dust and by dogs lying on the blankets in the daytime and the Aborigine lying on the blankets at night, cuddled against the dogs for warmth.

For many years, Aboriginal health programmes concentrated on the provision of hospitals and the treatment of diseases. This has not worked well. Aborigines do not like hospitals and are disinclined to use them. The emphasis has therefore moved away from therapeutic and towards preventive medicine, with Aboriginal health workers trained to educate the community to higher standards of nutrition and hygiene.

Jane, Chris's wife, a trained nurse, is also running a health care programme. 'They eat so badly. For one thing, they have a very sweet tooth, their tea is half sugar and all those soft drinks are not helping. I'm trying to change the food in the store to something more wholesome, like swapping the soft drinks for mineral water. But it isn't easy. For example, they have got used to white flour and won't eat wholemeal.' She also intends to tear down the 'dog boxes' and build a centre where she can teach spinning and weaving to the women.

Her son declined to let me join his forty-minute 'School of the Air'. He was shy and felt badly out of touch because poor reception had meant that he had not been able to tune in to the School for the past couple of weeks. It won't affect his education, since the 'School of the Air' is only a topping-up to the correspondence course. It was started in 1950 from Alice and provides a link by two-way radio between Outback children across 772,000 square miles (2 million square kilometres). One minute a teacher can be talking to children on a cattle station, the next to a mining camp or Aboriginal settlement.

Docker River is like Warburton, a huge government reserve; once again our first call was on the store and the storekeepers, Richard and Jane. Jane used to be a nurse in Alice until she met Richard, and Richard's career had been chequered before he decided he'd team with Jane and try life on a settlement. He'd been educated at schools in Switzerland and England before doing university courses in engineering and law, abandoning the latter to globe-trot and, as he put it, squander an inheritance. By the time he arrived in Alice his trade was that of house-painter. In Alice he painted the post office and got ripped off. 'I didn't get paid and it took me nine months of hassle to get the money. People here are more corrupt, it is as simple as that. They don't have the same business ethics one finds elsewhere.' He was appointed to Docker by the Aboriginal community and reckons he got the job because of Jane's qualifications as a nurse. The reserve has one full-time sister and an Aboriginal health-worker, but they liked the idea of having another trained person.

And yet once again he found a store full of problems. 'I inherited large debts and I can't be too sure what had gone wrong. Maybe there was some fiddling of the books, but I also think that the policy of giving credit was at the heart of it. The credits were never paid off. So I stopped credit immediately and sat down with the community and asked them to discuss with me how we were going to get rid of the debts. Well, we cut the lines drastically – but then we had to; many suppliers with unpaid bills refused to do business with us – and then we decided to add one hundred per cent mark-up on everthing until the bills had been cleared. When they are paid off the community will then decide whether to lower prices or use the profit to improve the store. We could use a new roof!'

He could indeed. Although the store was large and neat and tidy – Jane dislikes disorder – the roof was made of tin strips, making access easy for those who wished to do a little stealing. 'They do it mainly because they are bored and mischievous, and they get quite clever at it. They prise up the strips from the roof and then put them back when they leave. Once, the only way we realized they had been inside the store was because they left footprints up and down the wall!' The store may have been neat and tidy, but it was also pretty empty. The truck was late. 'We are right out of flour and sugar, and the Aborigines get withdrawal symptoms when the sugar runs out because they use so much of it. Many of them are diabetics.' Jane, like Judith, is trying to introduce unsweetened fruit juice as part of the campaign for improved diet.

I sat and watched the store in operation for a while. It was late afternoon and there was a steady stream of customers wanting soft drinks and warm sausage-rolls from the hot tray. These had come from Alice deep-frozen, and were served with airline packs of tomato sauce. On pension day they claim that a queue of 200 people wait to do their shopping. A few put money into envelopes and ask Richard to keep it for them, but most spend the money as soon as it arrives – and run short before the next cheque. 'It is easy for them to get in a muddle, you know. They wander off to Alice for a while and have their cheques moved there, and then when they arrive back here there is a time-lag before the cheques are transferred. That, of course, is when they come asking for credit. And it is not easy to refuse.'

Jane and Richard had been in Docker for over a year, earning $A13,000 each and free food and lodging. On the whole they like their life, but is is not without problems. 'There are plenty of them now, with all the building work going on.' The building work (as Paul Rumple, the community adviser, was to explain) was yet another line in Aboriginal housing: this time a wooden square with wide verandahs and a tin roof. The designers had at last realized that the Aborigines preferred to use the inside as a store and the outside for sleeping. The verandahs would enable them to throw their mattresses and blankets in a suitable spot to avoid the wind and the dust. The community had voted for this design some nine months before and had had to wait for delivery, and with each batch there were, of course, components missing.

Housing for Aborigines in Outback areas has caused many disappointments. When Whitlam came to power in 1972, he vowed that within ten years the Aboriginal population would be housed at levels reasonably compatible with the rest of society. Success in urban areas was a little easier; it could be assumed that those who came to live in towns were willing to accept Western concepts. In rural areas, where the Aborigine had never lived in a house, no one knew what was wanted, and attempts to find out defeated the impatient. The story goes that when Aborigines were first shown models of houses where the roof could be lifted off to display the inside, they argued that they didn't want houses where the roof could be taken off so easily. In the end they were cajoled, by those who wanted to get busy building, into accepting white-style housing. That they couldn't handle bedrooms and bathrooms and kitchens soon became evident. Back to the drawing board. Many styles have since been tried. The square box with wooden windows that push out and with verandahs is a vast improvement on a piece of canvas slung against a tree, and it seems appropriate for the moment, or longer. Maybe the rural Aborigine will never want a fitted kitchen.

My first few days looking at settlements were depressing. Of course it was Jack's aim to get people to talk about their problems, in case there was anything he could do to help; nevertheless, the sight of poverty and the sounds of frustration lowered my spirits. The gap between white intentions and black desires, as far as they are known, seemed so wide. It hasn't been easy for either side to understand the other, but in the last fifteen years, through the stumbling and the mistakes, much has been learned. Policy-makers now know three fundamentally important facts: first, the Aborigines need to be on land that means something to them, not just any old land to which they have no commitment and from which they will drift at any opportunity; secondly, they do not like being herded into groups of up to 500. This may be the level at which it is economically feasible to offer schools, hospitals and running water, but rural Aborigines are used to living in smaller extended family groups, and they find being mixed up with other tribes anathema to them. Thirdly, they find living in a 'them and us' settlement ('them' being whites, distanced in demountables and often behind a wire fence) saps their confidence and initiative. While the whites are there to be leaned upon, what incentive is there for them to do more for themselves?

These three discoveries have led to what is known as the Country Camp movement: Aborigines moving away from government settle-ments and attempting to return to their hunter-gatherer life-style, but wanting a modicum of white comforts (a water supply, a store, a vehicle, and radio communication for keeping in touch with larger centres). This causes headaches for governments, both State and Federal; the cost of providing even basic requirements for small groups of up to 100 is high. It provides headaches for Aborigines,

The Ribbon and the Ragged Square

too. Once they decide they need *any* white comfort, they need white help to make it work, and are then in danger of re-creating the same dependence from which they sought escape.

During my last few days in central Australia I was to visit two such camps and was to be cheered, not so much by what I saw (which was still inadequate), but by what I heard which, because it contained a sense of understanding, also contained a sense of purpose.

Christopher Duff and his wife, Elaine, have been at Blackstone for three years. He is buoyed up by enthusiasm rather than boned-out by frustration. 'This place has moved fifty years in the three years I have been here. The place was bankrupt, not even the generator worked, so that food was constantly being ruined – a real problem when we got supplies trucked in only every two months from Western Australia. The fuel used to come from there too in barrels, and by the time it arrived some were split and had clearly left a trail of oil across the desert. When we got up to twelve split barrels we said nothing and simply paid for it, but when we got up to twenty-nine I became suspicious. I realized something was up, and when I examined the drums I could see that those that had split on the journey had sand around the break, but there were many others without sand. They had been loaded empty. We existed in those early months by returning the empty drums, there were piles everywhere and they were worth $A15 each. That was all diesel of course, we used to have to lug our petrol from Warburton.' Jack delivers the fuel now and the community has its own petrol pump. 'We resisted this for some time because of the fear of petrol-sniffing, but so far it has not become a problem. There have been other dramas instead. The Aborigines run the pump themselves and their relatives are constantly bludging – asking for the stuff or taking it on credit and then not paying. At the end of the week the books don't balance of course, and their answer to that is simply to walk away and get some other fella to do it. Teething troubles. She'll be right. They got to learn to hack it.'

Health has improved. When he arrived there was malnutrition, but the community has developed a liking for fresh fruit because it needs no preparation, and some vegetables – carrots and tomatoes – because they too can be eaten raw. Trachoma is on the way out, mainly because the new houses keep the Aborigine out of the dust and they have learned to keep the dogs off their blankets. The housing is the same square box with an inside light and push-out windows and verandahs that I saw at Docker River. Here, Chris has encouraged the community to plant bamboo to act as a dust-breaker and to put up a stone wall around each plot to act as a wind-breaker. The result looks pleasing.

And so does the school. We had arrived at eight a.m., in time to watch Murray run up two flags, one Australian and the other Aboriginal, to signal the start of the day. There is also a swimming pool to encourage the children to attend classes. The school-room is a large tin hut with a torn roof, and inside there are pretty blue and red chairs and a ritzy quartz clock which shows not just the time but the date and the day. I suggested that Murray might prefer a new building to a quartz clock, but he said that it was not important, the building worked well enough. I looked through the schoolbooks and read essays by children on how their fathers hunted for kangaroos and their mothers hunted for rabbits.

The community also has a plane which it shares with other breakaway camps. 'It was my idea. I put it to them that it was costing too much to get things flown in and that if we had our own plane it could also be used by the mob to go on trips to Alice. We charge $A50 for that ride, and they usually go when they want to buy a car and then spend three days driving it back. It took them eight months to make up their minds to buy the plane because the first question was, where was the money coming from. I asked them that question and they said "The Government" because they got used to things being provided for them. "Pigs," I told them, meaning "Pigs might fly". So then they suggested using the profit from the store, and I had to remind them that they had bought a Toyota land-cruiser out of that and that the only sensible thing to do was to raise the money from the communities who would be using it, by taking donations from each member. They didn't like that, but in the end they agreed and I think we did it by docking $A10 off each of them for many a month.'

Stability has given much to Blackstone. Murray has been there just as long. 'Yes I know we are unusual. White people are the heart of the trouble out here, you know. They come with the very best intentions but they can't stick the frustrations. They are not as adaptable as they think. They won't listen to those of us with experience; they come with grandiose plans, make misguided decisions, and when things fail they get downhearted. Then they go off on leave and simply don't come back, leaving the community without anyone for six months or so, which means that the next person has to start from scratch. I know that when Elaine and I went off on leave, for the first time, the community did not expect us to return and were surprised when we did.

'I'm worried now about staying too long and becoming the old man around here. Five years is enough, I think. And you mustn't be too impressed by what you see. It's all window-dressing. My methods are not necessarily the best, the community is much too dependent on me and I allowed this to happen to get things moving; but I know that if I left, things would crumble. And that's not right. Up the road at Wingelina it looks awful, but the guy up there has six people, six Aborigines running the place with him, and while this means they have not achieved so much because it is all so slow, he reckons that if he left, the community would struggle on.'

He was right about Wingelina. It did look a mess. I watched an old woman sitting in the dirt beside her 'home' made of tin stretched across two empty barrels, alternately blowing up a red balloon and letting it down and then doing the same with a blue balloon. At one point she got up and walked to the boot of a rusty old car, opened it and took out a can of soft drink. Everywhere dirty dogs were scratching themselves. I could see neither trees nor houses, let alone a school-room with a swimming pool. Indeed, Jack was there to discuss moving his storage tanks, which seemed for some reason to be too close to the site chosen for the school. When it came.

The Aboriginal playwright, Robert Merritt, who grew up on a mission station and in camps on the fringe of a New South Wales country town, has said: 'We've been on a merry-go-round for two hundred years. It is not possible to walk in a straight line, to be immediate masters of our destiny, after such an experience.' They needed time to find their feet, and now they need to be encouraged to stand on them, to pursue true self-determination. Some Australians are unwilling to offer genuine autonomy to Aborigines; they cannot bring themselves to believe that the Aborigine has the capacity, and they also fear a form of *apartheid* if Aborigines are allowed to return to their lands and run their own show and keep the white man out with fines if he enters uninvited. But in a land so vast, it does seem to be the answer.

Since the middle 1970s, a small but influential group of white people, calling themselves the Aboriginal Treaty Committee, has been working for a constitutional basis for a new black–white relationship. In 1979 they recommended that a formal treaty should be signed: a treaty that would 'recognize and restore Aboriginal land, compensate for land and life-styles lost, establish conditions for land use, protect Aboriginal civilization, give Aborigines control of their affairs, so that they may end the humiliation, recapture their dignity and embark on a future of mutual peace and friendship'.

They call the treaty *Makarrata*. It is an Aboriginal word for 'thigh', the fleshy area in which an aggrieved Aborigine spears the cause of his grievance. The latter, after expertly dodging the thrown spear, finally allows his accuser to dance close enough to him to permit the spearing. By so doing, he accepts the retribution. In this way, both parties look good and both keep their dignity intact. Somewhat loosely translated, it means 'the end of a dispute and the resumption of normal relations'. The basis for their treaty is simple: they state that Australia was occupied by Aborigines prior to 1788 and that there was a nation exercising sovereignty over the continent and that that nation was 'state-ful', that is, it had recognizable organs of government. Australia was therefore acquired by conquest and not by settlement, and the descendants of those conquered should now be compensated. They want Australians to admit that the first white settlers made a mistake in simply walking in and taking the land. The treaty is not merely to assuage hurt pride, however: it has practical value. The terms would establish once and for all the rights of the Aborigine; give him land, self-government, and money, not as charity to be fought over each year, but a percentage of the national budget, as a right. The committee would like to see the treaty signed in 1988. Otherwise, they say, there will be no cause in that year for the Aborigine to celebrate.

Neville Bonner made this point all too clearly. He was the first Aborigine to serve in the Senate, and in 1975 he urged the Senate to accept that the Aborigines had been wrongly dispossessed and that this fact deserved recognition and recompense. The Senate voted unanimously in support of his view.

I met Neville Bonner early one morning in Brisbane as he was about to catch a plane to Alice Springs. His wife had arranged the meeting and, as he wasn't too clear about the purpose of my book, he quizzed me about it and in particular about the timing of publication. By this stage in my journey I had been asked the question so often that I mumbled something, without thinking, about Australia approaching its two-hundredth birthday.

'Its what?' he said softly.

'... the two-hundredth anniversary of European settlement.'

'The *what?*' This time there was no mistaking the emphasis.

'The two-hundredth anniversary of the conquest of Australia by the British.'

He chided me, deservedly.

After Wingelina, Jack and I headed for Coober Pedy and then for Adelaide. Storms made it impossible for a light plane to land at Parafield, so we changed tack for Orroroo and landed in a paddock, scattering the sheep. The storm had redrawn the route of my return to Adelaide; it meant I could ride back by car with another Ampol executive who happened to be visiting Orroroo. This enabled me to drive through the Barossa Valley, through the district called Clare, to see the damage caused to the wine industry by the freak weather conditions. The drought had been bad enough; it had depleted the vineyards before the bush fires had frazzled the land and further lowered the output. And now the storm and the flash floods. The roads were still waterlogged and in places our progress was slow, slow enough to view the blackened land with increasing sadness. Burnt trees had been uprooted, and mud washed down by the floods had smothered the vines. The Adelaide *News* commented: 'This place is getting like Pharaoh's Egypt. Any day now I expect to hear that we have been smitten by a plague of locusts.'

The journey ended with two surprises. We arrived back in Adelaide in late afternoon and I decided, first, to collect my mail. Two minutes after I left the car, and just as I reached Rundle Mall, I stopped, rooted to the spot, dumbfounded by the sight of so many people so close to me, so brightly coloured, moving so purposefully, so fast. In ten days – in so short a time – I had grown accustomed to the space and the speed and the subdued colours of the Outback. I had forgotten the city. In Giles I had listened to Jane, Chris's wife, tell me how she loathed going into Alice; that she found it an unpleasant effort to be in so large a place. I had listened, and yet I had not understood. And now I understood as I faltered, transfixed, surprised by the distaste I felt as a small figure bumped into me and hurried on. Two small specks in this huge land – and still not enough room to avoid each other's paths. I shall not forget that moment, but at the time I could not dwell on it. I was anxious to collect my mail and to collect my luggage and move into Craig's house. Travelling like this, cut off from family and friends, it takes no more than a few hours to form new friendships, real enough, though transient.

I had promised myself at the beginning of my journey that I would follow new paths and make new plans as opportunities unfolded. I did not wish to drift completely from one chance conversation or unresearched idea to the next, but neither did I want my journey to be planned like a military operation, with no time for detours and no inclination to accept an unexpected invitation. I had promised myself that, if people invited me into their homes, I would respond with enthusiasm and not with hesitation born of suspicion and of the fear that such offers were not genuine but merely gestures. Some, of course, *are* merely gestures; some are meant at the tine but later evaporate amid a host of changed circumstances. Three times so far I'd heard the words: 'You must come and stay while you are in Sydney . . . Canberra . . . Adelaide . . . '; three times when I had sought to act upon the invitation I had met with 'Look, my marriage is going through a rough patch and it would not be a good idea to have you around' or 'My dear, I've got the dates muddled up and we are going to be away and I can't really ask the housekeeper to keep the house open for you' or 'Oh, what a boring clash, my wife's brother is about to arrive'.

With these three instances in mind, I had become a little wary, and I did hesitate when Craig said, as we neared Adelaide: 'I don't know why you are staying in a hotel, maybe you prefer it, but I have a spare room and you are most welcome to it.' Travelling like this, constantly and for a lengthy period of time, a hotel can offer much-needed solitude, time to think without a care for others – but not all the time. I reminded myself of my promise, and accepted Craig's offer with gratitude, and found myself in North Adelaide in a new town-house, accepted and welcomed by a lively group of men, younger than myself. Craig, when he wasn't working for Ampol, organizes a team of bouncers – guys who patrol clubs and rock-concerts, whose height and width and sense of presence keep gate-crashers and trouble at bay. His house was a meeting place for the group, and for others who fancied a beer. It always seemed to be full, and I much enjoyed being around, fitting in, tagging along, and clearing off when they wished to plan a hilarious and ambitious stag-night for one of their number. The storm which had caused Jack to land in a paddock, scattering the sheep, had yielded a delightful bonus.

CHAPTER 9

Festival City

Adelaide is different. South Australia is different. They know they are different and they are proud to be different and they make much of their difference. It's simple enough: Adelaide was never cursed with the custody of a single convict, nor did she grow up willy-nilly as a service centre for fortune-hunters. She was colonized by private enterprise, her creation carefully planned by an idealist who believed that Australia would never flourish while it was weighed down with felons and paupers, temporary officials often with little interest in the place, and self-seeking squatters with even less interest; and who had imaginative views on how he might redress the balance by creating a settlement of free, honest and committed men who would work to build a colony exemplary in every way. His name was Edward Gibbon Wakefield who – with the delightful irony that makes Australian history so colourful – developed his scheme while a convict, encased in Newgate Prison and charged with abduction.

Wakefield's plan (which has already been glimpsed in Chapter 4) hinged on selling land in small quantities and at a price high enough for those who bought it to settle it and work it to their own benefit and that of the colony. His aim was to attract the small capitalist, sober and industrious. He deplored the way in which land was either given away or sold cheaply in huge parcels, much of which then lay idle, untilled and untended. To provide the labour for the small landowners, it was decided that the money raised by selling the land would be used in part to fund the passages of young agricultural workers, sober and industrious, who would be content to be employees while they saved enough to buy their own acres. Healthy young artisans and tradesmen to service the needs of the growing community would also benefit from assisted passages. His idea was adopted in other colonies to boost their populations as transportation came to an end. But here in South Australia the scheme was to be attempted from scratch, untarnished by the past and endorsed by Wakefield's personal attention. The vision was grand; the venture was to be self-supporting and, thus freed from purse-string domination from London, this colony would speedily become self-governing.

To this end a company was formed selling land at £1 an acre (about a half-hectare), or in a package containing a city acre plus an 80-acre (32-hectare) country block for £81. Initially few shared Wakefield's enthusiasm and the enterprise was a struggle at the beginning; by and by, however, the first shipload of dreamers and radicals and men on the make sailed in 1836 to a place they called Adelaide, after King William's wife. Their hopes were high. Jeremy Bentham suggested the colony be called 'Felicitania'.

Their hopes soon faded. The history of those early years is one full of bickering and bitchery and tales of quarrelsome men fighting for supremacy. The idealistic scheme was flawed and fragile: flawed by the splitting of authority between a governor and a board of commissioners who were responsible for selling the land, spending the revenue and selecting the immigrants; and fragile because of the calibre of some of the men involved. Colonel William Light was the good news. As Surveyor General, he was responsible for choosing the site of Adelaide, for the planning of the city and for the surveying and division of the rural areas. His efforts were thwarted by a governor who by all accounts was a menace and whose opposition to Light's plans slowed things up to such an extent that immigrants were arriving before the place was ready for them. This mess resulted in a bankrupt colony within four years. The South Australia Company was disbanded, and the British Government took over the colony and ran it along with the others – a galling defeat. But by 1845 the colony was at least on a less shaky footing, which much energy devoted to wheat, wool, barley, fruit, wine, beef and lamb. For all the early mistakes, the chosen immigrants did conform to Wakefield's ideal: no idlers, no convicts, no military, no dissipated young gentlemen. The majority came from London and the Home Counties, very few from the North of England or from Ireland. The Scots were considered ideal: 'Good practical farmers who possess capital and families to assist them are, above all, the best qualified for this colony.' From the start, South Australians were snobbish towards the rest of Australia; they strove hard to do everything in a superior way. Their motivation came in part from their sense of difference, but mainly from their religion, for it was a fundamental part of Wakefield's plan to create a paradise for non-conformists, a haven for dissenters. The founders wanted no Anglican domination in Adelaide; they also wished to avoid 'Pope worshippers', mainly because they equated Catholics with Irish convicts. Both were accepted (the Anglicans tended to be Evangelicals, eager for reform) but both were always to be outnumbered by the combined non-conformists: Methodists, Congregationalists, Baptists and Presbyterians were to occupy positions of influence, and of the lot the Methodists had the greatest impact.

For all its lofty aims, drink turned out to be a major problem here too; this – not surprisingly – upset the Methodists who soon started a temperance movement. Alone they could do little, but, when joined by the Women's Christian Temperance Union, the face of Adelaide was to change. The women wanted the vote, not towards any liberationist ends, but as a weapon with which to combat drunkenness and gambling and sin of any kind. In 1894 the women of South Australia got the vote; from that moment and for many many years – indeed until the 1960s – Adelaide was draped in a dowdy Puritanical shroud. It is said that the seamy side remained, underground, while on the surface all was prim and pure. Maybe some sought back-street pleasures, but the majority seemed happy enough, creating a State which they could claim offered a better standard of living than elsewhere and, in the process, chalking up any number of 'firsts'.

By the turn of the century, as well as votes for women, South Australia had introduced the eight-hour day, workers' compensation, and industrial arbitration, and many more pace-setting reforms were to follow. As for a 'superior standard of living', even official Federal documents dare to claim that there are no slums in

Adelaide; that more people own their own homes; that there are more television sets and cars but less congestion, less pollution and a lower crime-rate. Such a list, aided no doubt by her sturdy origins, makes Adelaide a quietly confident city with a healthy self-esteem which in turn makes her people open and generous and easy-going and eager to please. High praise, I know, but this was my experience at all levels. Those from other States are often heard to mutter that 'Adelaide is up itself', a crude if picturesque way of declaring that the city has an unjustifiably high opinion of itself. My view is that, through a mixture of diligence and luck, the high opinion is justified.

The diligence of all those sober and industrious settlers was bound to throw up sober and industrious leaders, none more so than Sir Thomas Playford who was to lead the State for twenty-seven years from 1938 and during that time master-minded the introduction of manufacturing (mainly cars and other consumer goods) to ease the burden of wealth creation from the rural sector. And then came the luck: flush with affluence in the 1960s, the State became restless, bored with years of unbroken Conservative rule and bored with its drab image; right on cue came Don Dunstan to sweep away the dullness and the last vestiges of Puritanism and to liberate the Labor Party, not just in South Australia. Dunstan first took office in 1968; he quickly became tagged socialism's success story, which must have helped to prepare the rest of the nation for the Whitlam years. He was young, attractive, well educated and very unstuffy; he embraced a trendy life-style, which included growing herbs and vegetables and keeping chickens in his backyard. His clothes kept him in the headlines: he wore pink shorts to Parliament, and formal dress meant polo-necked sweaters and Nehru jackets. He kept the State centre-right on economics but veered centre-left on social reform and ensured that South Australia stayed ahead with progressive legislation: he legalized abortion ahead of other States, introduced comprehensive consumer protection laws, a state lottery and late closing for pubs (which for years had been forced to call last orders at six p.m.). He also loosened censorship and pronounced himself in favour of nudist beaches. Adelaide was no longer merely the City of Churches. Some considered him autocratic and self-opinionated, but to most he was a bright light and so popular that he managed to survive the 1975 landslide against Labor which marked the end of the Whitlam era. The light went out eventually; Dunstan was forced to resign through ill-health. He is now, somewhat surprisingly, head of tourism for the State of Victoria.

Even with Dunstan gone, his influence remained. The city would never again be described as dull – orderly, perhaps, the kind of town where everything has its place. The River Torrens marches through the centre, ensuring the continued separation of the residential north from the commercial south. The centre is corseted by a grid of streets crossing at right angles, containing a few modern frills like shopping malls and smart new hotels, the whole lot enfolded by parkland which forms a figure of eight around the city. Orderly, then, but never dull: no city where you can see cannabis growing in pots in gardens is likely to be dreary; no city where you can sit in a pub discussing the latest State proposal for the legalization of prostitution, brothels and massage parlours could ever be considered dowdy.

Luck remained, too: when the time came to start establishing high technology in Australia (albeit a little slowly and belatedly), Adelaide would claim a head start. The outskirts of the city already housed a huge electronic research establishment, the Defence Research Centre, which dates back to the 1950s when the empty interior of South Australia was used by the UK and by Australia as a rocket range and nuclear-bomb testing site. This acted as bait when other firms were invited to put down roots in the neighbouring Technology Park: the giants EMI–Thorn and Texas Instruments are there, as well as a host of smaller companies. Indeed, it is one of the smaller companies that generates most of the gossip – for it is here that the CSIRO (Commonwealth Scientific and Industrial Research Organization) finally came out of its ivory tower and into the market place. The division of Computing Science, world leaders in the design of silicon chips tailor-made for specific tasks, has allowed its staff to form a commercial company called Austek to develop and sell its software far and wide. It may sound small, but it is a large step linking the research community with industry.

Adelaide would like to be known as the capital of High-tech. She has always attracted epithets: City of Churches, City of parks and gardens, and 'High-tech' has an advanced ring to it; but it will be a while before it supplants the tag the city has worked for decades to achieve: 'Festival City'. I'll return to Festival City when I've added a tag of my own: City of Wine. The hills around Adelaide and the land within a couple of hours' drive of Adelaide produce some sixty per cent of Australia's wine, from the very finest to vast quantities of cask wine, plonk for picnics and barbecues and beach parties. The cask wine comes from the Riverland – the land beside the Murray River – from the towns of Renmark, Berri and Loxton, the site of Australia's first irrigation scheme. These are pretty towns, made so by the Murray River and by the lushness that is the hallmark of irrigation. They are much visited by those attracted to the river and the paddle-steamers, which may no longer be an essential form of transport but are retained, along with the houseboats, to provide peaceful holidays and a taste of the past. The towns, too, are much admired for their strong community spirit: hotels are owned by the community and the profits used to improve the towns' amenities, and the distilleries are owned cooperatively by the grape-growers.

In the first place the Riverland was devoted to the growing of citrus and stone fruits and a distillery was built merely to cope with the surplus grapes not needed as dried fruit; but in time brandy-making grew in importance and led to the making of fortified wines and thence to table wines. Few people realize the importance of the Riverland as a wine-producing area, because for years the crush was sold in bulk to other wine makers to blend and bottle and, as there is no labelling requirement to list the origin of the grapes, the Riverland remained anonymous and ignored. This is no longer the case. The distilleries of Berri and Renmark merged in 1982 to form Consolidated Cooperative Wineries, producing an annual crush of more than 50,000 tonnes from some 1,000 grower members. The merger has produced a new force in the Australian wine industry, dedicated to upgrading grape varieties and to marketing at least half the crush under its own labels. The move reflects important changes: serious wine lovers no longer ignore grapes from irrigated areas; and wine in a bag or cask is going upmarket with bottle quality being sold in two-litre casks. In fact, eighty per cent of Australian wine is sold this way and cheap plonk, particularly the whites, sold in four-litre casks, easily outshines the cheap wines of Europe, at a price that is little more than the cost of mineral water. Until the early 1980s there was no tax on wine in Australia; it now stands at ten per cent, adding a handful of cents to a cask and as much as $A1.50 to the best of bottles, a difference which annoys the top end of the market.

Experts argue that with eighty per cent of the market given to cask wine, the remainder is divided into fifteen per cent 'average' bottles and five per cent top quality. The top quality wines are quite remarkable. The Adelaide hills have produced what is indisputably Australia's finest red wine: Penfold's Grange Hermitage. The first vintage of Grange was in 1952. It is made from shiraz grapes (the Australian synonym for 'shiraz' is 'hermitage') which is matured in small, new American oak casks, and further matured in the bottle and never released under five years old.

Close to Grange, in the cool Mount Lofty Ranges, at Petaluma the white wines reign supreme. Bollinger, one of Champagne's most respected firms, has been so impressed by the products of this winery that it is investing in Petaluma and helping Brian Croser, said to be the best young winemaker in Australia, to produce a premium South Australian sparkling wine from Champagne grapes and by the painstaking Champagne method. This investment is the greatest compliment the French could pay the Australian wine industry and underlines the advances made in Australian wine in the last thirty years. Len Evans, the country's best-known and most ebullient wine expert, is fond of recalling his early days in Australia, when he arrived from Wales in 1955 and asked for a glass of white wine in a Queensland hotel. 'What are you,' the hotel-keeper asked him, 'some kind of poof?' In Darwin he fared no better when asking for wine with his dinner and being told: 'Look 'ere, the dining-room's for eating and the bar's for drinking.' Evans claims that since then Australia has seen the most extraordinary change in eating and drinking habits of any country in history. This may be an exaggeration, but it is true that from the mid-1950s to the mid-1980s Australia has gone from being a non-wine-drinking country to one where the average consumption is now more than two cases a head per year. And the industry has gone from producing brandy distilled from left-over dried fruit to wines with reputations the world over.

The same thirty years saw the rise of the Adelaide Festival from a local hop to a date in the international artistic calendar. For three weeks during March in each even-numbered year, Adelaide takes the centre stage in Australia's cultural life; writers and musicians, actors and dancers, playwrights and composers from other States and from overseas converge on the city to create an international event of which any country would be proud. The city fathers began dreaming of such a festival in 1954. At first they aimed for a single concert hall, but the scheme grew when Don Dunstan became head of the State and was willing to invest heavily in the arts; and so in 1972 when Sydney opened her Opera House, Adelaide opened her concert hall, and then followed it two years later with a further complex of three theatres. The Festival began in 1960 in a small way and grew in step with the buildings. There have been conflicts and conquests and controversy and combat – but when the day comes the city unites behind its festival and no seat is left unsold. Festival directors – the city likes to have a different one each time – enjoy the luxury of knowing that for three weeks Adelaide will happily sample anything, and this tempts them to toy with the avant garde as well as with the trusted classic, and to encourage the home-grown as well as to fly in international stars.

For the rest of the time it is a different story. Many people described Adelaide to me as an event-orientated society; its citizens see culture as a vast social banquet at which they can feast every two years and then fast in between. Culture is not seen as an intellectual stimulant and an integral part of life. The theatres on the banks of the Torrens struggle outside the three weeks of the Festival, and managers tend to settle for an anodyne string of imported musicals from London and New York in order to see their books balance. But then most people in most countries see cultural activities as pleasant additions to life rather than as essentials; and most governments have to battle with the problem of allocating scarce resources to encouraging artistic endeavour, only to wince as they watch a tiny minority of the population bother to embrace the product. Is Adelaide any different? Is Australia any different? Does she deserve her reputation as a philistine nation? The short answer is: no – she does not. But she got saddled with the reputation early on, and lack of self-confidence has not only prevented her from ridding herself of the image but has in some perverse way encouraged her to cling to it.

The earliest reference to an uncultivated society that I've come across appeared in one of the first novels to be published in Australia – in 1848. Thomas McCombie's *Arabin*, which chronicles the life and times of a doctor who emigrates to New South Wales, describes the Australian-born as 'matter-of-fact men with very few elements of originality in their composition and ignorant of the pleasures to be derived from the arts ... the majority of the colonists have little taste for that which the more refined and polished long for, because their mode of life is rough and their education but limited'.

What else would be expected? If you dump boatloads of illiterate convicts and poor people on the shores of an empty continent, is it so surprising that all their energy is given over to building a community and that in their free time they prefer to frolic in the sun rather than bother to learn to read and write, let alone yearn for the arts? Education was not made compulsory until 1872 in Victoria and until 1880 in New South Wales; before that much of the early writing came from the pens of the newly arrived. McCombie is now forgotten, but Marcus Clarke is not: his account of convict brutality in *For the Term of his Natural Life* is a classic. However, the emergence of the first generation to receive schooling coincided with the moment when the Australian-born outnumbered the overseas-born for the first time, thus providing men of talent with a potential audience; the 1890s saw a flowering of ballads and poetry, of short stories and novels. In these years Australia was full of self-confidence: gold had made her rich, her citizens had the highest standards of living in the world and the British fell over themselves to invest in the country. The creative work best in a confident climate. Miles Franklin's *My Brilliant Career* dates from this period and is now well known outside Australia, having been immortalized on film, but the best-known novel inside Australia is undoubtedly Joseph Furphy's *Such is Life*, an admirable portrayal of the on-going battle for supremacy between the rough and resourceful Aussie and the superior and supercilious English gentleman. It was, however, the ballad writers who ruled. The ballad has always flourished in societies in which few people depend on the written and printed word: the ballad poem telling a straightforward story in rhyming, easily memorized, short stanzas travels happily from mouth to mouth. Banjo Paterson has an assured place in Australian life for it was he who wrote 'Waltzing Matilda', the unofficial national anthem, and 'The Man from Snowy River' (also made into a film which received some overseas recognition).

Banjo Paterson loved the bush. His rival as a ballad poet, Henry Lawson, did not. Their verse 'debate' amused the readers of the *Bulletin* where much of their work was published. And it was Lawson who bridled most at the unfair competition indigenous writers had to face from London. In the preface to his first book of short stories, in 1894, Lawson wrote: 'This is an attempt to publish in Australia a collection of sketches and stories at a time when everything Australian, in the shape of a book, must bear the imprint of a London publishing house before our critics will condescend to notice it and before the public will think it worth its while to buy.' He was right, and five years later when the situation had not improved Lawson declared that the best Australian writers and artists were being driven overseas by lack of recognition at home, and then he set sail for London himself. What could he hope to achieve there? The competition was ludicrous: his contemporaries included George Bernard Shaw, H. G. Wells, Thomas Hardy, Joseph Conrad, Rudyard Kipling and Henry James.

And so the die was cast. There is not and never has been a serious shortage of artistic talent in Australia, but from the beginning when it sought to find an audience it was swamped by competition. A nation with more secure origins and higher self-esteem might have fought this encroachment, but there was something timid in the Australian character which allowed men to wilt before the intimidating mass of Anglo-Saxon achievement. The self-confidence of the 1890s was too new, too shallow to withstand the depression which followed, dashing hopes in many spheres; instead of fighting, the embryonic artistic community was battered by competition and allowed constant unfair comparisons to sap its will. From this it was one short step to accepting that the only worthwhile achievements came from overseas, and against these the artistic community did not measure too well. Of course it did not. The comparison was foolish and a better one, if the comparisons must be made, would have been to look to the achievements of the first hundred years of America: this would have been heartening. This habit of making comparisons has continued to dog Australian endeavour. I have seen contemporary critics persist in lining up Henry Lawson against his overseas contemporaries and then condemning him as a writer of jingoistic clap-trap, a scribbler of impossible plays, lead-booted short stories, dreary doggerel and prose 'that was as lumpy as porridge, raw as fog, indigestible as gum leaves, trite as respectability, dull as Ockerism'.

I'm sure I shall be forgiven for claiming that after the splurge of the 1890s no novels of any worth appeared for the next fifty years. There are exceptions – mostly from writers who chose to live abroad. Henry Handel (Ethel) Richardson wrote *The Getting of Wisdom* and the trilogy *The Fortunes of Richard Mahony* during the first three decades of this century, but she had left Melbourne for Germany and London. And Christina Stead wrote *Seven Poor Men of Sydney* (1935), *The Man Who Loved Children* (1940) and *For Love Alone* (1944), but she had quit Sydney for Europe and America.

Poetry tried hardest of all to stay alive and to break free from servile imitations of European forms. In 1938, in Adelaide, the Jindyworobak movement aimed to rid their art form of alien influences and turned instead to Australian culture, to the Aborigines and Dreamtime for their inspiration. The Jindyworobak is an Aboriginal word meaning 'to annex' or 'to join', and the movement was founded by Rex Ingamells who was determined that Adelaide could and would offer an alternative to the overseas-inspired literature of Sydney and Melbourne. The movement lasted ten years and did not produce great poetry; instead it produced great squabbles. Other poets described the Jindy movement as the Boy Scout school of poetry: 'They have the same boyish enthusiasm for playing at being primitive; they lay the same stress on the moral values of bushcraft and open air, and they promise to be pure Australian in word and thought and deed.'

The Jindys and other schools of modern poetry were to be dragged down in the end by an elaborate literary hoax which caught the popular imagination in 1944 and is therefore worthy of attention. Two Sydney poets, James McAuley and Harold Stewart, who clung to more traditional verse forms, set out to prove that the experimentalists wrote gibberish. To this end they wrote a stream of nonsense poems without meaning and heavily reliant on random quotes; they then invented an author called Ern Malley who had been a tram driver in Melbourne and who was by now dead. His imaginary sister sent the poems to *The Angry Penguins*, an experimental magazine edited by Max Harris, and he proudly published them in a special issue with a grand introduction and a note of sadness about the loss of such talent.

At least such antics kept the literary scene lively until the 1950s when Australia, economically flourishing once more and rapidly turning away from Britain, was ready for some self-examination. It was at this moment that the critic A. A. Phillips invented the phrase 'the cultural cringe' to try to jolt his country out of its complacent acceptance of English domination. 'The core of the difficulty', he announced loudly, 'is the fact that at the back of the Australian mind, there sits a minatory Englishman.' And Australia was ready to listen. Patrick White had already returned to his homeland, looked around, found it wanting, but – instead of fleeing again – uttered a few harsh words and then settled down to help put the situation right.

In all directions stretched the great Australian Emptiness, in which the mind is the least of possessions, in which the rich man is the important man, in which the schoolmaster and the journalist rule what intellectual roost there is, in which beautiful youths and girls stare at life through blind blue eyes, in which food means cake and steak, muscles prevail and the march of material ugliness does not raise a quiver from the average nerves.

It was the exaltation of the 'average' that made me panic most and in this frame of mind, I began to conceive another novel ...

While Patrick White laboured to bring forth *The Tree of Man* in 1956 and *Voss* a year later, a campaign started to set up a chair of Australian literature at Sydney University. Such a suggestion resulted in an interesting debate about whether there was any literature worth studying; the answer came back with the burgeoning of a host of literary journals, *Quadrant*, *Westerly*, *Hemisphere*, *Nation*, *Australian Book Review*, two literary histories, and finally in 1961 that chair of Australian literature. Publishers began actively seeking new Australian writers and newspapers began reviewing their works. The reading public were the last in the cycle to change their habits. A survey in 1980 showed that Australians were still ignorant of their own writers, but there are now signs that they are finally beginning to take some pride in Australian writing.

The cringe has not been conquered, but at least it has been reduced to a twitch. I recall a distinguished Australian publisher and writer telling me that Australian literature was second-rate; I suggested that this was nonsense and hoped that he was offering the view as a pre-emptive strike: *he* feared that *I* might think that Australian writing was second-rate and therefore offered the view rather than receive the criticism. The vulnerable often resort to such contortions. For no one who has read Australian literature would wish to hang insulting labels around its neck. Patrick White, having won the Nobel Prize in 1973, still leads the field; and there are at least six other writers who would sit comfortably on anyone's list of top creative talent: Thomas Keneally, David Malouf, David Ireland, Frank Moorhouse, Peter Carey and Murray Bail. To this I would add at least another fifteen authors whose works give pleasure and further cause for national pride (see Bibliography).

As literature suffered, so did the performing arts. I have already noted J. C. Williamson's effect on lyric theatre; his hand on drama was just as deadly. When Williamson arrived, Australia did have its own actor-managers and actor-authors in George Darrell, Alfred Dampier and Bland Holt. Darrell's name survives. His plays were – and still are – referred to by Australian critics as 'bellowdrama', and his most successful work, *The Sunny South*, was dismissed by the *Bulletin* when it was performed in Sydney in 1883 as 'a headache in five acts'. Critics, particularly those of the *Bulletin*, were supposed to be championing indigenous works, but in fact they were fond of knocking and of noting 'with regret for the lovers of the artistic' whenever such works displaced Shakespeare from a theatre. I have no idea of the worth of these early dramatists, although Darrell's *The Sunny South* was revived as recently as 1980; whatever their status, they did not have the strength to survive once 'the firm' became entrenched. They disappeared and Australian drama seemed doomed; amateur companies performed the works of Ibsen, Shaw, Bennett and Maeterlinck; audiences flocked to Sarah Bernhardt and Marie Lloyd, and anything that managed to drop from indigenous pens was dismissed as trivial and imitative.

A few stalwarts struggled on. At the turn of the century, Melbourne playwright Louis Esson went to Dublin and discovered the Abbey Theatre where a band of writers and players were determined to put Irish life on the stage. He talked to Yeats and Synge and they told him to go back to Australia and create an Abbey Theatre there. No aping. No imitation. 'Keep within your own borders. The Greeks kept within their own borders and they were the greatest artists the world has ever known.' Yeats was most encouraging: 'You ought to have plenty of material for drama in Australia: all those Outback stations with shepherds going mad in lonely huts.' Esson took the advice, returned to Australia, turned his back on the cities and towns and looked to the bush and the past for inspiration. It didn't work. He and other playwrights wanted realism in three acts with a curtain between each. And how do you do that with the bush? Their characters sat around and nagged about the drought, the floods and the fires, and when the time came for something to happen – all drama derives from conflict – they had nothing to punch but each other. Unlike the Irish, they did not have political struggles to focus their dramatic intensity. Only one play survives, Esson's *The Drovers*, written in 1919. Imports reigned; imperialism flourished. Even as late as 1949, Tyrone Guthrie was recommending to the Australian government that the only way to develop the theatre was to send promising actors to Britain to be trained and then to be transported back to Australia as cultural missionaries

As with literature, drama got the break it longed for at the end of 1955 with the discovery of Ray Lawler's *Summer of the Seventeenth Doll*; at last a playwright had abandoned the bush and wandered into the city with characters who could talk to the audience in the language of the suburbs. The play came from Melbourne University's Union Theatre (founded in 1953) which was eventually to become the Melbourne Theatre Company and whose founder director, John Sumner, was to do more than most to create Melbourne's taste in theatre by constantly commissioning work from local playwrights. *Doll* (as the play is known) caught the public's imagination and for a while they could not get enough of things Australian; unfortunately, however, appetites were soon sated: there was not enough that was good. Audiences came, saw and went away with their prejudices confirmed: they didn't care for things Australian. Only two other plays survive this period, Alan Seymour's *One Day of the Year* and Richard Beynon's *The Shifting Heart*. The timid rabbit of a theatrical revival scurried away, leaving theatre managements once again looking to London. Some had sufficient energy to rail: against '*untalented* English homosexuals' who dominated the scene again; against actors: 'If one cannot protest against the employment of the Pommy poofter instead of the Aussie poofter, one can record dismay at the employment of fifth-raters who get nowhere near even spear holding in Drury Lane, yet who are invited to pit their puniness of vision, and a cock-eyed theatrical sense, against the perceptions of the highly sensitized Australian public.' They railed against directors 'who were not good enough to make the grade in England and who came to act boss-cocky to those Australians not good enough to make the grade in England'. You can hear the pain.

But nothing happened. Not until Betty Burtsall returned to Australia determined to re-create the energy she had seen off-off-Broadway. *La Mama* liberated Australian drama. Writers finally kicked their addiction to naturalism and Jack Hibberd, Barry Oakley, John Romeril, David Williamson, Alexander Buzo and Dorothy Hewett turned their attention to local plays and local language. The result has been the development of intensely colloquial scripts: vulgar, vital, vivid and looking at the life-styles and preoccupations of Australian life. Such plays travel badly; they need a kind of shorthand. David Williamson is the exception: *The Club, Don's Party, The Perfectionist* are all well established. Perhaps middle-class manners and mores are readily understood by the middle class anywhere; they have sufficient homogeneity.

The one-man show has also emerged as a peculiarly Australian form. Steve Spears' *The Elocution of Benjamin Franklin,* a one-man monument to pederasty, is internationally acclaimed; Jack Hibberd's *A Stretch of the Imagination,* a one-man monument to isolation, disillusion and self-destruction, hogs the home scene; Robyn Archer has cornered the feminist market with *A Star is Torn*; and then there is Max Gillies whose speciality is political satire. His show *A Night with the Right* hissed at Australia under Malcolm Fraser, and when Bob Hawke won the election he quickly revised his script into *A Night of National Reconciliation* and found he had an exhausting mini-*Mousetrap* on his hands. And I suppose I ought to mention Barry Humphries. No other country can boast a man like Humphries who, as Les Patterson, cultural attaché, or dressed as the woman, Edna Everidge, makes a fortune slagging off his country. 'I let no opportunity pass when I can portray my people as oafish tosspots, sentimental, inarticulate boors, slobbering, flatulent, flag-waving blatherskites.' I can only assume that this is another example of the pre-emptive strike: while Humphries is so successful sending up his own country, it denies outsiders the opportunity. But his image of Australians is behind the times – the sketches were first conceived in the mid-1950s – and yet in a perverse way Australians are proud of this man and seem prepared to overlook the fact that, in some ways, he does them a great disservice.

On the wider front it is true to say that the 1970s' bubble of creative energy has burst, causing slight fears for the future. Will the rabbit run away again? Stephen Sewell is probably the most admired of the 1980s' playwrights with *Welcome the Bright World* and *The Blind Giant is Dancing,* and there are signs that this time drama should survive the doldrums. The Australian Writers' Theatre has taken a Yeatsian stance in the western suburbs of Sydney work-shopping new plays with the help of professional actors and directors, and

Melbourne has a similar movement; but there is still too great a tendency to lean on London.

The fortunes of drama have tended to wax and wane for a number of interesting reasons, not least because the theatre is seen as the underdog and therefore treated as the underdog, and this status is clearly reflected in the standard of drama criticism, which is of much lower quality than in any other area of the performing arts. The development of good drama needs the beady-eyed attention of decent critics. Few newspapers have full-time critics, and no newspaper has a critic who travels from city to city to gain an over-view of drama development. For the most part the drama critic is offered far less space for his reviews and his few hundred words consist of a résumé of the story and a few under-explored comments and no serious attempt at analysis. It wasn't always so: the diminution of the status of the critic and the quality of criticism is often blamed on the rise of those theatrical public-relations persons who encourage editors to devote precious newspaper inches to interviews rather than to criticism. With drama unsupported in this way, talented dramatists are tempted away to more buoyant and more lucrative areas. A while ago, with the expansion of commercial television in the 1960s, John Romeril, one of the more political of playwrights, argued that: 'at any one time, well over three-fifths of the money, three-fifths of the performers, writers, musicians, cameramen, dancers and lighting technicians, are making advertisements'. More recently, Jack Hibberd saw the enemy as the insidious attractions of the synthetic media – television and the cinema. And there is no denying this.

In the beginning, the Australian Broadcasting Commission (as it then was) was happy to fill most of its air-time with BBC buy-ins, and the commercial channels were happy to fill their air-time with imported American products; but recent years have seen much indigenous programme-making, with plays carved from Australian literature and documentaries shaped from Australia's past, all of which demand the attention of talented writers, directors and actors. The latest fad for docu-drama and mini-series illustrates this to perfection. It started in 1983 with *The Dismissal*, a six-hour portrayal of the events surrounding the sacking in 1975 of Gough Whitlam's

Government by the Governor-General, Sir John Kerr; it continued with a ten-hour reconstruction of the 1932–3 'Bodyline' test match series; *Waterfront*, a six-hour dramatization of the dockland strike of 1928; *Eureka Stockade*, an equally lengthy look at the miners' uprising of 1854; and *The True Believers*, a dramatic reconstruction of the decline and fall and eventual split of the Federal Labor Party, beginning in 1945 with the election of Labor's Ben Chifley and ending in 1949 with the election that cast the Labor party into opposition for twenty years. All these programmes ooze commitment and passion and professionalism and prove that it isn't only the British who can turn history into art. But television's gain has been drama's loss, for the skills involved are interchangeable and the lure of large budgets, excellent viewing figures, plus overseas sales, has left the theatre unable to compete.

Television is not the only competitor for the same theatrical talent. There is the cinema whose increasing international prestige teases the most devoted from the boards and into the studios. The success of the Australian film has prompted many to ask: how come? The answer is, at least in part, that the Australians are more comfortable when they can cling to the life-raft of the *visual* as a prop for the word. In the theatre this is not possible; dialogue stands exposed, and indeed scripts are often the weakest part of a film (any producer will readily admit that the screenplay causes more than its share of problems).

The Australians began making films long before the current spate of successes; indeed, the country lays claim to having made the world's first full-length feature film in 1906 (its subject was the story of the Ned Kelly gang). But Hollywood killed the early film industry: by 1925, five years before 'talkies', Australia was importing ninety per cent of her silent films from America – not because they were better, but because they were cheaper. This not only deprived Australian film producers of money to make films; even if they managed to overcome this hurdle, they were denied a screening by distributors locked into American block-booking systems. The public gobbled up the American products. Not only was Australia, for five years in the 1920s, America's biggest buyer, but it also established world records in audience size and long runs. Talented men were left making newsreels.

The film industry was not born again until government subsidy of the arts as a whole became fashionable and, as a result, the Australian Council for the Arts was set up in 1968. This body gives advice to the government and also distributes government funds. By the mid-1970s the Australian Film Commission had been formed along with the Australian Film and Television School and every State followed the government's lead and set up a film investment corporation; the government also introduced generous tax incentive schemes for private investors. The figures tell the story. In the decade 1960–70, 13 films were made; in the 1970s, 120 films were made. Heady times – but serious film-makers also acknowledge that it was a silly business, too. Wealthy doctors and dentists looking for a respectable tax loss encouraged much rubbish to be made; some of it was never released. The world saw the best and was saved from having to watch the disasters. Such films as Fred Schepisi's *The Chant of Jimmy Blacksmith*, Bruce Beresford's *Breaker Morant*, Gillian Armstrong's *My Brilliant Career*, Peter Weir's *Picnic at Hanging Rock* and *Gallipoli*, Phil Noyce's *Newsfront* showed the world that there was more to the Australian film than Errol Flynn and Peter Finch.

The mood now is one of uncertainty, with film-makers hoping that the boom won't be followed by bust. Money is tighter although tax-incentives, changed somewhat, remain; new productions average around twelve a year. On the whole – and with the notable exception of the *Mad Max* sagas – the products remain distinctively Australian and wholesome, untarnished by the coating of sex and violence of American film-makers. On the whole the talented have not been tempted to Hollywood, at least not to stay; they may go for one film and then return. This also applies generally to other areas of the arts: people no longer feel that they must work abroad to prove themselves; they are content to capture the home market and, if needs be, remain unknown abroad. Equally, Australian audiences no longer hang back, reserving their seal of approval for those who have earned their reputations elsewhere.

As they sat dreaming of their concert hall, the city fathers in

Adelaide in 1954 had the right mood for the right moment for, if I had to pick out any one year to mark a significant changing point in cultural attitudes, it would be 1954: that is when the thinking and the talking started. Since then much has happened, and since then Australians have travelled greatly and come to realize that they are not so badly off, not so artistically inadequate; they have no need to feel inferior, no need at all – particularly if they can resist the temptation to compare themselves to London and New York.

I have every sympathy with Australia's turn-of-the-century plight: the swamping that induced a fifty-year sleep. But that is over; there will be little sympathy and no excuse if Australia continues to lean too heavily on outsiders to fill either their bookcases, their theatres or their top posts. I recall my bewilderment when it was announced that two senior positions at the Australian Broadcasting Corporation (Managing Director and Head of Television) had been awarded to Englishmen. I also recall my amusement on hearing that passed-over executives would rush home in the evening to play a chorus or two of 'Waltzing Matilda' to exorcize their irritation at working for Poms when they considered they could do the job themselves! The decisions clearly showed that emerging cultural confidence is inclined to waver. At least the newspapers had the courage to denounce the situation: once upon a time such appointments would have been taken for granted.

I hope this hiccup is the cringe having a final fling, for it goes against everything that I had learnt in numerous conversations with authors and publishers; with playwrights and theatre directors; with film-makers and music-makers; with directors of galleries and opera houses and community arts centres. Hours of stimulating conversation may have shown doubts and hesitancy, but all revealed a genuine desire to balance the need for Australia to maintain her cultural links overseas and to encourage the best to visit Australia with the need to offer solid commitment to indigenous talent.

CHAPTER 10

Silver City

I almost overlooked Broken Hill. Most people do. When the media discuss Broken Hill, which is fairly often, they are referring to a company of that name, a company which by any criteria – sales, assets, profits or size of work-force – can claim to be Australia's largest public company. The Big Australian, as it is known, is a broadly based natural resources group with interests in iron ore, steel, oil, gas, gold, copper, aluminium, manganese and other minerals, and with activities throughout Australia and overseas.

It is of course named after a place called Broken Hill where one September morning in 1883, Charles Rasp, a German-born boundary rider from a nearby sheep station, went clambering about the jagged, humpbacked broken hills and found what he thought was tin. Returning to his station he persuaded six other men to put up money for mining leases and within two years had formed a company called Broken Hill Proprietary (BHP) which within a year had stock valued at £1.5 million. Rasp had not found tin; he had discovered a silver–lead–zinc lode so massive that it triggered the transformation of Australia from a pastoral to an industrial nation. Needless to say, Rasp and his six men became among the richest in Australia; the company performed handsomely for its shareholders, mainly because those sheep people who knew nothing about metals had the sense to hire an American mine manager at the huge salary of £4,000 a year; in its heyday the mine employed some 2,000 men underground, hacking away at ore so rich it was all a strong man could do to lift a football-size chunk, or so they say. BHP is no longer in Broken Hill. By 1939 it had exploited the best of its lode and moved off into iron ore. The divorce is sour: outside the city, the company is talked of with pride and the place with pain; inside the city, the place is talked of with pride and the company with pain.

Broken Hill is in the far west of New South Wales, 750 miles (1,200 kilometres) from Sydney – too far away to be of much interest, especially in the early days when a visit involved a trip by sea to Adelaide and then two days overland. Broken Hill is only a few miles from the South Australian border and only 300 miles (480 kilometres) from Adelaide, and is therefore thoroughly orientated towards South Australia. Adelaide provided many of the first shareholders and many of the first workers, so much so that by 1897 Broken Hill had twenty-seven churches, all but nine of them Methodist, and forty-seven hotels and plenty of hangovers.

Even so, economic benefits and relative proximity have not produced a rosy view of the place. The files on Broken Hill in the library of the Adelaide *Advertiser* revealed an intriguing image: the place has a problem. Somewhat predictably after 100 years, the mine managers are warning that the end is in sight; that unless a new discovery is made there will be nothing left to dig by the end of the century. The miners stubbornly refuse to believe such a forecast; they have heard it all before, it is the kind of stuff companies put out to stop unions making big claims. However, the soft small voice of common sense has made them realize that 100 years is not a bad life for a mining town and perhaps they ought to try and attract secondary industry – just in case. But no one seems that eager to help the town of 25,000 people, the town that created so much wealth for the country. It seems to be a place to be avoided. One report suggested that if you lived there you had to obey the orders of the Kremlin, that individual rights were a joke and the town a disgrace to Australia. Alan Whicker, a BBC commentator, had also condemned the place and called it 'The Walled City'.

Reading this, I felt compelled to hop on the next plane. These days it is possible, but tiring and tedious, to drive along a bitumen road, and I took it for granted that such a city would have enough prestige and traffic to warrant regular flights. There is one a day.

One minute before departure, a girl marched the flight on to the tarmac of Adelaide International Airport and, pointing to an eight-seater, cried, 'All aboard.'

'No,' countered the pilot and, looking the six of us up and down, distributed the seats according to our weight. On really hot days the planes dare not fly full. The Outback *is* the Outback.

One and a half hours later, green dots appeared amid the miles of wasteland, green dots denoting parks and sports grounds sprouting with the help of water from a dam on the Darling. The descent was not spectacular, not nearly as pleasing as the view of Alice; slag heaps and the scars of open-cast mining do not make a pretty picture. The airport was small enough for me to take in everything at one glance, and my next glance sought a taxi; there were no taxis. The man behind the Avis sign had a telephone on his desk and I asked if I might use it to phone for a taxi and he said yes, but then added that he was about to return to town and would take me. The Walled City was friendly.

The ride into town was short, along a straight road at the top of which stood a head frame, the top-knot of a mine shaft, and down streets called Chloride, Oxide, Cobalt and Argent. The place seemed awash with clubs: the Musicians' Club, the Sturt Club, the R S L Clubs, the Social Democratic Club, the Alma Sporting Club, but their number was seriously rivalled by art galleries – I'm sure I counted twelve. Broken Hill is the home of the bush-painter; the home of the artist who paints the Outback at a price people can afford and in a way which may not win prizes but which ensures sales. There were also several swish modern buildings that would not look out of place in Canberra and which competed for pride of place with the ornate offering of the late-Victorian Town Hall and the verandahed splendour, also Victorian, of the Court House and the Post Office. The city under sentence looked remarkably assured, and within an hour I was to discover that it also sounded assured.

The Royal Exchange Hotel does not have telephones in the rooms and all calls have to be handled by the reception desk, so after I had contacted several mine managers and the Mayor, Rex became curious and wanted to know why I was there. He used to run the Commonwealth Bank before he was transferred to Sydney and was back on holiday and helping out his friend, Dennis. I *had* to meet Dennis, he said, and Keith who runs the TV shop and Ray who runs the Sturt Club. They'd all tell me that Broken Hill was a special place full of special people and much misunderstood by outsiders. And so they did. Utopia, Keith called it. Community pride was overwhelming. The mine managers were tolerant of the town's blinkered view that there would be no end, that something would turn up; that a new ore body would be found or new technology would make it worth pursuing low-grade stuff. School teachers were tolerant of the fact that kids insisted on leaving school at sixteen, even though there were no jobs. There was no trouble, either; the unemployed played netball and basketball rather than indulging in petty crime.

Broken Hill's problems, they said, were of others' making, either through greed or ignorance. For 100 years the town had been milked by the Federal Government's tax demands and the State Government's royalty requests; it was about time, they chorused, that those bullies gave something back. The Federal Government should provide an airport where decent-sized planes could land, and the State Government should forgo royalties to encourage companies to undertake further exploration. This town *works*, they insisted; it has a system that works; it has stability. If only outsiders appreciated this, then they would rush to start new industries. But they don't.

They don't because of the town's image. Broken Hill is a Union Town, a town run by the unions. This either puzzles or petrifies outsiders. It's why they stay away. Inside the town, people understand the system; it does not threaten them; they are fully aware of the advantages; they appreciate what the Barrier Industrial Council – the parliament of trade unions – has done for the town. And they are proud of a system which enables the entire work-force to negotiate an agreement every three years. There may well be strikes during these negotiations, but once settlement is reached there is peace and stability. Inside the city, people are at a loss to understand the fears and negative views of outsiders.

The Barrier Industrial Council came into being in 1923 after an appalling strike which lasted eighteen months. It was a far-sighted plan by Andrew Fairweather, a mine superintendent, to bring the men and the mines together, not merely to make music over wages and working conditions, but to work for much-needed improvements in the town which until then had been a shabby shanty with a short-stay work-force: men came, set on saving a certain sum of money and then leaving. Fairweather wanted improved hospital and medical services, welfare schemes, housing loans and support for cultural, educational and sporting facilities. He was *years* ahead of his time and he had to wait patiently for the mining companies to catch up with his thinking. By 1937 he was President of the Mine Managers Association and in a position to nudge his vision into place. Alongside him, Paddy O'Neill, the first President of the Barrier Industrial Council (BIC), fought with the weight of union might to transform Broken Hill.

Today half the town's work-force of 6,000 is employed in the mines, and the other half in areas servicing the mines and the miners. That makes eleven unions, all of which are affiliated to BIC; membership of a union is compulsory; Broken Hill is a closed shop. The rules say that youngsters entering the mines must be born in the town or have lived there for at least eight years; skilled workers from outside can only be hired if it can be proved that no resident can do the job. There are rules to say how, once employed, these men must behave towards each other (but more of that later); married women may work, but must give way to single women if there is a job shortage. There is one newspaper in the town, the *Barrier Daily Truth*. It is owned by the BIC and funded by compulsory union levy. It is delivered to the door each morning – and if there are five union members inside then there are five *Truths* on the mat.

Once there were two papers; the Murdoch family owned the *Barrier Miner*. They tried to buy the *Truth*, but it was not to be. The *Barrier Miner* folded; its building is now a car park. One day each quarter, all workers must wear their union badges to prove that they have paid their subscriptions; should a worker show up without a badge the rest of the work-force refuse to work with him (or her).

To a stranger, the BIC presents an awesome spectacle; undoubtedly some of its rules are time-warped and out of tune; others are irritating, and some intimidating. The point is that if you do not like the spectacle, then at least you must respect it, and if you can do neither, then you will not be happy in Broken Hill.

If the BIC is awesome, what does that make its president? The Boss of Broken Hill – the King of Silver City – Mr K. of the Kremlin – Joe Keenan. In those files back in Adelaide it had said that if he decided to like you he would call you 'brother' and do anything for you: if he did not, then he would call you all the names unfit to print. On the whole it was thought he had contempt for intruders, particularly journalists who came into town for a few hours, had a drink in a bar or two and then went away to vent their spleen on the Mecca of Australian workers. I anticipated an uncomfortable meeting – and I was wrong; it could not have been more pleasant. Joe Keenan did not call me 'brother' but we clearly liked each other, and he did everything possible to help during the remainder of my stay. Back home, in London, his was the first Christmas card to arrive.

Joe Keenan is a small man, a smart man with slicked-back hair. He looks strong. He worked underground for forty-four years and has been President of BIC for fifteen; even though he is now retired, the Council keep re-electing him. I can understand why. He is among the most amiable of men, unpretentious, tough-talking and direct, and with a commitment to trade unionism and Broken Hill that is total. He knows that the conditions and prestige the BIC has earned since 1923 have not come easily. He can recall the town before refrigeration and air coolers, before five weeks' holiday and high wages; before there was ventilation underground and much attention paid to safety. He can recall a prideless, purposeless place: a dusty dump with dirt roads where men on night shift had to snatch sleep in noisy, insufferably hot tin huts, and where men on day shift had little to do in the evenings except shuffle through the gutter from one pub to the next.

Joe Keenan was born in England, in Cumberland where his father was a miner. The family left for Broken Hill in 1925 when Joe was nine. His father, a veteran of the First World War, died young, leaving his mother with six children. 'I left school at fourteen and got the loan of a push-bike and went looking for work. I was too young for the mines so I became a swagman, following shearing sheds, getting odd jobs. When I came back a year later, Mum met me at the door and I told her that I had £28 which was a fourtune in those days and I gave her £20 and kept the rest because I wanted to buy a trumpet. The trumpet cost £8 but I only had £7 10s. because I wanted the rest for union fees! Then I worked three nights a week at clubs for 18/6d. a night. And this I did until it was time to go down the mines, and along I went to line up with all the others to ask for a job. At one moment I heard footsteps approaching the door and got up to open it. We were taught in those days to open doors and have respect for elders. The man said "Thank you" and asked me what I was doing there and when I told him I was looking for a job he gave me one. I did not know that he was the General Manager of the Zinc Corporation.'

And so began his lengthy marriage to the mines. Even after all these years, Joe Keenan is not willing to concede that the town must dwindle in size to become nothing more than a service centre for pastoralists. He claims that the educational and medical facilities could easily support twice the number, so he is not interested in talking about half the number. His first choice for the future would be based on irrigation: a satellite town based on Menindee, some fifty miles (eighty kilometres) away, where wool and cotton could be processed.

And he wouldn't say no to an atomic power station. 'Atomic power is not all for war. That's rot. That's like saying that because lead is used for bullets we ought not to mine lead. Atomic power stations are the only answer for the future. We get our electricity now from Victoria and it is very expensive, which again does not encourage industry to come.' Once he almost made it: Nissan once thought of setting up a factory to assemble cars. 'That would have been perfect. There were a few problems because the rates of pay in this town are higher than in other towns, but I told them that they could build outside the town and pay New South Wales rates if that would help them. The problem inside the town is the lead bonus, another imaginative scheme introduced in 1925 as a profit-sharing scheme. In the first ten years the bonus was so small it meant nothing, but there have been times when the bonus more than doubled miners' wages. When it got to this stage, the people in the town began to think that they ought to have a similar scheme, and so this was agreed. It has always caused problems. No one likes paying it and it does make our wages high. That's why I said the Japs could build out of town, but still nothing happened. I reckon it was because the State got greedy and started asking for too large a slice of the action.'

Could it have something to do with the image of union power?

'I've tried to answer that question so many times. I know Nissan wanted to come here because of the three-year agreement; this is the only place left on earth where a big company can *budget*. I don't understand the problem. This is such a friendly place and the BIC is like a forum; we all like each other; we went to the same schools; we belong to the same clubs, there is no class distinction – this is a working-class town. Of course we have problems, employment for women is one, but it is better now that tourism has expanded and coachloads come over the border to play the pokies, because they don't have gambling in South Australia. People make too much of that rule. We have more married women working per head of the population than many other towns, but we don't like to see our young girls forced to leave town because they can't get a job, that's why we have the rule. But it is hardly ever used and is mostly in unskilled areas.'

Broken Hill has all the answers – but they do not supply a solution. All the city gets is government reports with conclusions printed on blue paper and the appointment, by New South Wales, of someone called a coordinator. He lives in Sydney (which, as far as Joe is concerned, might as well be London), and only visits Broken Hill 'when he fancies a free meal'.

The town is a victim of its past record, a record which had the place labelled 'the greatest centre of industrial turmoil in Australia'. It was. But then all it has ever done is mirror the industrial climate outside; mirror the trade-union history of the country.

When the lode was discovered in 1883, the unions in Australia were in peak condition, having slowly built up strength since the Gold Rush of the 1850s which brought skilled labour from England and, with it, craft unions. The first unions were solely concerned with skilled workers, and it was to be another twenty years before the unskilled were unionized. By then, of course, Australia had made an important decision: its inhabitants had opted to ignore future needs in favour of a high standard of living and high wages which could only be achieved with labour shortages. Thus immigration was to be curtailed and the assisted passage, seen as a threatening source of cheap labour, was to be phased out. By 1890, the unions had suffered few setbacks and were flushed with success and confidence; the employers were prosperous and wealthy; and Australia had the highest standard of living in the world. Trollope had got it right a few years earlier when he had described Australia as a working man's paradise compared to England. And then the whole thing crumbled: the unions sought a closed shop and the employers wanted to preserve their rights to employ whom they chose. In 1890 this issue resulted in the nearest thing to a general strike; it started in the docks and ended in total defeat for the unions, a bitter blow with the widest of ramifications. The unions lost credibility and membership began to fall; with this, the unions saw the limitations of strike action and decided instead to see what would be achieved by the ballot box. The Labor Party was formed and the principle of arbitration as a way of settling disputes was accepted. In 1901 arbitration was adopted in New South Wales, and other States had followed by 1904.

As well as general disillusion with the strike as a weapon, the country was plunged into a severe depression in the 1890s; in such conditions, strikes are never popular and rarely worth while. Broken Hill was to learn this lesson in 1892: in that year and because of the economic climate, the mines introduced contract labour – paying men by what they mined rather than by hours worked. The miners went on strike for eighteen weeks before they gave in; contract labour was introduced; wages were cut by ten per cent and hours worked rose from forty-six to forty-eight. Sixteen years of peace followed both in Broken Hill and in the rest of the country. By 1908, however, the gains through political action and arbitration had ceased to satisfy trade unionists, and strike action once more became a weapon. Ironically, it was arbitration that triggered off the trade-union revival, for only organized associations of workers could appear before the courts and therefore there was a rapid rise in membership.

In Broken Hill in 1908 metal prices were down and, while nine companies agreed to keep wages level, four companies insisted that they could not pay and argued for a cut. BHP was among the latter – the giant, the Big One, the founder company arguing that it couldn't afford to pay! No one was willing to accept this, particularly since it was BHP that had argued at the outset that all companies, whether profitable or marginal, should pay the same. That was all right while BHP was the richest; now her lode was diminishing, however, she had changed her tune and was attempting to change the rules. BHP went on strike for twenty weeks. The other mines did not, thus keeping the striking miners in funds. Agitators were brought in.

It is part of Australian trade-union folklore that all shop stewards are Pommies, and in those days it was easy enough to prove. Tom Mann had worked in English coal mines and had been a leader of the London Dock Strike in 1889 before he took his activities overseas. France and Germany threw him out, and he ended up in Broken Hill to stir the miners. In the end, the Commonwealth Arbitrator decreed that BHP could not cut wages; it either had to pay the same wages as everyone else or cease working. BHP chose to remain closed until metal prices improved two years later. It is easy to see why the company is not prized in Broken Hill.

The outbreak of the 1914 War affected Broken Hill badly because it had to stop supplying concentrates to German and Belgian smelters and, while jobs suffered, the cost of living soared. The rest of the country was fretful, too. Australia was too far away from the battlefields to be able to make economic mileage as a supply base. In 1916, 1.25 million working days were lost through strikes; in 1920, 3.5 million days were lost. Needless to say, Broken Hill did more than her share to swell the number. From April 1919 to November 1920, the miners were on strike; for eighteen months the mines were closed. In his history of Broken Hill, Professor Geoffrey Blainey argues that this lengthy strike was possible only because it is a one-industry town, and shops and services had no option but to support the miners. Industrial disease was at the centre of the troubles, and the town remained idle while a State commission undertook a massive investigation into the health of mining employees. Pneumoconiosis, contracted by inhaling dust, was found to be widespread. When the strike ended, the concessions won by the unions were sensational – to use the word chosen by Blainey. Underground workers were awarded a thirty-five hour week; the night shift was abolished; sick men received pensions; holiday pay was introduced, and the wages of all workers were increased. Enlightened men were determined to bring a lasting peace to the metal fields and, as well as generous concessions, the Barrier Industrial Council was set up.

And there was peace in Broken Hill, just as there was industrial peace in the rest of the country. The setting-up of the Australian Council of Trade Unions in 1927 helped and, indeed, so did legal controls on union activities; it is fair to say that once again the strike weapon retreated as an industrial tactic while men faced another depression, another war (from which Australia's economy gained much, the South Pacific being sufficiently close) and two decades of unprecedented prosperity. By 1970 the strike was to become fashionable again as living standards achieved through the 1950s and 1960s became threatened and individual unions began to kick against the power of the ACTU.

Australia remains a heavily unionized country with sixty-four per cent of manual workers and forty-one per cent of non-manual workers in trade unions (compared with fifty-six and thirteen per cent in the USA, and fifty-three and thirty-eight per cent in the UK), but the pattern of strikes has changed. They are rarely lengthy; they seldom last longer than three weeks, most lasting between one and three days. Indeed, Australian trade unions make much of this fact to explain away the large number of strikes. Other countries may boast that they have fewer strikes – but in other countries the strikes last longer and are more damaging. There is little talk of politically inspired strikes, strikes against the capitalist system, even when unions are led by known Communists. The work-force is conservative and this keeps the unions conservative; and the word is that members are happy to appoint communist leaders because such men work with great energy to support living standards. This must be so; in Melbourne I talked to several communist trade-union leaders and they talked of little else: they were after a larger share of the cake rather than one baked to a different recipe.

And certainly this is so in Broken Hill. They are happy with their system. Joe Keenan can rattle off the occasions when the three-year agreement has been negotiated without a day lost, and he claims that a long strike these days lasts seventeen days. None the less the dog has a bad name, much to Joe's annoyance; a one-day garbage strike in Broken Hill still warrants front-page coverage in Sydney, whereas a longer strike elsewhere might be ignored. The BIC remains a bogey. This is unfortunate and, in many ways, unjustified. But history haunts and, during the period when Broken Hill most needed the outside world to reassess its view, Noel Latham grabbed every headline. The story of Noel Latham says it all.

Noel Latham was employed by Broken Hill City Council as a motor mechanic with supervisory powers. One day in 1977 he asked a labourer called Eric Wall to clean the radiator of a Council tractor. The machine was used by the sewerage works and cleaning it was a filthy job. It needed goggles and a mask. Mr Latham had done the job in the past, but on this occasion he asked Eric Wall to do it. Wall refused; he said it was not a labourer's job. Latham reported the incident to his foreman who in turn reported it to his boss, the acting City Engineer. The latter personally asked Wall to clean the tractor; again Wall refused, and was suspended.

The procedures were all in line with the requisite local government Act, and in any other place the quarrel would have turned into a routine demarcation dispute. But in Broken Hill there are other considerations. The BIC has its own rules; there is one dating from 1941 which says that reporting your mates to the boss is not on. If there are any problems, they should be reported to BIC and anyone reporting his mates to the boss and getting them sacked is liable to be fined not less than £5. Latham was called to a meeting and fined $A50. He refused to pay the fine and in retaliation the BIC instructed his union, the Amalgamated Metal Workers Union, not to issue him with his badge until the fine was paid.

Now we know what happens when men appear for work on badge day without a badge; his fellow workers can refuse to work with him. And this is what happened. A strike followed and, in an attempt to resolve the crisis, the Mayor offered to pay Latham's fine. This was not acceptable to the BIC who were anxious that Latham should abide by the rules. The Mayor resigned and the new administrator said with some reluctance that the only way he could end the troubles was to fire Latham because 'his continued employment is prejudicial to the provision of local government services within the city'.

Latham's response was to take action in the New South Wales Supreme Court against the seventy men who had refused to work with him. One final attempt was made at reconciliation. Indeed in a face-saving 'Let bygones be bygones' agreement, the BIC agreed that an anonymous person could pay Latham's fine and he could go back to work. But when he turned up, he found his overalls in knots and urine in his boots. The men did not want to work with him.

The situation returned to square one and Latham was once more suspended by the Council, and eventually his employment was terminated. Latham pursued his court case. It went on for four years and finally the Supreme Court awarded him $A110,000 in damages against forty-one of the men who, the judge considered, had directly intended to harm him. The other thirty, the judge concluded, had no such intentions – they had merely followed the other men off the job, blind followers of ringleaders.

Thousands upon thousands of words have been written about the case. Writers had a field day reducing the complex battle to a collision between two great Australian myths – mateship versus individual rights. No one in Broken Hill likes to talk about the case any more. The BIC levied the work-force to pay for the court case and to pay the fine. Noel Latham now has a caravan park on the edge of town.

Joe Keenan wrote to me some time later with his view; his words were sparing: 'We have inherited many things that we class as sacred within the ranks of the Trade Union movement. One of these is to remain faithful and true to the Cause, and never do anything detrimental to a fellow worker. To cheat, to steal from your mate, or complain to the "boss" and get a person the sack is the most despicable and heinous crime in our Organization.' Must the Council rewrite the rule book to reflect a world of shallow ties, and of working men without loyalty?

The case damaged Broken Hill. The journalist who wrote the article suggesting that the place was a disgrace to Australia claimed there was no such thing as individual rights in the Silver City and there was little for an employer to do other than hand out the pay-packet. The BIC does the rest. That's why people stay away and new industries refuse to be enticed.

Broken Hill's situation is not special; mining towns die, the world over. Australia has more ghost towns than most places. Men go to dig and never intend to stay; they do not fight the inevitable. During the time of which I write, the town of Mary Kathleen in the Northern Territory, where uranium had been mined, shut up shop. Television coverage was plentiful: it showed contented men closing their doors and walking away; it showed auctioneers arriving in town to sell what was still useful; it showed other companies buying up demountable housing to transport to new and developing fields.

But Broken Hill is different; she is the grand old dame of mining and she wants a new lease of life. She cannot see herself reduced to a staging post for pensioners on cheap coach tours; she cannot see herself as a quaint film-set, even though she is proud of having provided the backdrop for many a film: *Mad Max II, Sunday Too Far Away*, and the television series *A Town Like Alice*. The film-makers love the landscape, the clear desert light, the dry climate and the well-established transport links to big cities. The 27,000 inhabitants of Broken Hill love all that too, and they relish their place in history above all. Recognition of this status is everything; a future is what she wants, not a sentimental burial with full mining honours.

In an ideal world I would have left Broken Hill by train and I would have stayed on the train until I reached Perth, for there is little in between except the Nullarbor Desert. I longed to do that; I felt in need of a restful two days and two nights on the train, and I particularly wanted to travel on the Indian Pacific, the train running through Broken Hill and linking Sydney on the east coast with Perth on the west coast, a distance of some 2,500 miles (4,000 kilometres), which claims to be one of the great railway journeys of the world – and, unlike all other claimants to the title, this one is relatively new. The Indian Pacific came into being in 1970 after the nation had spent seven years and $A275 million transcending the idiocy of varying State railway gauges. Before that, both passengers and freight had a disjointed journey with several changes.

Such a silly state of affairs came about through yet another battle between the Irish and the English. An Irishman called Wentworth Shields was responsible for planning Sydney's first railways in the early 1850s and with a true anti-imperialist gesture he rejected the suggestion that the track be built upon the English gauge, 4 feet 8½ inches wide, which dates from Roman times and is said to be the distance between chariot wheels. Instead he opted for the Irish gauge of 5 feet 3 inches. Victoria and South Australia – also building their first railways – agreed to abide by his decision. However, Shields quit his job for some reason; his successor reverted to the English gauge and, by the time he got around to telling the other colonies, it was too late for them to change their plans. A few years later, Queensland started a trend for the narrow gauge, 3 feet 6 inches, and before long this out-miled both the Irish and the English. No one cared about the inconvenience; the colonies were fiercely competitive and not at all concerned with cooperative gestures; and in any event it was a while before anyone appreciated the difficulties caused by such an independent stance; the first railways were not destined to link the capital cities, but to link inland areas with ports on the coast. Some 120 years later, with inter-State traffic tired of fiddling around at the border, the English gauge, renamed the standard gauge, won the day, and the romantically inclined railway traveller was rewarded with a sixty-five hour strain-free stretch.

My wish was to pick up this train when it stopped at Broken Hill. It was not to be. The Indian Pacific was not running; it had been cancelled. It wasn't a strike, you understand, for all the men had been transferred on to other lines. And it wasn't a national scandal either; no one seemed at all bothered. The line is mainly used by tourists and pensioners travelling at half fare, and neither group has any political clout. Furthermore the line makes a heavy loss and, by not running, money had actually been saved; gossip had it that the administration didn't care whether it ran again or not.

The line loses money because it is hugely inefficient. Booking offices along the route are issued with a quota of tickets to sell; when these are exhausted, would-be travellers are told that the train is full, even though the next office down the track may have an unused quota. To right this ridiculous situation, a computer was rumoured to have been charged with the task of issuing tickets. At the same time, Indian Pacific management – a clumsy body involving three States and the Federal Government – was trying to attack losses by reducing manning levels. They reckoned that the train would run smoothly with one conductor to two cars, instead of one to each car. The unions were unhappy, especially since they anticipated more work if the computer did its job properly and improved the passenger load. So a five-member committee was looking at the mess and meanwhile the train had been shunted into a siding. Consequently I had to return to Adelaide by plane, there to see if I could clamber aboard the Trans Australian, a parallel service running from Port Pirie to Perth. The track is the same, they said, and so is the rolling stock and I wouldn't be able to tell the difference.

At one stage it seemed highly unlikely I would be given the chance. The booking office denied all knowledge of my telephone reservation and claimed that all the sleepers, both first- and second-class, were booked. I could have a seat; I could sit up all the way to Perth and they would wait-list me for a sleeper cancellation. On the day of departure a shared second-class sleeper became available. Of course the train does not leave from Adelaide, but from Port Pirie 140 miles (230 kilometres) north; the gap is bridged by a Greyhound bus journey which did nothing to enhance my feeling of embarking on a luxury train trip. The customary stop was at one of the dirtiest Shell roadhouses imaginable; when I commented on this to the driver, he turned and walked away.

I was glad indeed to find myself at Port Pirie, pushing a pigeon-toed wire trolley towards the baggage check-in, a suitcase being an unwelcome companion in a second-class sleeper that was bound to be little bigger than a double coffin – and a little bigger than a double coffin is exactly what it turned out to be. Furthermore the coffin ran along the length of the train rather than across the width, thus ensuring that passengers rocked and rolled the night away. The design is not ideal and, although the compartment looked cosy enough for one passenger, the thought of sharing it with a stranger filled me with claustrophobia.

I went in search of a glass of wine. It was nearly five p.m. and I needed to celebrate the simple fact that I was at least on a train. The bar car does not sell wine, but the kindly attendant sent me off in search of Trevor in the dining car. He'd sell me a half-bottle. Cuddling both it and glass, I wandered back to the bar and found my way blocked by my conductor who said: 'Would it make you smile if I kept your compartment for you alone? There is another girl due to get on at Port Augusta, but I can put her somewhere else.' I replied that it would not make me smile; it would make me grin from ear to ear all the way to Perth; and so the deed was done. There was plenty of space on the train; the old system had hiccuped again.

What, I asked, was I missing by not going first class?

'Nothing at all, now that you have a compartment to yourself. In first you'd have just the same, with a bit of carpet. It's the doubles that make all the difference. They go across the train, so there is much less roll and you also get your own lavatory and shower. Nice, they are. But I wouldn't worry yourself. You'd be bored up there – full of old people, it is.'

I drank to my luck in a bar car full of be-shorted, be-jeaned, be-thonged kids who seemed determined to drink themselves across the desert. They didn't have coffins, they were sit-ups. And I mourned the loss of a great railway journey. For I could tell already that this was no Orient Express. There was no trace of grandeur or glamour, no sense of occasion; just a perfectly ordinary train running on a lengthy piece of track. None the less I showered and changed for dinner and deliberately chose the second sitting at six forty-five rather than six p.m., first because it was quite early enough to eat and secondly because I fancied lingering over my vegetable soup, lamb and peach melba. But it was not to be; the first sitting gave way to the second sitting and the second sitting gave way to the staff sitting. And there was no lingering. My companions were a couple from Perth who had driven across the Nullarbor to Melbourne – 'for the hell of it' and to attend an oil conference – and were now returning with their car carefully stowed among the freight. They'd enjoyed the drive, but it was a once-only experience, and they were full of stories about how easy it is to fall asleep at the wheel, mesmerized by miles of nothing. There was also Sandra, an English girl who had spent a happy year in Sydney in computers, but who was forced to head homewards as her visa had expired.

By seven p.m. it was dark outside, but what did it matter? There was nothing to see. Mile after mile of treeless reddish plain. It had been raining and there were puddles by the track. Someone said that, when it rained in the desert, the place was transformed into a multi-coloured carpet of wild flowers. Not here. Not yet. The blue sky had turned to grey and now to black. Soon we would be rounding the last curve and then it was straight ahead for 300 miles (500 kilometres); the longest stretch of straight track in the world. Reading and sleeping was the best approach. There was nothing to miss; the place is empty.

The place is so empty that it was chosen by the British and the Australians as a suitable site for nuclear tests in the 1950s. Out there in the darkness there is a place called Maralinga, a few miles north of the track; and 120 miles (190 kilometres) north of Maralinga is a place called Emu. Between them they saw nine atomic tests. Until recently, no one had given a thought to either place, but now they are the subject of controversy, together with a third site, the Monte Bello Islands over on the west coast. There were three tests there, making twelve in all, and it seemed fine at the time – and necessary. Now those funny old newsreels make painful viewing as both sides, Australia and Britain, boast of their successes. It is different now. Servicemen have been claiming that they have contracted illness due to radiation exposure, and there have been persistent reports that Aborigines wandered into the test areas in spite of attempts to clear them from the danger zones. An Australian Royal Commission in 1985 recommended that the British Government should compensate the evicted Aborigines and pay the cost of cleaning up the three sites.

At Monte Bello in 1965 they dropped the 'dirty' bomb, so called because it is now thought to have been three times larger than anyone believed at the time, and the explosion appears to have been carried out in less than ideal weather conditions, so that radio-active dust blew over the northern half of Australia rather than out to sea. Down here in the South the story is much the same: there were seven explosions at Maralinga between September 1956 and 1957, and they totalled the size of the 'dirty' bomb. The accusations surrounding them make gruesome reading: it is argued that political pressure ensured that some tests took place in dangerous weather conditions; further, it is said that, under cover of the known nuclear tests, experiments took place in which trainloads of the mentally deficient travelled along this very track, were off-loaded at Watson and taken to bunkers at Maralinga. Furthermore it is stated that, when the tests officially stopped in 1957, 'minor experiments' continued until 1963 involving radio-active material and allowing highly toxic plutonium to be spread over a large area.

The official view is that no one was exposed to radiation during the tests and that any problems now coming to light were caused by human error, by people not wearing the right protective clothing and generally disobeying the rules. However, at least one service widow, whose husband had been at the Emu tests and who was subsequently discharged from the army as unfit and who then died of cancer, has been awarded damages of $A250,000. The Australian Veterans Association says that it expects 300 further claims. There were 2,000 Australian servicemen in the area, 500 British and of course the Aborigines who may have escaped the round-up. Maralinga is their word for 'Field of Thunder'. Out there, the darkness holds many secrets.

I had opted for the second sitting for breakfast at eight fifteen a.m. and had rather expected to be woken with a cup of tea. All the brochures show a steward or conductor handing teacups into compartments. So they do – if you ask: but how many passengers know to ask? Another attempt to cut down the work-load and enable one conductor to handle two coaches. The same goes for the bed-making process. If you wish a conductor to unlatch the thing from the wall then you must ask, or fumble for yourself.

The breakfast table was full of gossip. Two young people in the 'sit-ups' had become friendly during the night and, in need of a little privacy, had gone in search of an empty sleeper. There, in an unguarded moment of passion, one or the other had pressed the 'call attendant' button and were surprised on being disturbed. The conductor was not well pleased, and heated words were exchanged before the couple were removed and several other passengers were awakened by the commotion.

In the bar car I tried to be sociable, and at one point Sandra and I had struck up a conversation with a young man with dark, gypsy good looks and a shirt open to the waist who claimed to be a redundant butcher on holiday from the North of England. He became a pest. There are few things more obnoxious than English yobbo behaviour, and I did my best to ignore his silly shouted comments from the next table. In the end, however, I retaliated and, in a suitably resonant voice, suggested that I was ashamed that an Englishman should behave in such a childish way and requested that he quieten down. A group of young Aussies clapped and cheered, and I decided that this was a suitable moment to make a dignified exit.

I passed the day peacefully writing letters in my cosy compartment, having decided that the bar car was best left to bored folk who need beer and noise to pass any journey.

The major event of the day coincided with sunset. As the sky glowed in glorious pink and gold, we drew into Kalgoorlie, a gold-mining town, and we were invited to leave the train for a while. Kalgoorlie is famous; it boasts the Golden Mile, the richest few acres of gold-bearing land in the world. Some say that there is even more gold beneath the earth than has been taken out in the last eighty years, and they are certainly busy finding out, for the town that nearly died in the mid-1970s has revived with the help of the price of gold. Once again it became worth spending millions of dollars sinking deeper shafts. In the mid-1970s the figures wouldn't add up and the mines closed, all but one, leaving sun-blistered rotting headframes to cast shadows over the lives of a community already conditioned to a cycle of boom and bust.

But Kalgoorlie is lucky; the place has always been lucky. When gold was first discovered in 1893 by Paddy Hannan, it seemed of doubtful long-term worth because there was no water in the area. Then in 1896 a man called O'Connor decided to lay a pipeline all the way from Perth. The project cost £3 million, even though the pipeline was laid on the surface to save the cost of trenching, and was beset with problems; O'Connor, towards the end, lost his nerve. Convinced the whole thing had misfired he committed suicide before the water began to gush. Even today, the pipeline is considered to be one of the great hydraulic engineering feats of the world.

Kalgoorlie is famous for more than gold. Kalgoorlie is famous for Hay Street and its whorehouses. For several hundred yards along either side of the street there is a collection of single-storey houses, most with frontages resembling horseboxes. Each night the tops of the stall doors open from six p.m. onwards and coloured lights silhouette each girl as she awaits her customers. They are totally unperturbed by the sight of tourist buses cruising the street with eager noses pressed to the windows. The madam of madams is called Mona. She is in her eighties, usually dressed in something long and floaty and vulgarly coloured, and she runs her brothel according to strict rules. Her girls come from out of town, most of them from broken homes and unable to hold down a nine-to-five job; they must not appear in the local hotels and they must be medically checked each Monday. Sex talk outside the bedrooms is not allowed; nor is bad language, nor is beer. Prices are high: $A25 for fifteen minutes up to $A250 for an all-nighter. 'All night' begins at one thirty a.m. and ends with a hot breakfast at eight thirty.

No one in Kalgoorlie wants the whorehouses closed; they reckon they are a safety valve for the town; they keep the streets safe for women. In Kalgoorlie there is no rape. Of course, whorehouses are illegal, and every now and then politicians in Perth feel obliged to order a clean-up; Mona ends up in court and is ordered to pay a token fine of $A200. There is illegal gambling, too: a game called two-up played by spinning two pennies in the air and betting on whether they land heads up or tails – a simple game with little opportunity for cheating. The serious two-up games where large sums of money change hands are played out in the bush, several miles from town, and no woman is allowed within spitting distance. In town, everyone knows it is played at the United Nations Club. The town would like the game to be legalized. Not that it would make much difference; raids are infrequent and, again, the fines are nominal.

Our little tour ended with a glimpse of an Olympic-sized swimming pool which was built in 1937, the first in Western Australia, and with the information that Herbert Hoover was a mining engineer in Kalgoorlie before he set his sights on the presidency of the United States. The town of Kalgoorlie, or 'our Kal', added a welcome touch of vivid colour to the washed-out world of the Nullarbor, and a memory to an unmemorable, un-great railway journey. By six a.m. the following morning, the Trans Australian had rid itself of its passengers and its freight, and had slid away into a siding for a rest.

CHAPTER 11

Made of Iron

Perth is an appealing, pleasing city, perched proudly by the side of the Swan River, its high-rise buildings proclaiming its recent prosperity. It makes a pretty impression from certain angles, notably from Riverside Drive which, as its name suggests, follows the Swan, and from Kings Park, 900 acres (365 hectares) of greenery overlooking the city and offering panoramic views. From some angles, however, it appears rather bland, blurred almost, as though more time is needed to weather its features, to take the edge off the newness. For much has happened to Perth in the last twenty years and its youth shows; and much is still happening – and this shows, too. At a glance one can see why Perth is the country's fastest growing city – scaffolding is everywhere, new hotels, new offices and shopping plazas, all large and not all a delight to either the eye or the ear. But then I'm no fan of shopping centres. The shopping mall is agreeable with its freedom from traffic; but the centre is a suffocating concept with its glare-giving escalators and walkways and piped music – particularly offensive from tinkling bells trying to better Beethoven's 'Ode to Joy'. Such centres make developers rich and, yes, they seem to please most shoppers who like to feel enfolded as they wander from boutique to bank to bookshop. *I* need to see the sky. 'Sandgropers', as Western Australians are called (presumably because the State is rather sandy and Perth and surrounding areas are *very* sandy – indeed a wit told Trollope that it was the best country he had ever seen to run through an hourglass) – sandgropers like things to be under a roof, one roof.

Their predilection for umbrella'd shops is mirrored in their taste for huge, one-stop holiday resorts; there is one to the north of the city, called Yanchep Sun City where, within walking distance, you can have your boat, your bungalow, your bar and your baker lined up like a matching set of luggage, neatly fitting together like a nest of tables. I like it not, packaged and processed, sealed and without surprises. Well, it fills the space – the huge space. Western Australia is the size of India with a population of just over one million. These unified endeavours do not only fill the space, they also fit the mood, and it is the mood rather than the monuments of Perth that I recall with ease. It is something more than heady optimism and rampant expansion: Perth bounces; it swaggers. In the nicest possible way it is saying, 'We have got it, so we'll flaunt it.' For a long time Perth didn't have it; for a long time she was poor, and now she is rich; for a long time she was a failure, and now she is a success; for a long time she was ignored, and now she is fashionable. It's a rags to riches story. No wonder she swaggers.

Perth and Western Australia were slighted in the beginning and they have lived long with the knowledge of that slight. The western coast of Australia was discovered many, many years before the eastern coast, and time and again it was passed over by explorers as hardly worth the stop. The first recorded visit was in 1616 by a Dutchman, but it was to be more than 200 years before a settlement was considered, and then the decision was made out of fear. The British thought that someone else might take that western section – that someone being the French, who were nosing around in nearby waters. So, fearful for their trading routes rather than the land itself, in 1826 they placed a garrison down south at Albany and then set about populating the Swan River area with high ideals. At this time it was fashionable to scorn the convicts and vow to keep the ruffians out. Their presence not only lowered the tone of the place, it also ensured generations of Bill Sikes look-alikes. Thus it was agreed in London that land should be parcelled out free to settlers according to the money they were willing to invest: one acre for every 1/6d invested, something like that – and it didn't work. It was a daft scheme which allowed men to accumulate vast areas of land which they then could not and did not tend. The rules were changed. The land was to be sold at 5/-, 12/-, £1 an acre and allocations would be restricted to workable plots. But this was no answer. Who would buy in such an isolated place when they could buy for the same price in the eastern States? In the end, after twenty years of struggle, Perth called for convicts to come to its aid. That early slight, followed by such a defeat, was indeed a poor start. The discovery of gold at Kalgoorlie helped somewhat but, none the less, Western Australia remained a mendicant State, dependent on Federal aid until after the Second World War, despised, a drain on resources, too far away. Indeed Western Australia was so fed up with her lot and her relationship with the other States that in 1933 the electorate voted by two to one to quit the Federation, but London vetoed the move. Then in the 1950s came the discovery of iron ore, a story so important that I will return to it in a moment. And ore was followed by nickel, bauxite, alumina, oil and natural gas, diamonds even. Perth was on her way.

And then to cap it all, in 1983 Alan Bond and the Royal Perth Yacht Club won the America's Cup. A small thing, you might think, a mere sporting trophy, but it is more than that. It was won after ten years of effort, and it was no mean achievement for insignificant Perth to wrest the Cup from the mighty New York Yacht Club which had retained it for more than 130 years. It brought Perth into focus, made her fashionable, demonstrated that she had won her stripes. Actually she had won them two years earlier, in 1981, when seven of the eleven cricketers in the Australian test team came from Western Australia. That brought internal recognition; the America's Cup brought international acclaim.

Of course, there is money in this victory. Many have warned Perth not to make too much of the return match in 1987, but she insists on making the most of her luck and will spend millions of dollars promoting the State. And who can blame her? The America's Cup had become a non-event, something of interest to yachtsmen only. Alan Bond's victory has breathed life into the sport: two dozen challengers, a record number, have come forward for 1987; Italy's Costa Smeralda Yacht Club, backed by the Aga Khan, has been appointed liaison between the Royal Perth Yacht Club and all the challengers who will compete for the right to meet the Australian Defender – and there are some seven Australian syndicates, including Alan Bond's winning team, who will be fighting for the right to that title. There could be as many as 500 races in the elimination series; from the first race in 1986 to the final in 1987, Perth is expecting 300,000 extra – and wealthy – visitors.

And money is what Perth is about – for the moment. This is not to say that the place is brash and brainless. She has her arts complex and her annual Festival and a courageous theatre called Hole in the Wall and a courageous publishing house, the Fremantle Arts Press, propelling Western Australian writers towards their share of recognition. But dollars are driving the place, producing the bounce and swagger. In the eastern States they warned me to watch out for that WATF – that Western Australian Tired Feeling. But as soon as I arrived I knew this to be outdated nonsense, a remnant of the time when the only good reason for going to Perth was the climate. Perth claims the best in Australia, hot and dry in summer and warm and wet in winter, and has thus attracted its share of the sick and retired. The image lingers. The first person I met, the receptionist in my hotel (or, rather, self-service studio run as an hotel), had moved there from Tasmania for the benefit of her husband's health. And the newspapers still carry articles on the famous who settle in Perth to hide their aches and their old age.

Alan Bond's father left England and chose Perth for health reasons. Alan Bond stayed to make dollars. Starting life as a sign-writer, he made his first fortune buying and selling blocks of land, and now his interests run from brewing to brick-making, from transport to television, from resources to retailing. Perth is rapidly spawning an aggressive breed of entrepreneurs. Of the top 200 richest families in Australia, Western Australia claims 29, putting her third behind New South Wales (74) and Victoria (57). In the eastern States one is aware of the wealth, but it is taken for granted and is certainly not the subject of everyday gossip. In Perth, the tourist buses trundle slowly down the richest street, the guides pointing out the prices of the real estate. Jutland Parade, Dalkeith, a suburb on the road between Perth and the port of Fremantle, overlooks the Swan River.

It is not a long street and its houses are either relentlessly suburban or relentlessly modern. And they are owned by the usual assortment of builders and property developers and company directors of varying status – and doctors. The doctors in Perth are wealthy; it must be all those sick and retired folk.

The wealth of the street is such that it once made the front cover of the *Bulletin* because it is not just the richest street in Western Australia, it is the richest street in Australia; and it contains not merely the most expensive house in Western Australia, but the most expensive house in Australia. This rather undistinguished lump of white concrete with its seven bedrooms and three garages belonged to Michael Edgley, born Melbourne, educated Perth and promoter of ballets, circuses, sporting events, rock concerts, films and musicals. He put a price tag of $A4 million around its unlovely neck. (Edgley then moved to Sydney where he subsequently put an even higher price tag around the neck of something a little more elegant.) In Perth there was much interest in the man who wanted the white concrete. His name is Danny Hill, born Northern Ireland, arrived Perth in 1959 with a pocketful of peanuts and a job as a barman, and who is now signing cheques as a mining magnate. I think that means he mines the stock market, but anyway, it is the kind of rags to riches story that Perth adores.

Of course not all Western Australia's multi-millionaires fit the Cinderella image. The richest man in the State, Robert Holmes a Court, a former lawyer with aristocratic connections, arrived in Perth from South Africa (via New Zealand) without the rags, but busied himself accumulating further riches through transport, resources and the media. I did not know that Holmes a Court was the wealthiest man in the State. I was told that that title belonged to Lang Hancock; indeed, I was assured that he was the richest man in Australia and that his income topped $A30,000 a day. Lang Hancock found iron ore in the Pilbara region, 1,000 miles north of Perth. He is the man responsible for kick-starting the engine that was to turn Australia into one of the world's biggest producers of iron ore. Before he found the stuff, the official view was that Australia did not have major iron ore deposits; an embargo had been imposed on exports in 1938 and was firmly held in place until 1960. Finding the ore was easy. Hancock (along with the State Government) then battled to get the embargo lifted and scoured the world for someone prepared to develop the Pilbara.

Hancock is a man they like to call names. To some he is King of the Pilbara – the Flying Prospector – the folk hero – the buccaneer who stomped the world in big boots and a big hat, Texan style, advocating mining *über alles*. To others he is an ultra-conservative madman – a tunnel-visioned maverick – a self-seeking braggart. The truth is rarely pure and never simple and, such is the complexity of the tale, I will offer a mere outline. If iron ore had half the opulent image of oil, then I'm sure someone would have turned Hancock's home at Witternoon into another Southfork.

Hancock is a thick-set man, with the thickest of necks and glasses to match. His biography is entitled *Rogue Bull*; when we met, he gave me a copy and patiently pieced together his life story, something he has done many times in the last thirty years. He was never poor. He was the son of a pastoralist who did well with sheep, and his first stroke of luck was to stumble over a lump of asbestos. At the time he was a boy hunting dingoes near his home; his find was of little value, so the family turned the blue-veined rock into a door stop, and there it remained until a visitor tripped over it some years later. By then its worth had increased. It was 1934 and the Depression; Hancock, in partnership with a school friend, Peter Wright, made his first dollars using donkeys to hump the fibre from an isolated gorge. The money enabled him to buy his own plane and to leave his isolated homestead during the Big Wet, and head south for a season in Perth. In November 1952, Hancock and his wife, Hope, left – later than was wise as the rain had already started and huge banks of cloud surrounded them. None the less they decided to make a dash for it; they could not fly over the cloud; they could not fly through the cloud; they had to fly under it – very low indeed – and in this position Hancock could not help but notice the deep-red walls of the gorge. After the Wet he returned to the gorge again and again, landed and took samples to be assayed. The tests showed that the rocks were rich in iron ore, miles and miles and miles of it. So began the ten-year fight. At first no one believed his find. What was one man against the official word that Australia had no major deposits? And how was he to know that the export ban was part of a murky diplomacy? (It seems, so the story goes, that in 1930 BHP had found iron ore further to the north of Hancock's site and that the Japanese heard about it and sought partnership with the Australian giant in order to guarantee supplies of a raw material they badly needed and which they lacked. The USA vetoed this; they wished to contain Japan, cut her off from such sources and inhibit her development; the Australian government, anxious not to flout American foreign policy, decided that the best way out was to ban all exports of iron ore on the pretext that its own reserves were too low. That way the Japanese would not be offended. Pressure from America was irresistible, not least because of Australia's own White Australia policy, which did not lend itself to allowing the Japanese to have a share of the ground. The British Ambassador to Japan was not very pleased with this decision. He believed in freedom of access to raw materials and he reckoned that such a move would only encourage a country like Japan, a 'have-not' in terms of raw materials, to arm itself in order to take what it required.)

Lang Hancock knew none of this. 'All I knew was that the odds were terribly against me. They just wouldn't believe me. It took a lot of putting over. There was no way I could raise the money myself; I had to interest the multi-national steel makers and I wrote to them one after the other. One after the other they wrote back and said "No". What was the point of them being interested when there was no chance of an export licence? Will your government give me a permit, they would ask; and I would say, let's go together and argue the case. Everyone dithered like jellyfish.'

The nub of the matter was that the Western Australian government made it clear that they did not wish to negotiate with anyone who was negotiating with Lang Hancock. The government wanted to develop the Pilbara as a package; but Lang Hancock had his own ideas and, instead of the two working together for the good of Western Australia and Australia as a whole, there was much antagonism. So the iron ore remained in the ground for ten years, until

1962; by then the embargo had been lifted and a deal agreed with Rio Tinto-Zinc, a British company. Hancock's royalties were to make him a very rich man, but he was not the sort of sandgroper to sail into the sunset in a yacht and gloat over a brief moment of glory. He had other plans: he wanted the Pilbara to become the Ruhr of South-East Asia; he wanted to promote the building of a railway line across Australia linking the iron ore to the coal in Queensland, with a steel mill at either end. Nothing came of the plan. Hancock continued to dream of Australia becoming the richest nation on earth, however, and when uranium was discovered he turned his brutal energy and his friendship with Edward Teller, the father of the hydrogen bomb, to trying to persuade men that nuclear energy was the force of the future. He argued the hind legs off any environmentalist – or 'eco-nut', to use his phrase – who was willing to take him on.

He had inadvertently flown in his tiny plane through the aftermath of the Monte Bello explosion; through the radio-active cloud. Others were shocked; he was nonchalant. As far as he is concerned, he lived to tell the tale; he lived to produce a healthy daughter; he lived to enjoy healthy grandchildren. That others may have suffered is not in doubt – as he has said so often, if you are going to make an omelette, you have to be prepared to break a few eggs.

'Our uranium is a wasted asset. Australia was ready to go in 1973. We could have captured the cream of the world's market. We could have solved our power problems. We could have solved our unemployment.' But Australia dithered and compromised; she mined a little, but not as much as she could have. The moment for uranium has now passed, Hancock argues.

But the moment for Hancock never seems to pass. For his seventieth birthday in 1979, his only child, Gina, who is heavily involved in her father's affairs and totally in agreement with his ideas, organized a two-day jumbo flight around 'the world's richest country' for the media, politicians, businessmen and industrialists. Her mission – for his birthday – was to 'Wake up Australia!'. She wanted them to see the potential for investment and she wanted them, with the help of films and talks on board the jumbo, to understand the need to develop their own country. Far too much of the world is dependent upon Africa – and South Africa in particular – when instead it could be dependent on Australia.

They came, the plane-load, they saw and they went away. Nothing happened. Hancock shrugs. 'If only free enterprise could get on with the job – but we no longer know the meaning of the phrase. It has got lost in the fog of a mixed economy. But my message remains the same: "Dig or Die". The fundamental basis on which all modern civilization rests is *mining*. Can you imagine a world without steel, aluminium or glass? Without minerals we could not harvest our food, till our soil, build our machines, supply our energy, transport our goods. Our horn of plenty starts with a hole in the ground.'

By the time he had detailed his vision, I had a picture of Australia as one vast hole in the ground – but he would not let me get away with that. 'The area mined at the moment is tiny, maybe one per cent! We could improve on that without turning the place into a quarry.' All right. But then I didn't like his willingness to invite every Tom, Dick and Harry of an overseas company to, in his own words, 'come and play in his backyard, bringing, of course, their own marbles [money]'. Neither did he. None the less, he believes that, with all its faults, the greed of capitalism is the only force there is. And he won't give up. As we sat there he unfolded yet another plan: to invite immediate past principals – ex-presidents of nations, ex-heads of big commercial enterprises – men who have a wealth of experience at top level, to persuade Reagan's administration to visit the resource-rich land and tempt the two countries to work together to safeguard each other's interests.

I could see why they call him all those names; but whatever Lang Hancock is or is not, he wins my admiration for doggedly pursuing a vision to open up a desolate and remote area of Western Australia. I decided to visit the Pilbara so that I could appreciate the magnitude of the task of setting up a mining community 200 miles (320 kilometres) from the coast and 1,000 miles (1,600 kilometres) from Perth, which is itself the most isolated of Australian cities. An area where once there was nothing now has a thriving community. I wanted to see how it compared with Broken Hill.

But first I had to see Karri and Jarrah. They may well sound like a couple of newly made friends, but they are in fact a couple of distinguished eucalyptus trees. Karri is the more spectacular: it is huge in both height and girth; its trunk shoots skywards for maybe fifty feet (fifteen metres) before branching out. Many a painter of the Australian landscape has depicted men dwarfed by trees, and maybe they had Karri and Jarrah in mind.

The two, highly prized as timber as well as admirable to view, thrive several hundred miles south of Perth, encouraged by a distinctly Mediterranean climate which favours farming, the growth of quality grapes and the production of some classy wines. Perth has long produced wine. Trollope said he did not drink such wine with delight, but with awe and trembling and in small quantities. Grapes grown further south in gravelly loam and in cooler temperatures would have pleased him more. But no one thought to plant the area until around 1970, after an agricultural scientist had pointed out the merit of the warm (rather than hot) dry summers. Since then, the area around the Margaret River has claimed the attention of experts who reckon it can produce wine to rank with the best in the world. The Leeuwin Estate's Chardonnay 1982 has been rapturously received, even at $A20 a bottle. Leeuwin is owned by Denis Horgan, a wealthy merchant banker, and is a lavish operation, in contrast with most of the Margaret River producers who have 'boutique wineries' and often other jobs. Kevin Cullen, a local doctor, began wine-making with his wife, Di; she has now taken over, and her Sauvignon Blanc has won many a medal. At Cape Mentelle, David Hohnen is one of the few professional oenologists. He trained in California, a fact which is reflected in his predilection for deep-coloured, full-bodied wines with high tannin levels. He has introduced Zinfandel to the area, but Cabernet is his medal-winner.

From fine wine and tall trees to toasted sandwiches and coffee in cracked cups, that's how it was to be. I was back on the bus again for my journey north to Dampier. And playing games. Last time on the bus (coach) journey from Melbourne to Adelaide I had, if you remember, taken a vow of silence; I did not speak unless I was spoken to and, as a result, I had remained silent. This time, having no desire to remain silent for upwards of twenty hours, I decided that, at each roadhouse stop at least, I would initiate a conversation. However, I had no desire to talk for a while. The bus left soon after seven in the morning and that is much too early to be sociable. In any event there was little opportunity. The bus was not crowded; there were maybe twenty people on board, a good proportion travelling singly. A group of Aborigines formed a club at the back and ate chips out of paper cups whenever we stopped. At 90 cents it was the cheapest food. I took my seat near the front and divided my attention between my mass of newspapers, Lang Hancock's *Rogue Bull*, my notebook, and eavesdropping on a conversation the driver was having with a balding American who was dressed in jeans and a check shirt, chewing gum and taking endless photographs through the huge front window of the fast-moving vehicle. Eavesdropping is not quite the right word: it implies that I had to strain to hear secrets; but there were no secrets and there was no strain. This American talked loudly, with the self-confident air of one who assumes that anything he has to say is of interest to his fellows. I learned that he lived in Indonesia, where he was working for a World Bank project building roads, and had decided to use his sixteen-day leave travelling non-stop around Australia. Eight nights on the bus and eight nights in hotels. He reckoned he'd have done Australia by the end. Well, at least he'd seen the roads, and roads were, after all, his business. The driver knew nothing about Indonesia and cared less, even though the country is his near neighbour. He listened.

The weather was good, the sky clear except for a few clouds that looked as if they had been hung there for decoration. There was little to view; the bus did not run along the coast, and through the window there was – as ever – scrub with, occasionally, a wattle bush or bottle brush to add a pretty splash of colour to the grey bitumen, the blue sky and the dusty rust of the bush. Sometimes the bitumen was light grey, which seemed in keeping and softened the colour change from road to land and from land to sky. Sometimes it was dark grey, providing a stark contrast to the surrounding more subtle shades.

Music came from the radio: 'I've seen fire; I've seen rain and I've

231

seen sunny days I thought would never end ...' I'd heard the song before, but had never found the words so apposite. The day settled down.

At the noon lunch-stop, toasted sandwich in one hand and coffee in the other, I looked around for a conversation. The American, whose name was Leigh, was the only person already seated, and I asked if I might join him.

'Sure,' he replied, and looked intently at his salad.

This provoked me into commenting that roadhouse food was not giving him a favourable impression of Australian cuisine.

'It's wonderful to me. I'm used to living on rice, rice and more rice,' and that took the conversation right back to Indonesia.

I know the country a little, having once visited it for three weeks as a travel writer, and I attempted to regale him with my story of a well-heeled bunch of Americans let loose on the remote island of Nias. We'd all been told not to offer the kids baubles and sweets, but of course the majority of the party did just that until we had scores of them following us for hours begging for money. We'd been told that our visit, for which a fee had been paid to the island's Head Man, was to provide money for a much-needed hospital – which, in part at least, justified our intrusion. But the sound of blaring transistor radios and the sight of other Western nonsense, while we sat around gawping at a special display of stone dancing, had made me question the validity of the visit.

Leigh knew Nias, but he didn't seem much interested in such social questions. He was an engineer interested in building roads.

I switched tack. 'Do you think you are getting the feel of Australia from sixteen days in the bus?'

'I'm not missing much, am I? I don't know anyone and, when I do get off for an overnight stop in a hotel, I do little more than have a drink in the bar. I'm certainly not missing beds. I'm used to sleeping on the floor, so the bus is quite a luxury.' He had lovely eyes and a thin, mean mouth which managed to look even meaner when he smiled.

It wasn't much of a conversation, and I was happy to get back on the bus and swap my Lang Hancock for a volume of short stories by Elizabeth Jolley, a West Australian writer with whom I'd had dinner before leaving Perth. Elizabeth Jolley is in her early sixties, a frail, grey-haired lady with glasses and a wholesome granny-look, and yet she writes books about lesbians and old people and young girls called Clever and Pretty and loves it when people call her work 'sick' and her characters 'depraved'. She shares her life with her husband (who is retired) and her cat (who is seventeen and doesn't seem to know where he is half the time, but she refuses to have him put down while he seems to be enjoying his food). She appears self-effacing and has spent her life being unassuming: an unassuming nurse; an unassuming wife; an unassuming mother who quietly wrote fragments and slowly pieced them together over the years and didn't contemplate submitting anything for publication until she was in her mid-fifties. Now she is busy being an unassuming author, bemused by the fact that academics dissect her words and read more into them than she admits to seeing herself. She thinks it's all rather clever. Elizabeth Jolley was born in England, in the Midlands, of an English father and an Austrian mother, but she has lived in and around Perth for some twenty-five years – long enough to be classified as 'West Australian'. We got lost in a long discussion about the moment when she stopped being English and started being Australian and what this meant to her writing. In the end she conceded that she considered herself English and her themes universal and found it difficult to define 'Australian-ness'. She agreed it was something more than describing pink sunsets and white gums, but to be more precise was impossible.

I enjoyed the meeting and I enjoyed my afternoon on the bus with *Woman in a Lampshade*, savouring the daylight hours and knowing that by seven p.m. I would no longer be able to read. It would be dark and the inadequate lighting made reading a strain rather than a pleasure.

We stopped again at six p.m. and I chatted to two Australian nurses who were working their way around the country. They were uncertain where to stop in the North-West, and I could not help. We were all first-timers, except Bob who'd been visiting his daughter in

Brisbane. He came from Dampier and reckoned it was the greatest place; but the girls knew that it was a small company town and had already decided to pass it by. I was glad to talk to Bob, for I felt a little apprehensive about arriving in Dampier in the middle of the night – three thirty to be precise – and visualized myself stumbling around in the dark trying to find my motel room where I had arranged to have the key left in the door. Bob assured me that the bus stopped right by the hotel and that there would be plenty of light, and he'd make sure I found my way.

The evening on the bus seemed interminable. I envied those who found it easy to sleep. I tried and had succeeded only in dozing when, a minute or two before midnight, I heard two bangs, followed by the sound of shattering glass. The driver swore and braked. I thought two tyres had blown and rose from my seat to investigate, along with two other passengers whose curiosity outweighed their desire to sleep. We had hit two kangaroos.

'It's a bloody hazard on these roads at night,' said the driver. 'They seem to come from nowhere and rush right into the headlights.' With that he set about fixing the headlights with tape and sweeping the glass from the steps. The bottom panel of the glass door had been smashed. The driver was irritated rather than perturbed. On one journey, on the same road, he'd hit fourteen kangaroos. Two was nothing. The smell was awful – and it couldn't have come from the bodies, which were some distance behind; it must have come from the bits that clung on impact.

In spite of the incident we arrived in Dampier on time and, as Bob had forecast, I had no difficulty locating my room, No. 3, at the Mermaid Hotel. I slept until eleven a.m.

It was Easter Sunday and the 2,400 inhabitants of Dampier (the centre of the 'All go Archipelago', according to literature produced by Dampier Tidy Town Committee) had clearly decided to sleep all day. There was no one around. The reception desk was closed. The kitchen was closed until evening. The bar was open and attending to the needs of three men, one of whom suggested that I'd be lucky to find anywhere open, but perhaps it was worth trying the Seafarers' Centre which had a Chinese take-away. Outside, the streets were empty. On a long walk I saw one man on a bicycle, three families on the beach and a handful of cars at the Yacht Club.

Dampier is not an attractive town; the site itself is not congenial. There are rocky slopes down to the water and my hotel was separated from the sea by a strip of rubble which was clearly thought not worth landscaping. Cyclones are the trouble, perhaps. To meet the threat, the endless lines of brick veneer houses were built on concrete slabs, reinforced with diagonal bracing, and the screened windows were designed to withstand gusts of up to 150 mph (240 kph). The houses have everything, they say, refrigerators and washing machines. Mining companies have to provide such things these days, otherwise they would be faced with a shortage of labour. The longer I walked, the more suburban the place began to feel, but then the architects and town planners had set out to achieve this very feeling. They reckoned that most of the workers would be coming from suburbs elsewhere and would prefer to find a similar environment.

From a distance the Seafarers' Centre looked pleasant, perched on a hill overlooking Hampton Harbour, but on closer examination it appeared rather run-down and ramshackle. One couple sat on the wooden terrace eating and drinking wine from a cask. I should have walked away, but it was two p.m. and I was hungry. Besides, this centre, which aims to provide 'for the spiritual, social and moral welfare of all seafarers, regardless of colour, creed or country', was sure to offer fresh fish, even if the surroundings were scruffy. A fat man in filthy clothes assured me that the sea food was fresh, but as soon as he began to pour the contents of a saucepan on to something called a 'sizzling dish', splashing both me and the table, I knew that it was not. I tried a forkful and rejected it. This disappointment cost $A8 – but then I had been warned often enough that the North-West coast was expensive. Distances and freight charges are the official reasons, but the local Member of Parliament writing in the *Pilbara Advertiser* is not so sure. The gap between prices in Perth and prices in Pilbara has grown too wide. I fear that lack of competition plays its part. The Seafarers' Centre's only rivals are the Nosh Bar and the Milk Bar. The motel, which charges around $A50 a night, has no competition at all. No wonder tourists are few, and those who do venture forth favour camper vans.

None the less the view was pleasant and the shade was welcome, and I sat and devoured, not food, but the pamphlets I'd found in my hotel room. I learned about Red Dog. Red Dog was a handsome kelpie who spurned domestication and chose instead the life of a hobo, accepting a lift here and a meal there and roaming as far north as Broome and as far south as Perth. Red Dog had his own bank account, opened by single men in the town to pay his licence and his vet bills. When he died in 1979, having sampled strychnine bait, a committee raised money for a sculpture of the creature to adorn Dampier Tidy Town Information Bay.

Dampier is adolescent, less than twenty years old; it needs 'characters' and it needs to create a history for itself. The place was first described in 1699 by the English explorer, William Dampier. But the coast and its group of islands (with improbable names like West Intercourse Island and West Mid Intercourse Island and East Intercourse Island and East Mid Intercourse Island) were for a long time of no interest to anyone except passing whaling ships and pearl fishers who built seasonal camps on these blobs in the Indian Ocean. Monte Bello is out there somewhere, too. Michael Kalis, the head of a large Perth-based fishing fleet, had told me that this stretch of coast was the haunt of drug runners. His fishermen sometimes came across them, and he had offered to patrol the area for a fee on behalf of the government. The fee was not forthcoming. Now whaling and pearls have given way to salt fields and a vast natural-gas venture and, of course, iron ore. When this was discovered, Hamersley Iron had to start from scratch: they had to build the port of Dampier and the inland towns of Karratha, Tom Price and Paraburdoo at a cost of some \$A300 million.

The last two, where the ore is mined by open-pit methods, are 200 and 250 miles (320 and 400 kilometres) inland, and the product is transported by rail on trains hauling 180 car-loads to the port where the ore is stockpiled and dumped into ships, all of which head straight for Japan. I went on a tour of the port operation – which was not a riveting way to spend an hour or two, but it did at least enable me to work out how that dog got its name. I returned, speckled with red dust. My intention was to travel to Tom Price on the ore train: a request which Hamersley Iron considered a little eccentric but none the less agreed to.

Peter, the train driver, and Dennis, his observer, got a surprise; no one had told them to expect a passenger; when I arrived, just before six a.m., they had departed, hell bent on an early get-away. Fortunately they had not gone too far down the track and a quick phone call pulled them up sharp and invited them to wait for me. I caught up by car. The pair eyed me cautiously as I clambered aboard, and their first response was exactly the same as Ike's had been when I had boarded the road train a month or so earlier. 'Can't imagine what you want to do this for ... it's a boring run. Nothing happens. We might hit a 'roo, I suppose, but you wouldn't know much about it in this thing,' Peter said, patting the first of the three engines needed to haul the mile-long load. There are only six stretches of the track where one can look back and see the entire train, and there are only a few points in the track where, empty, the train can reach 70 mph (110 kph) in its eagerness to breathe the air at Tom Price. That's why the three engines are necessary: to cope with the gradient. For most of the way the track is single; for most of the way the sidings and line camps have evocative names: dingo, emu, galah, gecko, koala, lizard, pelican, possum and wombat; for most of the way it was a glorious run.

Peter loves the job, even though night rides can be dull and the tracks can mesmerize. He used to work on the rigs off the coast, but his wife didn't like the system of two weeks away and one at home, so he became an engine driver, like his brother. Dennis had been a co-driver (or observer) for three years. He'd left the railways in Victoria to come to the Pilbara because the money was good. He'd like to become a driver, but then so would lots of others, and the waiting list is long. In many ways his job was the more interesting as he was constantly on the move, running backwards and forwards checking the three engines, oily rag clutched in one hand like a security blanket. Peter remained in one spot, moving the throttle to control the speed and, every forty-five seconds, pressing a button to prove he hadn't gone to sleep. Should he over-run the minute, a shrill whistle reprimands him and the brakes go on. 'We have a rule: if you let the whistle go, you have to buy your mate a beer!' The gesture of pressing the button was as natural to him as raising a hand to brush away flies.

I wanted to drive the train, of course, but waited a while before I risked a rebuff. It didn't come; they both readily agreed and even allowed me to run the minute to test the whistle. 'No speeding, mind. We had a new chap on here one day and he wanted to see how far he could push it. He got it up to a 110 miles [175 kilometres], but they can tell, you know. There's a tape which shows up everything, the speed, where you've braked, everything.' I didn't feel tempted to speed; that throttle is a handful for a beginner. I was enjoying myself.

After a while a bell rang, denoting trouble of some sort, and Dennis disappeared and reappeared to announce that the third engine had a water leak. That engine had been faulty before with the same problem. The bell rang on and off for the next hour. Dennis seemed in control; no one said much. We even had time to boil a billy for tea. Nice traditional touch, that: a kettle would have been easier to use since the billy doesn't have a spout from which to pour the water. But tradition is all, and with our tea we had another sample: we opened the hamper which accompanies each journey; inside were a whole chicken, cold meat, tomatoes, cucumber, fresh fruit, Vegemite, biscuits, fruit cake, bread, scones – the list could go on. 'One of the perks of the job. We take most of it home; the hampers would feed a family, so long as they don't get bored with the selection.'

We travelled steadily on through the blinding sun, through the slowly rising, reddening hills. Ahead we saw a red light and Peter picked up the phone to unravel its message. A train was coming down the track, loaded, from Tom Price and our train would have to pull into the siding to let it pass. At the same time Peter decided to swap engines with the train, since he needed three in good working order to take the strain of the last stretch; the other train, though full, could manage with two, since it had a downhill run all the way to Dampier. He explained to me in detail what was happening, while Dennis worked in the mounting heat to uncouple the engines from the 180 wagons. Then Peter disappeared to fiddle around with the track, and after about twenty minutes returned to the cab to await the signal to inch forward and negotiate the swap. I think we were sharing a joke at the time. I can't remember; I know that the water from the billy went everywhere and I recall a jolt and an immense shudder.

It was all over in seconds – we were derailed. The front engine listed to the right and completely left the tracks; the second engine clung on for dear life and managed to remain partially in place; the third engine, with impeccable balance, stayed put.

Peter knew instantly what had happened – what had gone wrong – what he had forgotten to do. He had moved one set of switches on the track and had forgotten the other. The second lot had been in position for only a short while. In the normal course of events the switches are controlled from Dampier, but they had been turned to manual to aid the engine swap.

'They'll have my bum for this – and I deserve it. It's a bad mistake, a bad mistake. This kind of thing just never happens. They'll probably suspend me until they have held an inquiry and the damn line will be out of action for a day or two.' He was anxious but calm.

We climbed down and met Dennis coming towards us along the track. 'We're in the shit,' he said.

I tried to stay out of the way. I felt my presence had contributed to the oversight. I'd distracted Peter with questions and chat.

Within minutes a four-wheel-drive appeared, and men poured over the track and over the engines. 'You'll be the first to be bailed out,' someone yelled at me.

After a while another car came along the service road and stopped. 'What's happened?' asked the driver. I explained, and he explained that he was the headmaster of the District High School in Paraburdoo returning from an Easter weekend on the coast. He authorized his young sons to leave the car and look at the derailed engines, and I asked for a lift to Tom Price. The last time I saw Peter, looking remarkably unruffled in his neat green shorts and shirt and ankle-length boots, he was deep in conversation with officials. As I drove away I recalled his first words: 'I can't imagine why you want to do this ... it's a boring run. Nothing happens.'

At Tom Price I learned that the company official who had been assigned to show me the town had gone off down the track to rescue me. Our cars must have crossed, each without a thought for the other. I checked into the Tom Price Hotel and had a beer.

Roger Nancarrow found me before too long; company towns like to chaperone their visitors in much the same way as they cocoon their inhabitants. Tom Price is not a bit like Broken Hill. Broken Hill has balls; Tom Price is a feather bed. In the beginning, it must have been harsh, creating all this comfort out of barren waste, but the first comers recalled with evident pleasure the spirit of the pioneering community before there was a shopping centre, sports facilities galore and lawns with sprinklers. In the early days you might have had to look to Perth for your shoe repairs and your drycleaning, but at least you could go to the pub of an evening and wander from table to table. Now, with a work-force of 1,200 and a community of 4,000, you are just as likely to find a sea of strange faces. In this oasis of material wealth you must moan about something. You can't moan about money: a gardener earns around $A18,000 and a mine worker around $A30,000 – and this surely is a large sum, when living about the twenty-sixth parallel entitles you to a twenty per cent tax discount; when the company gives you two free airline tickets to Perth a year and charges you a mere $A27 a week for rent (that rent including your electricity and water – a bonus indeed when the air-conditioner needs to run most of the time and the lawn needs a daily sprinkle). As for repairs and maintenance, all you have to do is pick up the phone to Town Services and your lavatory will be unblocked, free of charge, an extra set of keys will be cut or an old mattress removed. I know because I sat in the office and listened to the requests.

I thought I'd found Wonderland: a 'No worries, mate' town. And it is – if you are young, and happy for your life to revolve around your children, a hobby or two, say dressmaking and gemstone collecting, and any kind of sport from football to flying. There is a cinema and one television station, the ABC, and general knowledge nights at the club. But there are no generations. There is no granny to do the baby-sitting and cook the Sunday lunch; no Mum or sister upon whom to off-load details of the latest domestic row – they are all a thousand miles away. This causes stress.

The average age of Tom Price inhabitants is thirteen years.

The schools are partly to blame. Education is provided up to the age of sixteen. This means that parents with ambitions for their children either leave the town when their children reach the age of eleven, or they send them to boarding school. Most decide to leave, even though the company is willing to help with boarding fees and air fares. And this in turn means that with most high-flyers heading south, the secondary schools are left with the dregs. That is not my word; it was used to me many times. The 'dregs' are kids who can't work or won't work – in any event don't work, and lower the standards of the schools, which then means that even parents with borderline children or borderline ambitions move on. The town has been nagging the State to offer education to eighteen but there is little chance. It would only mean postponing the exodus, since there are limited job opportunities.

Hamersley is doing its best to create a generation. Once you had to leave when you retired, but now you can buy your house at $A150 a month over fifteen years, and stay if you wish. Some may stay, but often the scheme is used as a form of compulsory saving, since the company will happily buy back the house. Wonderland may be without wrinkles, but it is full of fear. Those who come for a short stay get trapped. They fear the inevitable drop in their standard of living if they move to the city, and they fear the effort; they become accustomed to the ease of living, and apathy and dependence dominate their thinking. Tom Price is an engineering achievement, but living a cocooned life is an addiction hard to kick.

I didn't stay long. My days ahead held other engineering miracles; other areas of even greater isolation; other glimpses of insoluble problems. Besides, to my delight, the Flying Doctor called me from Carnarvon, on the coast south of Dampier, and offered to pick me up on his way home to Port Hedland.

CHAPTER 12

The Flying Doctor

The Flying Doctor invokes a potent image; the two words together restore a certain magic that has been lost to them individually. Flying has become routine; doctors are no longer revered; but the notion of the Flying Doctor retains an element of romance. The doctors don't see it that way. The drop-out rate is high. It is an experience, not a way of life, an interesting year for the young doctor en route to a cosy hospital in a country town or a surgery in a leafy suburb. Urban life is comfortable; urban practices are lucrative; besides, the Australian is a conformist, and the professional with a choice, unlike the miner, would rather be among the crowd. The crowd is happy to maintain the image: to pay for the Royal Flying Doctor Service. In a sense, it is the cities' gift to the Outback – the cost is carved into three parts and paid by the Federal Government, the State governments and voluntary donations. There are fifteen bases, eight of them in Western Australia. Victoria, a small State, has no need of a base and has taken on responsibility for providing a service in the Kimberleys, in the far north of Western Australia.

The crowd, that is to say the population clustered along the coast, appreciates the romance. They like to feel linked to the Outback, even though they rarely know what really exists fifty miles beyond the city boundary. The Flying Doctor is that link and is also a tangible reminder of those beloved, overly romanticized pioneering days. Every schoolchild learns about John Flynn. The Reverend John Flynn, a Presbyterian, dedicated to improving conditions in the Outback through the Australian Inland Mission. His first concern, of course, was for the souls of men, but spiritual soon led to physical concern,

The Flying Doctor

for serious illness meant death in the Outback. He first had the idea
of linking the medical services with the aeroplane via the radio in
1914, but he had to wait until 1928 for his vision to come to pass.
The plane wasn't the problem, but it took until 1927 for a cheap,
pedal-driven wireless transmitter to be invented.

At one time Port Hedland had been considered as the site for the
first aerial medical service base, but Cloncurry in Queensland won
the day, mainly because it had a larger population but also because
it had already seen the dawn of commercial aviation in Australia.
Qantas had established an aerodrome there. Mud had caused the
creation of Qantas. In the wet season, mud made the roads impassable
and several Queensland graziers and a couple of wartime pilots sat
and pondered how they might establish a passenger mail and air
link between Queensland and the port of Darwin in the Northern
Territory. Qantas – the initials stand for 'Queensland and Northern
Territory Aerial Services' – was, in 1928, contracted to the Australian
Inland Mission to provide the first air ambulance.

The Flying Doctor does not fly himself; he has a pilot and uses his
plane like a chauffeured car. Greg the chauffeur and Michele the
nurse were alone when they picked me up in Tom Price. The Flying
Doctor was enjoying a day off in preparation for two lengthy days
holding clinics in the bush. As well as giving consultations over the
radio-telephone and dealing with emergency evacuations, the service
is much concerned with preventive medicine – holding weekly clinics
to catch problems before they become emergencies. The nature of
the work has changed since the early days when the area was mainly
pastoral. Emergencies on cattle stations now form a minor part of
the case load – there may be the odd accident during mustering –
but the base is mainly concerned with industrial accidents. There
are five pilots and three planes, two on call and one assigned to clinic
duty. Those on call expect about eleven night and twenty-four
daytime flights. The Port Hedland hospital can handle most things;
only about one per cent of cases have to be flown to Perth. They can't
cope with really premature babies, or the man who had been stabbed
in the chest and had a ruptured spleen. That same day, Greg and
Michele had flown a stroke victim to Carnarvon en route for Perth.

The Ribbon and the Ragged Square

On the flight, Greg and Michele prepared me for Port Hedland. No one seemed to like the place. The tourist office in Perth was at a loss to recommend a hotel to me; no one went there, they said. And the staff at the Mermaid Hotel in Dampier had said they had no time for it. Greg and Michele were there for the jobs. Michele said she'd be off tomorrow if she could get a transfer to the base in Perth, but the waiting list was long. Port Hedland, she said, was a man's town: the men didn't know how to behave in mixed company, and she'd never go into a bar on her own.

The drive from the airport to the town helped me begin to understand why the north-west coast was for so long ignored; why it daunted the Dutch and disappointed Dampier. The western shores are depressing, the coastline is so low and so bleak. The town itself is not happily situated; it is built on an island connected to the mainland by three causeways which run over tidal flats. As the land on the island is limited, a second section, South Hedland, has been built five miles (eight kilometres) inland beyond the tidal flats. This section, they say, was designed by a woman to resemble a maze. The woman eventually committed suicide. The two towns together house 17,000 people. If the place is so bleak, why have a settlement there at all? Geographically it has its uses; it has had its uses since 1863 when it was a service point for pearlers and then, when gold was discovered in 1888 at Marble Bar and Nullagine, several hundred miles inland, its usefulness became even more apparent. After gold the place struggled for a while, but now there is iron ore. Port Hedland is the main port for the mines of Mount Goldsworthy and Mount Newman. And it has the Flying Doctor base and that is why I was there.

At seven-thirty next morning it was already hot, already humid; there was much talk of a cyclone, even though it was April and a little late in the year for such elemental tantrums. As I waited for the Flying Doctor, I pondered the kind of medical problems I might find in the Outback in the next couple of days. They had to be different from those suffered by sedentary city folk whom I knew to be an unhealthy lot. The death rate from heart disease, cancer and strokes was just as high as in other Western industrialized nations, and a survey in the late 1970s showed that forty-five per cent of the population suffered from one or more chronic conditions, the most frequent being arthritis, hay fever and hypertensive disease; but the list also included a fair number of circulatory and respiratory troubles – bronchitis, emphysema and asthma. Some sixty-five per cent of those surveyed had consulted a doctor in the previous six months, eighteen per cent a mere two weeks before; fifty per cent had taken medication within the last two days, whether vitamins and tonics or heart and blood-pressure pills. Not a healthy nation. The image of a bronzed breed of sportsmen is a myth and as mis-leading as expecting all Frenchwomen to look like Bardot. Now the sportsman is just as likely to be found slumped in an armchair, a spectator in front of the television set. That's why they invented Norm and a campaign called 'Life. Be in it', designed to make Australians aware of the perils of inactivity, of obesity and lethargy. Norm is a neat bit of marketing based on the concept of knowing your national characteristics. It might be one thing for Chairman Mao to require his citizens to indulge in statutory daily exercise, but in Australia a touch of self-mockery is more likely to get some people climbing the stairs, strolling a mile, or spinning a frisbee with the kids.

Norm in the telly ads has the message: 'Throw a dart, look at art, it's good for your heart.' He's a T-shirt-wearing, pot-bellied, crude sort of a bloke, happiest sinking a few and referring to women as 'sheilas'. 'G'day, Norm's the name. Pull up a chair and cop a load of this ... you can leave the telly on if ya like.' He's lovable and a bit of a poet:

> Have you copped this bloke on the telly
> Interrupting me favourite show,
> With a tinny arranged on his belly,
> Reminds me of someone I know.
>
> Not that I'm against physical fitness,
> Don't get me wrong on that score,
> I could watch them fit blokes forever,
> But me thumb's inclined to get sore.

And I'm not against watching the telly,
Cripes, if that was to go on the blink,
A bloke would have no sporting interests,
It certainly makes a bloke think.

Now it's true I might wheeze when I'm walking,
Not that I've done much of late.
And it's true I've put a few stone on,
But at my age you always gain weight.

So what if I can't tie my shoelace!
So what if I can't see me toes!
I remember what most of 'em look like,
So there's really no need to see those.

So when this bloke says 'Life. Be in it.'
Be in it he says on TV,
I give him a nod and change channels,
'Cause I know he's not talking to me.

When the Flying Doctor finally walked through the door, I hope I hid my surprise. Ann Kearney looked very young; her shoulder-length hair, permed into a pre-Raphaelite look, was still wet, and she wore a print frock with frilled sleeves and white-rimmed sun-glasses. Somehow I'd imagined a trim uniform at least. Then I discovered that she came from Glasgow, had been in Australia for three months, during which time she had spent six weeks as a locum in Sydney and six weeks in Port Hedland. For all that, she was extremely self-assured and swept us into the plane, taking the seat alongside the pilot for herself. I sat with my back to the pilot, alongside a bed. Opposite me was Andy Cumming, the district medical officer, who was English and had been a G P in Adelaide for ten years before moving to Hedland for a one-year posting. We were dropping him at Marble Bar where he was taking a clinic. He liked to get away from the hospital one day a week, and on this day we was going to tour the tin mine, Endeavour, to look at the conditions. Most of his patients worked in that mine.

Marble Bar has the distinction of being listed in the record books as the hottest place in Australia. In 1923–34 the temperature exceeded 100°F (38°C) for 160 days. In the winter, the temperature regularly reaches 100°F in the daytime and plummets overnight to produce frost. The place is blessed with endless, ever-changing, colourful rock formations, and Andy suggested that I take careful note of the morning colours and compare them with the evening hues when we returned to pick him up. Thereafter we discussed the Australian health service, which had continued to puzzle me. A country so willing to import and copy things British from institutions to the education system, from architecture to clothing, from books to television programmes, had shown an unusual streak of independence and chosen not to copy the glory of the post-war British Labour Government: the National Health Service. There had been an attempt in 1944 by a Labor Government to introduce a comprehensive scheme of medical benefits, but it had failed because doctors resented what they perceived as interference with their medical judgement and feared what they saw as the first step to nationalized medicine. Further attempts were out of the question while the Liberal Party reigned for more than twenty years, and individuals had to fund visits to doctors and hospitals through private insurance from one of thirty-eight companies offering a variety of schemes.

Whitlam's Government in 1974 introduced the first attempt at universal health care, which it proposed to fund from a 2.5 per cent levy on taxable incomes. This proposal was rejected by the Senate and the scheme had to be funded by general taxation. The whole thing was only partly implemented when Whitlam was sacked in 1975, and after that the Liberal Government dismantled 'Medibank' (as it was called) piecemeal, making so many changes in an attempt to revert to private insurance that the electorate became heartily sick of the constant messing about with the organization and form of payment for such an essential service. In the end it was decreed that health care would be free for the unemployed, pensioners and families on low incomes; and the rest made their own insurance deal. This cost the average family about $A15 a week, but a tax rebate reduced that sum to around $A11, or $A5 for a single person. It was estimated that under this system half a million families fell through the net: those with incomes not low enough for a free card and not high enough for them to be able or willing to pay for insurance.

This system was clearly inequitable in its distribution of costs. The family with an average income found themselves paying about three per cent of their pre-tax earnings in insurance; a family with an income double the national average was paying less than one per cent. Not surprisingly Bob Hawke's Labor Government changed the system back to a modified Whitlam plan, based on a one per cent levy on taxable income. The insurance companies were not happy; their turnover would be cut in half, even if a sizeable proportion of the population decided to take out additional insurance enabling them to have a single hospital room and the surgeon of their choice. But the majority of the electorate welcomed the proposal warmly: for most families it would be cheaper. Only the highest income families (those receiving more than $A1,000 a week) would find it more expensive – and even then there was a maximum levy which limited their increase to around $A5 a week. The question of real concern is how the Hawke Government could fund the system on a levy less than half that proposed by Whitlam ten years earlier; it was speculated that before long the one per cent levy would have to be increased.

Andy Cumming, being a reasonable man, suggested that there was good and bad in both the UK system and the Australian system, however it was funded. 'In the UK, it is in the doctor's interest to have fit patients, for he gets paid the same whether he sees the patient twice a year or twice a month. In this country it is in the doctor's interest to have sick patients – he gets paid every time he sees them. This is good because it encourages the doctor to work harder and there are fewer waiting lists, but there is always the danger of over-servicing.' There is indeed. Some estimates put the cost of over-servicing into millions of dollars.

As for the standard of medical services in the Hedland area, Andy Cumming thought it was not as high as in the city. 'The service is good in parts, but on the whole it reflects the community as much as anything. There is an abnormally high incidence of *de facto* relationships, alcoholism and those living on welfare benefits. In other words there is a greater proportion of social misfits than in city areas, the population tends to be more transient, and such people do not demand excellence. Port Hedland, with a population of 17,000, could easily support an eye specialist and a dermatologist, but instead exists on monthly visits from Perth specialists. But then of course what kind of specialist would be happy to settle in this area for any length of time? We have enough difficulty finding locums.'

Ann Kearney's destination that day was Nullagine, once a small but thriving gold-mining community and now a small and rather futile community mainly of Aborigines, a handful of scattered and eccentric prospectors and the usual bunch of whites running the post office and store, the pub and the petrol station and the police headquarters.

The clinic and community centre is a neat one-storey building behind a wire fence. On the wall of the surgery was a reminder that all patients being investigated for sexually transmissible diseases should also be examined for syphilis, a long list of patients receiving regular medication with their details in an adjacent column, and a further column decreeing whether the patient was an Aborigine or a Caucasian. Inderal for controlling blood pressure was getting a good run.

The clinic started at ten thirty. Sally, the nurse, sat in an outer room screening patients and warning them of my presence; they were given the opportunity to ask me to leave during their consultation. None did. Ann Kearney's first patient was a white mother with two sons suffering from asthma. They needed new prescriptions for inhalants. Ann quizzed the mother on the cause of the problem, suggesting that it might be something other than 'physical exertion' which caused the wheezing; it might be house dust. The mother said little: she wanted a prescription.

The second patient was a white male prospector who had trouble with his eyes. 'Lots of styes,' he said.

'Let's have a wee look,' said the doctor, laying him out on a couch and popping drops into his eyes. He nattered all the while about his job, and about the heat and the dust and the flies that were responsible for his eye trouble. His lower lids were covered with fluid-filled cysts which he rubbed, setting up secondary infection. I peeped at his file and saw that he had been lectured on personal cleanliness several times before. Ann warned him again. She pierced a cyst or two and hinted that he might have to go to Perth for treatment. She'd decide next time.

Another prospector arrived complaining of coughs and colds and a chest infection. He received a lecture on the perils of smoking and an introduction to the thought of nicotine chewing-gum. Dr Kearney is efficient and abrupt and prone to lecture. Even as a locum she is not content merely to hand out prescriptions without an attempt to influence the patient's habits.

The first Aborigine appeared with a hand wrapped in a dirty bandage, which she removed to reveal a huge open sore in the palm of her hand.

'Looks like a burn?' said Ann.

'No.'

'What is it then?'

'Boil. Won't heal.'

The burn, it seems, might well have been caused by applying the wrong kind of cream. Ann ordered an antibiotic injection, explaining to me as the patient left the room that there was no point in giving a middle-aged woman pills: she would not have sufficient education to understand their purpose, nor remember to take them.

Screams announced the presence of a year-old baby, whose Aboriginal mother was bothered not only by the endless screaming but also by continual weight loss.

Ann questioned her closely on the baby's diet. 'Does she eat from your plate? Does she have diarrhoea? Do you know what that is?' She was getting nowhere. In the end, an examination revealed that the baby had an ear infection. Medicine was prescribed, Ann believing this time that the mother was young enough to know the value of the stuff.

Rachel said she was nine. Her records said she was nine, but she looked at least thirteen. (Aborigines are not much interested in ages and in birthdays; all their records list 1 March, 1 April, 1 September as 'birthdays' to please bureaucrats who do not like forms with empty squares.)

Rachel had a swollen toe. 'Where are your shoes? Ask your mother to get you some shoes.' Ann was infinitely patient with the girl, chatting to her about school, about sums, testing her ability to add five plus two and her ability to read. The girl was completely at ease with the doctor, who obviously had an interest in children.

Rachel was followed by two more Aboriginal women, one suffering a chest complaint and the other yet another infected boil. But they were different: they had been let out of prison to visit the Flying Doctor. One had been given three weeks and the other four weeks for disorderly conduct while drunk. They had been fighting. I went outside to find their escort, Darryl, the local policeman. He was young and shy, and he answered my questions in short bursts. In the previous three weeks he had handled twenty-two charges of drunk and disorderly, most of them women.

'Reckon they like it in prison. We give them three meals a day. Give them their own food and they cook it the way they like it. If I cook it they complain and want it another way, so I let them get on with it. No, we don't lock them up, either by day or by night. Where would they go? In the daytime they can sit under the trees outside the prison. They don't even wander off. Why should they? When they are free they sit under the trees all day without a drink. But they get three free meals a day and they reckon that's fair exchange. Aw yeah. I like the work. We're not flat out every day, and I have an Aboriginal aide to help me. It's the paperwork that's bad.'

Back in the surgery, the local JP's wife was huffing and puffing, and claiming a chest infection. She told us about her dog. He had recently lost a leg. A horse had kicked him.

When the clinic was over, Ann and I went to the pub and ordered lime juice and soda while Sally, the nurse, finished dressing an infected boil and giving injections. One part of the pub was partitioned off for the Aborigines; that section had no carpet on the floor and no chairs or tables. The white section had carpet squares and tables and chairs.

Ann and I discussed the morning's patients. Those awful sores are the result of alcoholism; all the drinking makes it more difficult for the wounds to heal, and many are diabetic too as a result of a heavily sugared poor diet. 'I know I'm only temporary but I think it is my business to lecture them on cleanliness and on diet and on smoking. Perhaps other doctors are happy just to hand out a prescription, but I am not. Nothing will change, that way. I also take no notice of those who are obviously hoping for a free ride to Port Hedland. I am perfectly capable of treating most of them, especially the children. The other doctor before me referred a lot of the kids, but that is because he didn't know as much as I do about children.'

Ann Kearney left Glasgow because she felt hampered in her career. She wanted to be a paediatrician, but the only jobs she was offered were those of general practitioner. Not that she minds being a GP, just that, if that is her fate, she'd rather accept it in a better climate. An agency in Sydney has given her a two-year contract and she may decide to stay, perhaps in Tasmania or New Zealand. For the moment she is happy in Port Hedland and hopes it will take longer than three months to find a permanent doctor.

In a mere six weeks she has settled in remarkably well. She likes her house, has acquired a dog and signed on for evening classes in French, photography and scuba diving. 'I don't want to waste any time, so I won't have a television in the house.' Nor was she bothered about Hedland being a man's town. She has none of Michele's hesitancy. She is so self-confident and talkative that I doubt if she would have any qualms about walking into a pub on her own.

On the drive to the airstrip we passed the Aboriginal camp with its strange balloon-shaped houses: parachute fabric stretched over a circular frame – a cyclone-proof concept, this one. The Aborigines do not sleep in them; they prefer to bed down in the creek. Ann Kearney chatted like a bird all the way to Marble Bar – I forget what about; it is exhausting to be with people who do not stop talking. It dulls the mind. At Marble Bar we picked up Andy and a hugely pregnant woman. Conversation lapsed; doctors are cautious about gossiping in front of patients.

It was still light when we arrived back at the airport and, as Ann Kearney headed off for an hour of scuba-diving theory, I headed off to the beach for a walk. Out in the bay there were five ships, four Japanese and one from Taiwan. They had been there for several days, and were destined to be there a while longer. The miners were on strike, caught up in a row over how many men were needed to hose down a truck. The Japanese get irritated when such trivial troubles delay their iron ore. It was hardly the moment to annoy them: they were driving a hard bargain with the Australians over prices, demanding a fourteen per cent drop to bring the Pilbara product into line with their other supplier, Brazil.

The walk left me in the mood for a beer and so I decided to brave the bar. The place pulsated with the somewhat old-fashioned sound of the Supremes lecturing the crowd on the subject of love: 'You can't hurry love,' they insisted twice as I waited to be served. 'You should be in here all day,' said the barmaid. 'That record is played at least twenty times.' A group of men played billiards; the rest propped up the bar. They looked hard at me, but if I ever met their gaze they immediately looked away. I took my glass and sat at a table by the window watching the waitress toss tin ashtrays on to Formica-topped tables where they spun noisily until they came to rest. I dipped into a volume of short stories by West Australian writers and alighted on one by Robin Sheiner who that morning, according to the local paper, had published her first novel about Perth during the war years. Perth was popular with the US Navy; they thought the girls were pretty and the city perfect for having a good time. The continuous flow of American servicemen changed the lives of many Australian women who formed associations with them, even married them, even went to America as war brides. Sheiner had talked to many of them as background to her novel and seemed shocked at some of the stories. 'I thought permissiveness was invented in the 1960s, but it seems that during the war people did not feel morally accountable in the same way as they would have in a world at peace.' In Sheiner's short story, *Brothers*, she described a pale man who walked into a restaurant 'with the thin bravado of those who habitually dine alone'. As I walked to the dining-room I toyed with the image and hoped I offered no such impression.

The next morning we left again at seven thirty, this time for Telfer, almost twice as far as Nullagine and a small, closed, exclusively white gold-mining community. The Chief Pilot was bothered that I did not have permission to visit the town. However, John who was flying us was not fussed. On board was Evan Bayliss, the medical registrar of the hospital, heading for Jiggalong, an Aboriginal community. He went there once a month to attend to what he described as serious cases, diabetics and those with kidney problems. He lived in Perth and this was his second stint in Port Hedland. He'd agreed to it as the trade-off for another job he wanted in Perth later in the year. 'There are a number of kidney problems and we don't know why. Maybe it's the heat. People sweat a lot, pass little urine and what they pass is concentrated, and this may be affecting the kidneys. I've got two patients, Aborigines, who ought to be on regular dialysis, but this would mean living in Perth, which would kill them. It's better to leave them in Jiggalong and do the best we can. They just can't cope with cities. They have a bad enough time with Hedland Hospital. Last week a mother with a new-born baby discharged herself because she hated being there, and another left her baby and went on a blinder.'

He warned me of what I was going to find in Telfer; he called it the Pilbara syndrome. 'A lot of stress symptoms, tiredness, tummy pains, general complaints about not feeling well. These places may provide everything for their work-force, but they create their own problems. The men drink. They like to think they are pioneers indulging in a little frontier behaviour, but in fact they have got all mod. cons, and it's more like suburbia. The women get stuck at home with the air-conditioning while the men drink and gamble. Then they come to see the doctor with aches and pains – just like kids on Monday mornings getting sick to avoid school.'

It was raining as we landed at Jiggalong, and we teased Evan that we might not be able to get back to pick him up. It was not a good airstrip, and if it rained any more it would be impossible to land.

Our clinic at Telfer started at eleven a.m. There were a handful of common problems: a girl wanting contraceptive advice; a man wanting injections as he was planning a lengthy holiday abroad; another man with a rash. But Evan was right; there were some interesting examples of the Pilbara syndrome. A young female schoolteacher had been in Telfer for nine weeks and had suffered five migraines, bad ones that made her sick. In the previous year, living in Perth, she had had but one. Ann refused her request for valium and suggested that she needed a little more time to settle down. The teacher winked at me, maybe guessing that I was longing to ask her some unmedical questions! Later, gossiping to the others I learned that the school had problems. There were only two teachers; the other teacher had been deserted by his wife and children, who had become sick of the place. Many tensions resulted from his unhappiness. Then there came a most beautiful woman, immaculately dressed and with a wide straw hat protecting her pale skin. She looked miserable and was hostile from the moment she walked in. Unprompted, she declared she hated the place, hated Australia and longed to get away. She needed a gold injection for arthritis. She moaned about the chemist in Hedland who, she claimed, overcharged her. All prescriptions go back to Port Hedland and are then flown out on the next plane. Each prescription costs $A4 and a further $A4 handling charge.

Then came a man, a regular, complaining of chest pains and a racing heart. 'When I get these attacks, I take a couple of valium and sleep it off. I think there is something wrong with my heart.'

'Your records show that you have been checked for that, and it is not so. I'll give you some more valium.'

'I'm certain he's hoping for another free trip to Perth,' said Ann, after he had left the room.

A young girl asked me to leave, so I happily went outside to chat with Jean and Gloria who run the clinic. 'This place is awful for gossip,' said Jean, the nurse. 'I sent someone out of here with the Flying Doctor one day and within half an hour ten people had stopped and asked me what was wrong. I refused to tell them. I'm only a relief nurse, but I'd love to stay. There is so much to do here, with a young community of kids and babies. Mothers need to get organized to give one another a bit of a break. But they don't even baby-sit for one another and they certainly won't admit that they can't cope. Some of the kids just run wild in the streets after dark.'

The door opened and a head appeared: 'Who's on? ... which

doctor? Oh, *her* ... well, I'm not going in, then. She never stops lecturing us.' The head disappeared and the door shut.

'A number of people come out saying they can't get a word in.'

At lunchtime the mine's director of operations sought me out. He wanted to know how I'd heard of the place. It isn't on the map, it is never in the newspapers and security is strict. 'You can imagine how careful we have to be. We don't want people knowing about us; the gold has to be flown out in great secrecy.'

I assured him that I had never heard of Telfer until I met Dr Kearney, and that I had only the vaguest idea of where we were and that my information would be of no use to anyone. He seemed to accept this and told me a little about Telfer. The mine is seventy per cent owned by an American company, Newmont Corporation of New York, and thirty per cent owned by BHP. It had been in operation for six years and had a life-expectancy of only ten. This short life meant that the mine was not anxious to spend dollars on expensive infrastructure and therefore encouraged single men and girls to come to work in the town, rather than married couples with children and costly needs. The work-force consisted of 150 singles and 50 married men, 20 of them with working wives, and 60 children.

'We don't boast about our facilities, but we do offer very high wages. Most people here earn between $A30,000 and $A40,000. They come here to make money and to save money. Often they come with a fixed target and when they hit that target, usually after about two years, they leave. One girl truck driver has saved $A20,000 in eighteen months. She's worked hard for that, ten hours a day, six days a week.'

I questioned him about the Pilbara syndrome. 'Yes, some people do seem unhappy. But they don't seem to want to leave. They keep that target fixed in their minds. That is the incentive. I'm not sure I know what they are saving for, but I expect it is to buy a plot of land or to put a payment down on a house. That's why we encourage the young singles.'

Telfer made a weird impression: a temporary place with no community spirit; a place with problems which people hid as they piled dollars into the bank. I'd like to have seen more, but that was not encouraged. I was therefore pleased to discover that we were taking a patient back to Port Hedland – a long flight and plenty of time to talk. I'll call him the patient; I didn't ask his name. I instinctively felt he would be more comfortable anonymous.

The patient was a driller; he handled a big machine which drilled holes into which explosives were placed to break up the rock, for others to cart away and mill. He'd spent the last fifteen years travelling the bush as part of a team of three. They worked for a contractor who sent them anywhere, from Albany in the south to Darwin in the north. 'It's a cheap way of seeing the country,' he joked.

He had something wrong with his knee, a swelling which would not respond to treatment. He'd had one spell in hospital already and during that time they had diagnosed diabetes.

'That gave me a shock, I can tell you. I had to cancel my holiday in Manila and stay three weeks in hospital while I got used to the injections. I'm still having them, but they hope they might be able to reduce me to pills in the end. No drinking, they said, and I'd been having twelve stubbies a day. I'm on soda water now and I hate it; but I'm saving money, even though the mines subsidize the beer. It costs twenty-five per cent less in Telfer than it does in Hedland. The mines encouraging me to drink? No, I don't think so. I'd drink that much anyway, whatever the cost.

'Telfer's a terrible place. Just like being in jail. I've been there for sixteen months and I may stay another year. Things improved a few months back when the contractor running the mine moved out and Newmont decided to run it themselves, and they have turned out to be better employers. We are getting better accommodation for a start and the food is good – and plenty of it. We eat all the time. In the hospital at Hedland I lost eleven kilos [twenty-four pounds] in three weeks – that's a lot of weight! Mostly we just eat and work; there are two shifts: one operates from six-thirty a.m. until five p.m., and the other from five p.m. until six-thirty a.m. They say they can't operate the mine economically with shorter shifts and more men. The men don't seem to mind: there's more money in it for them, and there is nothing to do in the place. We'd only be bored with more time off.

As it is, we drink and play darts in the evening; and on our day off, Sunday, we play golf. You have to get on with the other men at all cost. If two guys get caught fighting they are both bundled in to the next plane and sent home, no questions asked and no matter who caused it. It's one of the rules. I understand that one, but there are others that I don't understand. If you want a car you have to ask permission and you have to have it registered. They like to keep an eye on you. I haven't bothered. I borrow one from the company from time to time.

'After six months of working six days a week, I got ten days off and a free flight to Perth, and since then every three months I've had another ten days off and another ticket. Not bad, is it? And then once a year there's twenty-five working days off together. Most of the time I go to Kalgoorlie to see my daughter. Her mother is there too, but I don't have anything to do with her. I once bought a house in Perth and tried to live in the city, but it didn't work out. Drillers are needed, but not in Perth.'

The patient was not a young man and, even though he painted a gloomy picture of life in Telfer, he did not seem unhappy. I doubt if he would demand more than darts and a drink from an evening wherever he was living – although he did say be missed the chance to fish. Time has altered the miner. In the early days of the Gold Rush, or the beginning of Broken Hill, men were self-selected for their adventurous spirit and their strength. They had to ride a horse, or even wheel a barrow piled up with their belongings, for days and days to reach a mine site. Now they pop into an employment agency, collect an airline ticket and take a punt on what they might find, knowing that they can quit after a few weeks if things don't work out – lesser men with comfort in their bones and dollars dancing in their dreams.

The sky was dark with dirty-looking waterlogged blobs. Those in the middle distance resembled a child's drawing of a cloud delivering its dashes to earth, hyphenating the journey through the humid air to the dehydrated dusty sponge below. The absence of a blue sky changed all the colours, made them deeper, more substantial. The landscape looked like a cloth imitating camouflage; shades of green and patches of brown would appear: a mineral peeping through. Manganese, said the patient, but only a touch or two tingeing a ridge, nothing useful. As we reached iron ore country, the rain painted chicken-pox upon the soil. Pink pools of water lay on the surface and were surrounded by circles of deeper pink where the water had begun to soak in. We managed to collect Evan from Jiggalong.

By evening the weather had worsened, and by ten o'clock a fine old storm was playing noisily outside my second-floor motel room. The wind howled across the stretch of beach between me and the sea, mercilessly chased by thunder and lightning. It didn't bother me. The weather report had predicted a storm but had firmly ruled out a cyclone; even the preliminary Blue Alert had been abandoned. Anyway, it was cosy inside my motel room as I scribbled thoughts into a notebook. I had just written a line expressing surprise and perhaps disappointment that, on the whole, Outback ailments mirrored those of the rest of the population when the light snapped off. Blaming the lightning, I fumbled around in the dark and went to bed. Forty-five minutes later the lights snapped on again, and after that interruption I awoke only once in the night and hazily recall a door banging time and again and the sound of something which might have been a dustbin lid hurtling across the yard.

I finally got out of bed just before seven a.m. to find the storm raging with even greater vigour than the night before. The room was muggy; there was no air-conditioning. There was no electricity: no lights, no way to boil a kettle. The telephone line was dead. I opened the curtains, stepping on a soggy carpet where the rain had seeped in; through the rain-spattered window the sea and the sky appeared the same colour: a sepia, sorrowful sight. I went to the shower: no water. I fetched the jug of water, no longer iced, from the fridge and washed my face and brushed my teeth and clambered into the nearest clothes, anxious to reach the main building and find out what was going on. As I reached for the doorknob, I paused. What was the wind speed? Would I be able to stand up? For the first time the word 'cyclone' came into my mind, and I looked around to see if there were any instructions on what to do if caught in such a dramatic event.

There was nothing to guide me, so I went outside, walking slowly and cowering into the side of the building to avoid the rain as well as the wind. As I crossed the open space between two buildings, a gust of wind knocked me sideways and I instinctively ran to clutch the nearest upright pole of a verandah. When I reached the Reception, I found the door locked and my knocks on the darkened glass went unheeded. Within a second I'd convinced myself that I was the only person alive in this ghost hotel. Then I saw a man frantically signalling me to go round the back, past the swimming pool whose protective glass sides were smashed to pieces.

'Where have you been?' asked a fellow guest.

'Where have you been?' chorused the manager, coming up behind. 'Didn't you hear the Red Alert? Didn't you hear the police racing through the town with their sirens blaring? Didn't you hear me pound on your door?' He sounded exasperated, and I was too stunned to answer – I'd slept through my first cyclone. 'We were worried about you. There's a Jap missing, too.'

Seeing my bewilderment, he offered to get me some coffee and propelled me through the kitchen which, with the aid of gas, was busily providing breakfast, into the specially built, cyclone-proof, windowless dining room. It was lit by candles and looked inviting. Some thirty guests were sitting talking in groups, and children played on the floor between the tables.

'Come, let me introduce you to some people. You are going to be stuck in here for hours.'

Two cups of coffee later, most of the group had exhausted jokes about the funny Englishwoman who could sleep through anything. The mood was heightened; people seemed over-excited and talkative. Throughout the room battery-operated radios offered news bulletins. The reports sounded grim: winds up to 150 mph (240 kph), trees bent to the waist. The cyclone – or, rather, the eye of the storm – had passed some thirty miles away, so Port Hedland had missed the worst. None the less there was anger in the voices: inaccurate weather forecasting had caught people unprepared. They hadn't brought in their boats; they hadn't boarded up their windows; they hadn't filled their baths with water. The only other item on the news was the postponement of the mass meeting of striking mine employees that had been scheduled for nine a.m.

At my table an Army major, who had been posted to Hedland to form a Pilbara reserve, fretted about his house; he was living in the hotel with his family while it was being built. Most people had not experienced a cyclone before, but inside the hotel they felt safe and were thoughtfully worried about those living in the nearby caravan park. For the moment there was nothing anyone could do. While the Red Alert is in operation no one is allowed out; flying debris forms the greatest danger, and some wind strengths can lift a car. The power and the water supplies were not victims; they had been turned off to minimize damage. They were restored soon after eleven a.m., when it was obvious that the weather conditions were improving. The Red Alert remained until one thirty. After the excitement and evident danger had passed, the mood changed; something of an anticlimax prevailed. Children became fractious and whined, and I was glad to get back to my room and a long hot shower.

The town worked hard to get back to normal. That afternoon, wherever I walked, men were chopping down dangerous-looking branches and sweeping the gutters so that the rainwater could run away. Hedland had been lucky; the damage was minimal. None the less the town looked drained, defeated by the struggle rather than invigorated. She looked in need of a good rest.

I went to the office of the Airlines of Western Australia to book a flight to Broome. The next one was at two thirty-five a.m., arriving in Broome two hours later. 'You look as though I've asked you for a thousand dollars,' said the counter clerk.

I didn't like the idea of a night flight and elected to wait until the following morning at nine twenty-five a.m.

'I wouldn't. If I had the chance to get out of here, I'd be on the next plane.'

In the tourist office there is a book where people are invited to record their views. 'I think I'll stay,' was the last entry. And immediately above that, just one word: 'Hole'.

CHAPTER 13

Pearls and Diamonds

Broome is the glamour spot on the north-west coast. This tiny town sits upon a small hook of land jutting into the Indian Ocean. It also sits on the edge of the district known as the Kimberley region, firmly in the tropics and only eighteen degrees south of the Equator. It has the kind of climate and the sort of history that evoke thoughts of Maugham and of Conrad. It is lush and lazy. There are no offfice blocks; the bank still has sloping wooden desks and whirling fans. There are no buses, but many bicycles occasionally ridden by stately-looking men in tropical white shirts, shorts and knee-length socks. There are no parking lots and no shopping precincts; instead, large houses, perfectly designed to suit the climate with wide verandahs and shuttered windows, stand back from the roads, shaded by shaggy palms and huge mango trees, surrounded by bougainvillaea and frangipani and other exotic shrubs. Such houses are favoured by millionaires; few in Broome can afford them, but plenty in Perth seem to need them in order to escape from whatever it is that is making them rushed and rich. They used to belong to the pearling masters in the days when Broome was the pearling centre of the world, in the days when Broome was better known than Sydney in the salons of Europe.

Broome did not have a Maugham or a Conrad to chronicle its eccentric early life, more's the pity; but it had Ion Idriess and *Forty Fathoms Deep* which at least tries to relay the mystery of pearl diving and the way in which men fought and cheated and lied and died over tiny baubles which gave passing pleasure to the wives of the wealthy. There was little mateship in this treacherous business; no man who found a pearl could afford to share his joy without risking betrayal.

Pearl fishing started along this coast in the 1850s, further south at Shark Bay where smaller oysters yielded smaller pearls with greater frequency. It was then an unregulated free-for-all; soon that area became over-fished, and men ventured northwards in 1883 to make Broome the centre of the industry. By then, too, the pearl shell had become of great value for buttons, and the pearl itself was of subsidiary importance. For all that, the diving was still dangerous and best left to Aborigines and Asiatics, as the Malays, Chinese, Indonesians and Japanese were then called. By 1910 there were 400 luggers in Broome and a population of 5,000 busily supplying the world's mother-of-pearl. Plastic ruined all that.

Everywhere you go in Broome they will willingly talk about the days before plastic; it is a place which lives *in* the past to some extent, and *on* the past to a great extent. A museum keeps all the bits intact and a thriving historical society keeps the memories alive. Those who leave are drawn back regularly for a draught of the past: of the days when families were large and girls were not allowed to work but spent hours fanning their mothers on those wide verandahs, waiting for the next party. There were lots of parties, beach picnics and dances and get-togethers on Sunday morning where the girls, outnumbered four to one, would whisper of their conquests over lemon squash and the boys, elsewhere, would embroider theirs over beer. Those days were prosperous and even lazier. The blacks who were not divers formed a serving class to potter around the houses of the pearling masters and dig their gardens. If there were tensions in this racial melting-pot, it was not between blacks and whites but between the coloureds. There was a well-remembered riot in 1920, which started when a Japanese diver was stabbed on board a lugger by a Timorese, and ended five days later with three dead and with the despised Timorese having earned a degree of respect. The Malays wore arm-bands to indicate their neutrality.

One round of the riot took place on the verandah of the Continental, then the only hotel in town and the centre of its social life. It is still there but revamped now to offer air-conditioning and television in the rooms, a bar designed to look like a sailing vessel and a drive-in bottle shop. However, they have kept the wrought-iron scrollwork and the wide verandahs on the main building and hidden the extra rooms amid tropical plants. Despite competition from three new motels, the Continental still acts as the main meeting-place. I stayed in this hotel and one night went to eat in the bar where counter meals were served. Of course, it was full of men – but bars usually are, so I thought nothing of it as I paused before the menu, until the manager appeared by my side and suggested I might like to eat in the dining room. 'You will be much more comfortable there and you can charge your meal to my account.'

I bristled slightly at the thought that – in the nicest possible way – I was being invited to leave, but then decided that he was genuinely concerned for my comfort and would prefer to see me dining alone in a nearly empty dining room than dining alone in a bar crowded with men. In any event, to allay lingering suspicions of a men-only policy, I invited the local doctor to meet me in the bar the following evening for a drink. The stand went unnoticed.

Western Australia encourages doctors with entrepreneurial flair. In the south they own wineries, but up here in the north they own petrol stations, caravan parks, shops and property. Peter owns the lot; he symbolizes the new breed of businessman who has filled the power vacuum left by the pearling masters. He arrived in Broome in the early 1960s when land was cheap and the place somewhat depressed, but he foresaw a new life for Broome as a deep-water port serving the cattle industry in the Kimberleys. Now the abattoir, hacking up cattle for hamburgers and packing it for shipment to the USA and Japan, is one of the largest employers and, with gas off the coast and oil inland causing a regular traffic in mining executives, the town has less reason to be depressed. It is tourism, however, upon which the doctor has pinned his hopes and his investments. He noticed the increasing number of Australians who retire early and take off in their camper vans to explore their country, and he is ready for them with the beachside caravan park, petrol station and shops.

Others are eager, too. The tourist office is unmissable, since it is housed in a Douglas DC3 which, while under charter to an oil-drilling company, crash-landed in 1974 and has now been resurrected. Tourist office literature tells you to note how the reflection of the moonlight on the mud flats gives the impression of a golden stairway to the stars.

Not everyone is happy with this emphasis on tourism; it can be a divisive business, for it favours white employment, shoots up land prices and enables only a few to get rich. There were several moans that Chinatown was being destroyed and an impressive amount of criticism over the increase in ugly modern housing designs imported from Perth, based on brick, dependent on air-conditioning, and totally out of keeping with the tropical climate.

Some visitors who make the pilgrimage are indeed disappointed. I read a couple of accounts by journalists who complained that the town had lost its lustiness; that it had become flabby, double-chinned and weak at the knees. The writers were male; they had come to Broome hoping to witness fist fights in the Roebuck bar as evidence that the town was wild and wayward enough to warrant the journey. To me, particularly after Dampier and Port Hedland, Broome was acceptable without the violence. I loved the way every transaction turned into a conversation, whether in the post office or in the library where they claim they can get any book within two weeks, and where the librarian opened on a closed day so that I might return my books before leaving and he might return my temporary member-ship fee and tell me more about how he spent his spare time looking for crocodiles on the Fitzroy River.

Perhaps I also found it less disappointing than some because I came across a corner of Broome that was struggling to retain links with the past, a corner that was determined to fiddle with nature and produce cultured pearls. This is skilled work indeed, and costly and laborious and risky and much more interesting than I had expected. The whole business of choosing an oyster of the right age and size, of opening it at a carefully chosen moment and dropping inside a tiny spherical shape and hoping that the oyster would accept the foreign body as though it were a grain of sand and then continue to grow, coating the sphere with nacre to form a pearl, is fraught with difficulties. The oyster doesn't like being tampered with and often dies or rejects the bead or, in defiance, produces a misshapen lump that is of no use to anyone.

The idea is old. The Chinese were pretty adept at the process in the thirteenth century, but the secrets of the technique lapsed and it was left to the Japanese and the Australians to try and revive it in the 1890s. But the powerful pearling masters of Broome felt threatened and the government of Western Australia passed a law banning the cultured pearl. Between 1922 and 1949 anyone caught experimenting was liable to be fined and imprisoned. The Japanese continued the research and by the mid-1950s were ready to return to Broome with their knowledge and start a joint venture. For some years their pearl farm at Kuri Bay brought millions of dollars to Broome – but now it is floundering. Cyclones have wrecked pearl beds, an elusive marine bacterium has killed off thousands of oysters, and competition from Indonesia is eating away at the profit. Indonesian divers seem happy enough to work for $A15 a month, while labour costs in Broome are high. The pearl from these waters looks doomed.

John Fox-Lowe, Bill Reid and Ian Turner are not quite ready to give up. The conditions for pearl oysters are still good: the huge twenty-foot tides ensure a rich supply of food, and the fact that the water temperature drops below 68°F (20°C) for a few months each year allows the nacre coating a period of slow, fine growth. Their company, Broome Pearls, funded by the Kalis fishing empire from Perth, is small; the future – if there is a future – is likely to rest with a few small companies where owner-operators can lavish intensive care upon their oysters without counting the hours.

That Sunday I found the three sitting in a shabby room, muttering about mommes and kans, the measures used to weigh pearls, and poring over $A70,000 worth of pearls of varying shapes, a sample from the next harvest. There was no air-conditioning and with humidity reaching ninety-five per cent, the only thing that was cool (and then only briefly) was the beer. The three learned their craft working for the giant Kuri Bay Company and branched out on their own in 1978, and each year they have watched their increasing skills produce a better harvest. Ian and John were divers, a job which has changed little since the early days, except that it is now safer;

but it still means being underwater for eight hours a day and it is still highly competitive. There may be plenty of shells down there on the sea bed, but often they are not easy to see, and often they are not of the right size, between $4\frac{1}{2}$ and 7 inches (11.5–18 centimetres). John's description of divers elbowing one another aside had me thinking that perhaps the fist fights took place underwater these days – but then divers are well known for their 'back deck' storytelling.

These modern pearlers put to sea in their lugger, a converted prawn trawler, in teams of seven for ten days at a time. If they are lucky, it takes around three months to catch the shells they need. The carting of the shells to their new homes, on piled-up racks beneath the sea, is one of the trickiest parts of the operation. Bill, who used to do research into the elusive disease, believes that it is during this transition that the oysters are most likely to succumb to the bacterium. He reckons it is a bit like moving from the country to a high-rise block in the city, a change traumatic enough for humans, let alone young oysters. They are constantly watched during the settling-in period and are sometimes given up to a year to get fat and lazy before the surgeon comes to operate. 'Surgeon' is the right word, since the men who perform the insertion of the tiny spheres made of Mississippi mussel shells are paid as much as top medical surgeons. Their skill is prized and there are not more than 100 men in the world capable of the work, most of whom are Japanese. Broome Pearls hires a specialist, but Ian has been learning and the other two claim that even the Japanese are impressed with his work.

'It requires intense concentration, and constant decision-making – where to put the bead and which size of bead to use, and it also requires a constant rhythm – a bit like making mayonnaise. At the end of the day I'm whacked.'

As the oysters need to be out of the water for as little time as possible, the operating is done at sea in a specially designed raft. When the oysters are returned once more to their high-rise homes, they are again closely watched and checked for two years. 'It is not exactly a fast way to make a buck,' said John, 'but then we started with the easy stuff, making half pearls which end up as cheap pendants, and that is not nearly so interesting. Apart from anything else, the Australians don't have much idea about jewellery, and the stuff that sold well in our workshop at the edge of the bay was the kind of thing that would delight a nine-year-old.' His harvest is sold to Japanese dealers – 'the only people who understand pearls'.

The threesome had what is best described as chequered careers before they joined forces. Much of Bill's time was spent overseas with the United Nations doing research work, and John scorned the chance to join his father's milk-selling business in England at the age of twenty-one, appalled to discover his entire life mapped before him. Uncertainty and adventure were more in his line: delivering boats halfway around the world, diving for scallops in Scotland and abalone in New South Wales. Diving for abalone in Eden was where he met Ian, who was doing the same.

Ian had read engineering at university but thoughts of a conventional career were abandoned when he received his call-up papers for Vietnam. He fled, and remained on the run for sixteen months before the police caught him. 'I knew they would in the end because I had been one of the leaders of the Draft Resisters Union. I was sentenced to a full eighteen months in prison, but Whitlam came to power after I had served just over ten months and all draft-dodgers were released.' Ian talks lightly of his time in prison. He was given a protected job, mending the prisoners' clothes. 'I had this computer-like sewing machine and had a laugh putting scalloped edges on the men's overalls and sewing on their patches with orange cotton. The screws were not amused; they didn't appreciate the need to make the best of things.'

The future of the Broome Pearl could hardly be in the hands of more likeable or more intriguing men, but, for all their enthusiasm and dedication, the majestic past has gone. A natural pearl may be found every couple of years, but no one fights and cheats and lies and dies any more. And I doubt if men will fight much longer to keep alive the ailing cultured pearl. Broome will lose its focus, but it will not disintegrate – it will not be allowed to disintegrate. There are too few people in this far corner as it is, maybe 20,000 in the whole of the Kimberley region. Politicians will doubtless come up with some scheme to use the land and the labour force and prevent the population drifting away. They encouraged the Americans to invest $US30 million in planting sorghum for animal feed by donating $A3 million for the storage silo. It remains unused. They say that the fertilizer failed to arrive from Texas; that the ships caught fire on the way; anyway, there is no sorghum. Taxpayers do not like to hear such stories, but they comfort themselves with the thought that it was a good idea at the time and that the principle is correct, the principle being that *someone* must be encouraged to live in the tropical north. The sparse population unnerves people; they fear that the empty north will prove too attractive to the crowded Asian countries and that they will be tempted to come and take possession.

Such fears are not fanciful in Broome. They know how vulnerable they are: it is written in history. On 3 March, 1942, the Japanese attacked Broome airstrip and Roebuck Bay. At the time the town was serving as a refuelling stop for planes evacuating Allied military personnel and their families from Java. That March morning, there were sixteen flying-boats in the bay. Because of the shortage of accommodation in the town and the difficulty of taking people off the flying-boats, many Dutch refugees had spent the night on board the flying-boats. Within an hour they were ablaze, along with twenty-two aircraft. Two American planes took off; one escaped to Port Hedland and the other crashed into the sea, killing thirty-two airmen. No one knows how many aboard the flying-boats were killed as there was no precise record of who was on board. The Japanese were happy with their military target and made no attempt to fire on the town; in any event, Broome was defenceless: the best it could muster was a volunteer defence corps firing rifles.

Broome suffered just as Darwin had suffered a couple of weeks before when Japanese bombers, launched from an aircraft carrier only 200 miles (320 kilometres) offshore, shelled the harbour, sinking half a dozen vessels and damaging a dozen more. Some 243 people were killed: Darwin couldn't cope either. Indeed, the aftermath was a mess, with abandoned buildings being thoroughly looted not least by the military police guarding them. It could be argued that the bravest and the best were away fighting the war in Europe, but that begs the question: could she have coped if they had all been at home? The answer is probably not, and it continues to be probably not.

In the mid-1970s, a former Defence Minister said: 'Australia would not be able to protect Botany Bay on a hot Sunday afternoon.' The remark, defended as an off-the-cuff quip, was broadcast around the world. The word in the mid-1980s was much the same: 'We couldn't beat anything more than a band of raiders.' The difference now is that the mood in Australia is encouraging the development of an independent defence capability, instead of relying on jokes and the hope that, in the event of trouble, others will come to its aid. Australians believe that if there were a major threat to Australia, the United States would come to their assistance; but they no longer believe that they should base their entire defence policy on the inevitability of that assistance being given. After all, where was Britain in 1942? Arguing the toss, with Churchill ignoring the Japanese threat to Australia and demanding that more troops be made available to him in North Africa and Burma. Curtin, the wartime Prime Minister, in an historic speech called to America for help: 'Without inhibitions of any kind, I make it clear that Australia looks to America, free of any pangs as to our traditional links of friendship with the United Kingdom.' America responded and became the saviour in Australian eyes; after the war, the new relationship was cemented in 1951 when the Pacific Security Treaty, better known as the Anzus Pact, was signed by Australia, New Zealand and the United States. With this pact which committed the signatories to 'act to meet the common danger', America took over Britain's role as protector. The US still has that role; but it is viewed these days with a touch more realism and caution, which has encouraged Australia slowly to develop an independent defence capability costing around $A5.5 billion a year, or less than three per cent of the gross domestic product, a sum still low in comparison with Britain and America.

But then it isn't nuclear, and it isn't likely to become nuclear, although a leaked defence report, which was not denied, suggests that Australia should closely monitor the development of nuclear technology in its region so that, if any neighbours decided to acquire such weapons, Australia would be in a position to do so just as quickly. Meanwhile the defence research establishment outside Adelaide is working on its own submarine detection system, having discovered that gear bought from its allies' and designed for cold northern climates is not effective in the tropics where the seas are warmer and often shallower. There is Jindalee, too, the over-the-horizon radar located at Alice Springs which could give Australia the surveillance it needs over the north-western approaches if a situation like that of 1942 is to be avoided. Yet a third project is a hovering rocket which acts as a decoy, tricking missiles into tracking an expendable missile rather than a ship; this answer to Exocet, however, needs American interest, so that the rocket can be mass-produced at a price that makes it 'expendable'.

These war toys (together with the purchase of others), a combined force totalling 72,000 and an enlarged reserve are planned – by the time they become operational in the 1990s – to enable Australia to cope with any local difficulties. But what are the difficulties likely to be? Public opinion polls show that just over half the population believes that if there is a threat to Australia, it is most likely to come from Indonesia. Even so, the dangers are perceived as slight; only seventeen per cent fear Indonesian intentions; another fourteen per cent fear either Russia or China. Defence Department documents echo these low-level fears; indeed, their prognostications are reassuring, promoting a view that all is quiet on the Australian front. The worst they might have to battle with is low-level harassment from Indonesia. That, the Defence Department say, is all Indonesia is capable of, and no one seriously believes that Indonesia's 140 million people have any designs on Australia itself. It is the neighbouring islands that have to be watched. In the mid-1970s Indonesia invaded and annexed East Timor and some would have liked Australia to have taken a stronger stand over this; they claim that Australia did not do so because she needs to keep Indonesia as a warm ally rather than provoke her into becoming a potential adversary. They also argue that not standing up to Indonesia encourages her to cast greedy eyes on Papua New Guinea. It is for these reasons that Australian military capabilities should command Indonesian respect.

The Ribbon and the Ragged Square

Some others argue that Australia should go further and aim for armed neutrality. These are the people, and they are a growing band, who dislike having American bases in Australia. A Nuclear Disarmament Party fielded candidates for the Senate for the first time in the 1984 elections; only one candidate was elected, in Western Australia; proving that the majority of Australians still support the Anzus treaty and that any attempt to dismantle it is politically unacceptable. New Zealand's row with America in 1985, when the country refused to allow the US destroyer *Buchanan* into a New Zealand port on the grounds that it might be carrying nuclear weapons and which looked for a while as though it might scupper the treaty, found Australia firmly backing her protector, rather than her neighbour. Australians have become used to huddling under the wing of major powers; it may not be a blanket insurance policy but it does afford some protection, even if the price to pay is high. From the facts that are available, the presence of American bases does seem a high price if it increases the likelihood that any Soviet attack on the West would start with the USSR knocking out the bases. But there again, Australia is used to paying dearly.

In the early days when she depended upon the might of the British Empire and the reach of its navy, the cost in providing men to fight on European soil was so high that it has scarred the minds of those involved. In the first instances it was easy enough: the first time the Australians set foot overseas to fight with the British was in 1885 when the history books record that 750 men from New South Wales were involved in a skirmish in the Sudan. It is a matter of little significance. Then came the Boer War, when 16,000 enthusiastic men went to South Africa and proved themselves able horsemen. Around 500 were killed and there were 1,400 casualties, not enough for anyone to question the point of it all or loyalty to Britain. However, all that changed in the 1914–18 War. Again there was initial enthusiasm and volunteers aplenty, but the losses were appalling: that war was full of battles that cost thousands of lives for acres of ground. At Gallipoli, a futile battle against the Turks which ended in defeat, 33,000 died, including some 8,000 Australians. On this occasion the Australian soldier won his spurs; his willingness to fight and his ability to fight gave Australia greater recognition within the Commonwealth. Despite the fact that it was not a victorious battle, 25 April 1915 inspired Australians, and that day each year is still celebrated as Anzac Day, and Australian historians still manage to enshrine the occasion in glory. There is much talk of chivalry at Gallipoli; of mutual respect between the Australian and the Turk, and of the day when the fighting stopped so that the dead could be buried with as much reverence as possible. But none of this is to be found later in France where the war was ugly, where the troops were ground down by the gore of war and were not sustained by glory; where the accounts admit lost nerve, lost sanity and cowardice. In September 1916 at Pozières, 23,000 Australian soldiers died. There is little talk of chivalry; instead, historians quote: 'Many a man smiles when he is told he will never fight again' ... 'poor wounded devils you meet on stretchers are laughing with glee'.

The horror of all this filtered home in letters, where it mingled with a Catholic-led denunciation of a war which some perceived to be a capitalist-inspired desire to protect trade routes rather than a fight for freedom and justice, and caused a significant drop in volunteers and a resounding 'No' to two attempts to introduce conscription. Australians were indeed questioning the point of it all and of their loyalty to the British. By the end of the war, Australia had 60,000 dead and a quarter of a million wounded – a higher casualty rate than any British force. Such heavy losses entitled her to a separate seat at the Paris peace-talks in 1919, but the importance of this soon paled while the scars remained deep. It took many years before novelists could try to disentangle the thoughts of a nation disillusioned by war and baffled by ties for which they had paid so dearly.

The Second World War solved the problem with Britain: in 1942 and for the first time in its history, Australia stood alone to fight its own battles, not the battles of the Empire. However, the fact that she had to call for help from yet another power resulted in history repeating itself, as it so often does. American protection led to Australia getting involved in more wars. Korea came first: when South Korea was invaded by the communist North, the United States gave military support to the South, and Australia promptly made armed support available to help America. Such action was dressed up with a big bow and described as a 'Forward Defence Policy', that is to say fighting the enemy, dreaded Communism, on other people's soil in the hope of preventing it spreading to your own shores. Such a policy led Australia to support, eagerly at first, the Americans in Vietnam, and then once again to question at length the point of it all and the demands of loyalty. Nowadays, most Australians, whatever their politics, agree that they should not become embroiled in America's troubles unless they concern Australia directly, and that they should act far more independently without endangering the Anzus treaty. There is no need to be a sycophantic yes-country. The gains from such an unpalatable position are non-existent, for in the end such a super-power is sure to act to suit its *own* needs, and not because it feels an overwhelming bond with a country with whom it shares common parentage and a common language.

At low tide in Broome, it is still possible to see some of the mangled metal of 3 March 1942, lying in the mud amid the mangrove swamps. Slowly, however, the wrecks are disappearing and with them the heightened sense of gratitude and commitment to America that Australia has felt for so many years. What still remains is the awareness that despite a policy of 'populate or perish' which was formulated out of fear at the end of the Second World War, there are still too few people in this vulnerable corner. Development of the north has been slow because it is extremely costly, and most politicians have regarded the area as a hopeless liability to which they give money grudgingly, rather than a potential asset to which they give money willingly. The road south of Broome to Port Hedland has been surfaced for only a few years, providing access in all weathers; the road north is as yet unsurfaced, although it is promised, and while I was there the track was impassable, submerged by the flooding Fitzroy River. I had to fly to Kununurra, a town which owes its existence to those Japanese bombs, a town which is a tangible monument to regional planning, and a tangible reminder that European man is not at ease in the tropics; his body rejects the climate and his mind has yet to understand its nature.

Kununurra became a government town because of the Ord River.

The Ord has consistently enticed men and encouraged them to exaggerate the merits of this remote area. When Alexander Forrest first ferreted around the Kimberleys in 1879, he said that the Ord, which he named in honour of the Governor, 'may yet prove to be the Queen of Australian rivers'. He was dazzled by much else, too: the trees with luxuriant foliage, the vast open plains heavy with pasture, and the surprisingly friendly natives. He returned to Perth and pronounced his find 'a cattleman's paradise'; pastoralists in the south-eastern corner of the country, destroyed by drought and hindered by the high price of land, eagerly accepted his excitement and believed that the only thing wrong with the place was its remote location – and even then they were certain that where one man dared others would soon follow.

The pioneers who drove their herds from New South Wales to settle the Kimberleys are revered in these parts, none more so than the Durack family, whose zig-zag route from Cooper's Creek formed a two-year, 3,000-mile (4,800-kilometre) trek for 7,500 cattle, only half of which survived. Undaunted, the Duracks built their home, thatched its roof, named it Argyle and enjoyed a brief period of optimism when a nearby gold find invited an influx of men and provided a market for their beef. In time, the Duracks were to acquire 7 million acres (2.8 million hectares) of land amid much hardship, according to the family's account of their lives in *Kings in Grass Castles*. The cattle struggled against red-water fever; the settlers struggled against malaria; the buildings struggled against white ants eating away the foundations; the whole community suffered from a lack of accessible markets and a lack of interest by successive governments in Perth, and endless problems caused by the deterioration in relations with the Aborigines. As for the climate, it must have been frustrating watching the deluge of monsoonal rain; seeing the rivers in torrent running away to waste and knowing that within a few months that same ground would be parched, cracked earth. Alexander Forrest was right when he said that rainfall was reliable – indeed, there is an annual cycle, but it either rains in great indigestible gulps or not at all.

The Duracks stayed until 1950. Their house, Argyle Homestead, still stands – but not in the same spot. The Ord has been dammed; a lock covers the original site, and the house has been moved stone by stone to form a museum, the show-piece of a tourist development. The Duracks would not have minded the uprooting; it was one of their number, Kim, who first talked of the need to dam the Ord to provide irrigated pasture of high quality all the year. In 1941 he finally persuaded the government to set up an experimental research station to help the beleaguered pastoralist. Then came the bombs, and an irrigation scheme no longer seemed a pipe dream, merely a costly but wise way to encourage settlement. The first farms were allocated in 1962, and today very few are commercially viable. Many mistakes have been made as men struggle to understand the vagaries of tropical agriculture. But there is hope.

Bill Withers is still full of hope – and he was one of the early arrivals. He was in Sydney in the early 1960s working on the cloud seeding programme when he heard about the Ord and decided to apply for a farm, but he didn't have the right amount of capital or sufficient expertise. None the less he chose to settle in Kununurra and open a store, and after the store there was a petrol station and then for eleven years he was Liberal MP for North Province, which gave him plenty of time to analyse the area's problems; he also travelled far and wide comparing and contrasting remote-area farming in India, Africa, Russia and Canada.

He became the area Member of Parliament because he considered that decision making in the south was adversely affecting the north; he quit when they made constituency boundary changes which displeased him. Anyway, he wanted to put into practice some of the many highly individualistic ideas of which he had talked much; he wanted to inject a touch of free enterprise incentive into a government town where the leasehold agreements not only tell the farmers what to plant but even when.

'The Kimberley Research Station was supposed to have the answers, and that is why they were to tell the farmers what to do. But in the early days many of the so-called specialists were untrained in tropical and irrigation agriculture and really we were all learning together. Many of the early crops were not successful, and cotton, for example, ended in failure. I think it was because we planted the wrong type for the area but, whatever the reasons, it was eaten by insects and a total failure. Cotton is not planted now and other early crops, sorghum, rice and sunflower seed, have also been replaced by maize and soya beans and peanuts, bananas, mangoes, water-melons and many vegetables that can take advantage of out-of-season high prices to offset the distance they have to travel to their markets.'

Sugar, too, looks like becoming a big success. I went to the experimental farm and saw it growing and it looked magnificent, yielding twice the amount to the acre as farms in Queensland, Australia's main sugar-growing area. The success of sugar could make a spectacular difference to the prosperity of this area, particularly if a major company can be persuaded to build a mill. But nothing is easy in Kununurra. The success of this crop has awakened State rivalry, and Queensland is displeased at the thought of competition and has been using its considerable clout to block expansion.

Bill Withers's ideas include building his own home from local materials – a large and elegant home, well suited to its environment; cultivating worms on a commercial basis because he believes that the worm is an excellent fertilizer; and keeping chickens. All three are unusual in Kununurra. Houses are suburban-looking boxes imported from Perth; no one else is breeding worms nor are they keeping chickens.

'The current system does not encourage the keeping of pigs, ducks and chickens, the kind of subsistence farming that helps cut costs. This is because houses are in town and farms are outside town and the farmer goes to his farm each morning just as he would an office. This is bad. It is bad for the wives who do not feel part of the farm and it also means that the farmer cannot keep chickens and so on, because he cannot keep an eye on them after dark when the dingoes are about.'

Bill had met me at my hotel and, soon after we began to talk, he became restless. The light was fading and he was worried about his chickens, worried that the dingoes might be prowling; so he suggested we go to his farm and lock up the chickens and then continue to talk. We drove out of town, locked up the chickens and wandered back to the house via the lakeside jetty. It was dark, insects swarmed everywhere, dogs leapt in and out of the bushes and, as I approached the jetty, a six-foot crocodile plunged into the water.

'It's only a crocodile,' said Bill, holding the lantern over the water so that I might get a better view. 'He's quite tame; freshwater crocodiles usually are.'

I must have looked unnerved, for several days later I received a letter apologizing for the dogs and the dingoes and the darkness and the insects and the crocodile and the fact that only after my departure had Bill been struck by the thought that such surroundings might unsettle a stranger. It was the insects that really bothered me: they eat strangers.

Bill Withers is the kind of determined optimist one expects to find in such an area. There are others, too. The Research Station showed me their projects with great confidence. Past mistakes are accepted as inevitable; all irrigation schemes take a decade or so to get going, they argue; now they are well on the way to discovering crops which are not only well suited to the climate but which could become financially viable in the long term.

They are even attempting to solve the hundred-year-old problem of the pastoralist. Compared to other areas in the north, properties in the Kimberleys are still poorly developed; fencing is minimal, denying pasture management, stock and disease control and causing high mustering costs. Owners have traditionally overcome the problems of poor pastures during the long dry period by having millions of acres and playing 'spot the cattle'. The Research Station's suggestion is either to grain-feed the cattle for a month before they are sold so they can regain the weight they lose during the dry or, indeed, to finish them in irrigated pastures; but cattlemen can afford to do this only when beef prices are high.

There are fewer problems with diamonds. A mighty market-rigging operation controls supplies by stockpiling production when prices fall and releasing them when prices rise. The main difficulty with diamonds is finding them – and they were found in the late 1970s in huge quantities (enough to increase the world's supply by forty per cent) some 120 miles (190 kilometres) south of Kununurra. The diamond world, which in effect means De Beers and the Central Selling Organization, practically jumped out of its skin when it heard about the Argyle diamond field. It feared that its cosy world would come apart if the Australians refused to join the South African cartel and instead sold their diamonds themselves. In the end, Ashton Joint Venture (AJV) decided that in the early stages of their development they had enough to do, without having to set up a network of men with suitcases rushing round the world. Until 1990 anyway, some seventy-five per cent of the area's diamonds will be sold through the CSO. The decision was made easier by the belief that only ten per cent of the find would produce diamonds of gem quality; the rest would be for industrial use.

Kununurra was delighted by the diamond find: it had earned a place on the map for something a little more glamorous than an irrigation scheme, and of course it has benefited from the find – but not as much as it had first hoped. The idea of grafting the diamond work-force on to the town was discarded as impractical, since the journey by car takes two hours and to commute by air each day was hardly cost-effective. To build a complete town at the mine site had also been discarded early on. AJV, having studied other remote mining communities, decided that many industrial and other problems were caused by a frustrated work-force longing to get away from such a hemmed-in life-style. The solution they settled on belongs to the oil rig. The bulk of the force remain on site, working for eighteen days, and then are flown to Perth for nine days' leave. A handful of senior staff live in Kununurra and commute by company plane to the site. This means that Perth benefits more than anywhere from the diamond find, but Kununurra is satisfied with its share.

Another reason for not building a complete town on the site was to shield neighbouring Aborigines from the impact of such a settlement. There are three groups within forty miles (sixty-five kilometres), two out-stations of around 25 and a larger reserve of 250. There are no formal land rights for Aborigines in Western Australia (though progress towards this is being made) and therefore the traditional owners of the land cannot command royalties; none the less cooperation and some form of compensation had to be agreed.

One small group, Glen Hill, were eager to accept help for their community; the other two were slower and more suspicious; but, in the end, all agreed to receive annual sums of money for capital improvements which in the first years totalled around $A1 million. AJV has been criticized for its handling of the Aborigines; they have been accused of rushing through agreements with handfuls of leaders; but such accusations surround any meeting of men and mining, and AJV are in fact proud of what they term their 'Good Neighbour Scheme', proud enough to let me visit both Glen Hill and the diamond fields, even though others had told me that no outsiders were allowed near the site.

One morning at six a.m., I flew from Kununurra to the site, and switched to a helicopter for the hop to Glen Hill where Neil, one of AJV's two community relations officers, was making a weekly visit. The distance between the two is only fifteen miles (twenty-four kilometres) but the ride by road is rough. The Aborigines did not want bitumen, for fear of encouraging tourists; they agreed instead to trade up from track to dirt road; and dirt roads, of course, need regular re-grading.

Glen Hill is little more than a clearing in the bush, beside a water-hole: so small, so neat and so well kept that it looked idyllic. The half-dozen houses were made of brick with iron roofs and wooden-posted verandahs. In some instances this basic structure had been left unadorned, with beds (predictably) arranged on the verandah rather than inside the house; others had beds inside the house and adornments almost lavish. The Aboriginal elder, to set an example to the village, had extended his house with a structure that looked like a car port, using wood from nearby trees. At one end a mango tree had been planted, and in time the whole would be covered in vines to provide much-coveted shade. Washing hung on lines between the trees. Some distance from the houses, there was a block of showers and lavatories, and a generator to provide electricity to each house as well as street lighting. Away to one side there were horses in a fenced paddock. The community lives by its horse-breaking skills. AJV had provided all that I saw, from the fencing and the stockyards to the community vehicles, the housing and the generator.

The weekly meeting took place at a table under a tree, and with only men present. Children hung around, but the women watched from a distance, sitting on the steps of their leader's house. They could not have heard anything; Aboriginal voices are soft and low. The occasion was similar to an old-fashioned parish council meeting where groups of concerned citizens nagged members to put right a host of niggling complaints. In this case, it was the wicked white ant, a fault in the generator and a query or two on social security cheques which Neil, acting as postman, had brought with him from Kununurra. The weekly meeting is a much-welcomed prop. The community has no desire for a resident white adviser, but they value regular visits. Their next project will include more housing, as the community is expanding, and a school. Word had it that all and sundry, both black and white, had warned this group against negotiating with the mining bastards. But John Toby had his own plans. He had lived at Turkey Creek, the large camp, and had quarrelled and gone to Kununurra, but living on the fringe of a white town suited him no better and, when he saw the chance to achieve the kind of life he desired, he took it. Fortunately, claims to the land at Glen Hill meant he was in a position to trade access to AJV for all that he needed to make a start.

Our stay was brief and we returned to Argyle Prospect, to what men hope will be the richest diamond patch in the world. It covers more than a hundred acres (forty hectares), and no one knows the depth of the diamond pipe, at least 400 feet (120 metres), but for the moment diamonds are being found in the surface ore which is lying there waiting to be shovelled and carted and crushed and washed and sorted. I watched the entire process undertaken within the tightest security and was most intrigued by the sorting, carried out by six girls huddled over desks, tweezers moving with pace and precision, picking carats from dross. A painstaking and dull job; the sorters have music piped to their ears through headphones to minimize the monotony and their eyes are checked regularly. I asked to try my hand but was not allowed into the closely guarded room; instead, a tray was brought into an outer room and a security guard stood at my elbow while I poked and prodded the gravel-like concentrate, plucking out tiny specks of raw diamonds which looked more like glass from a shattered windscreen than coveted objects of considerable worth.

Lilian Kirkwood has been a sorter for eighteen months. She works twelve hours a day, sixty hours a week, for which she earns $A350 and from which she saves $A250. When she reaches her target of $A20,000 she will head back to Perth. That money is to provide a fifty per cent deposit on a $A40,000 flat. Her future security lies in that flat and not in a career which she could have had if she had finished her university course. Having abandoned English literature as 'impractical', her life has been a series of adventurous jobs, like cooking for tourist groups tramping through the bush. On one such trip, she passed through the Kimberleys and returned to sort diamonds.

'There's a limit to what I'll sacrifice for money, but two years seems about right. The first time I went to Perth on leave, I blew $A2,000 in twelve days taking all my friends out for meals, but I decided that would not do or I'd never reach my target. I reckon I'll be ready to leave in about another six months. Last time I went to Perth, I stood at a bus stop and took great delight in waiting for a bus. It is surprising the small things you miss. Life here isn't bad. We get up at five a.m. and work from six a.m. until six p.m. and then, by the time you have had a shower and a meal and a beer in the mess, it is time to sleep. In the beginning I used to go to Kununurra for the weekends, but I hardly bother now. Everything is provided here. We have a pool and I send away for books and there are videos to watch and letters to write.

'We spend all our time in dungarees and steel-toed boots and rarely bother to change into dresses in the evenings. The girls are outnumbered six to one and there is really no need to encourage the guys: half a stubby and they think they are in love! The work is monotonous, but we have a change every now and then, moving to the machines and learning how to maintain them. The girls are often quite amused to find they can handle a spanner.'

Outside, the air is warm and a breeze moves fine red dust across the yard. It is the end of the wet season; the rugged landscape of jagged ridges and deep gorges, aptly named Ragged Range, is striped green imitating an improbable seed-packet lawn. No wonder Alexander Forrest thought he had found a cattleman's paradise. A camp site with mobile homes lined up like caravans, open-cast mines, a tailings dam and a treatment plant may mar the landscape for some, but one day they will be gone and environmentalists will be left to rearrange the land. It won't be the same, hills will be turned into flat land and flat land into hills. In the meanwhile, for a short time, there are people and there is prosperity in the Kimberleys.

CHAPTER 14

The Seventh State

It had been nearly a month since I had been in a town of any size; as I flew into Darwin, joining the last leg of the overnight flight from Perth, I wondered if the sight of a bustling airport – in my mind it had to be bustling, for Darwin is Australia's gateway to Asia – would induce another disagreeable moment of distaste similar to the one I had experienced on returning to Adelaide from central Australia. It was not to be. Instead, there were other surprises. There was no bustling airport: the terminal, scheduled for a multi-million-dollar update, was rather quaint, complete with ceiling fans and rickety plastic chairs and an atmosphere that was decidedly torpid and tropical. It hardly seemed the gateway to anywhere at breakfast time that Saturday morning. Any further reaction to my first sight of Darwin was smothered by the surprise of being met by the district sales manager of Airlines of Western Australia. I'd met Alan Nicholls in Broome, where we had chatted for a mere half-hour; on the strength of this – the slightest of acquaintance – he had decided that I should not arrive in Darwin without a warm welcome, and that is what I got, a delightful welcome from which evolved an invitation to stay with him and his girl-friend, Pat, who promptly set aside the rest of the day, while Alan headed for the golf course, to show me her town: the new Darwin.

The old Darwin was blown away by Cyclone Tracy on Christmas Day 1974. The old Darwin was like the airport, poorish, parochial and, being made mainly of fibro and timber, somewhat picturesque; a truly tropical outpost, embracing lassitude as a life-style. All that was gone, swept away by a mighty wind. The new Darwin is sturdy, a place designed by structural engineers who, as they pored over drawing boards, were concerned above all else that the place would not blow away again. Such men created modern Darwin with budgets and balance sheets before them. The result is Canberra in the tropics – but not the Canberra of arresting public buildings, rather the Canberra of Woden, of the suburbs, of government buildings and government boxes. The people of Broome are right to be concerned about the spread of such housing, for I could now see how it destroys the flavour of a place and creates instead a dull uniformity. I was surprised by all this, but I ought not to have been: I have seen Agadir, re-created after an earthquake to form a new low in contemporary ugliness. When men get the chance to start again, one cannot assume that they will improve upon the past.

But Darwin is not ugly, just architecturally a little dull and mercifully saved from further dullness by lush vegetation – even the central shopping mall is enlivened with tropical plants in pots and beds – and by vast, lonely beaches, emptied by large signs warning of the dangers of sea wasps (which aren't wasps at all but jellyfish with a deadly sting).

The old timers mourn the loss of old Darwin – those who are left. A fair number chose to stay in the south to which they were evacuated while the city was rebuilt, rather than face years of upheaval; others, if they were older, voted for retirement in Queensland. Maybe a quarter of the current population of 60,000 remember the old place and lament the arrival of planeloads of planners and architects and bankers who poured in, bringing with them their southern notions of development and their big-city standards. Driving through the suburb of Casuarina and wandering through its shopping complex, I sympathized with their view. Tracy had torn the heart out of Darwin; a transplant provided a new one, and with it came a new character.

It was inevitable. In 1974 Darwin was governed from Canberra, and therefore the Federal Government was responsible for the reconstruction. Reconstruction brought more than money; it brought a new population, many of them eager to cash in on the reconstruction boom. This new blood is just as much responsible for the change in

Darwin as the ink of architects. It is not inclined to lassitude and is determined to rid the north of such ways. What Tracy started, self-government continued. The Territory became self-governing in 1978 – which means it is largely responsible for its own affairs, with the Federal Government keeping control of uranium mining and aspects of Aboriginal affairs. It is not quite 'statehood', but no one is much bothered about that. Self-government was the most important step, and with it there emerged an energetic and impressive Chief Minister, Paul Everingham, who galvanized the Territory into believing that it was not the white elephant it had been painted since it had first been colonized in the middle of the last century.

Darwin, like Perth, was peopled through fears of French intentions; it was at first governed from South Australia, whose expansionist dreams had been fuelled by the descriptions of explorers who, like Alexander Forrest in the Kimberleys, were hoodwinked by the land they saw in the wet season and who had no idea of the contrast presented by the dry months. Even when this was discovered, South Australia hoped that the north would blossom with economic potential – especially when a little gold was discovered – and model its development on that of South Australia, with a port as capital surrounded by medium-sized farms for tropical crops and with the hinterland for pastoralists. For fifty years it waited for the Northern Territory to become a paying proposition: but it did not, and finally in 1911 it let the burden of debt pass to the Commonwealth.

Paul Everingham (who has since moved into Federal politics) won't have the words 'burden' and 'debt' applied to the Northern Territory. While not denying that the Commonwealth has poured and continues to pour millions of dollars into the place, he argues that the whole country stands to gain considerably from development prospects, particularly from those associated with natural resources. Indeed, he argues strongly, aggressively, for more money: for a railway line from Alice to Darwin and for a university which would not only stem the exodus of ambitious parents and gifted youngsters, but would also encourage research into problems specific to the tropical north. Alaska got both – yes, Alaska. Paul Everingham makes many a comparison with Alaska: their positions are similar.

Alaska once devoured US federal dollars but then, mainly due to oil revenues, found itself pouring dollars into federal coffers. He can see the same thing happening with the Northern Territory via a host of minerals from uranium, through bauxite and manganese to silver, lead and zinc. What this young and ambitious young politician is reluctant to acknowledge is that the uranium market is static, and that research in Japan and the United States is producing ceramics, fibre optics and so forth, which could well have the same effect on some minerals that synthetic fibres had on wool. Politicians live in a short-term world and he is not going to have its new-found confidence eroded by long-term fears.

The Territory is young – the average age is twenty-five – and hungrily looking to Asia as a market for its minerals; greedily looking to Asia to supply wealthy tourists to come and hunt buffalo; and eagerly hoping that the rich Chinese in Singapore and Hong Kong will come and use its casino; it has a lavish casino, with a special room set aside for big spenders. Darwin argues most emphatically that it is doing what the rest of Australia ought to be doing: courting Asia. Officials will tell anyone who will listen that Darwin sends a trade delegation to Singapore Trade Fair each year; invites the Sultan of Brunei to open the Darwin Show; and actively encourages the immigration of Asian entrepreneurs. There is a splendid irony in all this; it was the Chinese who were largely responsible for settling this part of the north, and a fine job they made of it – until they were invited to apply for repatriation as daft fears drove Australia to turn her back on Asia. The white Australia policy held back the development of the north and now, eighty years later, it is scrambling to catch up.

In those early years, in the 1870s when gold was discovered, the mine owners asked the South Australian government if they could import Asian labour from Singapore and Hong Kong. South Australia agreed for, having little gold itself, it had avoided the worst of the anti-Chinese feeling which had flooded Victoria and New South Wales; in any event, it wanted the north to grow, and the Chinese were willing helpers – they loved the place. One cook employed by a government official is often quoted as saying: 'This place welly good, by and by all China come, Emperor too.' An unfortunate forecast, given the fears; and soon many in the north began to think that this was happening indeed as thousands did come, outnumbering the Europeans. And they were not merely coolies, confined to the gold-fields, but skilled tradesmen, carpenters and merchants. And they worked hard and became known as 'the Jews of Asia', and such competition could not be tolerated for long. The depression of the 1890s brought men from the south in search of jobs; and fear and jealousy started a move to force the Chinese out. Some stayed, repatriation was voluntary, and those who stayed suffered years of segregation. Now the wheel has turned full circle: Darwin is proud of its Mayor's Chinese ancestors, proud of its mixed population – more than 100 overseas birthplaces were listed in the 1980 census – and proud of its lack of racial prejudice and its 'open door' policy. The boat people, refugees from Vietnam, many of them of Chinese origin, landed first at Darwin. Their boats sit sinking in the sand upon the shore, a statement of our times and an irresistible still-life for many a photographer.

The architecture may be a little dull, but the mix of people is as exotic as the lush vegetation. Of course, it is the climate that makes the vegetation lush and it has the same effect upon the people. The Territory has the highest murder rate in Australia, the highest rate of serious assault, the highest rate of rape, the highest rate of car theft, and the highest road accident rate. It also has the highest rate of imprisonment; the average for Australia is 64 per 100,000 of population and in the Territory it is 212 per 100,000. Drink is the cause of much of this; studies have shown that seventy per cent of all crimes are committed under the influence of drink. Why should Top Enders drink to excess and be so proud of drinking to excess?

Peter McAulay, the Commissioner of Police, tries to find the answers. The climate is conducive, he suggests. That's true: the innocent pleasure of a cold beer on a hot day is not to be denied – but it doesn't account for the excess. The Northern Territory has the image of being a heavy drinking place and thus attracts those who like the life-style: many of them are young, many of them are itinerant male workers and many of them are running away from marriages and other problems which their inadequacies prevent them from solving: to head north and 'go Troppo' is a pleasant way out. There are also twenty-five per cent Aborigines in the Territory's population, and it is well known that they have special problems with drink.

To be drunk has not been a criminal offence for some years – there was no point, the courts could not cope – but the introduction of other laws has helped. The random breath test has improved the accident rate, and the new law which forbids drinking within two kilometres (a mile or so) of a sales outlet has done much to improve street drunkenness. The extent to which this has merely displaced the problem remains to be seen, but at least drinking in a pub or in one's own home is deemed to be less harmful and has certainly reduced minor disturbances and offensive behaviour in the streets.

If Top Enders' drinking habits are treated with light-hearted tolerance and jokes (one writer quipped that the Territory had only two exports – full public servants and empty bottles), the murder rate must surely be cause for alarm? Peter McAulay remained relaxed and forthcoming: 'At times the murder rate has been seven times the national average and it is consistently four times the average, but it is not organized crime or gangland killings. There is nothing sophisticated about murder up here. Let me paint the scene: it is Saturday night and a group of people are drinking in a beer garden. An argument starts, a bit of aggro develops between two men, one gets up and walks around the table and passes wind in the face of the other. Affronted, the man gets up and goes to his car and returns with his rifle. He then shoots the guy through the heart, hissing "Fart no more, you bastard!"'

By the time I had stopped laughing I had realized that McAulay was not spinning me a yarn, he was describing an actual murder case: the most unsophisticated of murders.

Guns are the problem, then? 'No. On the whole the use of guns for crime is not high. Around 30,000 people have licences and they need them for hunting, but the laws are strict and so are the penalties for those holding arms without a licence.'

Gambling, he argues, is not a problem either. The presence of a casino may have its social consequences: depleted savings accounts, mis-spent housekeeping money, a smaller sale for consumer goods; but there is no link between gambling and the crime rate. It is not easy to accept that casinos can be squeaky clean when their image, engraved by James Bond, is of murder and mayhem, but the first four to be built in Australia, two in Tasmania in the early 1970s and the two more recent additions in the Northern Territory, fight hard to be whiter than white. The owners argue that the four towns are small and devoid of other kinds of organized crime; that the governments have strong control, with permanent inspectors controlling all equipment and conducting daily checks on takings which keeps the protection racketeers at bay; and they take pride in proving that the presence of a casino provides much-needed employment and stimulates local industry. The story goes that when the casino opened in Alice Springs, the local shops sold out of shoes. The dress requirements decreed that thongs were not acceptable!

Elsewhere in Australia the picture is not so cosy. Some State or other is always in the throes of yet another expensive inquiry into whether or not to permit a casino. The big cities are fearful. In Melbourne, for example, they know that organized crime already exists, and thus argue that it would be foolhardy to build a casino as it would only be a matter of time before it was infiltrated, not to mention the attraction of adjacent crimes like loan-sharking.

I visited both Darwin casinos: the old, temporary one built into an existing hotel and about to close, and the sparkling, purpose-built Diamond Beach. I've never much cared for the atmosphere in such places: the true gambler always risks more than he can afford, therefore he plays seriously and the mood is hardly carefree. And this was no exception. The traditional gaming tables were surrounded by silent, earnest faces revealing not a flicker of amusement or fun. The jolly corner was the two-up table. Here there was laughter and humour as slim-hipped croupiers invited players to try their hand at arranging two pennies on a flat ruler and tossing them into the air, while the crowd had a bet on which way the coins would fall. I attempted to toss the coins, a movement that is not as easy as it looks. I also won ten dollars; but I came away, knowing that I could not cross that invisible barrier and fathom the mind of the compulsive and excessive gambler, any more than I could understand the compulsive and excessive drinker. The two have much in common and, while society recognizes the latter and is to some extent sympathetic and willing to help, the gambler with his problems is all but ignored. A hundred years ago, Henry Lawson suggested that gambling and drink were the country's greatest curse. Now, outstripped by corruption and drugs, they are but lesser vices.

Perhaps the newcomers with their new attitudes and their new laws and their big-city standards will, in time, rid Darwin of its addiction to drink, dry her out a bit and tame her crime statistics. After all, the image is better suited to the days of lassitude than it is to an Australasian city of steel and concrete with its arts centre, its own Parliament House, its plentiful supply of international hotels, and its casino which is surely the symbol of the New Darwin, rising as it does from the sand like a great white pyramid with its peak cropped, fearlessly facing Asia, a confident beacon to beckon the big spenders.

When politicians talk of tourism, of Asians flocking in, avoiding the Wet and the wasps, to hunt the buffalo, admire the national parks and, of course, divest themselves of dollars in that Special Room, sometimes they sound in their eagerness like Third World leaders of the 1970s, many of whom believed that the tourist dollar could perform economic miracles. Only sometimes – underneath, their dreams are made of sterner stuff; they want the rich to come as tourists and to return as investors. The Northern Territory missed out on the growth of the 1950s and 1960s, and only now is its thirst for development being assuaged by a skyline forever dotted with cranes, and with talk of deals, and with dreams upon dreams of a new Alaska with more than a drop of oil on which to base its prosperity and claims to statehood.

The Northern Territory did not miss out entirely on earlier booms: there was uranium. After the war the British government urged Australia to look for uranium, and there was joy when it was discovered in 1949, some sixty miles (just under 100 kilometres) south of Darwin, at a place called Rum Jungle. Men came from afar to gaze at the wonder that was to find its way into the American and British weapons programmes. The Governor-General came; the Prime Minister came; the Duke of Edinburgh came. In 1949 the world was naïve; environmentalists did not exist nor did the Campaign for Nuclear Disarmament. Uranium was another of the earth's goodies destined to make countries rich and nations powerful. Hiroshima did not make men cry 'Halt!'; it made them scurry to own a bomb of their own.

In 1949, Rum Jungle was a discarded plot. In the middle of the nineteenth century it had been seen as a suitable spot for small farms, but that was short-lived; and some time later a settlement flourished, where copper and tin were mined. In those days it was known as The Jungle which must have been someone's idea of a joke, since the area is mainly scrub with gum trees and a bit of tropical lushness where water lay below ground. The 'Rum' was added towards the end of the settlement's life when the mines were running out of copper and tin and the storekeeper refused to extend more credit to miners. One night, so the story goes, the miners in rebellious mood broke into the store; a barrel of rum was stolen and broken into, and the rum ran from the store through the dusty street and into the spring, making a happy mix. From then it was known as Rum Jungle. It was deserted that day in 1949 when Jack White found uranium.

By 1963 it had all been mined and milled and sold. New finds of copper kept the place alive for a few more years, then in 1971 Rum Jungle was deserted again. The miners walked away, taking with them anything of value and dumping everything else in a big hole in the ground where the uranium had been mined. Rum Jungle became an environmental abscess, an eyesore with rocky red earth defying plant growth and with fishless waters. Radium had of course been discharged into the environment during the mining, but this, scientists argue, is the least of the problems; the main concern is pollution from heavy metals such as copper and zinc. A few desultory attempts were made to clean the place up, but they were not successful and no one seemed much bothered. They are bothered now, now that the world is no longer so careless, and the Federal Government is spending some $A16 million to help nature reassert itself. One day they would like the area to become a recreational centre, a nice little picnic spot for day trippers from Darwin.

Rum Jungle was only a beginning; by the late 1960s, millions had been spent on exploration and there were several other much larger finds, and the business of uranium mining had become a matter of public concern. The stuff was a menace to mankind and an endless source of conflict for politicians. Liberal governments were happy enough to mine and mill; but after much argument, the Labor Party adopted an anti-mining policy with which it too was happy while it remained in opposition. When Whitlam came to power in 1972, the enthusiasm of some of his ministers for uranium mining caused political problems, so wisely he passed the buck to a public inquiry and asked it to answer all the awkward questions on the impact of mining on Aborigines: on the pastoral industry, on wildlife and the environment generally, as well as near impossible questions on the hazards of mining and milling, the safety of reactors and the problems of nuclear waste disposal and – the worst question of all – the fears of misuse and the effect upon nuclear proliferation.

The inquiry published its report in 1977 and the industry got the all-clear: 'The hazards of mining and milling uranium, if those activities are properly regulated and controlled, are not such as to justify a decision not to develop Australian uranium mines.' The safety of reactors and the problems of waste got much the same wordy approval – although they were not strictly Australia's concern but that of the purchasing country. Australia was happy to sell her yellow cake, but not inclined to eat it herself; the opposition to local nuclear power generation and enrichment plants is considerable. The fears for world peace made the inquiry (known as the Fox Report) uneasy, but they salved their consciences by declaring that a renunciation of uranium mining in Australia would have little effect on the world. The country would grab international headlines for a few days and then be left nursing its superiority while it watched customers running with their cheque-books to other countries less eager to pass moral judgements. At the time of the report's publication, uranium was at peak price of $US45 a pound. (Before the oil crisis, it had sold for $US6.50. By 1984, spot prices had sunk to $US21.)

However, the Fox Report did insist that uranium mining should be carefully monitored. A supervising scientist should be appointed to ensure that the mine obeyed all the rules and regulations; indeed, the scientist and his staff should help to formulate rules where none existed (for example in the handling and release of contaminated water); this same team should also monitor the mines' effect on the environment – on everything from mussels to magpie geese – about which so little is known; there is a limited amount to be gleaned from other nations, since these uranium mines are in the tropics.

Bob Fry is the Commonwealth's watchdog. His full title is Supervising Scientist for the Alligator Rivers Region, for it is within the three Alligator Rivers (East, West and South) that the uranium is to be found. For the moment there are two mines; from one, Nabarlek, the ore was extracted and stockpiled in one fell swoop and is now being milled; the other, Ranger, is larger. Two other companies have sought permission to mine, but so far this has been refused.

I met Bob Fry at a party in Sydney, soon after my arrival in Australia, and asked if I might visit the Ranger Mine and his Research Institute at Jabiru.

'Have you got a four-wheel drive?' he asked.

'No. Do I need one?'

He smiled tolerantly and suggested that I report to his office in Sydney for a briefing – which I did. After that, we arranged to meet several months later in Darwin, so that I could join him on one of his regular site visits.

Bob Fry is an unusual scientist, equally happy discussing the novels of Kingsley Amis and *The Angry Penguin*'s Ern Malley hoax as he is being cross-questioned on uranium and his career in atomic energy. His role as Supervising Scientist is not an easy one; it demands the skills of the diplomat and the politician as well as of the scientist. The Northern Territory would rather be left to do its own monitoring; they find his presence a constant reminder that Fox and the Federal Government decided that they were not capable of doing so. The industry find his presence a constant reminder that they are not trusted and therefore need an abundance of regulations and regulators. And then there's the money. Bob Fry has been battling for years for a permanent laboratory costing around $A7 million; meanwhile his staff work in makeshift workshops. A permanent laboratory might help him to attract staff. It is difficult enough to entice scientists away from the cities without offering them second-rate facilities, he argues. Ideally, he'd like a staff of fifty, half of them around the age of forty – at their peak. As it is, he has around twenty and most of them are young.

The forty-years-olds have children and they know the schools in Darwin are not good enough, let alone those in Jabiru. But that's only part of the answer: the Australian is not that adventurous or interested in living in the bush, and lack of applicants has meant widening the search, not all that successfully, to Britain, the USA and Canada. Arthur, an older scientist, had come from Scotland. He told me he had become tired of the way English universities dominated, and was glad to be out. He was also, after a few months, complaining about the science facilities at the local school and the fact that Japanese was taught by correspondence course! His answer was to cast his thoughts ahead to his next post, which he hoped might be in Canberra, and to send his family there, which would involve him in some expensive commuting. Bill, the computer expert, was about to leave. While setting up his programs he had been able to travel between Jabiru and Sydney, but now he was required to live in the area. His wife said 'No', even to Darwin.

The younger scientists seemed easier to please, bound together by an acceptance of nuclear energy – at least, as far as I could tell, none was opposed – and the chance to do some interesting fieldwork and original research. They had much enjoyed the early days, living in demountables in a closed, closely-knit community where miner and scientist mingled; where there was no radio, no television and the newspapers arrived once a week. Now the town of Jabiru is complete; the enlarged community of 1,200 has moved into a suitably large estate where all the roads look alike and only the trained eye can detect differences in the houses. With an enlarged population, the mingling has to some extent ceased and a gap has grown between the government employee and the mine workers. Lyn Barker, aquatic biologist, preferred the old days; but even now, she argues, she does not feel as anonymous as she did when living in Sydney, and she can hunt barramundi at the weekends and start the day with a dip in a billabong. This is not recommended. There are warnings of crocodiles, but none the less a group of us watched the sunrise one morning in the most glorious way: they swam, I paddled.

Lyn is concerned with fish. She gave me a guided tour of her tanks where different amounts of copper and zinc are being fed to varying sizes and types of fish to see how much they can take before it kills them. Aquatic life has a stressful time in the tropics. For five months it rains and rains, the plains are flooded and there is plentiful water; then, one month after the rain ceases, the rivers stop flowing and the creeks dry out, leaving only a series of billabongs in which the fish congregate, gasping for oxygen and longing for the rains to come again. Towards the end of the dry season, their lives are on a knife-edge and the by-products of uranium mining could easily tip the balance and kill everything.

Once again the emphasis is on heavy metals, for these are seen to pose the greatest threat. Not everyone would agree. The Northern Land Council, the body set up to look after Aboriginal interests, heard that a high radium content had been found in a batch of mussels, a traditional food source for tribal Aborigines. It caused a stir. The scientists at the Jabiru Research Institute were asked to comment and, after examining both the mussels and the billabongs where they were found, decided that, because of the age of the mussels, the increase in the radium could not be attributed to uranium mining directly, 'but only to such processes as erosion following site clearance'. Bob Fry argues that in the end site clearance was exonerated and that the highish level of radium found in the mussels was simply due to the presence of uranium in the area, mined or unmined. The scientists' answer was irritatingly precise, accompanied by a dash of comfort: the Aborigines living near the mine relied on Western food bought in shops and ate very few mussels.

The Research Institute reckons it will take ten years in all to produce worthwhile and conclusive answers to their wide-ranging environmental brief. They had to spend the early years assembling base data – finding out what was in the area – before they could even begin to examine the effects of mining. At the end, they believe they will be able to provide a model of natural life in the Top End, valuable in itself, and that they will also have evolved new measurement techniques which could be used for other environmental surveys.

Down the road at the Ranger Uranium Mine, they are not impressed. They have heard that the Supervising Scientist is aiming for a staff of fifty and an expensive laboratory, and they sum up such ambitions in a single word: overkill. Few scientists have bothered to visit the mine, and in return few miners have bothered to acquaint themselves with the details of the research work. Of course Ranger has its own scientists working on the all-important question of water management, and these two groups maintain contact to avoid duplication. But the rest get on with the business of making yellow cake.

The mine likes visitors, or so Lorna Wood assured me. 'We have got nothing to hide and we don't want to become like Pine Gap, covered in secrecy and surrounded by gossip. But we don't like deceitfulness. A group of Greenpeace members tried to hire a local tourist helicopter. The operator was unsuspecting at first, but when they asked him if he would take off the door so that they could film he became rattled. Checks soon revealed who they were.' Kakadu Wonderland Tourist Services claims to have taken thousands on a $A5, seventy-five-minute tour of the $A350 million mine. My private tour with Lorna took somewhat longer and was a jolly affair, mainly because Lorna is a vivacious lady. We headed first for the open-cast mine so that I could watch the ore being gouged from the earth.

There was dust everywhere. 'What is going on? I've never seen it like this before. This place is usually soggy and there is *no* dust,' said the imperturbable Lorna. 'Oh no, this would happen while you are here! Last time I had a television crew here, there was something wrong with the tailings dam,' she added, laughing and peering through the dust to see if she could catch sight of the two water-spraying trucks which should have been making continuous circuits of the mine. One had sprung a leak and the other had broken down.

297

We returned a while later to see them restored and doing a fine job – no dust. In the meantime I tried to concentrate my unscientific mind on complicated explanations of when and why this is added to that, by making incomprehensible notes: 'ground ore plus acid plus manganese . . .' my notebook records, 'ammonia added . . .' Lyn had talked about ammonia and said she would soon be feeding that to her fish.

Lorna, who is related to the mine manager, did a fine public relations job, assuring me that a worker on the site would receive no greater exposure to radiation in a year than I would during one X-ray. 'You've got more chance of being eaten by a crocodile than keeling over from radiation poisoning.' None the less the mine keeps detailed records of where each man is working, day by day, to arm themselves with documentation should there be lawsuits in twenty years' time. Nevertheless there is no shortage of applicants for jobs. 'When we got going they were queueing up; most of them are young, between twenty and twenty-five, and of course well paid. A heavy machine operator gets $A20,000 a year and pays a few token dollars for the rent of a nice house.'

There are a dozen Aborigines in the work-force. It is part of Ranger's agreement that they should employ Aborigines and train them in skills which could be of use in their communities. Allan McIntosh knows all about them. 'The nearest settlement is Oenpelli, which is some forty miles [sixty-five kilometres] away, and these Aborigines do not like being away from their families and their communities for too long; so if they are hired, they do not tend to stay. Those who do stay tend to be apart from the communities, the misfits, the outcasts, the ones who don't fit. This can be lonely for them, as Aborigines are not really kind to one another unless they are related. Some of the reasons for enmity go back a long way. Once upon a time it was OK for them simply to spear each other and be done with it; but this sort of practice is frowned upon by whites, and so enmity tends to rumble on and last a lot longer!'

Allan McIntosh, slow-speaking and avuncular, was responsible for negotiating mining rights and was awarded the MBE for his efforts. It wasn't a happy time nor an easy task. In those days the

Aborigines were against mining. The Fox Report of 1977 states this quite plainly, and equally plainly adds that this view should not be allowed to prevail. Since then, however, the situation has become less clear-cut. It seems that if suitable financial provisions are agreed, if care is taken to minimize social and cultural disruption and if wide consultation and slow progress are accepted, then Aborigines can be persuaded to agree to mining, even if reluctantly at times. Cynics say that those who appear to be pro-mining have become so because they have no alternative; they consider it in their interests to be agreeable, in order to negotiate the best deals. Others argue that the converts have realized that millions of dollars in royalties aid the prospect of self-determination; money is power to Aborigines, too. But to generalize about Aboriginal attitudes to uranium mining is unwise; their views are likely to be just as diverse as those of the rest of the community. The only obvious fact is that they were in the end persuaded to say 'Yes'.

At least in the end, when the mines have gone, they will have money and they will have another large chunk of land to call their own again, to add to neighbouring Arnhem Land. Kakadu, covering an area of more than 2,300 square miles (6,000 square kilometres) was handed back to the Aborigines in 1978; the traditional owners then leased their land to the Director of National Parks and Wildlife, to be managed as a national park on behalf of all Australians. Kakadu National Park is lovely, so lovely that it is included in the World Heritage list of exceptional natural reserves. It is made up of flat flood plains, gently undulating scrub with occasional rocky ridges, and imposing plateaux of ragged sandstone, criss-crossed with deep gorges. And it is rich in wild life and Aboriginal sacred sites and Aboriginal art. Conservationists began arguing that it should be declared a National Park in the early 1960s, but their pleas were ignored until uranium was found. The Park was declared as part of the package which permitted mining; a sop to opponents. Nabarlek is, in any event, part of the Arnhem Land reserve, but Ranger is an island in the park; the boundaries were carefully drawn to exclude the area to be mined, but once the uranium has been extracted it will be enfolded. The realist rules. Mining hastened land rights and hastened the declaration of a park: a strip of silvery lining inside a nuclear cloud. The mining area is small in terms of the total size of the park; one small patch is made ugly and damaged, for it is bound to be damaged; however, many scientists work to keep this to a minimum, but in return a much larger patch will now be carefully preserved and tended.

Alec Carter is the Chief Ranger. We spent the day together, talking, looking, taking photographs. The going was slow. The Wet had lasted overlong and many of the tracks were impassable, even in a Land-Rover used to swishing through water. And all day we saw only one other vehicle. Tourists don't come in the Wet; they wait for the land to dry out – and then they come in cars and caravans and tourist buses, and sleep in tents or in the allotted spaces for caravans or stay in the one hotel, now owned by Aborigines but run by whites. Ten years ago, Aborigines, anthropologists and seekers of minerals had the place to themselves. Now some 50,000 tourists pass through each year to admire the birds and the buffalo and the billabongs decorated with hosts of water lilies. The buffalo, made nervous by the presence of licensed hunters, lope away at the slightest sound – too quickly for me to catch more than a glimpse. The ranger has no time for the buffalo. They might have been an all-important source of meat in the last century but, brought in from Indonesia, they are not part of the natural environment and they do it untold harm. In contrast, the crocodile has no fear of people and does not flee. When they too were hunted for their skins, they would also slope off at the slightest sound; now they are protected by legislation and flaunt themselves fearlessly.

Big Bill Neiijie joined us for part of our journey. A senior member of the Bunitj clan, it had been his responsibility to guard sacred sites and to see, among his own people, that the men did not wander into the women's sites, nor the women into the men's, and that both groups were shielded from boys. Now he is a Park Ranger, paid for doing what he has always done, with the added worry of ensuring that the sites accessible to tourists come to no harm.

Bill, with bare feet, shorts, a T-shirt covering his pot-belly, and a shock of grey hair, had been to Jabiru for a meeting and was now returning to his home at Canon Hill. He'd left a week earlier, evacuated by helicopter, the waters too high even to contemplate driving. 'My, what a change in a week,' he said constantly, 'so dry ...' Bill doesn't smile; his face remained immobile even when, prompted by Alec, he told stories which displayed the driest humour.

'Bill, tell Linda about your visit to Perth.'

'Perth ... buildings made cars look like ants. Tall, tall buildings. I look for stairs; I never seen lifts before! I like Kings Park overlooking city lights. I tell taxi take me there and he wait for two hours while I watch lights going on and off. When I finally saw Darwin, I said "Phew, this nothing. You see Perth."'

Bill had gone to Perth for a short course before becoming a ranger. He is sixty and, he admitted, too old to learn. He had not enjoyed it, but he was glad to have gone so that he could appreciate what young people learn. 'Old generation must continue to teach the young, but also good for young to learn European ways and to read and write.'

I did not ask questions; Aborigines do not like to be questioned by strangers. It didn't matter. Bill talked when he felt like it and from time to time pointed out birds: sea-eagle, whistle duck and a stork called jabiru. There were scores of them, exotic-looking and with pretty names.

'My birds ... no one hunt them ... just to look. You have birds where you come from?'

'Yes, small birds, drab birds ... blackbirds, starlings and pigeons.'

'How far away; how long to get here?'

'Twenty-four hours by plane.'

'Long walk.'

And from time to time he would also point out a sacred site. 'Hawk dreaming. See hawk?' Once the idea had been planted in my mind, I could indeed make out the shape of a hawk emerging from a rocky ridge. 'Don't ask who built it ... don't know. You have tall buildings, we have tall rocks. Long climb, no steps. Hawk used to live there ... oh, long time ago. Can't take you to site. They'd kill me with spear!'

Canon Hill lay off the main track and, as we veered left along a much narrower but clearly defined route through the bush, there was a sign which read: PRIVATE KEEP OUT.

'My road. White fellows give humbug. Stay out.'

The settlement was small, a group of neat new houses, provided by the Parks Department. Bill proudly pointed to his and was gone; glad to be home.

Alec and I drove on to see Obiri Rock, a place of great importance to Bill and of the greatest fascination to white visitors: it contains a band of the most impressive rock art. How old it is no one knows, but the paintings depict both man and wildlife: the Tasmanian tiger, magpie geese, fish. Man is shown in X-ray form, as skeletons with internal organs, resembling the matchstick men of children's drawings. Aboriginal man is shown with spears and goose-wing fans and a string bag around his neck. European man bears rifles and axes. These paintings are under threat, not least from their own environment, from water running over the painted surface and seeping through the sandsone. As I walked around I noticed some curious lines of 'chewing-gum' on the rocks. They turned out to be silicon driplines which keep the water off the surface. I'm glad I spotted them and asked what they were: the answer made me think that man can sometimes interfere with nature to good effect. All day I'd been haunted by the recurring image of a classic political poster issued by nuclear disarmers: they had taken Constable's painting 'The Haywain', depicting an idyllic village scene, and had superimposed a missile upon the green. Uranium mines have no place in Kakadu National Park; no place in a day so pleasant and so peaceful. But they are there and eighty per cent of the Northern Territory's population of 130,000 are glad that they are there. It is the price that they are prepared to pay for progress and to rid themselves of the mendicant tag and the white elephant image; the price of prosperity and the pathway to the Seventh State.

CHAPTER 15

Wait-Awhile Land

Ian McBean has no time for uranium or any other contentious topic. Cattle is his business. Cattle used to be the backbone of the Northern Territory, but not any more. In the 1960s mining became the main money-maker; and in the 1980s tourism pushed livestock into third place. Ian McBean is not bothered by league tables. He knows that the cattle industry, country-wide, is of the greatest importance to the nation's wealth; and he knows that up here he is a man of stature. He is one of the few owner-managers in the Territory with some 20,000 head of cattle spread over 5,600 square miles (14,500 square kilometres) – more than 3 million acres. For years he made do with Innesvale Station and a mere 1,500 square miles (4,000 square kilometres); then in 1982 he bought Bradshaw and quadrupled his lot. It keeps him busy to the exclusion of all else, except his family. Anyway, he's not inclined to fuss much about the rest of the world; and the rest of the world gets little chance to fuss with him. The radio speaks out clearly at six a.m., but after that it crackles and hisses and is useless; there's no television; telephone calls on a radio telephone can be made only at certain times of the day; the newspapers never come into his homestead; the *Bulletin* arrives once a week with the mail and there is no rush to read it. Cattle prices are all that matter. And the weather.

At least I'd found true isolation. Other places had been remote and deserved to be described as isolated; but the ease with which I'd reached them, and the extent of communications once I was there, had robbed the words of meaning. Now I felt cut off. There was no light plane outside the door to whisk me away; no bus down the road. The nearest neighbours were at least an hour's drive away, and the nearest town, Katherine, two hours. And that is nothing compared to Bradshaw. You need a boat to get to Bradshaw.

John, Ian's manager at Bradshaw, came to meet me in Katherine. I'd made the four-hour journey from Darwin on the bus and stayed overnight at Katherine Lodge. The words may evoke thoughts of grandeur – but far from it; it used to be government-provided lodgings for itinerant workers and now, no longer run by the government but by Paul whom I'd met at the Casino, it continues to provide cheap accommodation for those intending to stay awhile. My room resembled a pair of well-worn shoes: every imaginable surface was scuffed and the place was a riot of colour – the cupboards were bright yellow, the walls green, the floor-tiles turquoise and the net curtains were purple. Each room was adjoined by a shared bathroom, and my sharers were two hefty blokes who had travelled from Perth in search of work. They'd found labouring jobs and seemed pleased. They also seemed embarrassed to find me there and hastily removed their dirty washing from our bathroom, which thoughtfully contained a washing machine. Eating involved buying a meal ticket for $A5.50 and swapping this in the canteen for soup, a choice of spaghetti bolognese or sweet and sour pork, a choice of fruit and jelly or sponge cake and tea. The television set was tuned in to a sports programme, and all around men ate without taking their eyes off the set or their elbows off the table.

By seven p.m., when the canteen closed, the sports programme had ended and there was only one man left. In silence we watched a current affairs programme and then I got up to leave, pausing by his table to offer an explanation: 'I've no appetite for old-time music halls.'

'Nor have I. I'm just waiting for the lads, they've gone off to shower.' The lads were his labourers. He, Denis, owned his own construction company based in Queensland and had been awarded a government contract to build grain silos in Katherine.

The lads soon appeared and the four declared that they were on their way to the Workers' Club for a beer; they invited me to join them. The beer came in a bottle without a glass; I decided that this was no time for dainty ways and soon marvelled at how easy it was to sip from the neck. There was music and it was noisy, but we managed an hour of fragmented chat about Australia – the land of opportunity, they assured me, provided you were prepared to put yourself out, travel, go anywhere for a job – and about Katherine, a town of some 4,000 people, a centre for the cattle industry, but also blessed with decent agricultural land if only people could decide what to grow. Katherine has a research station like the one at Kununurra, and it too has had its failures, mainly with rice (which the magpie geese ate, long before it got anywhere near its intended Asian market).

John arrived early next morning flanked by two teenage boys, Jeff and Dave, who would be joining him at Bradshaw under a government-funded programme to give work to unemployed youths in the south. Jeff had arrived the previous night and, having no money but much enterprise, had knocked on the door of the Roman Catholic priest and asked if he could pitch his tent in the garden. He could have stayed at the Lodge; the scheme would have paid his overnight expenses as well as his fare and his wages for three months. Dave had arrived that morning on the bus from Sydney.

'Hop in the back of the Ute', John said to the boys, 'and get to know each other.' The two hopped into the back and said not a word, and within half an hour they were asleep. 'I'll soon get some fat off them and some muscle on,' John said to me.

It seemed fair comment. He could not have been more lean; a slight, bronzed, attractive man with a finely-chiselled face. John, at thirty-six, had been all over the place before agreeing to manage Bradshaw for Ian. He'd seen the job advertised in *Queensland Country Life* and had been chosen from thirty other applicants. Bradshaw, he said with immense satisfaction, was the most isolated place in the world. 'For some of the year you can get there overland but the going is rough and slow. The best thing is to take the road and then just row *across* the river, but at times like this with the rain coming down, the land between the road and the river is a mess, and the only thing to do is travel up the river for an hour. It's very isolated for Beverley. She's my second wife and only twenty-four and she hasn't been off the property for eight weeks.' Silently I resolved to visit Brad-shaw.

Most of the journey to Innesvale was speedy but, once we had left the bitumen road, the last fifteen miles (twenty-four kilometres) along a dirt road were driven with care. This road had been graded a few weeks before when it was thought that the Wet had ended, but the recent rains had roughed the surface and many times we dipped into water where a creek had flooded. The previous night three inches had fallen. The soil, varying from red to leached brown, supported scrub and coarse grass and trees, eucalyptus trees, wiry-looking and well spaced. The sky, laden with clouds, muted the colours and threatened more rain.

As the homestead came into view, we dropped the boys at the men's quarters and drove up to the house, large and low and screened by trees. Ian MacBean, in his early fifties, and his wife Kay, in her late thirties, and their two tiny children welcomed me to Wait-Awhile Land. 'What else can it be? We are constantly giving in to the weather, we have to.'

Ian seemed agitated. He'd started mustering early, hiring extra hands to help him, and he minded about the men having nothing to do and about the newcomers, Dave and Jeff, sitting around getting the wrong idea about life on the land. John was eager to get back to Bradshaw and phoned immediately to check the conditions there; he reported with relief that he thought he could get through by road and boat. Over lunch of cold beef and salad, plans were made: John's chums visiting Bradshaw would leave immediately and head towards Innesvale; we would leave and head for Bradshaw. We'd meet, it was hoped, at the Victoria Pub, the half-way point, then John and the newcomers would continue to Bradshaw and we'd go to The Christening.

'You'll enjoy the christening,' Kay said to me; 'there are not many social functions like this around. It is probably the first one for ten years. You can tell that because there are fourteen kids to be branded and they stretch from twelve to a few months. The Roman Catholic vicar from Katherine has agreed to hold the Bush Christening, and I think he's quite tickled. He'll do the R Cs first and then the Anglicans.'

By the time we had met the Bradshaw group of three (one Aborigine, John's brother and John's brother's friend) and loaded up their van with a couple of crates of beer, plus John, Jeff and Dave, and watched the whole lot totter off into the distance, we had missed the christening ceremony. It had been very simple: a white tablecloth and a bowl of water; the vicar in flowing robes and everyone for miles around in their Sunday best. We were, however, in time for the party. Don Hoar who owns the Victoria Pub had arranged it all. The food was anything but simple: an extraordinary display, table after trestle table covered with complete pigs, huge cuts of beef, a variety of hot dishes and puddings that watered the mouths of those way past baptismal age. There were pavlova cakes decorated with kiwi fruit, mousses and chocolate cake and flans and an endless supply of wine and beer.

As expected, the rain came down in torrents, but no one let that spoil the occasion. The kids tore off their Sunday best and played in the mud until covered, then they raced inside to shower and emerged to repeat the joyful process over and over again. The adults sat in verandah'd splendour and ate and drank and gossiped, the men at one end of a table and the women at the other. The branding caused most chatter. No one used the word christening or baptism; after all, these were cattle folk and Banjo Paterson had given them a better word. He'd written a ballad-poem about a man called Michael Magee who tries to get his ten-year-old son sprinkled with holy water. The lad, listening at the keyhole, overhears his parents' plans:

> He was none of your dolts, he had seen them brand colts,
> And it seemed to his small understanding,
> If the man in the frock made him one of the flock,
> It must mean something very like branding.

The boy runs away; the vicar catches him and brands him in an instant; not stopping to ask his name, he uses the first that comes to mind – Maginnis, a brand of whisky. The child becomes Maginnis Magee and bush christenings become brandings.

For the rest, the men talked of the weather.

'How much you had?'

'Five and a half in two days.'

And the women talked of babies and weight. They thought Kay's Fiona, aged three, was rather small, and they thought Don's Simon, aged eleven months, was huge, big and fat. But then Ian was a small man, and Don was big and running to fat. Don never used to be like that. The gossip galloped. He'd always been so energetic and so ambitious. He owned several cattle stations and a pub at Timber Creek as well as the Vic and he was so busy building up the latter to take overnight trade *and* building an abattoir – a small one – that he only found time to sleep between ten p.m. and two a.m. Then one day a truck ran over him. It was his truck and he had been working on it and the brake came off. He hadn't been the same since; slowed down and gone to fat.

Soon after eight p.m. it was time to leave. Ian got one more round of drinks in plastic cups for us to sip on the journey home – and that included a couple of cans of beer for the Aborigines who were waiting in the back of the van. 'I teased old Don, I did. I said I reckoned it was the first time he had shouted a coon.'

That night I slept on the verandah. We all did. It runs right around the house which meant we could take a side each, one for Kay and Ian, one for the children and one for me. The McBeans sleep outside whenever they can; the verandah is enclosed by an insect screen and they like to fall asleep watching the stars and awake to the birds. I fell asleep to the sound of heavy rain upon the tin roof, which is hardly a lullaby, but the mind, if asked repeatedly, will eventually cut out anything. I awoke to the sound of the six a.m. news and to the sight, in the dawn light, of horses being rounded up. It was glorious: thump, thump, squelch, squelch. The weather was bad again; there would be no mustering. Ian put the men to work building a fence around the head stockman's house and filling up puddles near the homestead with gravel. 'They'd rather be doing that than nothing.' He had started mustering three weeks earlier than usual, and everything had gone so well. Now this.

Ian McBean is a battler, a man who starts with very little, who works against the odds to improve his lot, and whose hands remain rough and whose life-style remains modest. Such men are much admired. It's an image far removed from the farmer in the Western Districts of Victoria where sheep make men rich: rich enough to hire managers so that they can enter politics. And it's an image far removed from the squatter of colonial fiction, the farmers who in the early years of settlement helped themselves to land without government permission and then, when established, applied for leases: such men built replicas of English country houses, allowed peacocks to strut on the croquet lawn, dressed for dinner each night and expected their jackeroos or apprentice station hands to make up the numbers for tennis. Such young men did not come via government employment schemes but were the sons of other wealthy farmers, gaining experience away from home before they inherited. Of course, there are cattle barons with names like Vestey and life-styles like 'Dallas' – but there are just as many cattlemen who claim that their income in a bad year hardly matches the dole. Things have been rough for the cattle industry since the mid-1970s and, as Ian and I talked at Innesvale, the President of the Cattlemen's Union addressing the International Brahman Congress warned that unless the industry united, restructured and modernized, the next generation of cattlemen in Australia would be peasants.

Ian McBean was born on a sheep station in New South Wales. His dad owned it; but it was debt-laden and, once his father had a taste of the army during the First World War, he realized that this was his first love and stayed in for another eighteen years. The farm was sold. But Ian loved the land, and after school be began on the bottom rung of station life as a jackeroo. It is not a bad way to start; if you get a good boss you get a good training, especially if you are prepared to move around the country. Ian began on a horse stud, then moved to a mixed sheep and cattle station, both in New South Wales, before heading to Alice as a stockman, then Queensland as a horsebreaker and then back to the Northern Territory as a drover.

'At that time I never thought I'd have a station of my own, and the next best thing was a drover's plant. For that you need forty horses, three other men, a cook and so forth, and then you could take charge of 1,000 head of cattle and walk them maybe 2,000 miles (over 3,000 kilometres). It was always hard at the beginning of a long drive. We'd be up all night keeping the cattle together but once they settle down, maybe after five nights, you can reduce to a single watch, or shifts of two hours. I'd always do the last watch, starting at four a.m., so that I'd be around to wake the cook and get things going. I'd always let the cattle have a bit of a feed first thing; some drovers don't let them have anything then, but I reckon they are better for it. Then we'd walk them for six miles (ten kilometres) and stop for a while and in the afternoon cover little ground, three miles or four at most (four to six kilometres), letting the cattle eat themselves silly, so that by the time we were ready to pitch camp all they wanted to do was sleep.'

He conjured up striking comparisons with Chips Rafferty in *The Overlanders*, the British movie made in 1946 depicting a mammoth cattle drive from the north to the Queensland coast to save the herd from threatened Japanese invasion. Chips Rafferty had to put up with women and children too, and I couldn't see Ian allowing such a blot on a man's peace.

Ian MacBean spent twelve years droving. 'You'd work for thirty weeks, and then if you were careful you could manage on that money for the rest of the year. Most of us had no responsibilities so we splurged at Surfers Paradise on the Gold Coast and then took any old job to carry us over. How we let our hair down! People were quite pleased to see us at first and then the police would start suggesting that it was "time you drovers got back". The drovers' town was Camooweal, known as "the Weal"; we'd leave our horses there during the wet and when the dry came, lads would turn up from all over Australia, stony broke and looking for jobs.

'Sometimes I'd go contract mustering instead of droving, and that's how I came to know this block of land. And then the previous owners turned this block back over to the Crown and I thought I'd have a go at getting it. I'd married my first wife and it was time I settled down. I knew I had the experience but I didn't have the money, and my mates told me to get the block first and worry about the money afterwards; once you'd got the land you could always borrow the money. So I sent off my application to the Land Board. Anyone can do that and the Board either accepts or rejects the application. Those that are accepted then go into a ballot, a lottery, and if your number comes up then you go before the Board for interview. All this was done in those days to give the small man a go and keep out the city folk, the Pitt Street farmer. There's still some Crown land going but I reckon you'd need money these days. Governments are more interested in selling to foreigners and foreign governments. There's a station near here owned by the Sultan of Brunei, and that cuts us right out. We were better off when we owned the stations and sold the cattle to the Asians. We can't sell, now they have got their own.

'But in those days no money changed hands, and the land came with a covenant that said I had to improve the stock, increase the number of bores and the fencing and so on. If you don't improve the land and the herd, you can have your lease revoked; and if you do, then at the end of fifty years it can be leased in perpetuity. This place wasn't in good shape when I came in 1964. There were around 3,000 head of Brahmin cross but no bores, no fences, no buildings. I don't think a vehicle had ever driven over the land.

'When I heard I'd got Innesvale I went straight back to the Weal and swapped my house for eighty-seven horses and came back here with everything I needed, 120 horses, truck, caravan, dogs, wife and a couple of babies. We camped in the caravan for a couple of years while I got to know the land and thought about where to put the house. We're on a bit of a gravelly ridge here and it doesn't get too bogged in the Wet and I'd also spotted that this area was eaten out, so I realized it must have been sweet country if all those wild things had flocked here to eat with no one pushing them.'

It took a while to hear Ian's story. When he'd had enough of me, he'd say so and suggest we talk again the following day; while we sat in his office, the phone would ring out like a factory siren so that it could be heard some distance away.

'No, Allen, I haven't forgotten you, but this guy gave me ten dollars more a head than you could afford and you know how it is for me . . . raining like billy-oh here, you'd think it was the beginning of the Wet . . . buggering everything up.'

In 1973 just as Ian was beginning to find his feet, beef prices began to slide, and by 1975 the market had collapsed; rock-bottom prices persisted for four years and the period evokes bitter memories. Cattle were sold for a few dollars, processors made handsome profits and cattlemen went broke. There were, quite simply, too many cattle. After the Second World War Australia signed a fifteen-year agreement with the UK, which gave both impetus and stability to the industry; then in 1958 Australia entered the American beef market, gaining a much-needed outlet for poorer stock; the picture began to look temptingly rosy and the 1960s saw a spectacular expansion in beef production, many sheep farmers switched to cattle and dairy herds became beef. In 1975 cattle numbers reached a high of 33 million; it has now shrunk to 24 million.

Ian McBean did not go broke; he went back to contract mustering. For three years he hired himself out to others and left Innesvale ticking over. 'I had to do it. By the time I'd mustered my cattle and trucked them to the meat works, I was out of pocket. Those smart boys ruined everything; anyone who had an inch of land put a cow on it. It was bad for me; my marriage broke up and I could not meet my commitments. I had three kids and you are obliged to give them good schooling. I went to a decent boarding school and I wanted to do the same for them. Up here you have to send your kids away to school, so you might as well send them somewhere decent. I sent the eldest to Queensland and I've always felt he missed out on something by not going south. He worked here with me for a bit, but then left to go horsebreaking in America. I'd like to have him home. He'd be a terrific lot of help – but by the same token he's better off getting the wanderlust out of his soul. He's back from America now, but still breaking in horses and doing the rodeo scene.

'My middle daughter by my first marriage works in computers in Darwin and is engaged to a young man of property. I approve of him. Oh my word, yes. And my youngest, Doug, I sent to St Peter's, the best school in Adelaide, but at seventeen he wanted to come home and work with me. He's really settled down here, but at the end of this season, I'd like him to clear off for a few months. I don't want him to go sour and I don't want to put too much responsibility on to him just yet. And now I've got the two young ones. We'll probably get a governess for them when the time comes and eventually send them south, too. I love having kids around me. I've had them around me for twenty-two years and wouldn't want it any other way. But I'm not doing all this for them. I'm doing it for me. I'm not happy unless I have a challenge, same as in the cattle recession, no way was I going to sell up. No way!

'And when prices came good again in 1978 I had a fair number to sell and that got me on my feet again, and I began to plan so that it would not happen again. By the early 1980s I reckoned I'd reached the limit of my efficiency here at Innesvale. I had 5,000 cattle, which meant that I could turn off enough each year to run the place, but not enough to make surplus money to put in the bank to tide me over a bad year. I had to get bigger. Well, the only alternative was to try and improve the pasture so that I could produce top beef that ends up in the butchers' shops down south. But that is risky. I don't think the research boys have come up yet with anything that can cope with the rigours of this climate.'

So he decided on an enlarged hamburger herd and spent $A900,000 buying Bradshaw. 'I had to fight for it, you know. Some Singapore doctor wanted to buy it, but I enjoyed the fight, going down to Canberra and arguing my case. I really appreciated my education then. And now I've quadrupled my cattle and, I hope, only doubled my running costs. Of course it may turn out to be the wrong thing, buying all this land, but I am one of those people who believe you don't get anywhere if you don't have a go.' (Eighteen months later, he was to sell Innesvale and settle at Bradshaw, and John went to manage one of Don Hoar's stations.)

His main worry for the moment is ridding his herd of brucellosis and TB, which must be done by 1992 if Australia wishes to keep her American market. Many pastoralists argue that this will be the death of them. Exaggeration, they think, will persuade folk in Canberra to part with a subsidy to help with the work. On the whole, folk in the south, knowing little of the problems of the north, prefer to believe that the cattleman has an enviable life and does not need subsidies to make it more enviable. Mercifully, Ian McBean does not moan. It is a costly business mustering wild cattle from the outer regions of his empire, holding them for three days, and checking them again sixty days later; but he knows it is worth it to protect his market. ·

The rain continued for several days; the temperature dropped too to the point of chilliness, and the water went cold: usually the sun shines often enough for a solar system to cope on its own. The atmosphere was oppressive and the mood lethargic; I began to have an inkling of what the prolonged Wet could do to the spirits. The children became fractious. They got bored tearing around the verandah, bored with tapes telling them stories. Sam took to playing with dolls. I saw him, but later he denied it and said dolls were 'Yuk'. Fiona took to following me around, puzzled to see me so often with a notebook. Time and again she asked if I were making a shopping list, as though it were the only time she saw her mother with a pen. Kay looks after the books. Ian managed on his own before there was Bradshaw, but now Kay handles much of the paperwork. The inadequate telephone system prolongs her task and causes irritation.

If she could have one wish it would be for a twenty-four-hour system like city folk instead of a radio phone which entails booking all calls in advance and having them connected for a mere ten minutes in every hour. 'It is slow and frustrating and we are trying to run a business. We are employing twenty-eight people at the moment.'

The phone aside, she complains very little. She enjoys the isolation and puts off going to Katherine until her shopping list is a mile long and requires a full and exhausting day; she is content to spend many weeks on her own while Ian and the men are away mustering. She could receive television if they were prepared to buy an expensive aerial, but is happy enough with a video recorder – a boon to the Outback; friends in Adelaide tape programmes of particular interest, like *Brideshead Revisited* which she watched night after night with much pleasure, instead of in tantalizing weekly instalments.

'When I first arrived and sat around the table with all the men, I thought, "This is great," but now I think it is rather boring. All they talk about is cattle and horses, and I'm not that interested in either – I don't even ride. I know most of the station wives become involved and even do a little mustering, but it's not for me. I love the bush though, but just occasionally it would be nice to have another woman around with whom I could discuss the rest of the world.'

She's seen a fair bit of it. She was brought up in Adelaide, trained as a nurse and then spent three years in Europe and North America. 'It was necessary in those days. Australia seemed so cut off from the rest of the world. All the important news seemed to come from overseas, and certainly all the movies we saw were either English or American. I loved my years of travelling; it was easy to get jobs as a nurse, but in the end I came back to see my parents. I felt I owed it to them to spend some time at home, and also I felt in need of a bit of family love. I stayed a year and then went on my way again, this time to see the bush, the north. I went to Darwin – but didn't like the hospital much and was pleased when they asked me to move to Katherine for a month. I stayed longer, I stayed until I got involved with a bloke and then I left and went south. I was always doing that: every time I got involved I'd decide to take another course, get another qualification. Reckon I was a bit afraid, a bit wary of marriage. I came back to the bush after a while and joined the bush clinic going around the cattle stations. I made friends on one station and used to arrange a clinic in the area on a Friday so that I could stay the weekend. That's how I met Ian. But, true to my pattern, I went off to Sydney to do a course in Community Welfare as soon as I saw myself getting involved. It was a pretty emotional year; I didn't much like Sydney and I only half enjoyed the course. In the end I came back; and by then Ian had tidied up all his muddles and we got married one hot day in November.'

Ian is a fortunate man. While he gets visibly agitated by irritating things he cannot change, like the weather, Kay McBean could glide through those tedious days with Edwardian serenity, keeping to a rigid timetable (breakfast, six-thirty; smoko, nine-thirty; lunch, twelve-thirty; smoko, three-thirty; supper, seven-thirty) and coping with tiresome children. During a rainless hour, Kay took me for a long walk to show me the outbuildings, the horses being shod, the head stockman's house, the mechanic's caravan and the single men's quarters. The latter were basic indeed: a wooden barracks with separate, tiny sleeping cubicles, communal facilities and a wide verandah on which to share a beer. It's good enough, said Kay. The men spend only about a month in there; the rest of the time they are roaming 3 million acres (1,215,000 hectares). We also went to the blacks' camp (Kay's phrase); the Aboriginal men work for Ian, and three of the women work around the house for Kay. The camp consisted of a piece of canvas slung against a tree and a square tin hut; inside, mattresses were placed head to toe without an inch to spare.

Some yards away there was a tap offering running water, a lavatory and a shower. Two camp fires were burning and a handful of women and children hovered close, shivering in tatty cotton frocks. The women refer to Kay as 'Mrs' and Ian as 'Boss'.

'Cold day, Mrs.'

'No jumpers?' asked Kay.

'No jumpers, Mrs.'

'I'll have to see what there is in the store,' said Kay and asked one woman to pick up the rubbish lying around, the bits of paper and the empty beer cans; she told another that her child's clothes needed washing. 'When I first arrived, I used to come here once a week and talk to them about cleanliness and health, but it's like talking to the grass. I don't visit here more than once a year now.'

I suggested that the Aborigines might be better off in a wooden barracks like the men's quarters.

'Can't afford it. Anyhow, they are OK like this. They like living outside, except when it is cold and wet – and that's only about ten per cent of the time.'

Coleen came back with us to collect the jumpers. She works around the house with Rosie and Margaret; they get paid in jumpers, soft drinks and food.

Next day, Rosie said her jumper was too big. 'It can't be that cold down there if you think your jumper is too big,' replied Kay.

Some things change but slowly. All Australian schoolchildren read a book called *We of the Never Never* by Mrs Aeneas Gunn, the story of one of the first white women to follow her station-manager husband to the north and of her fight to gain the acceptance of both station hands and Aborigines. The book was made into a highly successful film, criticized only for its lack of mud and touches of sentimentality. At some time Gunn had managed Bradshaw, which made the book apposite; but it was my visit to the blacks' camp which etched the reference on my mind.

Ian's problems seemed never-ending. The mechanic's wife's brother died suddenly and the two took off immediately for the funeral; since they had only an ordinary saloon car, Doug had to lead them to the bitumen in case they got stuck in the mud. Then one of the Aborigines came to ask for time off so that he could go to Katherine where his girl-friend had given birth. He didn't have a car, but the head stockman, Ronnie, had said he could borrow his. It was not a four-wheel drive, so Ian said he stood no chance of getting through and he wasn't having Doug running down the track again. The boy could wait until the weather was better. And then Greg, a jackeroo with excellent references (so good that Ian and Kay had at one time considered inviting him to live in the house as company for Doug, but had then decided against it), asked for a half-day off to get his ute (utility truck) fixed. Greg had his request turned down. It's all a question of timing; Greg had made the mistake of calling at the homestead at lunchtime, just as we were tucking into our cold beef and salad. 'Not even a black would be stupid enough to interrupt us at meal times.'

On top of this came Vince – he was enough to ruin anyone's tinned asparagus and beef stew. Vince runs the scheme under which Ian had acquired Jeff and Dave, and he needed to go to Bradshaw to see that the boys were OK and to get them to sign a handful of forms. The rules said this had to be done within ten days of their arrival. Well, the boys had only been at Bradshaw a few days, so Vince could wait ...

Vince didn't want to wait. 'Look, all he wants is a day or two out of the office. He gets an overnight allowance which he pockets and stays with us or at Bradshaw. Not that I want the money, but it's the principle of the thing.' Ian explained on the phone to Vince that the only way of getting to Bradshaw was by boat, and that would mean interrupting John's work while he came down river to collect him. 'If you want that you can pay $A100 to hire the boat and for John's time.' Vince agreed to pay the $A100, much to my delight. It meant that I too could visit Bradshaw.

Ian drove me down the bitumen to meet Vince, in the bull-catcher, just for fun. It's like a small tractor and it splashes mud everywhere. The kids enjoyed the trip; everyone did – except the dog. He fell off and no one noticed.

'Of course I could have waited, but I fancied the trip. Let's go,' said Vince and he crashed his foot to the floor and sped away the miles to the Victoria Pub in record time. We stopped there to buy rum and whisky as gifts for John and to get more forms signed. Don has four boys under the scheme helping to build the abattoir. For seventeen weeks the Federal Government pays between $A75 and $A100 towards their wages, and during this time they are meant to get some training; at the end of this time, it is hoped they will be kept on. From the pub we drove to Big Horse Creek, a favourite spot for fishermen, left the car and hopped aboard John's twelve-foot (3.5-metre) aluminium boat with its outboard motor to ease our journey upriver. It was splendid, like a sepia photograph: the sky wasn't blue and the rain had muddied the water, and we saw two crocodiles. The banks on either side were only slightly raised and gently wooded, and cattle grazed to the water's edge. Bradshaw station was on our right and Auvergne station on our left; in front, where the river curved, was a ragged escarpment, our landmark; it led us to the homestead. The spot where we finally left the boat is also the spot where it is possible to cross the river, scramble across the land (when it is dry) and meet the road again at Timber Creek. It is also where the cattle cross. It must be an impressive sight to see 1,000 head walk into the water.

It took ten minutes to walk from the river bank to the homestead, which was a revelation. Years of neglect had not altogether managed to destroy a certain elegance and the distinct impression that the house and outbuildings had not grown piecemeal but had been carefully planned together. The homestead was imaginatively designed on two levels: the ground floor contained a huge living area with small bedrooms and bathrooms opening off it, and the upstairs contained the kitchen and more bedrooms. Outside was a swimming pool. Bradshaw's previous owners had been Arabs, who had hired a manager more interested in horses than cattle. Before the lease lapsed, the wealthy owners would fly in from time to time for a spot of fishing and some fun. Ian's first manager had been a dead loss too, and John and Bev and four-year-old Olivia had arrived to find a disheartening scene. 'We had an awful journey overland; the ninety miles (145 kilometres) took us eight hours, because the way was full of gulleys and rocks and creeks. It was so rough that the cat thought it was dying and Olivia kept asking why I was asking her to eat dust. Bev said little until we opened the front door and saw on the table in front of us evidence of a meal eaten months before – dirty plates. a jam pot and sauce bottle on the table. Then she said: '''What have you brought me to!'''

After two weeks Ian turned up to find out if they were prepared to stay: 'I feel sure he thought we'd go; there was so much that needed doing and the isolation is total.' But the telephone works; the radio reception is good and there is a video. It is the Victoria River which makes the difference; it acts as a vast moat without a drawbridge and creates a feeling either of peace or panic, depending on your temperament.

'It was difficult at the beginning; there were only the four of us: John and myself and Olivia and Tony, John's fourteen-year-old son by his first marriage. Olivia cried a lot and missed her friends, but now she has developed the most vivid imagination and talks all day to her dolls and her dog. Tony's a bit of a problem. I'm supposed to oversee his education by correspondence course, but I'd be happier to see him at school in Darwin. We are going to get there soon and see if we can sort something out. But I've little to moan about, although I do hate making bread and I do moan when the stores and the fuel get low. But I'm kept busy cooking for all the men, and we have already had our relatives to stay.'

The men are a handful of Aborigines and, of course, Jeff and Dave, whom we had come to see. Jeff and Dave – who had been so silent and sleepy at that first meeting – had rid themselves of tiredness and apprehension and babbled delightedly about their new home and their new life. They are sharing a neat room in the men's quarters which offered twin beds and a wardrobe and table and had its own adjoining shower. Jeff had put wild flowers into a jam-jar and offered to repaint the room in his spare time. They had learned to kill and cut up a bull. They signed their papers without reading them, declaring that they weren't that bothered about days off and other fine details. A short distance away the Aboriginal stockmen had similar quarters.

'It's a bit different from Innesvale, isn't it?' said John. 'That blacks' camp is a disgrace and I can't say I approve of the men's quarters there either – they just won't do in this day and age. Ian's a bit slow to accept change, but I feel that at heart he wants to because he knows it will be better for the business. But he's a real Scot, you know, a real Scot!'

That night, further to underscore the difference, we all, Aborigines included, joined together for a barbecue of steak and ribs and beer and wine. The Aborigines said very little but played happily with Olivia who insisted they help her dress and undress her dolls. John is full of ideas for Bradshaw. He'd like to tidy up the demountables and rent them out to the classy sort of tourist who like catching barrimundi. He'd also like to persuade Ian to develop the internal market by selling young half-fat cattle to the south, where better pasture would finish them off. 'We can build their bones and then get rid of them; that way, I reckon we could run both properties with four permanent staff in each. I know Ian likes all the business of big stock camps and months of mustering, but it is not necessary. It's the old way and the hard way.'

We left early next morning and raced back to Innesvale, making good time on the river and even better time on the road. Along the dirt track, halfway to the homestead, we found our path blocked by a helicopter. Brian had arrived from Darwin, the rain had stopped, the sky was blue, Ian was in good spirits: mustering could begin again.

Doug had intended to go up in the helicopter as 'spotter', responsible for sighting crafty cattle hiding in creeks and under bushes, but he seemed happy enough when I volunteered for the job. No one much liked the helicopter, least of all Ian who had neither the head for heights nor the stomach for all that ducking and weaving. He had a bet with Brian that I would not last long. I was determined that he would not win, but within five minutes I feared that he might. Brian had decided to test me to the limit; he swung high into the air then dipped sharply to the left, diving into the trees; as he brushed the branches he rose steeply again and swung violently to the right, diving once more into the bushes. The sky became the trees and the trees became the sky, all within seconds.

I shut my eyes. 'Hey, you can't do that ... you are meant to be spotting,' Brian yelled over the head-phones that are designed to minimize the noise. I ignored him, sickened by the violent movement and his macho antics. After a while I cautiously opened one eye and then the other, and decided there was nothing to fear; Brian could certainly handle a helicopter – and all I had to do was ignore the showing-off and it would stop. Within ten minutes my heart had stopped thumping and threatening to leave my body via my mouth; within fifteen minutes I could manage a smile as I spotted my first calf. It isn't that easy; my first attempts had turned out to be boundary posts, which had caused Brian to jeer. Within the hour it had all become the greatest fun as I leaned out of the open-sided helicopter to take photographs or chalk up another spot. Once we had spotted a calf we went lower and lower until the noise and the wind created by the chopper persuaded the calf to run for its life. Sometimes we were no more than a few feet from the ground. We hovered until a stockman realized we had found something and came galloping by to steer the stray towards the herd. Then off we went in search of another wild thing. Each twenty minutes or so, we landed and waited for Ian to find us for consultations. Brian gets paid for the time he is in the air and, at $A160 an hour, helicopter mustering is not cheap. We spent as much time that afternoon sitting in the bush gossiping as we did in the air playing hide-and-seek.

Brian was born in England and came to Australia via New Zealand. He hates being thought a Pom: 'There's a stigma attached and I want none of it.' As camouflage, he has developed the ugliest of accents and a facility with the word 'bloody' that would make an ocker envious. 'It's bloody boring work, this; but I earn about $A30,000 in eight or nine months, and that's pretty good. And I can tell you,

I'm sick of the sight of bloody beef by the end of the season. It's all you get to eat on these stations, eggs for breakfast and bloody beef the rest of the time, cold, roast, steak and stew. And I don't much like living in the homestead, either. I'd rather eat with the men and have a caravan for a bit of privacy.' It is only his second time at Innesvale; Ian had fired his previous pilot for leaving 'too many of the buggers in the bushes'.

'Last time I was here, John got stuck on the road to Bradshaw – flat tyre, that's all – and he didn't have a bloody spanner. An hour at $A160 just to hand over a spanner!'

The flies found us and swarmed all over us, humming with pleasure as we sat on the flattened glass around the chopper. 'Last of the season's bloody clouds. Take a good look. Within a week we won't be seeing one of the bloody things for another six months.'

Supper was late that night. At seven-thirty Ian arrived with a handful of warm, newly killed beef. It had been alive half an hour before. 'Wait until you taste this.' He was full of chatter as he wielded the sharpened knife across the chopping board. 'Where's that Brian? I want to know how long he was up there.'

'One and a quarter hours,' I answered.

'Oh, that's good. Less than I expected; you seemed to be up all afternoon. Well worth it. That paddock's clean now.' He knew by instinct and was happy.

My last sight of Innesvale came at dawn one morning. The moon was still in the sky; the horses already had their noses into high-protein feed-bags, and Kay was tending a boil under the arm of a thin, silent, bearded Aborigine. I pondered the origin of never never. Those who do not like the isolation say that it is because, once you have left it, you never never want to return. And those who love it say that it is because, once you have found it, you never never want to leave.

CHAPTER 16

North to Nowhere

I lost count of the number of people who advised me not to do it. When I first mentioned the idea during my early days in Sydney, an eyebrow would be raised to denote surprise; but the comments were less harsh and damning than those delivered whenever I admitted my desire to travel on a road train. However, by the time I reached Perth, the raised eyebrow had given way to the odd word of warning; by the time I reached Darwin, the warning had become an instruction: Don't. Peter McAulay, having persuaded me to reveal my plans, simply shook his head: 'No, that's a bad idea. Have you stopped to think about the sort of girl who gets involved with that kind of thing? Yes, I know you are a writer but the men you'd be with are hardly likely to make allowances for the difference.' Peter McAulay being the Commissioner of Police, I pondered his words, but decided to keep to my plans.

All I wanted to do was to spend a few days on a prawn trawler. Now, it seems that the girls who opt for life on trawlers, as cooks or deck-hands, are what used to be called good-time girls. They are attracted to the life-style and a plentiful supply of booze, drugs and sex. Even if they arrive innocently in search of straightforward adventure, they soon find themselves trapped into accepting the rest of the package. The stories are legion of young girls, not realizing the extent of the services they are expected to supply until they are way out to sea, and then in desperation accepting the attentions of one man in order that he be responsible for keeping the rest at bay. It sounded most unsavoury; but I also found it difficult to believe that all trawlers were orgy-prone – and anyway I wanted to go north to

Nowhere, to Karumba, a tiny fishing town in the Gulf of Carpentaria, where the Outback meets the Arafura Sea.

Everything north of Mount Isa is known as Nowhere: an impossible backwater, little more than a cluster of neglected former mining towns. But these tiny towns, having realized that they are helpless on their own, have come together and formed the Gulf Local Authority Development Association, in the hope that they can persuade the Queensland Government that the area could outrank Africa as a destination for international adventure tourists. But that's in the future. For the moment it is Nowhere, cut off for three months of the year during the Wet, and with poor communications at the best of times. They say smoke signals are more reliable than telephones.

It is easy enough to get to Mount Isa, a copper mining town sufficiently flourishing to be on schedule-flight and coach routes. From there, however, one needs to be patient and wait for the mail plane. I waited forty-eight hours, whiling away the hours doing very little – mainly walking by day, which is seen as an odd thing in these parts. No one walks. The car is king and the heat a killer, and the walker feels conspicuous. In Darwin I had walked to a party and been greeted by a fellow guest: 'I know you. You *walked* here, I saw you!' In Mount Isa I half expected the police to haul me in for suspicious behaviour. One morning I walked into the local MP's office, hoping to find out something about Karuma, but he wasn't there and his secretary had not visited the area. 'Don't worry. I'm sure they are very friendly up there, provided you don't behave like a Pom.'

At night there was a cinema, and the local papers to comb. They were not at all parochial and seemed to enjoy reporting that Sydney's armed-hold-up rate was now eight a day, mainly banks and service stations, and that down in Melbourne a State Member of Parliament had been banned from the superannuation fund because of her weight. 'Rubens liked women my shape,' she quipped; but the *Courier Mail* was not confident that its readers would understand the joke and added in brackets: 'Peter Paul Rubens was a European painter of the 1600s who chose full-bodied women as his subjects.'

The mail plane was slow; it was in any event a tiny plane not given to speed; it was slowed still further by the number of times it touched down, mainly to enable Aborigines to get on or off. None moved either way at Karumba. It is a white man's town. Aborigines sometimes pass through and stop for a drink in the town's bar; but they move on at dusk. No one knows why the Aborigines skirt Karumba; some say it was once the scene of a massacre, others that it was a burial ground, but no one really knows. They are merely happy enough with the fact. The Flying Padre had been in the day before to hold a service, something he does from time to time, and had stopped to chat to the congregation. 'How do you like it here?' he asked a woman he had not seen before.

'It's great, no coons,' she replied causing much embarrassment and supplying the town with twenty-four hours' worth of gossip.

'Normanton's the black town, you must have realized that when you touched down. They have tarmac and night lights and a proper building with lavatories. We have a shack. If you want any money from governments these days, you've got to be able to show a fair percentage of blacks or you don't get any. We don't get any,' volunteered one of the town's gossips.

I don't think they mind too much about their airport. It's lack of water that bothers them. They have none, and what they need has to be carted some thirty miles (fifty kilometres) at a cost of around $A35 for 1,000 gallons (4,550 litres), and then it is suitable only for washing. There are notices everywhere telling you not to drink the stuff. The town has been arguing with governments for fifteen years for help with a $A6 million project to build a dam on the Norman River which would help the town to thrive rather than survive. The government says it is up to the fishing industries who benefit from local resources to put up the money; industry replies that it is the government's job to look after the infrastructure and that, if they accept this responsibility, the firms will then move their processing plants to the area. As it is, the prawns and other fish are snap-frozen at sea, are off-loaded to a cold store in Karumba and moved quickly by refrigerated road trains to the Queensland coast for processing. Such an arrangement makes the town look temporary, as seasonal workers camp in caravans or demountables.

The main street is wide and dusty and it has a bank which opens one day a week, a tiny travel agency to chart all the comings and goings, a post office and milk bar and a huge supermarket selling everything from metal eyelets to watches, from clothes and stationery to food. The prices are exceptionally high; many of the food products had overshot their 'sell-by' datemarks; and everyone tries to avoid buying things from the lower shelves. Dogs – numerous dogs, because there is no vet around to spay them – like sniffing their way through the shop, lifting their legs at regular intervals. Dogs are just one of the town's troublesome Ds. The others are drugs and *de facto* relationships. Dope growing and trading seemed to be an established fact; but when I asked the local policeman about it, I thought he was going to throw me down the steps. Instead, he yelled at me. I'd made a silly error in misjudging his personality. I thought he was as laid-back as everyone else and jokingly asked about life 'in this lawless town'.

'Lawless town! What are you talking about? Drinking? Is that it? So what. No one gets hurt. The men walk back to their boats and, apart from the odd fight, no one gets hurt. Drugs, is it? You're on about drugs? What am I supposed to do about that? You'd need a special squad to do a raid and I'm only one man.'

'Gambling?' I queried, thinking that if I bullied him a little he might quieten down.

'Gambling!' he roared. There was no retrieving the situation. 'There is no gambling. I've seen no gambling, and no one has reported gambling to me. If they had, I'd do something about it. Look, up here we have a different set of rules for what is acceptable and what is not. The thing that worries me is how to keep my fifteen-year-old daughter away from those trawlers!'

Many a father must have said the same. For the girls do get muddled up with the trawlers. Some 300 prawn and 100 barramundi boats are licensed to work the Gulf, and about half use Karumba as a base. A mother-ship circulates among them at sea to collect their haul and provide supplies of fuel and food, but they like to return regularly to paint the town. The men don't want to marry the girls and the girls don't want to marry the men, and I soon got used to the whispering: 'That's the one with three children by three different men.'

Their meeting place, indeed *the* meeting place, is the bar at the Karumba Lodge Hotel, the town's only hotel. In fact, there are two bars at this hotel; the one inside named the Suave Bar and almost always empty, and the one outside, a great concrete slab of a place with a roof to keep out the sun and the rain. This is called the Animal Bar. The names say it all. Jim Mackie couldn't wait to show them to me. He runs the cold store for Fridgemobile, a subsidiary of the mighty Swire group. When he first arrived in Karumba, he had gone straight to his office to find a note saying: 'In the Animal Bar.'

'I couldn't believe it. I had to fight my way through the crowd and the noise . . .' he rolled his eyes skywards; '. . . these men start on the grog at noon and continue until they can hardly stand, then they stagger home to sleep, and return the next day to start again!'

He thought I'd be amused by all this, and anyway I needed to meet fishermen to find out about prawns and see if I could find anyone willing to take me to sea for a few days. Jim and his wife, Jean, would be vetting proposals.

In the Animal Bar I found the Australian caricatured by Paul Hogan: the classic ocker, the man dressed in shorts, T-shirt and thongs; ignorant and crude and loud of mouth and one helluva drinker. The place was not full but the noise defied belief. There were perhaps half a dozen women and as many children mingling in various groups.

The first group to whom I was introduced by Jim welcomed the interruption not at all. A squat fisherman with a pot-belly, red eyes and slurred speech said: 'What I wanna talk to you for, eh? What's in it for me, eh? You gonna pay me? Tell you something, if you come on my boat, you'll need a big supply of tissues rather than notebooks . . .' and as he roared with laughter at his own obscene wit, a similarly over-sized chum took up the theme: 'Aw, not now. I don't mind talking to you some other time. What about six o'clock tomorrow morning on me boat, eh? I'm at me best then, cuppa tea and a shit and I'm on top of the world at that hour, eh?'

Queenslanders like to end their sentences with 'eh' or 'hey';

sometimes the syllable has an upward inflection making every remark sound like a question, at other times it is used flatly like a verbal full-stop. As for the rest, I was not affronted. I have spent too many years in newspaper offices where men delight in booze, callous behaviour, rudeness and sexual innuendo – and besides, I had deliberately chosen to wander from the world of garden-party good manners, and these men were being themselves; if I didn't like it I could leave. I turned away instead and Jim tried again.

Bill Fulham was different, older, leaner and quieter: 'I can't be bothered with talking. I catch fish, I don't talk about it.'

I offered to buy him a beer, and when I returned he started to talk with ease and without prompting.

'Don't be put off by these guys. See that one over there in the red shirt? You'd never guess his boat cost him half a million and that in the last four weeks he has put $A50,000 in the bank – $A35,000 of that is profit!'

Bill was once a pig farmer, and now he yearned to breed quarter horses and exotic parrots. Meanwhile and for the last twelve years he has been a fisherman, catching barramundi from six a.m. until noon and mud crabs in the afternoon. His wife goes to sea with him, and so does one of his sons. 'My son is a fanatical fisherman, he never stops; when he starts picking on me, I know that he is tired and that it is time to pull up for a few days. That's why we are here now, but not for long. The place is rough. Last time, I had my boat with an outboard motor stolen. I hunted it down and sure enough it had been taken by druggies. I wouldn't go aboard their boat to reclaim mine; I knew they would just throw me in the water. So I went and found a policeman and he wouldn't go aboard, either – but he did a deal with them: return the boat, he said, or I'll bust you for drugs. They returned the boat.

'It's like a jail up here, full of wanted men, or men on the run from their wives and their debts, and drugs seem to be at the heart of much of it. Last time I was in Cairns, negotiating a market for my crabs, I was approached by this twenty-two-year-old who said he liked the look of my well-kept boat and was there a job going? I fell for the flattery and I needed a helper, so I took him on. Within a couple of days I realized that he had selected me because I had a bit of age on me and therefore would be a respectable cover for his marijuana growing. He finally came clean and showed me the seeds and invited me to go halves. I tipped him over the side and into the water. That'll give him a chance to sort himself out, I thought. I'd have picked him up eventually, but he found his own way back, and since then there has been no trouble. We work well together.

'Prawns? No, I'd never do prawns. You wait till you see the life. The money is incredible but the life is awful and it won't last. If the Japs ever pull out, we are done for, and I hear that they are already breeding their own. It'll all be over in four years. I think I'll leave tomorrow. I like to have a beer sitting in a comfy chair on a bit of green grass with a few flowers around me. Why should I stand here on this slab of concrete with all this damn noise?'

Through the throng I could see the sunset doing its standard tropical number, silhouetting palm trees against a pink sky, and I noticed, for the first time, a huge notice saying NO DOGS. In the Animal Bar, drunken men are given to kicking each other's dogs and this has caused more fights than anything else; thus the dogs are banned.

The next day, Saturday, Jean and Jim and their daughter, Jeanette, invited me back to the Animal Bar for lunch. 'It has quite a different atmosphere and offers the best fish and chips in the world for $A2.' It has and it did. The noise was no longer male-voiced but music from a juke box; few stood and many were seated at tables. Between the tables at varying intervals were tin buckets acting as dustbins for empty glass beer bottles. A sharp-looking barmaid was taking great delight in chucking the stubbies from a great height and often from some distance to make the greatest possible noise. 'I love doing it on Saturday and Sunday mornings to aggravate the hangovers.' People were pointing and laughing at a man wearing a T-shirt which said: 'Fat women shit me.'

Bobby, the bookmaker, sat at the next table, smoking and coughing and flashing a ring which was just too large to be a diamond, his attention divided between the radio at his side and the newspaper spread over the table. Other men at other tables were similarly occupied and silently sent their kids across with crumpled notes.

Steve came in to place a bet on a horse called White Wine in a Sydney race. He badly needed to recoup his losses from nine hours of solid drinking the day before – rum, rum and water, rum and coke. He'd had an excellent start to the prawn season but was short of cash because his boss, George, had yet to finalize a sale; and the telephone to Lizard Island, the ritziest of the Barrier Reef resorts where George was showing affluent tourists all they needed to know about big-game fishing, hardly helped.

'It's not the right time for game fishing, but he's there somewhere and this shortage of cash is a problem. I wanted to leave again this afternoon, and my stocks are pretty low.'

Jean and Jim like Steve; he is one of the few independent operators left in the Gulf. They offered to sort out the money and organize his shopping, from cigarettes to celery, from toothpaste to tomatoes, and send it out on the mother-ship. They also encouraged me to sail with him. I was full of doubts and I remained full of doubts until the trawler pulled away from the quay. After that, there was no point in having doubts; I'd made my decision – but, even so, I was unusually tense and ill at ease for some while. Steve noticed and I think it amused him. 'Relax,' he kept insisting as we sailed towards the open sea and he tried to interest me in his expensive radar equipment, including one piece which shows the sea below and charts the movement of fish in pretty bands of colour. Another screen soon showed a group of six trawlers, some distance ahead. 'Must be something there. Yeh, has to be.'

The other trawlers had dropped anchor, so it took us no time to catch up and pull alongside one of their number. Skipper Ralph explained that a spotter plane that afternoon had detected three mud boils (dark circles of sea) in the area which could prove to be banana prawns.

Steve was pleased with this news. We dropped anchor and ate steak, Steve and I and Marie, both cook and deck-hand, and Ernie, a Maori and Steve's right hand. There were many jokes, mostly emanating from Ernie who was never serious and who appeared to have lost his pet frog that normally lives among the pot plants. 'Look out for Knee-Deep, won't you. I called him Knee-Deep 'cos when I found him he was knee-deep in shit.'

The galley was well equipped, with a deep-freeze and a micro-wave oven, honey-coloured carpet and cushions and a stereo unit with tapes from the Bee Gees to Beethoven. At one end of the galley there were steps leading down to four bunks, arranged in twos, divided by a gangway: one side for Marie and me and the other for Ernie. Steve slept in the wheelhouse. The shower and lavatory were tiny; but the water was hot, even if the lavatory required help from buckets of water hauled from over the side of the boat.

After dinner, out came the marijuana, crumbled into a pipe and smoked communally. No one said a word when I declined to join. Soon the galley stank of the stuff and Marie started giggling. It was time for bed, but I found it hard to sleep; the sloshing of the water against the side of the trawler was like a cold, deliberate and regular slap; I was glad when dawn came and we began to search for banana prawns. Ernie took binoculars and scoured the sea for evidence of colour change. At the first hint, Steve lowered the try-net, a smooth operation done at the flick of a switch and taking all of five minutes. When the nets rose, they contained three prawns and a load of catfish. Steve cut one open to see what it had been eating – not prawns – and contacted Ralph on the radio. Ralph thought he'd found a patch but, since he didn't have a speedy, electrically operated try-net, Steve offered to shoot over and do a try. One hour and three tries later, we had found nothing; Steve decided to cut his losses and head away on his own, forget banana prawns, even though they are the choice catch, and settle for the night-time fishing of tigers and kings.

'It wouldn't have been much fun if we had found a big one. The big boys would soon have been over, using their booms to elbow us out of the way. They'd do anything to get a piece of the action, and their booms go right over this wheelhouse. They are spoiling things for us. They've got computers on board that do all the thinking and work out where the fish are likely to be.'

At the mention of a return to night-time fishing, Marie and Ernie were back in their bunks and fast asleep. Steve stayed on watch and, as the trawler slid steadily through the sea, told me his story. He'd worked with the Australian Broadcasting Corporation as an outside broadcast engineer between the ages of nineteen and twenty-three, but when the cuts came in 1975, at the end of the Whitlam era, he was confined inside and quit. During those years he saw himself as a settled sort of a guy with a steady job and a steady girl-friend. 'She was still at school and the daughter of a wealthy builder who thought I was too rough for her, so when she left school, he sent her off around the world. I suppose I could have gone after her, but I became friends with her dad instead and helped him build a boat. I'd always loved the sea and had taken part in two Sydney to Hobart races, and when I quit the ABC I drifted up the east coast and got a job fishing. They were crazy times, real good. We worked three or four days a week and I made $A24,000 and never looked back. I bought and fitted out a camper van and drove right up the coast to Groote Island, to the manganese mines, and got work fixing radios and closed-circuit televisions. That lasted three months. It wasn't for me, so I came to the Gulf and started work on the trawlers.

'I met George a year ago. He was skippering this boat himself then, and one day when the boat I was on hit a big one, we called him in. We got $A66,000 in eleven days. Not bad money, eh? When George found out that I was quite a good fisherman and that I could do all my own maintenance and didn't need an engineer, he asked me to take over his boat. He wanted to return to big-game fishing which he knew and loved best. One day I'll have my own boat, but this is OK, isn't it? I get seventeen per cent of the sale of the catch, Ernie gets nine and Marie gets five, and I reckon to make $A58,000 in an eight-month season. This season, my aim is to pay off my house in Cairns, and I already own one in Hobart.'

Steve is in his early thirties, a first-generation Australian; his parents came from Poland, where they were pig farmers. They now have a poultry and fruit farm. He isn't married. He claims to have fathered a child when he was nineteen. 'The girl had an IQ of 140 and was too bright for her own good. When she told me she was pregnant I said, "Aaah well, I'd better talk to your dad," so the old man and I went down the pub together and got legless and he told me not to marry her because she was nuts. And eventually she did spend some time in a mental home. She had the baby and gave it away. It was a boy and one day I'll find him. If he's in a good home and happy, I'll say nothing, but if he's a bit on his own, roaming like, I'll take him down the pub and talk to him.' Steve also claims to have another child in the Philippines. 'I went there for a spell and got the pox; when I went for treatment, the nurse said she was going to give me a jab. 'No way,' I said. I wanted to rage, have fun, and not go around holding myself, so she gave me pills that had been developed for soldiers – and within twenty-four hours it had gone! I raged with the nurse then. My daughter is two now and I send $A1,000 every now and then, but her mum earns good money.'

I left Steve to his book which was coverless and squashed open. It read: '... The trawler plunged into the angry swell of the dark furious sea ... everywhere there were sounds of inanimate pain; wood straining against wood, ropes twisting, stretched to breaking point.'

I went and sat in the sun, not an easy thing to do as trawlers do not provide either flat surfaces or comfy chairs for off-duty hours. None the less it was a glorious day and I propped myself in a corner and gazed out to sea, wondering how on earth anyone had ever thought the world was flat, the horizon was so clearly shaped.

'You meditating?'

'No, day-dreaming.'

'Marie's up and at it again. She can't stop, you know. I reckon she's on speed. Right now it's the windows, and she's roped me in to do the bits she can't reach.'

Ernie is delightful. I found out little about him – only because he joked with the answers to my questions – but, from what I could gather, he was once a lightweight boxer; he was once a horse rustler, rounding up wild things all over New Zealand; and his only ambition is to own a marijuana farm and smoke his way through it.

Marie is not on speed. She's tried it and hates it; she cleans all the time just to keep busy. She's twenty, muddled and moody, and quite clearly unhappy. I found her in the galley with a Mr Sheen and a duster in one hand and the other flicking over the pages of cookery

333

books. I offered to cook the evening meal and she brightened immediately and delved into the deep-freeze for the ingredients.

Marie is a surfie. She left school at sixteen and did any number of odd jobs to support her passion for the surfboard. She'd been on the prawn boats for five months and already this was her third. 'I've only been here two weeks. I took over when Steve quarrelled with his girlfriend and she left. They seem nice, don't they? They were nice to me in Karumba. They kept going around saying to other men, "Keep your hands off our cook".' Her first two boats had been anything but nice. 'I left the first because they didn't seem to like my quietness. I like to rage from time to time – but I like to be quiet, and that didn't make me popular; they said I didn't fit in. The second boat was OK to start with, and then I got friendly with one of the deckies and he made a pass at me which I refused and he turned nasty. I'm not going to sleep my passage on any boat. I like working hard and I'm here for the five per cent and that's all. I want the money for a car and a block of land and then I want to travel ... I'll be an air-hostess or something. Hope I can stick the season.

'My mother hates me being on the boats. My father left her with three kids when I was only a few months old. I don't know him at all, but I think he is Hungarian and I'd like to find him one day. Mum married again, but she's divorced again now and the man I call 'Daddy' has since remarried a much younger woman. They are real nice to me. I ring them all the time.'

The nets went down at six thirty. We ate at seven thirty, Steve taking his beef (cooked in cider with oranges) up to the wheelhouse. 'I hope you don't think I'm snobbish, but I need to keep an eye on things.' At eight thirty came the first haul. Steve played the skipper and stayed at the wheel; Ernie and Marie in rubber boots – and Marie with rubber gloves – positioned themselves either side of the large sorting tray which almost covered the back end of the trawler. At the flick of a switch the nets, laden, rose into the air and hovered in position above the tray. At the flick of another switch the nets opened and released a mountain of fish, one to the left side and one to the right of the tray. As well as tiger prawns, which clearly earned their name through brownish red stripes, and kings, which were yellowish and large, there were shells and crabs and sea snakes and bloaters and bits of coral and a large squirming octopus and various other sea creatures with threatening spikes on their backs.

While I gawped at this sight, Ernie and Marie, using wooden bats, deftly swept the intruders back into the sea along chutes linking the trays to the side of the trawler. Some were dead: fish for other fish to feed upon. Once they had been removed, the kings and the tigers were separated and sorted according to size and placed in buckets. Those already damaged were hurled into yet another bucket, one day, somewhere, to be served up as prawn cutlets. Meanwhile each bucketload was dipped in a solution to kill bacteria and to prevent blackening and then plonked into polythene-lined cardboard boxes, marked carefully, stapled down and finally pitched below deck to be quickly frozen. That first catch, weighing a mere sixty pounds (twenty-seven kilograms), had been dispatched within half an hour of the nets being raised. The deck was then washed down, cups of tea were drunk speedily, then Marie and Ernie returned to their bunks, completely attuned to snatching their night-time sleep.

The whole process was repeated at midnight, at three a.m. and five a.m., the only difference being that on these occasions I donned boots and gloves and cautiously attempted to help the sorters. There was a warm breeze; spotlights lit our inky darkness and, in the far distance, lights from other ships twinkled, destroying the feeling that we alone were at work. The hi-fi blasted us with rock music – and at one point a group unknown to me rent the air with the inappropriate suggestion that 'Nights Were Made For Loving'. I laughed.

'Enjoying yourself?' said Marie.

'Are you?'

'No.'

At six a.m. I celebrated the end of my first night as a deckie, stinking of fish, watching the sun rise and taking photographs of hundreds of birds that flew in our wake in search of their breakfast. We'd stayed too long. The middle catches of the night had been so good, over 100 pounds (45 kilograms), that Steve had decided to go for a fourth. It was a bad decision; the catch was only forty pounds (eighteen kilograms), and now we were well behind schedule for our rendezvous with the mother-ship to take on fuel. We belted through the sea at our top speed of eight knots, but didn't make it; the ship had moved on. It had tried to raise us on the radio but we hadn't heard. 'Fucking inefficient,' muttered Steve without feeling. It had been his decision to drop the nets again, and now we had wasted both time and fuel for nothing. Another rendezvous would have to be made. A huge breakfast was eaten, mainly eggs which Steve swallowed like oysters, in one gulp. And then on a clear and sparkling morning the night workers slept.

The pattern was set: a silent ship until mid-afternoon and then chores, nets to be relieved of trapped, rotting fish, holes to be mended, the boat to be cleaned, until suppertime (and sometimes the most delicious garlic prawns), followed by an endless night, dozing between regular assaults on the produce of the sea. I found it impossible to adjust to this new routine and, after a couple of nights, I honoured the first catch and then fell asleep so soundly that nothing could wake me.

'Don't know how you did it,' said Steve. 'It was a noisy night. We let the chains go too far on the starboard side and the net sank too low, dredging up so much mud that the boat keeled. Should have thrown you out of bed!'

'It blew too,' added Ernie. 'Got quite cold. I did think of throwing a blanket over you, but I thought you'd snot me one if I woke you.'

Marie said nothing. She was glum and fussed about her figure and her face – and in particular her hands. She was so glum I half thought she'd quit at Mornington Island when we paused to refuel; but she didn't. The party must have cheered her. For, naturally enough, other boats were assembling for either fuel or supplies, so of course we'd shared a beer.

Maverick was the first to invite himself on board: an ugly little man with a woolly hat and the tiniest and tattiest of knickers. It's all fishermen wear. The conversation deteriorated immediately. 'Fucking beauty of a night, mate, must have made hundreds,' he said and they all joined in, comparing catches and prawns and money – and, eventually and inevitably, women. There was Pam in Darwin, eighteen and newly discovered, and then poor Isabella: 'Christ, our fucking cook, mate; she always seems to be having chicks' problems.' He left.

Others arrived. Beer turned to rum. The conversation stayed much the same. Marie and Vanessa consoled each other. They agreed the job would age them, that the hours and the sun and the salt water would wreck their skins – but they reckoned it was worth it for the money. I heard Ernie say that he had four children by four different women: 'It's not me they want, mate, it's babies.' The nets went down late that night.

I left the *Deliza* at Mornington Island. Steve and Ernie rowed me ashore in their dinghy. Together we scrambled up the beach and walked to the airstrip which we had located pretty accurately from the sea. We'd checked on the radio that a plane was due. It was the same plane on which I'd first arrived in Karumba.

'Sorry you're leaving,' said Ernie. 'But then I am sick of waiting on you!' I never did master the knack of swinging buckets of water over the side.

At Karumba a message awaited me. The headmaster of the local school wanted me to talk to his senior classes. 'Oh, you must do it,' said Jim, whose daughter, Jeanette, would be one of the group. 'We get so few visitors and the kids would love it.' Wally, the headmaster, took over: 'They are great kids. Our only real problem is the itinerants. This time last year we had forty new enrolments just for a couple of months. Not so many this year. It's a sign of the economic times. People can't afford to up-sticks and travel in the hope of picking up casual work. The senior classes are eleven- and twelve-year-olds; after that they go away to school, but we've got a handful of fourteens studying by correspondence. It's not a bad system; we've all had plenty of experience of teaching like that.' The headmaster was right; the kids were great.

After a sluggish start with dreary questions concerning what I thought of the Princess of Wales and whether I'd ever met the Queen, a girl popped up from the back row and said: 'Do you find us uncouth?'

I was so taken aback by the question that I played for time by asking why she had asked.

'My mother says that the English have such nice manners and the Australians are uncouth.'

I suggested that her mother had never been on an English building site, or in a pub at closing time or been part of a football crowd. On the other hand, I was prepared to admit that the English seemed obsessed with good manners. In every survey where people are asked to list the qualities they admire most, 'good manners' always sneaks to the top. Ugly things are hidden behind a veneer of good manners and, for my part, I added, I'd prefer an 'uncouth' person who was honest and kind to a well-mannered, callous crook. Fortunately, that was the only difficult question, and for the next hour and a half I was soundly quizzed on where I had been, what it was like, how I'd got there and why I had chosen to go there. Their interest in their own country was real enough; their knowledge, however, was pretty thin, and this served to underscore what I had already observed on my journey – that Australians know too little about their own country.

In part it's the fault of a British system of education which they imported and which served them well for some time and to which they have clung with insufficient adaptation for just too long. Schoolchildren can recite the Kings of England and the dates of all those Wars of the Roses and such like; but they have a skimpy awareness of their own history beyond exciting tales of early explorers – and even then each State tends to concentrate on its own adventurers and gloss over the exploration of others. As a result of this bias I had many surprises. Children within a boat-ride of the Great Barrier Reef knew that it was 'special', but did not know what it was or why it ought to be cherished. In Tasmania, two expensively educated girls who claimed to have passed out near the top of the State's Higher School Certificate could not tell me which Australian author they most admired. And in South Australia, 3,000 children aged between eleven and fifteen were asked in a survey to name famous Australians. About half managed to list a sportsman, but after that the guesses included Elvis Presley, Bjorn Borg, Benny Hill,

Prince Charles and Abba. These are extreme examples of course, and the situation has improved in the last decade or so; Australian content has been added – and has not always met with approval from parents. I read an article in the *Australian* in which a father with two children just out of primary school declared:

My two children have been bored witless by an interminable recital of the sparse facts of Aboriginal life and culture. There has been such a succession of repetitive projects on how Aborigines live in the bush and of Aboriginal art that they never want to look at another bark painting nor watch another school-touring troupe of Aboriginal dancers ... When I went to school in Britain we were swept away into the magic of the *Odyssey* at eleven, and we had been familiar with Alfred and Guthrum and the epic struggle of Saxon and Dane since the age of seven.

Despite such reactionary sentiments, many of the best academic minds are determined to expand and improve Australian studies, in both schools and centres of advanced education. Since each State looks after its own educational affairs, there is no clear nationwide picture of what is taught and what is omitted, merely a general agreement that the amount is minimal and the quality often poor. The Committee in charge of Bicentennial Celebration for 1988 has agreed to fund a project assessing the current situation and offering pathways to improvement.

This legacy of an imported British system is sad enough, but there is another: Australia also inherited from the Mother Country a poor attitude to advanced education. Only thirty-two per cent of young people stay at school until they are seventeen to gain the Higher National Certificate, and of that number a mere seven per cent bother with tertiary qualifications of any kind. This is a significant improvement on the past: in the 1950s, only eight per cent of seventeen-year-olds were still at school, and only three and a half per cent bothered with tertiary qualifications; but even so, Australia remains an under-educated country, way down the international league table. In the United States the average number of years spent in full-time education (between the ages of three and twenty-four) is 16.7; in Japan it is 14; in the United Kingdom it is 13.2; and in

Australia it is 12.6. It is to Japan that the Australians dedicated to improving this situation turn most readily: in 1950, Japan had a mere one per cent of her labour force with tertiary qualifications; now she has thirty-nine per cent.

However, just as there is no complacency over the lamentable state of Australian studies, so there is no complacency about the general state of education. Everywhere I went I discovered committees and commissions examining ways to improve the overall standards of literacy and numeracy; seeking ways of keeping young people in school for the love of being there, rather than as an alternative to life on the dole; and eagerly propounding enticing changes for colleges of education as well as universities. Their shared objective is to change attitudes; in Australia there is hardly any community disapproval for those who leave school early, whereas in the United States, it is constantly argued, such people are called 'drop-outs'. All this is a central part of the Labor Government's policy; for not only is it realized that tomorrow's successful nations will depend on brain-based industries, it is also universally accepted that formal education is the greatest leveller – and to date there has been a disappointingly slight swing towards the lower socio-economic groups among those entering higher education. There is much wastage among students from working-class, immigrant and country families.

Karumba is, of course, one big country family. Wally said: 'My kids are not book kids. They will be through by the time they are fifteen.'

I left the Gulf of Carpentaria by refrigerated road train. Jim had arranged this while I was at sea. I was to join a convoy of three, travelling to Townsville with $A500,000 worth of prawns. Jim had selected Darryl because his truck was beautiful – it had every luxury: it was his home – and because Darryl was imperturbable. He smiled at everything, including the news that his gear-box was broken and a new one was going to cost $A7,000. Darryl's smile was indeed huge and radiant, giving employment to every muscle in his face. He appeared from the shower, tall and blond and most attractive in well-cut jeans, boots, checked shirt and huge hat. 'My truck's overheating, so I want a mechanic to come with me for the first part; you can go with Ian.'

I looked at Ian. He looked as though nothing would make him smile and his truck, thirteen years old and bought six months before for $A11,000 had few comforts. It was a boneshaker. Ian had an air cushion to protect his spine; my seat was straight plastic, torn, with foam peeping through. The air-conditioning had broken and the radio was struggling. 'I can only get that ABC programme which puts out Mozart and that organ stuff and I can't stand it. I'd like to listen to Country and Western from dawn to dusk, but I can't afford a tape deck.'

Ian is thirty-two; he looked forty-five and said he felt sixty. He was fourteen when his dad asked him if he wanted to leave school or go on. His dad said he'd pay if he wanted to continue, but he didn't. He was the last of nine children; seven are left, two having died, one drowned and another, an alcoholic, committed suicide. They all live close to their original home near Brisbane. Ian lives with his mum when he is at home, which is only a handful of nights a month; the rest of the time he lives in this old truck, sleeping in the dog box measuring seven feet by three (two metres by one). 'We all thought Mum would go first because Dad was so fit, and then he got cancer and was gone in six months. Mum's seventy-seven now and has arthritis; but the others all help to look after her and I ring home each week, and if I forget, she's on the phone to the boss asking where I am. Sometimes I walk into the house without warning her, and her eyes light up like a child's.

'I fell into trucks, I suppose. Loved them as a boy and was always getting rides on them. I often give it up now and for the first few months it's like a holiday, and then one day I'll be walking down the street and I'll see this truck going along and I'll think, "Shit, I wanna be behind the wheel." It gets to you. I couldn't work under a roof. I just like being on my own. You could shove me right out in the middle of the bush and, as long as I had plenty of tucker and enough stubbies, I'd be right.'

The convoy of three had left together but, within half an hour, Peter was out of sight. 'He always does this for excitement and thrills.

We decide on a rendezvous and he drives there as fast as he can and sleeps until we catch up. The boss wouldn't be too pleased to know the speed he went on these roads.'

They *were* bad. Ian was forever weaving to avoid pot-holes. He didn't always succeed, and I rose out of my seat as though it were a saddle. He'd left Karumba at four p.m. and intended to drive for twenty-one hours, stopping only for an evening meal and for breakfast. It's illegal, of course, but who's to know? Ian admitted taking pills to keep himself awake. He showed me the bottle; the label was tatty but I think it said Effidrine.

'There's one chemist in Brisbane that sells them under the counter. The trouble is, the more you take the more you need to take . . . and after a while your mouth feels bad. I wear false teeth and I usually keep them in a hanky in there . . .' he said pointing to the box from which the pills had come. 'I have to take them out, otherwise it feels like sandpaper between my plate and the roof of my mouth.'

We stopped at Burke and Wills for a meal. It's nothing but a roadhouse: a square corrugated-tin construction, open-sided and attached to a house. On one wall there is a picture of Burke and Wills and a dead camel with its tongue hanging out and long, pretty eyelashes. Above the food counter another picture portrayed a horse throwing a man. 'They'll be expecting us tonight, so I guess they will have saved us something.' Fish and chips and cauliflower; rock melon and two scoops of ice-cream.

Conversation hardly flourished and towards the end of the meal I heard Ian whisper to Darryl: 'Aren't you going to give her a ride?'

Darryl didn't answer, and I thought this a good moment to go in search of a lavatory while they argued about what to do with their extra passenger. But when I returned, Ian was still whispering, ever more urgently: 'Aren't you going to give her a ride?'

Darryl turned to me and said: 'You can come with me for a bit.'

I walked back to the trucks with the mechanic called Peter, asking him if he had fixed the over-heating problem.

He looked blank. 'What over-heating problem?'

'I thought you were a mechanic helping Darryl with a problem.'

'No, I know nothing about trucks. I'm Darryl's brother-in-law. I'm a cane harvester. I came along for the ride.'

The luxury truck was more comfortable, but I missed Ian's friendliness. Darryl had no intention of talking and snapped on the radio: Rachmaninov, Elgar, and Placido Domingo singing '*Questa o quella*' from *Rigoletto*. At the first yawn, Darryl suggested I hop in the back and get some sleep. Relieved to be out of the way and hopefully forgotten, I stretched beneath a blanket and began counting the potholes and cattle grids. Some time after midnight the truckies stopped to check tyres and drink coffee from a thermos, but I stayed hidden until Hughenden. It was dawn and breakfast was an hour away at a roadhouse in Prairie, after which I returned to Ian.

'Ah, you're back. That mechanic spoke only three words all night.'

'What mechanic?' I said. 'That's Darryl's brother-in-law.'

He looked as though I'd shot him. 'Christ, no! Oh, I hope he didn't make too much of that shit I gave him about Darryl's girl-friends. Yeh, I spent half the night going on and on about Darryl's women!' Ian was in fine form. 'I took two of those pills at midnight and that's why I didn't fancy any breakfast; they kill the appetite.' He bounced along, killing the miles with tales of the days when he had the energy to drive to Perth and back, and if I ever fell silent for too long he would pound the gap between us: 'Just testing to see if you are awake.'

We left Darryl, the man with the empty smile, on the outskirts of Townsville; road trains are not allowed to trundle through the town. Our truck had no such restrictions, and we drove on to the depôt. Ian was silent now and he looked grey as he slumped in a chair, too tired to head for the shower for which he longed, too tired to smile.

CHAPTER 17

A Slow Train to Johburg

Captain Cook came to grief on the Great Barrier Reef; he had to beach his boat *Endeavour* to repair the damage. Long before Cook, Portuguese explorers had happened upon the coral heaps and named these hazardous waters Coste Dangereux. Soon after Cook, Matthew Flinders, charged with making a complete survey of the Australian coastline, warned that only those with strong nerves should approach this particular stretch. For years, then, this complex structure of thousands of coral reefs, sometimes near the shore, sometimes miles out to sea, sometimes scattered and sometimes huddled together, and spreading from Papua New Guinea to just south of the Tropic of Capricorn, was considered nothing more than a navigational hazard through which trading ships needed master mariners to guide them. Anthony Trollope and Mark Twain passed this biological wonder without a word. Perhaps it was just as well. Ignored, the Reef could continue, unhampered, its slow, slow growth of thousands of years. For, once this mysterious underwater garden caught man's eye, it became a punch-bag to be thumped until it oozed money.

It began in the early 1960s, with the development of snorkelling and scuba diving and underwater photography. Some were happy to look with awe and take photographs to show the world or to help scientists unlock the secrets of the sea. Others were not. Someone, realizing that coral is composed of almost pure lime which needs little treatment beyond crushing and knowing that the sugar-cane industry urgently needed cheap lime, decided to dredge and blast and mine the southern end of the reef. The coral is dead, they said defiantly. The coral was dead because it had been infested by crown-of-thorns starfish. This mishap was first noticed in 1962, and today scientists are still arguing over the cause; some say it is part of a natural cycle; others that the starfish's natural predators have been removed – fish for human consumption, and shells for human collections. Yet a third group deduced that since the infested reefs are among the more accessible, human pollution is the cause. Whatever the reason, a laudable group of conservationists succeeded in blocking the mining proposal and the dead coral was allowed to rejuvenate in peace.

No sooner had that battle been won than the conservationists realized in 1969 that the Queensland Government had given title to the reef to various oil prospectors. The thought of oil rigs alongside idyllic tropical islands and coral cays, and pipelines crashing through a unique eco-system destroying organisms that are to be found nowhere else, is as surrealistic as a uranium mine in a national park or a cruise missile on a village green. Wags had a field day: it was suggested that the crown-of-thorns starfish be trained to gobble up the inevitable oil leaks and that the entire reef should be dredged up and replaced by a plastic replica – made, of course, from the newly drilled petroleum. A Royal Commission took the matter in hand; and this was followed by a legal battle that had State and Federal Governments at loggerheads. Then, nicely timed, the *Torrey Canyon* tipped oil all over the Cornish coast of England, and at Santa Barbara in California there were leakages from several more tankers. Pictures of oil-soaked birds, dead fish and blackened beaches did as much as anything to help the conservationist cause and keep greedy hands off the Great Barrier Reef.

All this publicity attracted visitors in increasing numbers, and in 1975 the Federal Government declared the area a marine park and set up an authority to manage it and to zone it for specific use, keeping a balance between preservation and recreation. It took ten years for the Great Barrier Reef Marine Park Authority in Townsville to bring the entire 1,200-mile (1,900-kilometre) stretch under protective legislation, earning it a brickbat for slowness and charges from conservationists that it is on the side of controlled exploitation. That would be about right. The Authority is in favour of tourism in

345

designated pockets and dedicated to educating the public, to ensure that damage is kept to a minimum while at the same time enticing those at home and abroad to view the Eighth Wonder of the World.

I must confess that the joys of the Reef eluded me for a while. I walked upon the coral at low tide some distance off Hayman Island, a middle-priced holiday resort, and found it an interesting experience. I visited Green Island, a down-market day tripper of a coral cay which boasts 1,000 visitors a day, being a mere seventeen miles (twenty-seven kilometres) – a dash by hydrofoil – from Cairns. The crown-of-thorns starfish banqueted here in the early 1960s and again in the late 1970s, and I saw the devastation through a glass-bottomed boat and wandered through an underwater observatory to look at the fish. Again it was interesting but not magical – and my reactions in no way squared with the awesome accounts of those who donned diving gear and disappeared beneath the sea. I resigned myself to the fact that poor swimmers and those who fear the water once they can no longer stand up in it are going to find the mysteries of the reef forever elusive.

And then I was invited to visit Lizard Island. It is the northernmost of the Great Barrier Reef tourist resorts, the smallest, having only fifteen rooms, and the most expensive, costing around $A120 a day. Brochures advise guests to leave their 'Dior ball-gowns' at home, but none the less the place has an understated elegance. For three months of the year it is monopolized by men fishing for marlin; but for the rest, it is open to anyone who can afford it. The island is also shared with a research station, operating under the auspices of the Australian Museum and offering facilities for field work to fourteen tropical marine scientists from around the world. From Barry Goldman, who heads the resident team, I detected a cool cooperation between pure scientists, applied scientists and tourists. The presence of applied scientists, mainly Japanese combing the reef for leads to new drugs, has meant the station has acquired a decent boat capable of tackling the outer reef in all weathers; the presence of tourists, whose carelessness often causes Barry to fret, at least means that the conservationist cause is better understood and that any future threats to the reef will be met with opposition from a growing number of people who, having seen the reef, know that it is something more than a few rocky mountains under the sea.

Over at the Lodge they tolerate the scientists; the station provides guests with an interesting alternative to an afternoon on the beach, and Peter and Michelle sometimes invite the resident researchers to dinner. 'But it's a bit like inviting the plumber; we have little in common. They are conservationists and our guests come here to *kill* fish .. ' (with, of course, the help of George York in whose trawler I'd prawned the Gulf). And it was here that I met Gary Low who, I'd venture to suggest, is the best diving instructor in the world. On my second morning I sat down next to him at breakfast, visitors being encouraged to mingle like house guests rather than cling to separate tables.

'How are you going to spend the day?' he asked between mouthfuls of steak and eggs.

I explained that my options were fairly limited as I had a fear of deep water.

'I'll put that right,' he said and, when I didn't respond, added: 'Well, I can try. What have you got to lose?'

What, indeed? By lunchtime I was snorkelling way out of my depth, confident that Gary was never beyond reach and so enthralled by what I saw that for a few minutes at a time I could forget my fears. The next day, childlike with excitement, I had my first scuba diving lesson and discovered Wonderland: scores of different kinds of hard coral with aptly descriptive names – staghorn, brain, needle, plate, mushroom; delicately coloured soft coral gently swaying in the current; sponges and a wealth of marine plants; crabs and clams, sea slugs and glorious sea anemones; and fish, dazzling fish of deep blue and bright yellow, seemingly oblivious of my presence. It was magic. I was no longer the sceptical listener to the awe-struck accounts of others; instead, the superlatives tumbled out and I was in danger of becoming a Reef bore.

I hated leaving, but I couldn't linger. I had an appointment with the slow train to Brisbane. The train is so slow that they say its signature tune is 'I'll walk beside you'; it is so slow that it took seven hours to cover the distance from Cairns to Townsville; the reverse journey which I had done by coach had taken a mere five hours and had included stops, and it would take thirty-six hours to complete the 1,000-mile (1,600-kilometre) journey. It was built at a time when the State had so little money that it chose the narrowest gauge: 3 feet 6 inches. For all that, it is a popular train and fully booked. Since it departed at six forty-five a.m., my first inclination, having found my seat, was to take my copy of the *Cairns Post* and find a cup of coffee. Within minutes a bright, bubbly, fast-talking Canadian girl had sat down opposite me. She had been in Australia for three years studying for a Ph.D. in plant pathology at Sydney University, and that had been time enough for her to assess the country. Her main conclusions were that she had had to tone down her natural energy to cope with, rather than be irritated by, the Australian approach to life and that she had found Australian relationships superficial. 'This applies to both sexes. I've found it difficult to get close to people. They are happy to tell you their life story at first meeting, but it doesn't develop from there.'

Her observation is not incorrect. Australians are inclined to make quick and superficial friendships; it is a gift I rather admire and from which I benefited much, but then I do not relish soul-searching sessions and claustrophobic entanglements nor chase after such concepts as 'closeness', which is used, all too often, as a euphemism for dependence. The Canadian, on the other hand, clearly showed her exposure to the North American obsession with analysing and quantifying what makes a good relationship and inevitably resorting to an overemphasis on verbal communication. Her difficulties may also have something to do with the fact that Canadians are not much admired in Australia. The image that Canada presents to the world is that of a dull country, under-occupied, devoid of a clear identity and utterly swamped by another culture. It's an image Australians find too close for comfort.

Our conversation was sufficiently engrossing for me not to notice that we had an attentive audience, but no sooner had the Canadian vacated her seat to find a shower than it was occupied by a young man who asked if he might borrow my *Cairns Post*. He returned it rapidly and admitted that the request had merely been a device to start a conversation. Graham had been fascinated by what he overheard and wanted to share his views, which were somewhat different. Graham, twenty-three, a petroleum geologist newly graduated from London University, had been in Australia for two months. He'd quit England disillusioned and depressingly bitter, having been unemployed since leaving university. All his young life he'd believed that education was the passport to a trouble-free future. His father was an estate manager in Salisbury, and Graham claimed to have gone to the worst kind of comprehensive school where no one was interested in studying and where he had had to push himself. 'Only four kids from that school had gone to university, and when I went home and told my mum that was what I wanted to do she said, "University is not for the likes of us." I shall never forget that remark, but I went and had to work bloody hard to get through, only to discover that job opportunities in England are few. It's not just me; only a handful of my friends have got jobs and the rest were spending their time writing letters that were never answered.'

He'd come to Australia on a holiday visa, hoping to find work, and meanwhile he was delighted by what he saw – particularly of girls. 'They are not necessarily stunning lookers and often they don't take sufficient care of themselves – they have hair on their legs – but they are very forward. They do not wait to be approached by men, as they do at home; if they like the look of you, they come up and tell you so. They'll just pick you up at parties or walk up in a pub and suggest you buy them a drink. It's great.'

Now this is not a young man boasting. I had seen this happen at a party in Sydney and I had seen it referred to in newspapers – an art school boss had been asked to explain why he was living with one of his students and had replied: 'She walked up to me and said "I fancy you, can I move in?"' – and at a rather more interesting level I had noticed that it was a fairly constant phenomenon in Australian novels; whether written by men or by women, the woman is often portrayed as the initiator. The fact that Australian girls make the running has also been remarked upon by social commentators, together with the aside that, to Europeans, the girls often seem quite shameless in their pursuit of men. The explanation offered was that the girls have to do this to counter the indifference of men.

This does not mean that men never proposition women, as I was about to learn from another train encounter. We met at breakfast when I was not in the best of spirits. I'd learned at eleven p.m. the night before that economy travel on this slow train offered sleepers but no sheets, blankets or pillows. A sleeper is merely a plastic-covered triple bunk. My night-time companions, a middle-aged woman and her mother, took pity on me; they knew the rules and had tracksuits to sleep in, plus a pillow and a blanket in their luggage – I'd stored my luggage. They offered me a thick sweater and then placed newspaper upon my bunk and, once I was in position, tucked more newspaper around me. It gets cold at night in May, and by morning my limbs ached. A hot shower did much to alleviate that and I hoped that breakfast would do the rest. A waitress ushered me to an empty space at a table already occupied by three people: two elderly women and a well-built, fit-looking bronzed male in his mid-thirties. No one spoke and after a while, to break the silence, I asked if anyone knew where we were.

'Gladstone, we are just about to come into Gladstone,' said the man we'll call Bob. 'Used to be a beaut fishing port, now it is an awful place, just a huge sprawling port. Bauxite is brought down from the North to be turned into alumina, so there's a large smelter; and then millions of tons of coal from inland fields come through here on their way to Japan. It must be one of the country's biggest ports, but there is no quality of life. Everything in Australia is so short-sighted. No one thinks of the future: immediate bucks is everyone's goal. Look at that drought a few months back – all those farmers overstocking on sheep and turning the place into a dust bowl. And it's *my* country, the bastards.'

He revealed that he used to own an electrical company in Townsville which serviced stations in the area, but all that was over. 'I was going to a job one day on my motorbike – now that was a bad management decision, I should not have been on a motorbike – when some bitch in a car, taking her kids to school, ran me over. I've had two years on disability pay and I'm fighting the case in the courts.

When I get the compensation I'm going to start a centre putting some stuffing into kids, teaching them the things I was taught in the Army. I reckon the Army spent a quarter of a million training me and I didn't even get to Vietnam. Don't know why. I reckon they were training us for some special mission that never happened. But my centre is in the future; for the moment I'm living rent-free on my father's property with my wife and kids.'

I mentioned that I'd noticed him the day before, playing with a couple of children in the bar car. Everyone had noticed: he was telling two small creatures that no laughing was allowed, then tickling them until they became hysterical. Perhaps they were his kids?

'No. No, they're not mine. They belong to a woman who fancied me. Her husband has just left her with three kids. I only met her yesterday. See, I know I'm attractive to women and I like it when they make their position clear. I'm not interested in all that messing around; waste of time, all those games. And I make my intentions pretty clear, too. But I'm not crude. I don't go around saying, "Fancy a poke," like a lot of my mates do. I was in Sydney once, on the ferry, and this bloke spotted a very young girl in black stockings and he just said in a loud voice, "Wanna fuck?" and she just turned round and said, "Yes." My friend Euan has got the best approach. He'll walk up to a girl in a bar and say: "My name is Euan and my game is screwing and how am I doing?" If the girl says, "Piss off," then that's just what he does, and if not then he's away.'

I steered the conversation back to his plans for a centre to toughen up kids; and he told me about the joys of camping in the bush and teaching kids about survival. Then suddenly he said: 'It's getting hot in here. I'm going to find a shower. Will you join me?'

Of course, I pretended not to hear and went on talking about his boy-scoutish enthusiasms; then, after about another ten minutes, he said, 'I do need that shower. Now are you coming with me? Just say yes or no, but don't try and ignore me.'

'No,' I said.

He gathered himself up to his full six foot three inches and left, leaving me to reflect on his stylish proposition and the aplomb which enabled him to seem indifferent to rejection and incapable of embarrassment.

'Sex in Australia,' said John Pringle, author of *Australian Accent*, 'is healthy, frank, open and often somewhat animal; there is rarely any sense of reserve or sophistication.' I won't argue with that, nor with the fact that the flummery of love, the courting or wooing, is of little concern to a lot of men – Germaine Greer has been telling us as much for years. Several other highly intelligent women also tried to convince me that the Australian male is fundamentally a misogynist. Why else, they argue, are there so many homosexuals gathered in Sydney?

The Australian male is a victim of history, a dire history that could not be eliminated in one generation. The first bunch of convicts to land at Botany Bay were boorish men who became even coarser through the hardship of those early years, a hardship that could only be alleviated by rum; there were no women around to act as a civilizing influence. There were no women for rather a long time. It is accepted that sodomy was widespread in the penal settlements and no doubt continued when men got their freedom and took off for the bush. It was either that or borrowing Aboriginal women in exchange for tobacco and bread, and treating them with brutal contempt. Neither alternative engenders fine feelings towards women, nor serves as a suitable apprenticeship for those who sought to 'settle down' one day.

By about 1840, attempts were made to correct this imbalance by shipping out the contents of Britain's poor-houses and orphanages; but even so, there were never enough women to go round, and it was not until 1900 that the numbers began to balance; in that year there were 110 males for every 100 females; 1916 was the first year in which females were as numerous as males – and then only because many men were away fighting in Europe. A century without women is bound to have had an effect on men: at best, it leaves them shy and awkward; at worst, it leaves them actively hostile to women and preferring the company of men; and in the middle, it creates a vast band of indifference. If your ancestors are sodomists and gin-jockeys, then I can see it may take several generations before you get around to seeing any value in sending Valentine's Day cards. And this indifference has taken its toll on women; treated like doormats, prized only for child-bearing, they grew to lack charm and femininity. John Pringle decided that this legacy left the Australian woman with a characteristic expression that is hard, suspicious and contemptuous.

But much is changing. Men are questioning and there is some intelligent debate; there are also some unedifying spectacles of middle-aged men discovering their inadequacies and rushing around trying to 'get in touch with their feelings'. That perhaps is an inevitable step. Women are no longer rushing off to Europe in search of their romantic ideal, nor indeed are they staying at home to be doormats. There is no need. They are at last a majority: the 1981 Census revealed that there were 119,000 more women than men in Australia, a fact of political significance that has not gone unnoted by the present Labor Government. Legislation outlawing discrimination on the ground of sex was rapidly implemented; since March 1983, 100 women have been appointed to public bodies, and in the Federal Public Service there are now three female deputy secretaries. And there are 65 women with taxable incomes over $A100,000 compared with 2,500 men. It's a start, but there is much left to do: women figure highly among the unemployed, earn less than men when employed, and have restricted careers – either because so many of them (thirty-eight per cent) leave school at fifteen or because more than half of those with post-secondary education choose to become teachers and nurses. In other words, the plight of women in contemporary Australia is no different from that of her sisters in other industrialized countries: the law is on her side, but the facts are not. However, my hunch is that Australian women have as great a chance as any others of narrowing the gap between what is promised and what is possible – provided they do not waste too much time fretting over the 'awfulness' of the Australian male. And they do fret a lot, particularly the educated ones, and the words they use most often to castigate their educated opposites are 'devious', 'untruthful' and 'unstraightforward'. Such men exist. And – alas, alas – such women exist, too.

Not on the slow train, however; everyone was deliciously direct. Kids squabbled and swore and a young mother said, 'Where did you hear *that* word? Well, I don't want to hear it from you again until you are fifteen.' Old ladies complained about the food and the service and the boredom, although they had to agree that by car it was a cow of a journey; and old men needled each other: '*You* ought to have had the experience of killing someone ... watching the light dying in a man's eyes ... what section were you in – bloody transport, I suppose?'

Outside, Queensland rolled by, chilled by the month and made dank by the rain. There were houses on stilts twinned with water towers; there were wooden-fenced paddocks protecting well-fed cattle, lots of trees and lots of towns; more than half the State's population of 2.5 million live outside Brisbane, a large proportion compared with other States. Since leaving Cairns which has a population of 50,000 we had passed through two other towns with populations of more than 50,000 (Townsville and Rockhampton); three with more than 25,000, and a handful with more than 10,000. Queensland is, then, more decentralized than other States. It has always been so. Brisbane was settled as a penal colony in 1824, a sort of Sydney overspill. However, as soon as free settlers began arriving, they began to push northwards, in part to get away from the tainted first settlement (which was peculiarly harsh, especially under one commandant called Logan who had his own stern and pitiless ways with lazy rebellious convicts) but also because the north's tropical lushness offered much: gold at Charters Towers, sugar at Mackay, tobacco and bananas. In Queensland the north was settled a lot more successfully than elsewhere, so much so that when the colony gained independence from New South Wales in 1859, the new State argued strongly that Brisbane, stuck down in the southern tip and close to the border with New South Wales, should not be the capital. Brisbane won, but for many a long year it remained a sleepy, tropical, provincial place, with none of the force and kudos of the other State capitals. It got some attention during the Second World War when it became a garrison city and General MacArthur established his headquarters in Queen Street. Even so, it remained a provincial backwater and only seriously started coming into its own in the 1960s.

Now it is the third largest of the State capitals, eagerly pursuing an international image and grand enough by 1982 to host the Commonwealth Games. In 1985 it opened a mammoth cultural centre, on the south bank of the Brisbane River, housing two theatres, a concert hall, an art gallery and a museum, a library and restaurants, all beautifully landscaped, and proudly announcing that anything the other States could do it could do bigger.

The rapid growth of the last twenty years has not spoiled Brisbane; it still remains a pretty, sub-tropical city, with the Brisbane River looping its way between hills and under bridges. The river and the hills are the city's chief assets for they have dictated terms to developers who might otherwise have been tempted to pour concrete somewhat indiscriminately, in much the same way as they have done further south on the Gold Coast. The University of Queensland is a fine example. It was founded in 1909, but the campus has expanded dramatically in recent years to encompass sixty departments (and one of the most adventurous and widely respected publishing houses in Australia, the University of Queensland Press), and yet the site remains glorious and the visual impact supreme. The first buildings were set around cloistered courtyards, rather like Oxford and Cambridge, and the later buildings are defiantly modern, but both have had to surrender to the setting, a loop in the river, with the main buildings on a rise surrounded by playing-fields and parklands.

Geography has also dominated residential areas; the smart addresses and the expensive houses are up on the hills where the rich can catch the breeze, and the valleys on the whole contain the smaller, terraced properties. Central Brisbane, on the other hand, bows to history, rather than to hills. One glance reveals that only a few notable buildings came before 1900, including the impressive Treasury building which dates from 1888 and has been dubbed one of the finest Italianate buildings in the southern hemisphere. Most of the eye-catchers have arrived since 1960 – with one exception: City Hall. City Hall was built in the 1920s and it remains a focal point;

whenever people are stuck for a rendezvous they invariably meet on the steps of City Hall or in King George Square opposite. For the rest, Brisbane offers the stranger an easy time. Queen Street is the main street and all the female streets run parallel to it – Ann, Adelaide, Elizabeth, Charlotte, Mary, Margaret and Alice – and all the male streets, William, George, Albert, Edward, run at right angles. But the ease does not stop there; Brisbane people are warm and friendly, welcoming and direct. They'd deny it, of course. The whole of Queensland jealously guards its image of being suspicious of outsiders and cool to strangers. This was not my experience. The friendliness of rural areas had culminated with the most delightful of gestures at the end of my train journey. I had got to know a family travelling in the next compartment; we had shared a meal together on the first evening, and after that the odd chat and glass of beer. They were leaving the train at Caboolture, some forty miles (sixty-five kilo-metres) north of Brisbane; as we approached the station they called me into their compartment and said: 'We have taken you to our hearts and we hope you will think of us from time to time,' and they handed me a gift wrapped in Christmas paper. Inside was an ornamental candlestick with tiny red candles. 'Good luck,' they added – and were gone.

I expected such warmth to evaporate in Brisbane, city folk are always more reserved and hesitant; but it did not happen – indeed, there were similarly delightful gestures on the most unexpected occasions. It was winter and I'd now left the tropics; feeling cold and conspicuous in my cotton clothes, I'd braced myself to do some shopping, a chore which gives me little pleasure. Not only did I receive the most immaculate service but the assistant even offered to lend me clothes of her own while the items I had chosen were obtained in the right size from another branch. When I declined, she speeded up the process by collecting the clothes herself.

And then there was Keith. He drives a taxi; one Friday night when it was raining so hard that the blue dye left my shoes and stained my feet, I hailed him for a journey to the airport where I anticipated a meeting with a passenger changing planes. Incorrect information meant that the meeting did not take place and I was combing the crowd, looking puzzled, when Keith appeared beside me: 'You have an expression on your face which says "This shouldn't happen to me".'

'Nor should it,' I laughed and asked him to take me back into town. As we neared my temporary home, he asked if I'd mind waiting a minute and disappeared into the darkness, reappearing to place on my lap a bottle of wine. 'For you. No strings attached, but you've had a disappointing evening, haven't you?' He also refused to take the fare. 'Now, don't insist,' he said. 'Don't spoil it.'

These instances are not merely pleasant memories, they are important because they made me question the image of Queensland. If it is said that they are suspicious and unwelcoming to outsiders, it could mean that they reserve such treatment for inter-State rather than overseas visitors, or it could mean that the image is wrong: hollow words mouthed often enough to become a myth. I believe this to be so and I believe that there are other inaccurate images, the worst of which states: 'Queensland is vastly different from the rest of Australia' or 'Queensland is another country'. It is almost a State slogan and newspapers write articles trying to prove the point. The *Australian* devoted a complete page to proving such a thesis from a handful of statistics and a few inconsequential facts. The trivia included the realization that Queenslanders take more headache pills; that they have bigger feet; that the State gets struck more often by lightning; that Brisbane hosts the national Biggest Beer-Belly contest. The facts state that Queensland has the highest number of Aboriginals and refuses to give them land rights; that it spends far less on education and has far fewer formally educated citizens; that homosexuality is banned; that nude and topless bathing is banned; that poker machines are banned; that sex is censored from movies, and *Playboy* sold only under the counter.

All States could cobble such a list together – but the point is that they don't. Other States are happy to do it for Queensland so that they can sneer, and rib the place, refer to it as red-neck land, label it the Deep North. And Queensland is happy with this because it likes to be thought different. But Queensland is not different. It is Australia writ large; aggressively so; defiantly so; unpretentiously so. Australia has an Aborigine problem; Queensland has the biggest problem. Australia is under-educated; Queensland is the least educated State. Australia welcomes foreign investment; Queensland begs for it. Australia wants growth; Queensland worships it. All Australian States have known a little gerrymandering; in Queensland it is legendary. All Australian States are chauvinistic; Queensland would rather secede than be ordered about by Canberra.

Since 1968, the image of Queensland has resided in Sir Johannes Bjelke-Petersen, or Joh as he is known throughout the land. Joh is a most unusual politician. He noisily proclaims Queensland to such an extent that it is often referred to as Johburg by those who do not like his political line. For years he ruled as head of the Liberal National Party Coalition, but now his National Party is strong enough to rule without Liberal help. Joh despises unions; he hates the reputation they have given Australia through their strike record and through wage demands which make Australian goods uncompetitive in the export market and costly at home. He despises tariff protection which props up costly Australian manufactured products, particularly cars. Queensland has no car industry and would much prefer to open doors to overseas vehicles and cancel import duty. Joh would prefer to drive a Mercedes Benz than an over-priced Australian car. He also hates the holiday penalty which the unions have won for the hotel and catering trades and which adds 17.5 per cent on to bills at weekends and holidays; he reckons it maddens tourists to see such surcharges on their accounts. He does believe in low taxes, or no taxes. Overnight he abolished death duties in Queensland; there was such a stampede of people trying to buy property to establish residency that other States, and finally the Commonwealth, had to follow. He doesn't believe in Australia for the Australians. He'd do away with the Foreign Investment Review Board and let everyone in. As for foreign aid and the United Nations, he is not interested in either, and if he had his way he'd pull Australia out of both. He leans towards law and order and has both a pronounced dislike of loud-mouth minorities who like to take to the streets and march, and a profound antipathy to marijuana-smoking drop-outs. Ironically, many of them choose to make their home in the far north of the State in tropical bliss, away from the madding crowd. The police once blitzed such a community outside Cooktown, rounding up the boys and girls and razing their hovels to the ground. The outcry saw the police being charged with arson and the courts acquitting them. As for Aborigines, Joh could talk all night on the subject. He wants the blacks to live like whites and then qualify for financial aid like everyone else. He does not believe in land rights, and the notion of blacks issuing whites with passes to visit their land is abhorrent to him: apartheid by another name. And as for land rights workers, he reckons too many of them are black Commie militants and they'll get nothing from him.

Joh is in some ways an easy man to interview. He likes to talk about Queensland and he expects journalists to sit and listen. He regularly feeds them stories to keep them quiet and calls it 'feeding the chooks'. He seemed pleased to see me.

'Max Christmas,' he said as he walked towards me. Max Christmas is a prosperous Gold Coast estate agent (and no relation), but I appreciated his attempt to remember my name.

His conversation was a lengthy commercial for the State: 'I'm here to promote stability and security and an atmosphere of confidence in which there can be rapid business development. Did you know that 1,000 people a week are crossing the border and moving into Queensland? I want to focus the attention of the rest of the world on this State and let all the others fade into insignificance – that's why I'd like the next Expo and the next Olympic Games to be held in Brisbane.

'I know what this State wants. I've been around a long time and I've served it faithfully and well. I believe in personal contact and I don't take people for granted. I'm constantly on the move, meeting people and letting them know that I am a servant of the people. And most of the time I use just common sense when making decisions; I say: is it right or is it wrong?'

I asked him about Australia's future as a republic, knowing him to be an admirer of the monarchy: 'I'm not so proud as to disown my relatives. If you were my friend when I was little, then you will remain my friend now that I am grown up. But the Royal Family is about the only important link with Britain. If Britain didn't have the Royal Family, it would never be mentioned here. Britain has gone to water over defence; the United States is the only country prepared to defend us against all the Communists in the Pacific. And Britain dumped us when she joined the EEC, and so now we're not interested. We turn to Japan, America, Korea to get our bread buttered, but not to Britain. She lost a prize jewel in Australia.

I tried to ask him about reports that the Labor Party was gaining in strength and popularity, but he cut me short. 'I'm not interested in negative thinking.' The phone rang then. His wife Flo wanted to say 'thank-you' for the flowers. It was their wedding anniversary. Flo is a National Party Senator representing Queensland and is famous for her pumpkin scones. Joh and Flo are a great vote-catching team.

Johannes Bjelke-Petersen looks like the film-maker David Lean. He is in his seventies, autocratic and very wealthy. He was once dirt poor. His father was born in Denmark, a well-educated schoolmaster who became a Lutheran pastor when he arrived in Australia, plummeting the family into poverty and relying upon his wife, Joh's mother, to supplement their income by selling butter and maize from their farm. Joh, who had polio as a child, left school at thirteen to help her, and at the same time pledged himself to get his family out of poverty. At the age of twenty-one he asked his bank manager for £100 to plant peanuts and to put a deposit on a tractor. All day and all night he worked. But never on Sunday; that day he read the Bible. He made himself rich by the age of thirty-six and decided in 1947 to enter Parliament and make Queensland rich. He was lucky to become Premier at the time of the mineral boom, but even so his raw philosophy of risk-taking and hard work has helped the State to blossom. Opponents may call him a 'Bible-bashing bastard' and a 'pugnacious lay-preaching peanut farmer', but Queensland is no longer the Cinderella State, and Joh claims that by the year 2000 she could be one of the richest places on earth.

People like strong leaders. Queenslanders like their new-found riches and their new status and the fact that they have a Premier who does not bow to Canberra. Progressive social legislation has certainly lagged behind in Queensland under Joh, but then the State offered much in the past. It produced the first Labor government in the world on 1 December 1899, and for some fifty years the electors believed that their interests were best served behind the Labor banner. In those days it was poor but progressive. It was the first State to introduce compulsory voting and a free hospital service, the first state to abolish hanging and the only State to eliminate the upper house. It also elected the first and only Communist to State office and the first and only Aborigine, Neville Bonner, to the Federal Senate. And while it was poor and progressive it also failed to produce any sportsmen. But in recent years it has produced Andrew Slack as the captain of Australian Rugby Union's Wallabies; Allan Border, the captain of the Australian cricket team; and Wally Lewis, captain of Australian Rugby League. I meant to ask Joh whether he felt responsible for this. No doubt he would have answered that he had brought out the will to win. I doubt if he would have mentioned Jack Howe.

CHAPTER 18

Sheep and the Robot

On 10 October 1892, at Alice Downs station in Queensland, Jack Howe sheared 321 sheep in seven hours and forty minutes, using hand-held shears. It was a world record, and was to remain a world record, surpassed only by the use of mechanical shears in the hands of another Queenslander in 1950.

Jack Howe became part of bush folklore; a much-admired man, not just for the speed with which he sheared sheep. He was also a staunch union man at a time (the early 1890s) when the shearers chose to challenge the squatters in that fateful confrontation between capital and labour. The squatters were a fine target: most of them were imported English gentlemen, well educated and well-off, and they had dominated the State's legislature and played the lord on their lands, having brought with them their master–servant attitudes which they imposed, in a rigid hierarchy, on those who worked for them. Shearers were low on the list. They were considered foul-mouthed drunken reprobates and feared for the way they maintained solidarity among themselves and stirred up trouble.

The shearers, despite this odious relationship, took a long time to organize themselves to the point where they could strike back. The first meeting to agitate for better conditions took place in Queensland in 1874 when a handful of shearers argued for a fixed price of £1 per 100 sheep; a day starting at six a.m. and ending at five p.m., with one hour each for breakfast and dinner and fifteen minutes for each smoko, and Saturday working to end at four p.m. But the shearers were itinerant workers, often of no fixed address, and scattered among thousands of sheds; it was not until 1890 that they were sufficiently unionized to act. The timing was wrong. The 1870s and 1880s had been boom time, triggered by gold discoveries – but all that had changed. The overloaded economy, running on overseas borrowing, slumped; banks went bust; drought came and there was high unemployment. Squatters lowered wages, counting on non-union men to undercut the market. The violence was nasty, and the union leaders ended up in court in Townsville, charged with conspiracy, and convicted.

The shearers were not the only strikers: waterside workers and miners were all flexing their muscles – to no avail. The outcome was a defeated union movement and the beginning of the Labor Party in which men could fight through the ballot box rather than through strike action. The only major change for the shearers during this period was the introduction of contract shearing, whereby shearers were engaged by a contractor who organized their 'runs' and negotiated with the squatters. The system is still in operation; station owners do not give orders directly to shearers, they act through the contractor. For the rest, little has changed and fights within the industry continue. The shearers were on strike during my visit. The issue was whether or not to allow the introduction of wide combs, cutters with four teeth instead of three. Ironically, Australia has made such combs for years, but for use in New Zealand where the wool is coarser and ends up as carpets. Nowadays the wide comb is considered sufficiently refined to be applied to fine wool. It is also speedier and, while this will enhance the wage-packets of those in work (for shearers are still paid by the number of sheep they shear), it could also lead to unemployment. The big fear is that New Zealanders, who have free access to Australia, will come in droves to take work from the hands of Australian shearers. After all, they are skilled in the use of wide combs and are said to find conditions in Australian sheds more attractive. There were no strikes in Queensland; the industry had agreed to keep the ban on wide combs.

To walk into the shearing shed on Victoria Downs in Morven, eight hours' drive due west of Brisbane, was like walking on to the film set of *Sunday Too Far Away*, a film made in the mid-1970s about another shearers' strike, one which they won. It was eight a.m., and

Noel and John and Jim had already been working for half an hour, their timetable as rigid as ever: seven-thirty to nine-thirty; ten to twelve; one to three: three-thirty to five-thirty. Outside, it was freezing; the first frost of the winter had thrown a morning coat of white across the grass. Sheep squashed into pens shut their eyes and lifted their faces towards the watery sun. Inside the shed it seemed no warmer, but the three shearers were stripped to their singlets, ignoring the draughts caused by the chutes through which the shorn sheep tumbled. At the back of the shed, a large area was reserved for sorting and baling the clip. From time to time a young wool-classer would collect the wool which a young jackeroo had swept from the floor and dumped in bags. The classer would then spread it on his sorting table for classification. 'Long', 'short' and 'pieces' was enough for this mob, they were only lambs. Opposite the shearers the sheep waited in pens, watching and being watched by another young jackeroo.

The three shearers worked silently. Noel who had been shearing for twenty-eight years worked carefully. Beside him were pain-killers and a bottle of cough mixture and in front his dog, Digger, was tied up, keenly following everything. 'I shouldn't be doing this, not now, my back's not up to it any more,' he said.

Jim was speedy enough. He's a New Zealander and has been shearing for only a matter of months. John was the team leader. He called me over as he grabbed a lamb by the horns from the pen, flicked it on to its back and then dragged it by its front legs, belly upwards, towards the shears. 'Been in a fight, this one, look – half a horn missing,' he said, jamming its right front leg high behind its head, leaving its left front leg dangling and shoving its nose under his armpit. 'He'll be OK now, so long as he doesn't move. Our contract says if you damage one you have to pay, and this is a stud lot so it could cost some money. But you can't help the odd nick, that's accepted, particularly with these; they are not combing well. Rain's been at them. Here we go, nice long run down the belly, get rid of all that; then clean up the back legs and on to the side of the head and the neck, and then just wait for those final blows right down the back from tail to head.' I winced as the comb went close to the lamb's eyes, but the creature seemed complacent enough, or was it just stunned by the experience of losing its first fleece? It awoke quickly when it was tumbled unceremoniously through the chute to join the rest of the naked flock in pens a few feet below.

I watched, mesmerized, for some time. The three all followed the same pattern of blows and only slightly differed in the way they held the sheep between their legs. It must be the toughest of jobs, struggling with hefty wriggling sheep, bent double all the time, forever handling a vibrating comb. Within the hour John had badly nicked the belly of a ram. As it began to bleed he hastily threaded a needle with black thread, dragged the poor creature to the door for better light and swiftly sewed six stitches. 'Ah, don't fret,' he said to me. 'Sheep are tough, they don't feel pain the way we do. But I'll tell you one thing, I wouldn't want to come back in the next life as a sheep!'

At nine-thirty a.m. precisely, the men downed tools for half an hour to eat sandwiches and scones and drink tea. John came straight to the point. 'What do you know about these wide combs?' I told him what I knew. 'Well, you're on the right track. We reckon the wide combs could be fourteen per cent more efficient, and that's got to mean a loss of jobs, hasn't it? All the newspapers are saying that Queensland is not joining the strike, just to make the others look bad. They don't seem to grasp that we are not in the strike because the cockies in these parts are not trying to introduce them. A guy called White turned up in Charleville the other day with a team of wide combs and he was run out of town. No, I don't know how it's going to end. We don't want New Zealanders taking our jobs, that's the main issue. I suppose in the long run the combs will be accepted. For one thing, youngsters don't choose to become shearers these days, so the numbers will fall anyway. How's that class war of yours getting on in England? I suppose with your education you wouldn't notice it too much. I reckon that education is good. If you've a point to make, you can get up and make it. Some kids in the Outback can't even read and write at all, and that's not good.'

John continued to entertain us all with a stream of questions which he answered himself. 'What do you make of that Lady Di? I reckon she's a right bitch, but the Queen's all right. If you've got to have one, she's OK. And that Koo Stark, she made a right fool of Andrew.' I congratulated him on his fine store of gossip. 'Well, got to keep an eye on you Poms. C'm'on, why don't you try your hand at shearing?'

I had some difficulty hauling the sheep across the floor, less difficulty getting it into position, and great difficulty handling the electrically-operated comb; it seemed to have a mind of its own and great capacity for destruction. John watched patiently; Jim watched impatiently and in the end stood behind me, grabbed hold of my hand and guided the comb through the wool. 'That feels different, doesn't it? Now, hold your hand still and you can't go wrong.' My shearing produced a decidedly prettier sheep than the rest. It had as much wool left on it as I had succeeded in getting off.

Towards the end of the morning, William Roberts, the son of the station's owners, Lionel and Mary Roberts, came over to inspect the work. William is the studmaster and at the age of twenty-four has great confidence and a quiet, natural authority. He had been educated at one of the best public schools, King's School near Sydney, an established choice for the sons of landowners. From King's he had become a jackeroo. 'It's the best way to learn. Some agricultural colleges are quite good, but I prefer to learn by doing, and if you can get a good station the opportunities are endless. I was in Victoria, there are real studs down there, much more intensive. In comparison we seem to diddle around up here. I should have stayed longer in the south, but I wanted to get married and I felt that this place had been static for long enough and needed some new ideas.'

Together we looked at the three pens and examined the work of Noel, Jim and John. Jim's shearing was not good. You could see the blow marks quite clearly in much the same way as you can see the joins in badly hung wallpaper. There were also too many such marks, indicating that he had yet to master long sweeping blows. And there were too many nicks.

'I'll have to have a word with someone about this. As the contractor is not on site, I'll have a word with the classer. We realize that these shearers are not the best, but it is all we could get. We've booked ahead for the major shearing, but with all this rain holding everything up, we had to take what we could get.'

At lunch, cooked by Mary Roberts and eaten in the kitchen of the homestead, Noel and John talked of their divorces with some bitterness and of other shearing sheds with much affection and amusement. 'This one isn't typical. You should come with us next week. We're starting on a big one; a six-hander which will probably last two weeks – and there'll be no going home at night. We'll be camping out with our own cook. That'll show you what it is all about. And don't you take any notice of all that stuff about shearers not wanting women around, we'd enjoy it.'

After lunch I watched William and the two jackeroos, Simon and Paul, attend to the needs of the shorn sheep. First they forcibly squirted yellow liquid into their mouths to kill worms; then they squirted red liquid down their backs to keep lice at bay. This the sheep didn't much like; it must have stung their naked skin. After that their horns were trimmed, and then they were free to roam, but not too far. There was more in store. 'These shorn buggers sure like to walk. Once that fleece is off, all they want to do is trot away.' Simon and Paul kept a close eye on them and from time to time sped off on motorcycles to round them up. The motorcycles had become a valued asset to sheep stations. It is reckoned that one can do the work of three men and three horses, and that the dogs don't get so worn out. They cut their running time by leaping on to the back of the motorcycle and riding pillion until they are close to the sheep.

I think the shorn sheep strayed deliberately. They'd been warned about mulesing. 'Mule' is the name of the man who had the bright idea of cleaning up sheep's bottoms so that they are not so attractive to blow-flies and thus less prone to infection. His idea involves cutting away excess skin in the area. The operation is brief and bloody: the lambs are placed in a cradle on their backs and held in place by boiler-suited jackeroos. Within seconds, William's sharp scissors had done the deed and the wound was drenched with powder. The lambs react as if they have been given an electric shock. In a daze they are tipped to the ground and left to limp away. It isn't a pleasant business, but it is much to the benefit of the sheep in the end.

Simon and Paul were eager to try. The Robertses usually take one jackeroo a year from England, but their latest recruit had quarrelled with Lionel and left, so he, having been unwell, decided to take on two local boys. They were quiet and well-mannered and, although they have their own quarters, they eat with the family; care is taken to provide them with a modicum of social life which includes tennis parties (a favourite pastime in these parts, even in winter), and being allowed to borrow a car for evening visits to Morven, some twenty minutes away, for a drink or two.

Victoria Downs homestead is large and comfortable without being luxurious. Mary and Lionel Roberts have struggled to get their property together and to educate their four children privately. The youngest child, a daughter, is still at boarding school, and their three sons all went to King's School; the two elder sons chose university and careers away from the land: one is an accountant and the other a doctor.

'I suppose it cost me $A30–40,000 to educate each of the older boys, but it has worked out well. Will is the only one who loves the land, he is the only one I could work with here. We think the same way. If I didn't have Will, I don't think I could keep going. I've a bad hip; all sorts of health problems occur once you reach fifty, and Mary has her problems, too. Will and his new ideas keep us going and I let him have his head; after all, in ten years' time it is going to affect him more than me. He may be young, but he is very capable and works extremely hard – which worries me. He expects so much of himself and of others.'

Mary makes no secret of the limitations she finds in station life. She has a university degree, but chose to marry at twenty-one and give herself up to a life of children and sheep. She'd have been just as happy in the city, with access to theatres and music and stimulating conversation. But she's made the most of life in Morven, painting and attending occasional Flying Art Schools, teaching Bible Classes, and generally being a pillar of the community. At the age of fifty she also realized a long-held dream to go to Europe for several months, at first with her doctor son and then on her own to indulge her love of the theatre and opera.

Lionel has no desire to leave his sheep – except to go to the races. He comes from a long line of doctors, but broke the mould and after school (also King's) took to the land, starting as a jackeroo and eventually becoming a station manager in New South Wales. By 1959 he had married Mary and taken over Victoria Downs. 'The land was owned by Mary's grandfather who was one of the first to have a merino stud in Queensland. When he died he left the property to his children and they in turn left it to their children. By the time I came here, the land was owned by many, including Mary, and I was merely the manager. But we decided to buy the others out slowly and by 1970, with the help of the bank, we owned the lot. I suppose it may well be worth $A1 million now.

'Looking back I can divide the past into five-year spells; one year would be very good, one year we'd make a loss and three years would be pretty average. In the 1960s, things went well enough and we managed to have a cook and a housekeeper, but in the 1970s that slipped away. It was a bad time for both cattle and sheep. Cattle were in over-supply and I know several graziers who just walked off the land; and as for sheep, we were hit by the oil crisis and by synthetics. What saved us was the introduction [by the Wool Corporation in 1974] of a reserve price scheme which each year sets a floor price, below which wool is not sold; instead, the Corporation buys and holds it. Of course you can't do that with cattle, because beef is a perishable commodity. I've got about 250 Herefords here, and I don't know what the answer is – it is so unpredictable, and sometimes the problems sap your energy, both physical and mental.

'As a stud we face added difficulties. In times of drought we cannot simply sell off our sheep, otherwise we'd lose the genetic influence and have to start again. This means we have to hand-feed which is an expensive business, although we do get something back from the government in a really bad period. Certainly numbers are falling on the land. The nation's flock stands at around 140 million – and that's low, compared to the past.'

Once wool was central to the Australian economy – they say that Australia grew up on a sheep's back – but not any more. While the country still produces one-quarter of the world's wool, it accounts for only ten per cent of the country's exports.

The shearers were adamant that I should join them. I hesitated, but finally decided to take my last coach and head back for the coast. I minded the Outback cold. On occasions the heat had sapped my energy – but on the whole I found it manageable. The cold was different; it lasts for maybe eight weeks a year and no one bothers about it; coal fires, electric blankets and the odd paraffin lamp see them through. They would rather put their resources into coping with the heat. On my last morning at Victoria Downs, the temperature outside was once again 32°F (0°C), and inside it registered 41°F (5°C). I left the shearers generating their own heat, and Lionel drove me into Morven to catch the eight a.m. coach. At that hour on a Sunday morning the tiny place, which consists of two pubs, a café, a post office, a garage, a petrol station and a school, was showing surprising signs of life. The draper's shop, which doubles as the newsagent, was open and busily selling newspapers.

For the rest of the journey in the near-empty bus, people were few; the landscape was everything. The land was impressively green, but I'd been warned about that; the torrential rain, which had flooded some areas badly enough for some stations to be cut off and dependent upon air-lifted food, had left the land looking rich and fertile. Most deceptive, they said. It hadn't looked like this for twenty years. I'd heard much about the rains on the journey to Morven, which I'd done by car with the editor of *Queensland Country Life*. We'd stopped about halfway at a Poll Hereford sale which had been postponed from the previous month because of the rain. It had been a gathering of major breeders, a smart affair with plenty of Burberry raincoats and expensive boots, and corgis running on the lawn. The only people in jeans, apart from me, were the cattlegirls whose job it was to spray the calves with water and then dry them with a hair-dryer so that they ended up looking like fluffy toys. There was much talk about 'superior genetic material', 'first embryo transfer calves' and other things I didn't understand. Anyway, that day a new Australian all-breeds female record had been set: a cow with a heifer calf had been sold for $A43,000. This calf had been produced with the help of the most expensive bull ever imported into Australia, an American creature called Beartooth Advancer, owned by a syndicate.

There were no such excitements on the return journey, just the sight of cotton growing, sunflowers being harvested and the odd wheat silo, so my thoughts returned to the shearers. They had been so concerned about wide combs that they hadn't wanted to talk about robots or other scientific threats to their existence. Since the mid-1970s, however, the Wool Corporation has been spending much money encouraging research into alternative shearing methods. They'd first thought of biological defleecing, giving the sheep a pill which stops the wool growing for a while; the formation of this weak zone means that the fleece could literally be pulled off the sheep. There was much relief when it was discovered that the hormone in the pill had no adverse effect upon the sheep or the wool, but the problem is that different sheep react differently: in some instances the fleece would fall off, not waiting to be pulled; in other instances, nothing happened at all. The research continues, but has given way to the robot, the rank outsider. The robot will replace the shearer, and one day a shearing shed will look like those television advertisements which show cars being made without a man in sight. I saw the prototype at the University of Western Australia, where James Trevelyan and a team of sixteen mechanical engineers, electronic engineers, mathematicians and computer experts are convinced that by the early 1990s they will be able to produce a robot to shear a sheep in three minutes and at a price that will be attractive at least to those with large flocks. For the moment the robot is a bit slow, taking about twenty minutes over one sheep. The secret for the future lies in an electric sensor, built into the cutter, which sends messages to a computer so that it can define a program to suit the shape of the sheep. By comparison, cars are easy; the pieces are all exactly the same shape and size. If all sheep were the same size, there would be fewer problems; but James Trevelyan predicts that, once they have completed a device that can be sensitive enough to handle skin, it could have many other applications: it could be used in the meat industry to replace abattoirs.

The robot shearer is not just a toy which amuses 'Tomorrow's World' type television programmes. It is very important to Australia; it is one of number of high-technology research programmes which together, it is hoped, will form exotic new industries on which

Australia's future prosperity depends. There will always be primary industry; there will always be resources, but these alone cannot be relied upon to provide prosperity. World trading patterns in these areas become more complex by the day, and Australia has little clout to safeguard her position. The USA has been leaning on Japan for some time to take more of its grain-fed beef, thus ensuring that Japan cuts back on her imports of Australian grass-fed beef. The European Common Market (EEC) is attempting to off-load its many surpluses on the Far Eastern market, including Japan, and once again Australia loses out. In the resources sector Japan, which has been buying sixty per cent of Australia's coal, has decided to cut back not only in volume but also in the price it is prepared to pay. All this has made Australia think again and turn its attention, not before time, to its ailing manufacturing industry which has been limping along, propped up by tariffs and import quotas. These industries are now getting help with reconstruction but, over and above all else, high technology is getting a major boost.

Australia has always been good at research and hopeless at development; the ideas flow free and are then handed to overseas companies for development. This, it is argued, is because most research is not in the private sector, as with the major Western nations, but in the hands of the government, either in the universities or in the Commonwealth Scientific and Industrial Research Organiza- tion where too little emphasis is placed on commercial development, with the result that pioneering research has failed to emerge as products to form new job- and wealth-generating industries. The Hawke Government has decided to shake off this lack of dynamism and to nurture high technology by offering attractive tax deals to those willing to provide venture capital and to companies willing to expand research and development. As well as pushing others, the Government has also increased its own funding and identified sixteen key areas – sixteen 'sunrise industries' – to receive particular support, including biotechnology, computer software, custom-made chips, scientific instruments, industrial ceramics, lasers and robots.

One man has been responsible for formulating government policy, generating media attention and gaining public acceptance in an area which tends to threaten people (high technology to the layman is equated merely with loss of jobs): Barry Jones, the Minister for Science and Technology, is an impressive man. He put his thoughts into a book, *Sleepers, Awake*, in the early 1980s and before the present Labor Government was elected, and worked tirelessly to promote the ideas it contained. This wasn't so difficult; Australia is used to listening to Barry Jones. Years ago, when he was a teacher and university lecturer, he constantly appeared on 'Mastermind' type quiz-shows where his phenomenal reading speed and almost total recall made him a revered figure. He gets irritated when taxi drivers remind him of his past fame, but even now, in his fifties, his powers of retention are undimmed. At our meeting he wandered around his office packing his briefcase for his next meeting while keeping up a flow of conversation littered with statistics and quotes from Woody Allen, Marx and Keynes. Hardly pausing for breath, he raced through Australia's past problems, slamming into the evils of short-term political thinking and cursing Australia's under-educated population.

'The assumption that most working-class children were virtually ineducable was a universal belief in the nineteenth century, and this assumption is taking a long time to break down. But break it down we must. The resource-rich nations are being left behind. The resource-poor nations – like Switzerland, Sweden, Japan and Singapore – are rising very rapidly. And the major factor in their development has been the proportion of export earnings directly attributable to intellectual input: invention, research and development, design, patents. More than sixty per cent of the annual export earnings of Japan depend on brain-based industries, while Australia's figure is less than five per cent.

'We can do better than that. At the end of the last century we had a sense of confidence and were innovative. In those days the tyranny of distance operated in our favour. We were so far away and so cut off that we had to be independent and think for ourselves. Then came the First World War which made us feel close to Britain again, and at the same time the world began to feel smaller and it became possible, every time we had a problem, to run to others to sort it out, rather than work it out for ourselves. Technology is part of culture and, just as our culture has been derivative, so has our technology – and it's got to stop and stop quickly. We are way behind in the race to new technology and cannot afford to hesitate now. It is touch and go whether we can catch up, but we've got to try.

'Just look at our film industry. I'm the greatest film buff, but look at the characters in our films. They are all recessive; they are all looking backwards, reflecting a simple world, a pastoral world, a gentle world that disappeared years ago. Now look at American films: the central character always has an objective, always knows where he is going. The Australian has no objectives – and even if he manages to find one, he is easily deflected.'

Barry Jones is not easily deflected. He has set up a Commission for the Future; the name attracts derision, but the mission is anything but laughable. It aims to spread knowledge and stimulate debate so that others can share Jones's enthusiasm for technological change, rather than be frightened by it. It aims to curb the passivity and fatalism that is engendered when people do not understand what is happening, when words like computers and robots and biotechnology and genetic engineering are meaningless. Such a state provokes the anxious to neo-Luddite actions while the rest of the community sits back, bewildered. As long ago as the mid-1960s, social commentator Donald Horne advised Australia to start thinking about the future, otherwise, he warned, she would be in danger of losing her much-loved tag, the Lucky Country. Horne wrote pessimistically: Barry Jones is optimistic, and optimism is attractive and can be relied upon – if anything can – to produce the will to move forward. Besides, many people of differing political persuasions told me that the Hawke Government had assembled the most able bunch of men in years, and this may ensure that optimism is rewarded.

My last coach ride ended in Brisbane, and I immediately hired a car to drive the final 600 miles (965 kilometres) to Sydney. I dislike driving; I only hired this vehicle to prove that I had been right not to have bothered before. There were no problems, no burst tyres or accidents, but then I drove at a leisurely pace through the daylight hours, stopping as soon as darkness fell. The first thirty miles (fifty-odd kilometres) out of Brisbane until the border with New South Wales belong to the Gold Coast, glorious beaches alongside a thin strip of land which has been devoured by developers since the 1960s. At one time the Gold Coast was described as a millionaires' playground: it is now everyone's playground, and not a square inch has been left untouched. There are large hotels, small hotels, endless apartment blocks for those wanting retirement homes; there are caravan parks and camping sites, and shops and used car lots, and garish signs and gaudy posters from the Queensland Tourist Board warning of the evils of skin cancer. The thirty-mile strip resembles Miami, not just because it is an intensely developed and highly publicized resort, but because everything is geared to the tourist dollar. Organized entertainment abounds; there is a pet porpoise pool, performing dolphins and seals, a bird sanctuary, a car museum, a miniature railway, and many other man-made distractions shrieking a welcome from the roadside. I'd already spent a Sunday exploring the Gold Coast, so on this occasion I drove through thinking of Trollope's gloves. Trollope said that one does not buy a pair of gloves for a friend by measuring one's own hand; thus, when one finds a pair of gloves that do not fit, that does not make them worthless and useless. The Gold Coast is a pair of gloves which do not fit my hands – but then, thousands love what it has to offer, and thousands return each year to sample its delights.

Over the border, the northern coast of New South Wales is more agreeable. It is the same narrow strip of fertile land between the sea and the great Dividing Range, and there are rivers, and hills called mountains, and forest land; but it is not over-developed – although, to be fair, it too has its garish moments. At Coff's Harbour someone has thought fit to build the biggest banana in the world, a gimmick of reinforced concrete on a wooden frame, and I gather you can walk inside and learn all about the growing of bananas.

Byron Bay is, for the moment, far removed in mood from the Gold Coast. It is a small town on the easternmost tip of Australia named by Captain Cook after the poet's grandfather, John Byron, who commanded HMS *Dolphin* on a voyage of discovery in 1764. It attracts the trendy, appealing to Shirley Maclaine and George

Harrison and anyone else who loves the surf and spurns city style, at least for a while. Marie, the cook on the prawn trawler, had stayed here for the surf. They say you can pick out the police vehicles: they are the only cars without board racks. Byron Bay became attractive to the 'Radicals' in the early 1970s. It started in 1973 when a place called Nimbin, a handful of miles from the coast, staged an Aquarius Festival to which many hippies came and a small number decided to stay. I drove through the hills to Nimbin and found it rather tatty. On what might have passed for a village green a group of long-haired folk strummed guitars around a camp fire. I had a cup of coffee and returned to Byron Bay. Or 'Boring Bay', according to some T-shirt slogans. The beach is everything; the small, low-lying hotels are laid well back and could not be said to harm the scene. Early one morning I walked along the beach for two hours and saw only one man and a dog. Both were friendly. 'See you around town. Maybe we'll have a drink,' said the man after I'd paused to acknowledge the attentions of the dog.

Back at my small hotel, the manager was less courteous: 'It's gone ten o'clock. You staying or going?'

I checked out and sought breakfast in a tiny café in a neat plaza. 'Scrambled eggs? Oh no, I hate doing eggs, hate to touch them. If you really want them, why don't you come around the back here and make your own?' So I did.

Byron Bay has been under threat from developers for some time, but conservation-minded residents who would welcome controlled development are fighting to avoid another Gold Coast. Alan Bond, the financial wizard from Western Australia and winner of the America's Cup, has been persistent in his attempts to build a vast marina. In the beginning, the local paper reported that he intended to build a sales office in the shape of a golf ball, rising thirty-five feet (more than ten metres) into the air and just as wide. A local beef farmer, calling himself Fast Bucks, suggested that the shire might just as well approve the building of a fifty-foot (fifteen-metre) statue of Alan Bond holding the America's Cup! There is no sign of either and, to date, the locally nesting little tern has not been disturbed.

By the time I reached Newcastle, an industrial city built on coal and steel some 100 miles (160 kilometres) north of Sydney, I began to sense journey's end. It was a wet and wintry Sunday and my spirits sagged. I don't think it had much to do with the miserable weather; it had more to do with a sense of loss. I was experiencing a moment of sadness for all that had happened in the preceding months and which could not be repeated. At the outset of my journey I had anticipated that my spirits would sink from time to time as I arrived, tired, in yet another unknown town and checked into yet another unknown hotel. But this had not happened – not once in sixty-five changes of bed. The only gloomy moments had been during my first weeks in Sydney as I had struggled to plan my trip: moments when I had wondered why I had been so anxious to quit routine and cut myself off from all that was familiar; moments when I questioned why I had not been content to travel, as I had done for many years, for a mere four or five weeks at a time. But once a plan emerged and my journey started, I experienced neither low moments nor loneliness. I was much too involved, certain of my motive which was inquiry, and motivated by my curiosity which grew rather than dimmed with the passing months.

Australia is like her national stone, the opal. Glanced at casually from too great a distance, the stone can seem colourless, but once you get close and let the light fall upon the opal it becomes vivid, brilliant and full of interest. While aimless wandering without a goal can be enjoyable, travel accompanied by inquiry, by study, is to me infinitely preferable. My wanderlust is fed not simply by a yearning for adventure or misadventure, but by curiosity and by the knowledge that each day is different and offers endless possibilities and that, unfettered except by two bags and a typewriter, I could pursue each new idea at will. All I needed was imagination, energy and enthusiasm; with those three companions it is impossible to be either lonely or dispirited. I do not travel for the pleasure of arriving home to gloat and gossip; nor do I travel for the pleasure of proving that, in the end, home is best. Home is wherever I happen to be, and for the past months Australia had been my home. And now it was coming to an end.

CHAPTER 19

Land of Exuberance

Sydney had changed. It had shed the sloth of summer for the brisker mantle of winter. It looked the same: the sky was still blue: the sun shone most days – albeit more weakly: and the trees kept their leaves, which is a glorious thing for a tree to do even if it does detract from the delights of spring. The new mood and the new pace were welcome, and Sydney was most welcoming. It felt like coming home.

I was pummelled with questions: 'What do you think of us?' ... 'What line will you take?' ... 'What was the most exciting place?' ... 'Who was the most interesting person you met?' My brain, which by now resembled an over-used piece of blotting-paper, reeled and refused to supply my tongue with all-revealing, mirth-provoking quips. I took refuge in music; I went to the Opera House for three nights of Verdi and, not having heard a note of music for six months, wallowed anew in one of my favourite pastimes. I marvelled, too: if I had been told that I would spend six months without music, I would have said that it was not possible. But it was. My soul had been otherwise engaged and had not yearned for musical refreshment. I also returned to my favourite restaurant, E.J.'s, and walked between the tables, saying hello to acquaintances as though I'd lived in Sydney for years. E.J.'s is like that, particularly on a Friday. On that day each week, at a large round table in one corner, the friends of Richard Hall, journalist and writer, gather to chat. Present are other journalists and other writers, and journalists who have crossed over into publishing and politics, a handful of academics, a film maker or two, and even a Roman Catholic priest (in mufti, of course, and wearing his writer's hat). Not all the group turn up every Friday at lunchtime, and some days the group is joined by visitors from Melbourne and Canberra. The Friday table is now a well-entrenched part of the Sydney scene, having been started in the early 1970s by much the same group of people at a different restaurant, the 'Bon Goût', or 'Tony's' in honour of the founders, Gay and Tony Bilson, who are said to be the first Australian chefs ever given public acclaim. Gay Bilson now owns the grandest of restaurants, the Berowa Waters Inn, some distance from Sydney, where the wealthy arrive by seaplane. E.J.'s and its owner, Susie Carleton, filled the gap, and when the restaurant is empty of other guests, she joins the round table (should she wish to leave, she gives the keys to her trusted friends, to remain as long as they wish). I've sat at the round table until six p.m. – and I'm sure this table outsparks the Algonquin for its contacts and knowledge, for its friendliness and humor. The Whitlam era and Labor politics is what brought the group together in the first place, and is still the subject which nourishes the group. Politics and corruption, and there was enough of both happening in Sydney at that time to keep the courts and lawyers and the newspapers and the gossips at full stretch.

The Premier of New South Wales, Neville Wran, was in trouble. A television programme had alleged that he was involved in attempts to ensure that the former head of the New South Wales Rugby League, Mr Kevin Humphreys, had his case discharged when he came to court accused of fraudulently misappropriating money from the Balmain Rugby League Club. A Royal Commission found that the Premier was not involved, but that the former chief stipendiary magistrate, Murray Farquhar, had been. Mr Farquhar was found guilty of attempting to pervert the course of justice and was sentenced to four years in prison.

With the judiciary already under a cloud, a High Court judge, Lionel Murphy, was also found guilty of attempting to pervert the course of justice. He appealed successfully and was acquitted at a re-trial. However, further allegations were being investigated when he died.

This all came to light after a journalist had unearthed details of illegal telephone-tapping carried out in New South Wales in an attempt to expose drug-trafficking. The phone-tapping tapes revealed a host of other nasty practices, including race-fixing and illegal bookmaking. Sydney was beginning to sound like a mini-Chicago, but that was to be an understatement: a maxi-Chicago was waiting in the wings. It was spawned in Melbourne, where a commission examining the Painters and Dockers Union, which was accused of ghosting payrolls, discovered that the union had also conspired with tax-evading businesses to 'lose' key records, running into millions of dollars. These 'bottom of the harbour deals' were in turn the tip of yet another iceberg. The commission, under Frank Costigan, pursued fraying ends until it had produced a document which said that some forty people, whose names were concealed behind code words, were caught in a web of organized crime and drug dealing. Mr Kerry Packer, the media magnate, revealed himself to be one of the codes, denied the allegations, started an action for defamation against Fairfax newspapers and received abject apologies.

That drugs rings exist in Sydney came as no surprise to anyone. In the summer of 1981, an Antipodean drama was played out in the Lancaster Crown Court in England, where a trial lasting 123 days and costing more that $A1.5 million revealed Terry Clark to be one of the biggest heroin dealers in the world. He was a New Zealander, but his empire was based in Sydney; Richard Hall has charted his unsavoury story in a book called *Greed*.

Each of these scandals broke at different moments, like episodes in a well-turned whodunnit; they then rambled and rumbled along like a television series that no one could bring to an end. Would Sydney one day sink under this alleged weight of corruption? Sydney gossiped and Sydney shrugged. There was no outrage. Professor Manning Clark was so puzzled by the muted response to the Costigan Report that he wrote:

It is as though in questions of human behavior very few feel any genuine moral passion, any sense of outrage at human performance. After the holocaust against the Jews, the dropping of two atomic bombs, and the Vietnam war, we have all supped so much on horrors that we can no longer be roused to anger, no longer make the right responses. In an age of doubt and confusion we cannot agree on what the response should be.

The man on the Sydney surfboard responds very simply. It is just possible that his response is muted because he is dazed; but it is more likely that he is not surprised at all and merely dives into the surf, muttering, 'What do you expect?' Certainly the taxi-driver who drove me past the Royal Commission before which the Premier was appearing had it all worked out. 'What is going on in there is a waste of time,' he said – and then got on with telling me that he drove a taxi and collected the dole at the same time. The message is that no man is better than the next, so why should any man behave any better than the next. This may sound cynical, but it is an attitude founded in egalitarianism and nurtured by realism. There can be few societies today that still believe that the police, politicians and rich men are beyond reproach. Other societies, when they discover that such figures are flawed, drown in a deluge of hypocritical outrage; Australians prefer a more sober approach. Of course it is a shock to discover that the law can be bracketed with politicians and police, but the Sydney response was suitably down to earth. While they gossiped and condemned, they also noted that the law officers were 'doing a favour for a mate'. We all do favours for mates, don't we?

There is a myth in Australia that its citizens are anti-authority. Maybe the early Irish settlers were anti-authority because that authority was English, but most people are not anti – they merely have no undue respect for authority. This is particularly so in New South Wales, where the first police force was composed of ex-convicts and where many of the first administrators were seen as second-rate men who came to Australia and pretended to be 'swells'. Such men did not deserve respect and they did not get it, and those early responses have lingered.

I wondered why corruption at this level should have come about. A handful of thinkers, including Hugh Stretton from the University of Adelaide, suggest that it is all part of the 'New Greed' which has come over people after a period of stagnation that ended in the late 1960s – a new greed which has resulted in the widening gap between the rich and the poor, and which embraces those who have made fortunes out of non-productive and predatory activities, such as property; those public servants who have engineered fat-cat index-linked pensions; those doctors who over-service and over-charge, and those lawyers and accountants who dream up new tax-avoidance schemes. Perhaps the new greed is an example of that wretched pendulum which cannot resist excessive swings. For years it remained jammed through lack of confidence, and once it was freed it was bound to encourage some people to go too far. But the host of Royal Commissions and exposés do indicate that the new greed has poisoned itself and that the pendulum is now being forced into a more appetizing position.

Other explanations that were offered for the way things are were shallow and single-stranded: it's the Irish – it's the American influence – it's the Asian connection – it's the Italian mafia – it's the Chinese-American mafia. No one at any time mentioned the British connection. This is not because the British connection is above suspicion; it is because the British connection is of diminishing significance. Many ties which in the past bound the nations have been severed, either wholly or in part. The most important tie of all – that of Britain as protector – vanished on that fateful day in 1942 when Winston Churchill turned his back on Australia. Then came Britain's move into the Common Market, which accelerated the pace of an already diminishing trading relationship, and now the trade between the two is negligible. Immigration restrictions followed; Britain no longer allowed free access to Australians. Australia retaliated, and now visas are required for visits by Britons and job opportunities are comparatively few. Legal links still exist, but the High Court in Canberra is rapidly replacing the Privy Council as the final court of appeal. The only tie of any significance involves money: British investment in Australia is considerable and is likely to remain so, now that the financial system has been deregulated and a few British banks have been made welcome.

For the rest, the links are ceremonial, convenient, cultural and, above all, personal and emotional. After all, the bulk of the population remains of British origin, and some 8 million people in the United Kingdom are said to have relatives living in Australia. When the bush fires raged through Victoria and South Australia, the telephone lines between the two countries were blocked for days with people seeking information and reassurance. Ironically, with links at their weakest, air fares are at their cheapest; an increasing number of Australians visit Britain, and the traffic between Britain and Australia is very much on the rise – and not just with those visiting families and friends, but holiday-makers with no ties, and even professionals wishing to compare and contrast their expertise. All this makes for a growing awareness between the two countries, and in some ways serves to cement the remaining convenient links. Australia likes to say that it is a republic in all but name, thereby granting itself the best of both worlds. Sometimes I feel that people are a little embarrassed to admit that they are reluctant to take the final step, rather like a kangaroo that takes forever to leave its mother's pouch. It is rumoured that the Hawke Government will time its next election to coincide with the euphoria released by the Bicentennial celebrations in early 1988; if returned, it may use the tide of well-being and nationalism to introduce a referendum to remove the monarchy. It *is* only gossip, and it presupposes that by then the population will have made up its mind what it would prefer instead. I saw no signs that it had given any thought at all to the alternatives, and seemed to shrink from the obvious American model.

Since 1942 America has taken over Britain's role. This is a tidy move, since America could well be seen as Australia's step-father: if the United States had not turned Britain out, then the latter might not have bothered to colonize Australia. At any rate America is now Australia's protector; it is the principal source of foreign investment, and trading links between the two are strong if somewhat unbalanced – Australia imports from America twice as much as she exports. But even though the links are profound, the two countries have little real knowledge of each other. As with Britain in the past, the two rely on assumptions: each assumes that the other is similar and makes little effort to go beyond superficial comparisons. These include similarity of size, similarity of climate (at least with the West Coast of America), and similarity of background. Both countries were originally inhabited by so-called primitive peoples who were unceremoniously displaced by the British; both countries struggled to develop their lands and make them attractive to waves of immigrants, first from the United kingdom and then from all over Europe. The only major difference was that America had to fight for her independence and Australia did not. Britain had learnt a lesson and gave the Australian colonies the right to rule themselves in the 1850s. This assortment of twin-like attributes enables the two countries to feel a special affinity, and Mark Twain was one of the first to over-emphasize the mirror-image when he visited Australia in 1897.

The Australians did not seem to me to differ noticeably from Americans, either in dress, carriage, ways, pronunciation, inflections or general appearance. To be sure, there were fleeting and subtle suggestions of their English origins, but they were not pronounced enough to catch one's attention. The people have easy and cordial manners from the beginning; from the moment the introduction is completed. This is American.

The perpetuation of sameness was to continue; Sir Robert Menzies offered his view:

We [Australia and America] were born in the same era, sprang from the same stock, and live for the same ideals. Australia and America share an affinity that reaches to our souls. We see the world from similar perspectives, though no two countries could be on more opposite ends of the globe. We share values shaped on the new world frontier passed on to us as our heritage. We live in freedom and will accept no other life. We govern ourselves in democracy and will not tolerate anything less. We cherish liberty and hold it safe providing hope for the rest of the world.

And an American Ambassador to Canberra in the early 1970s went one step further by claiming:

One can emigrate from America to Australia or from Australia to America without really leaving home. Historical roots, language and literature, cultural experience, family values, civil liberty, religious freedom, sports, television – all these form the symbiosis of Australia and the United States.

Such exaggeration has given neither country much incentive for deeper analysis. Australians none the less are quite happy to feel that they have an intimate knowledge of America, acquired through hours of imported television which has enabled them to learn that Kojak enjoys pastrami on rye. Their contact with Americans has been minimal; maybe 70,000 live in Australia at any one time (either permanently or on loan from American companies), and the only occasion on which Americans were on Australian soil in significant numbers was during the Second World War, when some half a million passed through and were greeted with the same ambivalence as they were in Europe. Many people resented the way in which their superior rates of pay enabled them to monopolize the best hotels, the taxis and the women. They seemed particularly to dislike the way in which the Americans liked to enjoy themselves on Sundays. There were clashes and resentment, and even a riot in Brisbane with one soldier killed and several wounded. No need for riots now, just glimpses of envy for the way in which such a relatively young country has amassed so much wealth and power; and further glimpses of resentment of the sort that any small nation feels when it is beholden to a super-power.

In return, Americans have remained ignorant of Australia even though surveys show that Australia is the country to which they would most like to emigrate, and other surveys show that the return rate of those who do emigrate is seventy per cent. They go to Australia expecting to find a better-America, and then feel cheated and go home.

One American researcher listed the complaints of those who came expecting to find Arizona in the days of Geronimo, and found it hard to adjust to suburban Australia. They included a dislike of fifty varieties of poisonous snakes; flies in plague proportions, and beaches made intimidating by unwelcoming sea creatures (including sharks); Australians who were more difficult to get to know than they had expected and an accent they couldn't fathom. Apparently they had a hard time working out that 'horse rice' meant 'horse race' and that 'veggies' was short for 'vegetables'. They complained about poor roads, weekend surcharges on bills, and big bellies overhanging swimming trunks. However, they did appreciate seeing car parks without armed security guards and watching people stroll in the parks after dark and having taxi-drivers who not only handed them the correct change but often rounded down the amount from, say, $A2.10 to $A2. But in the end what drove them back to the United

States was a longing for American vitality and a desire to be 'back in the world' and rid of isolation. They came to get away from red tape and crime, and found that Australia had both; they came for cheap land and lower prices, and found neither. Yet no one talks of 'Whingeing Yanks'; I believe they reserve that epigraph for Ethel Sloan – in 1978, she wrote one of the few Americans'-eye views that I found. *Kangaroo in my Kitchen* is an unpleasant book written by a housewife who accompanied her advertising-executive husband to Sydney for a couple of years. She arrived half-expecting to find Aborigines spearing lizards in the streets, rugged bronzed gods shearing sheep by the wayside and kangaroos at two a penny. She found cockroaches aplenty, women with such wrinkled skins that they looked like their husbands' mothers, and salesmen who refused to sell her a car without her husband's signature. Fortunately, not everything written by Americans is devoted to superficial research and daft comments. In 1985, *Daedalus*, the journal of the American Academy of Arts and Sciences, published an issue devoted entirely to Australia. The seventeen essays are of the highest standard: they prove the distinctiveness of Australia and refute the charge that she is a carbon-copy of any other society.

While it is possible to find excuses for the assumptions of the Americans, it is much harder to understand why the Japanese arrive in Australia so ill-prepared for what they must know to be a totally different culture. Japan is Australia's main trading partner – there are 3,000 Japanese living in Sydney alone – and yet, according to one survey, seventy per cent said they had not received a briefing before leaving Japan, and as a result they do not mix well and stay within their own community.

In Japan, the koala bear is the dominant image of Australia: there are pop songs about koalas, there are documentary programmes shown on television about koalas, and there is even a Koala Press which produces a quarterly bulletin for Australophiles. Even so, there is no clear picture of Australia, other than the fact that it is a large country from which come iron ore, coal, beef and wool. This might be fair enough if connection with Australia was seen as limited to trade. Many, however, profess a much wider interest, and it can only be assumed that Australians have not taken advantage of opportunities to feed this interest. There are Chairs of Australian Studies in Harvard and in London and in Dublin, but no one has thought to pursue Japan. Only a few Australian books are available, and yet the Japanese are said to have a great appetite for reading in English.

Takeadi Hori started to fill the gap in the early 1980s by writing a slim volume for Japanese businessmen in which he tried to explain Australian people and customs. Quite clearly he feels that, despite the demise of the White Australia policy, the Japanese are not totally accepted and are treated in a way which makes them feel over-sensitive. Hori describes his own research. He and a group of Japanese friends would get on a bus in Sydney on a regular basis and deliberately sit in separate seats. He discovered that an Australian would sit next to a Japanese only when all the other seats were occupied – and then would pick the most Western-looking. Fortu-nately, he recounts his tale with humour, as he does the numerous occasions when he was served last in a pub, even if he was the first in the queue. For all the perceived slights, he describes the Australians warmly; he says they are kind-hearted, fun-loving and used to the outdoors – beaches and open spaces; that they tend to be simple-hearted, simple-minded, generous and rough; they are given to biased views on international affairs, naïve egotism, optimism and deliberate exaggeration. He finds some difficulty in explaining what he means by simple-minded, and gives as an example the members of an audience at the opera who often whisper to each other during the performance and who applaud whenever they are impressed, even in the middle of an aria. He has similar difficulty describing small towns:

Each small town greets visitors with a community set resembling that which is to be found in many Hollywood-produced Westerns. The main street is invariably flanked by a drug store, a milk bar, a pub (the local drinking spot), a bowling club and finally a Returned Servicemen's League (RSL) Club. The RSL is a nationwide friendship organization of war veterans and each club expands its facilities by using the huge earnings it makes from poker machines. Large-scale clubs serve as leisure centres, many equipped with more than twenty billiard tables, a library, gymnasium, Olympic-size swimming pool, sauna baths and an 18-hole golf course. The club is reminiscent of the busy atmosphere of Japanese ice-cream shops of old, and of the close personal relationships of the traditional Japanese neighbour-hood. The poker machine hall is overwhelming. In contrast with the bright, honky-tonk air of the Japanese *pachinko* [pin-ball] parlours, the poker machine hall looks like a factory at work producing discomforting, low metallic noises. The sight of old women with their double chins, and wearing bright-coloured hats, drooping over the rows of slot machines gives the illusion of lot-feed chickens in a ceaselessly-lit poultry farm.

Every foreign visitor is intrigued by the RSL Clubs. Their wealth causes raised eyebrows, and the sight of the slot machines producing the wealth usually causes a sneer. Perhaps they need Trollope's gloves. The pokies are the Australian equivalent of bingo. The Clubs – I visited one in Sydney – are impressive, having more trimmings than the Melbourne Club could ever afford. The decor and the atmosphere are different too; I doubt whether the Melbourne Club encourages members to plonk down their radios beside their drinks on a Saturday afternoon to catch the racing results.

Australians accept the ignorance of foreigners with good grace. They have got used to an imbalance in knowledge as in so many things. They accept that influential nations use and ignore less influential nations; it is the way of the world. But then the world has a habit of changing. In 1984, *L'Express*, the respected French weekly magazine, announced across its front cover that Australia was the Country of the Year. France is not popular in Canberra; Australian politicians do not like her testing nuclear weapons in the South Pacific. None the less, or perhaps in an attempt to bridge the gulf, *L'Express* ran a paean of praise for page after page, in which it castigated the French for taking so little interest in Australia. Cook may have discovered the country for the white man as long ago as 1770, but it was not until November 1983 that a French Foreign Minister thought to pay her a visit.

But our restricted vision of the world which made us neglect this antipodean island continent for so long is beginning to expand. Australia is now emerging on the edge of an ocean which people are calling 'the new centre of the world'; the Pacific, after the Mediterranean and the Atlantic, would seem to be the current centre of progress.

Asia is likely one day to be the new centre of world economic power. And where will Australia be then? It is to be hoped that she will be humming along happily, close to the hub of things, locked by trade and other mutual interests into friendly relationships with her near neighbours, the rulers of the Pacific. But, of course, there are always those who glimpse the future with a shudder of gloom and 1980 was a particularly bad year for predictions. In that year, left-wing academic Edward Wheelwright wrote:

Make no mistake, if we, the workers, do not take control of the big corporations at least, by the end of this century we shall be the biggest export platform in the world, with all the easy-access minerals ripped out of the ground, with us left with little natural resources, little new plant and equipment, and no new technology to compete with the masses in Asia. We shall be the poor white trash of South Asia, with our massage parlours open twenty-four hours a day!

In the same year, Herman Kahn, of New York's Hudson Institute, was invited by fourteen companies to visit Australia and predict its long-term possibilities. One of his suggestions was that 'Australia is slowly becoming something like the Persian Gulf – a vast storehouse of natural resources that may at some point become a target' – a target over which China and Japan might fight; a target which might entice Indonesia to become belligerent. He was fuelling Australia's worst fears: her 200-year-old paranoia that she is alone, isolated, a predominantly white democracy in a large empty continent, in a non-white region of the world with predominantly authoritarian governments; that she has no right to be there and one day the Asian bogey-man will come and get her.

Australia could not even celebrate the anniversary of the first 100 years of European Settlement (or conquest) without the spectre appearing. The *Age* of Melbourne urged a union of the States and, as one of the conditions of that union, a protectionist policy against the rest of the world to keep out the Indians, Japanese and Chinese who

... are eager to inundate us with the products of their myriad-handed cheap coloured labor ... We know of no foreign relations now save those we have with Europe and our own race; but the Asiatic, and not the European, is the competitor who threatens some day to dispute our claims to be the Greater Britain of the South, and against whom we shall have to legislate long before the arrival of the next centennial.

On 26 January 1888, the newspapers in other States were too busy looking back to spare a thought for the future. They celebrated in a quietly confident manner, not yet one nation and much aware that this was a Sydney occasion, rather than an all-Australia festival. Each noted that, in effect, the celebration was for the achievements of the past fifty years. The first fifty years were inglorious; Australia was merely the 'cesspit of England' (the *Brisbane Courier*) or, in the words of the *Sydney Morning Herald*, 'a distant prison'.

It was no band of adventurous colonizers, no fugitives from tyranny, no persecuted saints, that sought to plant the flag of commerce and liberty upon these shores. A hundred years ago, the Union Jack, unfurled for the first time on the Australian shore, waved only over an unwalled gaol.

The second fifty years, however, saw the end of transportation and the discovery of gold, and with the latter abundant labour and speculative adventurers by the shipload to create a country of which, by 1888, they were justifiably proud.

The *South Australian Advertiser* proclaimed that Australia was

... one of the freest, most prosperous and most promising communities under the sun ... a cluster of splendid cities, hundreds of thriving towns, a network of roads, railways and telegraphs and three million people relatively the richest in actual wealth, and having proportionately the largest commerce of any people in the world.

Australia seemed so blessed that some people on that day must have harboured hopes that in time Australia would rule the Pacific, as they dressed for the State banquet, watched the fireworks, attended the opening of Centennial Park, or the inter-colonial cricket match, or the band contest, or merely enjoyed a public holiday, reading in the morning paper that a shark had been caught in the harbour and inside it had been found a man's waistcoat with a gold watch in the pocket; that a steamer had arrived in Hobart from London with 300 stoats and weasels on board; that a meeting of miners had declared that first timers in the coal pits, unless they were the sons of operatives, were to pay for the privilege – £5 for the first six months. Halcyon days: no one could possibly have known that Australia had reached a peak of prosperity and confidence from which she was to decline in a few years' time in a depression that made men all too aware that luck passes. Nor could they have known that Australia's second century would, to some extent, mirror the first, with a sluggish fifty years of war and depression followed by a second fifty years of rapid growth and development.

No one now dreams that Australia will conquer the Pacific; the thought is a joke for playwrights. Jack Hibberd, in his haunting monologue *A Stretch of the Imagination*, has Monk O'Neill recalling a meeting with Les Darcy, the boxer. '"Monk," he said, "one day Australia, that great nation out there of soldiers and sports and athletes, cereals and wool, will one day rule the Pacific. England will one day lick the elastic of our boots. America will extend to us an equal hand. Out there, O'Neill, lies a germ . . . the germ of the future." Monk replied: "Cut it out, Les. You cannot extract sunbeams from a cucumber."'

Australia was not destined to dominate as had her parent country, Britain, or that country's other offspring, America. She did not inherit those fiery genes that produce rulers; she was instead to establish the habit of relying on her relatives, of enjoying life, of grasping the moment, of hoping for the best. These are attractive qualities: they have not made Australia the playboy of the Eastern world; she has a role to play and serious ambitions to expand her influence which will enhance her self-esteem. She has no cause to lack confidence.

She may not be the carefree, egalitarian Utopia that some had hoped to see. Such men are dreamers; they willed themselves to think that here perhaps, more than anywhere, humanity had the chance to make a fresh start. Man is imperfectible; so too are nations. None the less the poor who got away, the not-so-poor who followed and the rich men who have emerged have produced a country with much to celebrate in 1988.

For my private farewell, I hopped on the ferry to Manly. There was no special reason for choosing Manly – although it has a fine beach, fringed with Norfolk pines. The main reason was the ferry ride itself and the pleasure of seeing the harbour again and of entering Sydney Cove from seaward, a sight that never fails to excite my imagination, for in a glance the city reveals itself, offering a glimpse of the past, of the remaining old stone buildings, criss-crossed by the present, by expressways and by silhouetted sky-soaring buildings of glass and concrete. The trip also gave me time to focus my thoughts on what exactly it was I had come to cherish and was loath to leave. I gazed at the waves and treated my thoughts like tea-leaves, forcing them to reveal a pattern. It wasn't difficult. I knew that above all I would miss the spirit of Australia, a spirit so different from Europe with its centuries of indigestible history caked by a myriad of miserable mistakes. Australia, by contrast, is exuberant; its history is manageable, picturesque even; its mistakes make it interesting. It is, after all, an adolescent country, struggling with problems but not soured by them; like many an adolescent, it has a natural energy and enthusiasm to make light of its troubles and just enough wisdom to be proud of what has been created from the stockyard and carved out by the men of steel.

Trollope when he left felt inclined to shed a tear at the thought of not returning. I shed no tear: nothing will prevent me from returning.

Bibliography

Anthony Trollope, *Australia*. Trollope visited Australia in 1871 and 1872 and travelled widely, and this book is generally considered to be the most important visitor's account of Australia in the second half of the nineteenth century. In 1967 Queensland University Press published a scholarly edition with an introduction and copious footnotes explaining allusions and occasionally correcting his facts.

Mark Twain, *Following the Equator (a journey around the world)*, the American Publishing Company, 1897. Interesting but neither so detailed nor so perceptive as Trollope's account.

HISTORY, general

Australia is blessed with historians who produce concise and accessible accounts of the continent's development from the first settlement to modern times:

Geoffrey Blainey, *The Tyranny of Distance*, Sun Books, Melbourne, 1980
C. M. H. Clark, *A Short History of Australia*, Macmillan, 1982
A. G. L. Shaw, *The Story of Australia*, Faber & Faber, 1983

HISTORY, specific

Patsy Adam-Smith, *The Shearers*, Thomas Nelson & Sons, 1982
John Baxter, *Who Burned Australia?*, New English Library, 1984. An account of the bush fires of 1983.
Geoffrey Blainey, *The Rise of Broken Hill*, Macmillan, 1968

Geoffrey Bolton, *Spoils and Spoilers*, Allen & Unwin, 1981. Australia's environment and how it has been handled and mishandled.

————*A Thousand Miles Away*, Australian National University Press, 1963. A history of the settlement of northern Queensland.

Gavin Casey and Ted Mayman, *The Mile that Midas Touched*, Seal Books, 1976. The story of Kalgoorlie.

Edmund Campion, *Rockchoppers: Growing up Catholic in Australia*, Penguin Books, 1982

P. F. Donovan, *A Land Full of Possibilities: A history of the Northern Territory*, Queensland University Press, 1981

Robert Endean, *Australia's Great Barrier Reef*, Queensland University Press, 1982

Ross Fitzgerald, *From the Dreaming to 1915: A history of Queensland*, Queensland University Press, 1982

Colm Kiernan (Editor), *Ireland and Australia*, Mercier Press, Dublin, 1984. The transcript of a series of Irish radio broadcasts examining the influence of the Irish in Australia.

W. F. Mandle, *Going it Alone*, Penguin Books, 1978. This book takes specific episodes in Australian history to illustrate the development of Australian nationalism.

Ged Martin (Editor), *The Founding of Australia*, Hale & Iremonger, Sydney, 1978. A collection of articles exploring the reasons for the settlement of Australia.

John Molony, *I am Ned Kelly*, Penguin Books, 1980

Alan Moorehead, *Cooper's Creek*, Hamish Hamilton, 1968. The story of the explorers, Robert O'Hara Burke and William John Wills, and their attempt to cross Australia from south to north.

Alan Powell, *Far Country: A history of the Northern territory*, Melbourne University Press, 1982

Leonie Sandercock and Ian Turner, *Up Where, Cazaly?: The Story of Australian Rules Football*, Granada Books, 1981

Derek Whitelock, *Adelaide: 1836–1976*, Queensland University Press, 1977

Judith Wright, *The Coral Battleground*, Thomas Nelson & Sons, 1977. The fight to preserve the Great Barrier Reef from developers.

HISTORY, social

Australians like exploring who they are, why they are as they are, and where they are going. These detailed examinations of the Australian character and life-style are part of the continuing search for a clear identity and often end up being painfully self-critical.

John Carroll (Editor), *Intruders in the Bush*, Oxford University Press, 1982
Ronald Conway, *Land of the Long Weekend*, Sun Books, 1978
Bruce Grant, *The Australian Dilemma*, Macdonald/Futura, 1983
Donald Horne, *The Lucky Country*, Penguin Books, 1964
────── *Money Made Us*, Penguin Books, 1976
Jonathan King, *Waltzing Materialism*, Harper & Row, 1978
Craig McGregor, *The Australian People*, Hodder & Stoughton, 1981
John Douglas Pringle, *Australian Accent*, Seal Books, 1978

ABORIGINES

Geoffrey Blainey, *Triumph of the Nomads: A history of Ancient Australia*, Sun Books, 1978
H. C. Coombs, *Kulinma: Listening to Aboriginal Australians*, Australian National University Press, 1978
Kenneth Maddock, *The Australian Aborigines*, Penguin Books, 1974
Geoff McDonald, *Red over Black: Behind the Aboriginal Land Rights*, Veritas Publishing Co., Western Australia, 1982
Charles Perkins, *A Bastard Like Me* (autobiography), Ure Smith, Sydney, 1975
Henry Reynolds, *The Other Side of the Frontier: Aboriginal Resistance to the European Invasion of Australia*, Penguin Books, 1983

ARCHITECTURE

Robin Boyd, *The Australian Ugliness*, Penguin Books, 1963

DRAMA

Jack Hibberd (Editor), *Performing Arts in Australia*, a special issue of *Meanjin*, University of Melbourne, 1984
Peter Holloway (Editor), *Contemporary Australian Drama*, Currency Press, Sydney, 1981

IMMIGRANTS

Geoffrey Sherington, *Australia's Immigrants, 1788–1978*, Allen & Unwin, 1980

Geoffrey Blainey, *All for Australia*, Methuen Haynes, 1984

POLITICS

Blanche d'Alpuget, *Robert J. Hawke: A biography*, Schwartz, 1983

John McMillan, Gareth Evans, Haddon Storey, *Australia's Constitution: Time for Change*, Allen & Unwin, 1983

David Solomon, *Australia's Government and Parliament*, Thomas Nelson & Sons, 1977

LITERATURE

Geoffrey Dutton (Editor), *The Literature of Australia*, Pelican Books, 1964

G. A. Wilkes, *The Stockyard and the Croquet Lawn: Literary Evidence for Australia's Cultural Development*, Edward Arnold, 1981

In Chapter 9 I mention that as well as internationally acclaimed writers like Murray Bail, Peter Carey, David Ireland, Thomas Keneally, David Malouf, Frank Moorhouse and Patrick White, Australia has a host of lesser-known novelists whose work gives cause for national pride. Among them are:

Jessica Anderson, *Tirra Lirra by the River*, Penguin Books, 1980

Thea Astley, *An Item in the Late News*, Queensland University Press, 1982

Jay Bland, *Lavington Pugh*, Nostrilia Press, 1982

Blanche d'Alpuget, *Turtle Beach*, Penguin Books, 1981

David Foster, *Moonlite*, Picador Books, 1983

Helen Garner, *Monkey Grip*, Penguin Books, 1978

Rodney Hall, *Just Relations*, Penguin Books, 1984

Barbara Hanrahan, *The Frangipani Gardens*, Queensland University Press, 1982

Shirley Hazzard, *The Transit of Venus*, Penguin Books, 1981

Elizabeth Jolley, *Woman in a Lampshade*, Penguin Books, 1983

——*Mr Scobie's Riddle*, Penguin Books, 1983

Christopher Koch, *The Year of Living Dangerously*, Sphere, 1981

Roger McDonald, *1915*, Queensland University Press, 1979
Georgia Savage, *Slate and Me and Blanche McBride*, Penguin Books, 1983
Randolph Stow, *To the Islands*, Picador Books, 1983
Judah Waten, *Alien Son*, Sun Books, 1981
Michael Wilding, *Pacific Highway*, Hale & Iremonger, 1982

Short Stories

Kerryn Goldsworthy (Editor), *Australian Short Stories*, Dent, 1983
Frank Moorhouse (Editor), *The State of the Art: the Mood of Contemporary Australia in Short Stories*, Penguin Books, 1983
John Morrison, *North Wind*, Penguin Books, 1982

WINE

The Complete Book of Australian Wine, Len Evans, Summit, 1978

WOMEN

Miriam Dixson, *The Real Matilda*, Penguin Books, 1976
Anne Summers, *Damned Whores and God's Police*, Penguin Books, 1975

Index

Index

Index

Index

Index

FOR THE BEST IN PAPERBACKS, LOOK FOR THE 🐧

In every corner of the world, on every subject under the sun, Penguins represent quality and variety – the very best in publishing today.

For complete information about books available from Penguin and how to order them, write to us at the appropriate address below. Please note that for copyright reasons the selection of books varies from country to country.

In the United Kingdom: For a complete list of books available from Penguin in the U.K., please write to *Dept EP, Penguin Books Ltd, Harmondsworth, Middlesex, UB7 0DA*

In the United States: For a complete list of books available from Penguin in the U.S., please write to *Dept BA, Viking Penguin, 299 Murray Hill Parkway, East Rutherford, New Jersey 07073*

In Canada: For a complete list of books available from Penguin in Canada, please write to *Penguin Books Canada Limited, 2801 John Street, Markham, Ontario L3R 1B4*

In Australia: For a complete list of books available from Penguin in Australia, please write to the *Marketing Department, Penguin Books Australia Ltd, P.O. Box 257, Ringwood, Victoria 3134*

In New Zealand: For a complete list of books available from Penguin in New Zealand, please write to the *Marketing Department, Penguin Books (N.Z.) Ltd, Private Bag, Takapuna, Auckland 9*

In India: For a complete list of books available from Penguin in India, please write to *Penguin Overseas Ltd, 706 Eros Apartments, 56 Nehru Place, New Delhi 110019*

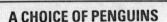
A CHOICE OF PENGUINS

The Big Red Train Ride Eric Newby

From Moscow to the Pacific on the Trans-Siberian Railway is an eight-day journey of nearly six thousand miles through seven time zones. In 1977 Eric Newby set out with his wife, an official guide and a photographer on this journey. 'The best kind of travel book' – Paul Theroux

Star Wars Edited by E. P. Thompson

With contributions from Rip Bulkeley, John Pike, Ben Thompson and E. P. Thompson, and with a Foreward by Dorothy Hodgkin, OM, this is a major book which assesses all the arguments for Star Wars and proceeds to make a powerful – indeed unanswerable – case against it.

Selected Letters of Malcolm Lowry
Edited by Harvey Breit and Margerie Bonner Lowry

Lowry emerges from these letters not only as an extremely interesting man, but also a lovable one' – Philip Toynbee

PENGUIN CLASSICS OF WORLD ART

Each volume presents the complete paintings of the artist and includes: an introduction by a distinguished art historian, critical comments on the painter from his own time to the present day, 64 pages of full-colour plates, a chronological survey of his life and work, a basic bibliography, a fully illustrated and annotated *catalogue raisonné*.

Titles already published or in preparation

Botticelli, Bruegel, Canaletto, Caravaggio, Cézanne, Dürer, Giorgione, Giotto, Leonardo da Vinci, Manet, Mantegna, Michelangelo, Picasso, Piero della Francesca, Raphael, Rembrandt, Toulouse-Lautrec, van Eyck, Vermeer, Watteau

A CHOICE OF PENGUINS

A Fortunate Grandchild 'Miss Read'

Grandma Read in Lewisham and Grandma Shafe in Walton on the Naze were totally different in appearance and outlook, but united in their affection for their grand-daughter – who grew up to become the much-loved and popular novelist.

The Ultimate Trivia Quiz Game Book   Maureen and Alan Hiron

If you are immersed in trivia, addicted to quiz games, endlessly nosey, then this is the book for you: over 10,000 pieces of utterly dispensable information!

The Diary of Virginia Woolf
Five volumes, edited by Quentin Bell and Anne Olivier Bell

'As an account of the intellectual and cultural life of our century, Virginia Woolf's diaries are invaluable; as the record of one bruised and unquiet mind, they are unique'– Peter Ackroyd in the *Sunday Times*

Voices of the Old Sea   Norman Lewis

'I will wager that *Voices of the Old Sea* will be a classic in the literature about Spain' – *Mail on Sunday*. 'Limpidly and lovingly Norman Lewis has caught the helpless, unwitting, often foolish, but always hopeful village in its dying summers, and saved the tragedy with sublime comedy' – *Observer*

The First World War   A. J. P. Taylor

In this superb illustrated history, A. J. P. Taylor 'manages to say almost everything that is important for an understanding and, indeed, intellectual digestion of that vast event . . . A special text . . . a remarkable collection of photographs' – *Observer*

Ninety-Two Days   Evelyn Waugh

With characteristic honesty, Evelyn Waugh here debunks the romantic notions attached to rough travelling: his journey in Guiana and Brazil is difficult, dangerous and extremely uncomfortable, and his account of it is witty and unquestionably compelling.

FOR THE BEST IN PAPERBACKS, LOOK FOR THE 🐧

A CHOICE OF PENGUINS

The Book Quiz Book   Joseph Connolly

Who was literature's performing flea . . .? Who wrote 'Live Now, Pay Later . . .'? Keats and Cartland, Balzac and Braine, Coleridge conundrums, Eliot enigmas, Tolstoy teasers . . . all in this brilliant quiz book. You will be on the shelf without it . . .

Voyage through the Antarctic   Richard Adams and Ronald Lockley

Here is the true, authentic Antarctic of today, brought vividly to life by Richard Adams, author of *Watership Down*, and Ronald Lockley, the world-famous naturalist. 'A good adventure story, with a lot of information and a deal of enthusiasm for Antarctica and its animals' – *Nature*

Getting to Know the General   Graham Greene

'In August 1981 my bag was packed for my fifth visit to Panama when the news came to me over the telephone of the death of General Omar Torrijos Herrera, my friend and host . . .' 'Vigorous, deeply felt, at times funny, and for Greene surprisingly frank' – *Sunday Times*

Television Today and Tomorrow: Wall to Wall Dallas?
Christopher Dunkley

Virtually every British home has a television, nearly half now have two sets or more, and we are promised that before the end of the century there will be a vast expansion of television delivered via cable and satellite. How did television come to be so central to our lives? Is British television really the best in the world, as politicians like to assert?

Arabian Sands   Wilfred Thesiger

'In the tradition of Burton, Doughty, Lawrence, Philby and Thomas, it is, very likely, the book about Arabia to end all books about Arabia' – *Daily Telegraph*

When the Wind Blows   Raymond Briggs

'A visual parable against nuclear war: all the more chilling for being in the form of a strip cartoon' – *Sunday Times*. 'The most eloquent anti-Bomb statement you are likely to read' – *Daily Mail*

FOR THE BEST IN PAPERBACKS, LOOK FOR THE 🐧

A CHOICE OF PENGUINS

An African Winter Preston King With an Introduction by Richard Leakey

This powerful and impassioned book offers a unique assessment of the interlocking factors which result in the famines of Africa and argues that there *are* solutions and we *can* learn from the mistakes of the past.

Jean Rhys: Letters 1931–66
Edited by Francis Wyndham and Diana Melly

'Eloquent and invaluable . . . her life emerges, and with it a portrait of an unexpectedly indomitable figure' – Marina Warner in the *Sunday Times*

Among the Russians Colin Thubron

One man's solitary journey by car across Russia provides an enthralling and revealing account of the habits and idiosyncrasies of a fascinating people. 'He sees things with the freshness of an innocent and the erudition of a scholar' – *Daily Telegraph*

The Amateur Naturalist Gerald Durrell with Lee Durrell

'Delight . . . on every page . . . packed with authoritative writing, learning without pomposity . . . it represents a real bargain' – *The Times Educational Supplement*. 'What treats are in store for the average British household' – *Books and Bookmen*

The Democratic Economy Geoff Hodgson

Today, the political arena is divided as seldom before. In this exciting and original study, Geoff Hodgson carefully examines the claims of the rival doctrines and exposes some crucial flaws.

They Went to Portugal Rose Macaulay

An exotic and entertaining account of travellers to Portugal from the pirate-crusaders, through poets, aesthetes and ambassadors, to the new wave of romantic travellers. A wonderful mixture of literature, history and adventure, by one of our most stylish and seductive writers.

A CHOICE OF PENGUINS

Adieux: A Farewell to Sartre   Simone de Beauvoir

A devastatingly frank account of the last years of Sartre's life, and his death, by the woman who for more than half a century shared that life. 'A true labour of love, there is about it a touching sadness, a mingling of the personal with the impersonal and timeless which Sartre himself would surely have liked and understood' – *Listener*

Business Wargames   James Barrie

How did BMW overtake Mercedes? Why did Laker crash? How did McDonalds grab the hamburger market? Drawing on the tragic mistakes and brilliant victories of military history, this remarkable book draws countless fascinating parallels with case histories from industry world-wide.

Metamagical Themas   Douglas R. Hofstadter

This astonishing sequel to the best-selling, Pulitzer Prize-winning *Gödel, Escher, Bach* swarms with 'extraordinary ideas, brilliant fables, deep philosophical questions and Carrollian word play' – Martin Gardner

Into the Heart of Borneo   Redmond O'Hanlon

'Perceptive, hilarious and at the same time a serious natural-history journey into one of the last remaining unspoilt paradises' – *New Statesman*. 'Consistently exciting, often funny and erudite without ever being overwhelming' – *Punch*

A Better Class of Person   John Osborne

The playwright's autobiography, 1929–56. 'Splendidly enjoyable' – John Mortimer. 'One of the best, richest and most bitterly truthful autobiographies that I have ever read' – Melvyn Bragg

The Secrets of a Woman's Heart   Hilary Spurling

The later life of Ivy Compton-Burnett, 1920–69. 'A biographical triumph . . . elegant, stylish, witty, tender, immensely acute – dazzles and exhilarates . . . a great achievement' – Kay Dick in the *Literary Review*. 'One of the most important literary biographies of the century' – *New Statesman*

A CHOICE OF PENGUINS

Castaway Lucy Irvine

'Writer seeks "wife" for a year on a tropical island.' This is the extraordinary, candid, sometimes shocking account of what happened when Lucy
Irvine answered the advertisement, and found herself embroiled in what
was not exactly a desert island dream. 'Fascinating' – *Daily Mail*

Out of Africa Karen Blixen (Isak Dinesen)

After the failure of her coffee-farm in Kenya, where she lived from 1913 to
1931, Karen Blixen went home to Denmark and wrote this unforgettable
account of her experiences. 'No reader can put the book down without
some share in the author's poignant farewell to her farm' – *Observer*

The Lisle Letters Edited by Muriel St Clare Byrne

An intimate, immediate and wholly fascinating picture of a family in the
reign of Henry VIII. 'Remarkable . . . we can really hear the people of
early Tudor England talking' – Keith Thomas in the *Sunday Times*. 'One
of the most extraordinary works to be published this century' – J. H.
Plumb

In My Wildest Dreams Leslie Thomas

The autobiography of Leslie Thomas, author of *The Magic Army* and *The
Dearest and the Best*. From Barnardo boy to original virgin soldier, from
apprentice journalist to famous novelist, it is an amazing story. 'Hugely
enjoyable' – *Daily Express*

India: The Siege Within M. J. Akbar

'A thoughtful and well-researched history of the conflict, 2,500 years old,
between centralizing and separatist forces in the sub-continent. And
remarkably, for a work of this kind, it's concise, elegantly written and
entertaining' – Zareer Masani in the *New Statesman*

The Winning Streak Walter Goldsmith and David Clutterbuck

Marks and Spencer, Saatchi and Saatchi, United Biscuits, G.E.C. . . .
The U.K.'s top companies reveal their formulas for success, in an important and stimulating book that no British manager can afford to ignore.

FOR THE BEST IN PAPERBACKS, LOOK FOR THE 🐧

THE PENGUIN TRAVEL LIBRARY – A SELECTION

Hindoo Holiday J. R. Ackerley
The Flight of Ikaros Kevin Andrews
The Path to Rome Hilaire Belloc
Looking for Dilmun Geoffrey Bibby
First Russia, then Tibet Robert Byron
Granite Island Dorothy Carrington
The Worst Journey in the World Apsley Cherry-Garrard
Hashish Henry de Monfreid
Passages from Arabia Deserta C. M. Doughty
Siren Land Norman Douglas
Brazilian Adventure Peter Fleming
The Hill of Devi E. M. Forster
Journey to Kars Philip Glazebrook
Pattern of Islands Arthur Grimble
Writings from Japan Lafcadio Hearn
A Little Tour in France Henry James
Mornings in Mexico D. H. Lawrence
Mani Patrick Leigh Fermor
Stones of Florence and **Venice Observed** Mary McCarthy
They went to Portugal Rose Macaulay
Colossus of Maroussi Henry Miller
Spain Jan Morris
The Big Red Train Ride Eric Newby
The Grand Irish Tour Peter Somerville-Large
Marsh Arabs Wilfred Thesiger
The Sea and The Jungle H. M. Tomlinson
The House of Exile Nora Wain
Ninety-Two Days Evelyn Waugh